KETO DIET COOKBOOK FOR BEGINNERS

500 Recipes For Quick & Easy Low-Carb Homemade Cooking

Sandra Grant

2022

Introduction

I'm in the best (hottest) shape of my life. The kind of hot that makes you want to pinch yourself to validate if what you're experiencing is truly real life. I don't count calories. I dip my bacon in mayonnaise and snack on jars of almond butter with zero guilt.

My body has found its happy place. Weight loss is effortless (I've lost twenty pounds in two months), my skin is glowing, and I'm not a slave to pack-along snacks, cravings, or energy lulls anymore.

The secret? Switching into a state of nutritional ketosis, where the body goes from burning glucose as energy to burning fat as energy. In nutritional ketosis, the body becomes a fat-burning machine, effectively breaking down fatty acids into ketone bodies that are used, even by the brain, as fuel. And we do this by following an eating style of high-fat, low-carb and moderate protein, also known as "keto" or "ketogenic."

When I started my ketogenic journey, I couldn't believe how many options I had and how creative I could be in the kitchen. It was so freeing after living the typical fitness program. One thing that was hard about starting keto was all the contradicting information out there. But keto doesn't need to be difficult; it truly is as simple as including a fat, a protein, and a green vegetable in your meals. Don't make it more complicated than that.

I hope you will find tools within these pages that will make your daily life easier and less stressful. I know making the time to plan and prep ahead will save you money, time, and your health.

The Keto Basics

Though not mandatory (you can skip over this part if you don't care to know how this all works), understanding how the body functions and fully knowing what's at play here makes following the ketogenic lifestyle more meaningful. At least, it does for me.

To fully understand what's going on here, we have to start from the very beginning. And the digestive system is the very best place to start.

The Digestive Process

When we consume food...

1. The site of initial carbohydrate breakdown occurs in the mouth. Your teeth and tongue take the first steps in battering food into bits. As they are shredding and grinding, more saliva is squirted into the food to moisten and soften it. The saliva contains chemicals called enzymes, which break down the carbohydrates in food (this enzyme release triggers insulin to start prepping for action).

2. When you have finished chewing, you swallow, and the mouthful of food makes its way down the esophagus to the stomach. Food does not free-fall down to the stomach but is squeezed along by the muscles in the esophagus. This squeezing/pushing action by the muscles is called peristalsis (perry-STAL-sis).

3. The site of initial protein breakdown occurs in the stomach, where food is treated to a strong acid bath as it's churned around by the stomach's muscular walls. These walls are protected by a mucus lining, which protects the stomach from its own gastric juices (made up of pepsin enzyme and acids).

4. Up until now, carbohydrates have been broken down slightly in the mouth and proteins have been broken down slightly in the stomach. Fats have not had their turn.

5. Now, for the breakdown of fats and further breakdown of carbohydrates and proteins. Food is now a mashed-up milky liquid, thanks to the stomach. It enters the duodenum (the beginning of the small intestine) where it is treated with a round of enzymes and bile to break the carbohydrates, proteins, and fats down even further.

6. From there, the substance enters the small intestine—a twenty-foot-long, curly tube with a shaggy lining. The walls of the small intestines are lined with millions of tiny finger-like projections called villi. The villi absorb the usable parts of the broken down food into the bloodstream.

7. The non-useful parts of the food continue to move into the large intestines. The large intestines absorb some of the water and salt. The remainder of the material is compacted and then sent out the anus as solid waste or feces.

Carbohydrate Digestion

Carbs are organic molecules that are made up of carbon, hydrogen, and oxygen. There are three principal carbohydrates present in foods...

1. Simple Sugars (aka Simple Carbohydrates)
2. Polysaccharides (aka Complex Carbohydrates)
3. Fiber

Simple Sugars (aka Simple Carbohydrates) have three classifications, and several sub-segments below each class. It's a web of sugary confusion! The simplest of simple sugars are: glucose, fructose, and galactose. These are called monosaccharides—this is how all sugars end up in our body when all is said and done.

For instance, if you consume white sugar (sucrose), the body will break it down into glucose and fructose. If you consume a glass of milk (lactose), the body will break it down into galactose and glucose.

Then there are oligosaccharides—simple sugars that consist of several sugars bound together. These unique carbohydrates cannot be easily digested by our regular digestive path and have to go to the large intestine to be eaten up by the bacteria there. Examples of oligosaccharide foods are... onions, asparagus, garlic, banana, and chives.

Polysaccharides (aka Complex Carbohydrates) undergo substantial digestion before being absorbed. Starch is a polysaccharide—the main carbohydrate source for plant seeds and vegetables grown in the ground. Think potatoes, corn, rice, pasta, and cereal. Starches are broken down into glucose by the body.

Another polysaccharide is cellulose, a carbohydrate that is indigestible in the body, adding bulk to the stool.

Fiber is another form of carbohydrate, one that is present in many polysaccharides. Fiber's main purpose is to aid in elimination.

The body converts digestible carbohydrates (the parts of the carbohydrate that are non-fiberous) into glucose, which our cells use as fuel. Some carbs (Simple Sugars, aka Simple Carbohydrates) break down quickly into glucose while others (Polysaccharides, aka Complex Carbohydrates) are slowly broken down and enter the bloodstream more gradually.

The major takeaway here is that ALL dietary forms of carbohydrates are made up of sugar (glucose). Sweet potato, white bread, whole grains, candy, potato chips, fruit, kale—all contain components that become sugar in the body. So that you fully "get the picture" on this carbohydrate thing, perhaps it would be helpful for me to list some sources of carbohydrates, yes?

Okay, here goes...

Bagels, bread, stuffing, buns, croutons, pancakes, English muffins, pita bread, tortillas, corn, waffles, wraps, beans, oatmeal, cornmeal, lentils, flour, hummus, rice, quinoa, pasta, peas, potatoes, squash, sweet potato, cow's milk, rice milk, soy milk, yogurt, apples, cantaloupe, banana, apricots, dates, grapefruit, prunes, raspberries, watermelon, carrot juice, apple juice, tomato juice, cranberry juice, kiwi, alcohol, biscuits, cookies, Danish, donuts, muffins, fruit pie, cupcakes, chocolate, potato chips, pretzels, crackers, sherbet, ice cream, tortilla chips, Jell-O, granola, cereal, French fries, apple butter, barbecue sauce, oats, cranberry sauce, salad dressing, ketchup, jams, jellies, candies, mints, gum, soda, gravy, honey mustard, dipping sauces, plum sauce, hollandaise sauce, maple syrup, honey, agave nectar, coconut sugar, coconut nectar, noodles, lasagna, egg rolls, cream soups, soups, chutney, arrowroot, tapioca, chickpea flour, sorghum, millet, amaranth, muesli, shredded wheat, popcorn, rice cakes, pudding, custard, almonds, cashews, pumpkin seeds, gar- banzo beans, lima beans, green peas, carrots, pinto beans, navy beans, beets, onions, parsnips, bell peppers, spinach, greens, turnips, yams, white sugar, dates, date sugar, dried fruit, flour, pizza.

The key here is that, regardless of if you are consuming a simple or complex carbohydrate, it will turn into "sugar" in the body.

Introduction to a New Way

The "Healthy" High-Carb Approach

Our current high-carbohydrate eating style of whole grains, several servings of fruits and vegetables, and minimal intake of fats has been touted as "healthy." Now you know from the previous section that all forms of carbohydrate—fruits, vegetables, grains, sugars, and anything starchy—are primarily broken down into glucose and stored in your body as glycogen.

When you have more glycogen than what's needed for immediate energy, your body will store excess in the liver, then the muscles and, if everything is full, the excess is converted into triglycerides and stored in your blood. Psst... this is not a good thing.

Relying on carbohydrates for fuel is:

- Not sustainable; we can only store a couple thousand calories of carbohydrates at any given time.
- Preventing us from getting a handle on our blood sugar, causing endless cravings, various daily eating times, and weight gain.
- Leading to triglycerides being stored in the blood, the major risk factor to heart disease.
- Slowly killing us.

What is the Keto Diet?

What is the ketogenic diet exactly? The classic ketogenic diet is a very low-carb diet plan that was originally designed in the 1920s for patients with epilepsy by researchers working at Johns Hopkins Medical Center. Researchers found that fasting—avoiding consumption of all foods for a brief period of time (such as with intermittent fasting), including those that provide carbohydrates—helped reduce the amount of seizures patients suffered, in addition to having other positive effects on body fat, blood sugar, cholesterol, and hunger levels.

Unfortunately, long-term fasting is not a feasible option for more than a few days, therefore the keto diet was developed to mimic the same beneficial effects of fasting.

Essentially, the keto diet for beginners works by "tricking" the body into acting as if its fasting (while reaping intermittent fasting benefits) through a strict elimination of glucose that is found in carbohydrate foods. Today, the standard keto diet goes by several different names including the "low-carbohydrate" or "very-low-carbohydrate ketogenic diet."

Keto Diet Fat Burner vs. Sugar Burner

At the core of the classic keto diet is severely restricting intake of all or most foods with sugar and starch (carbohydrates). These foods are broken down into sugar (insulin and glucose) in our blood once we eat them, and if these levels become too high, extra calories are much more easily stored as body fat and results in unwanted weight gain. However, when glucose levels are cut off due to low-carb intake, the body starts to burn fat instead and produces ketones that can be measured in the blood (using urine strips, for example).

Keto diets, like most low-carb diets, work through the elimination of glucose. Because most folks live on a high-carb diet, our bodies normally run on glucose (or sugar) for energy. We cannot make glucose and only have about twenty-four hours' worth stored in our muscle tissue and liver. Once glucose is no longer available from food sources, we begin to burn stored fat instead, or fat from our food.

Therefore, when you're following a ketogenic diet plan for beginners, your body is burning fat for energy rather than carbohydrates, so in the process most people lose weight and excess body fat rapidly, even when consuming lots of fat and adequate calories through their daily food intake. Another major benefit of the keto diet is that there's no need to count calories, feel hungry, or attempt to burn loads of calories through hours of intense exercise.

What is Ketosis?
Nutritional ketosis is a state where your body is "deprived" of glucose; achieved when carbohydrate intake is decreased and protein intake is moderated. In this state, you switch to using fat as energy instead of carbohydrates. This process—of using fat as fuel—produces ketone bodies that are converted into substrates for the Krebs Cycle (energy production). Once you're in nutritional ketosis, the storage of triglycerides in blood no longer applies. Blood sugar and insulin levels are reduced, levels of HDL cholesterol increase, and the visceral fats around your vital organs are "eaten up" as fuel.

In nutritional ketosis, we're tripping the metabolic switch, leading to so much more than just weight loss.

The Keto Beginning is about finding our body's happy place and using fatty acids and the generation of ketone bodies as a reliable fuel for constant, steady energy. The brain, the heart, our hormones, and every cell in the body loves ketones.

Ketones are a highly renewable energy source that our major organs use effortlessly to promote lasting health in a blood sugar-balanced environment.

This is nutritional ketosis, not to be confused with diabetic ketoacidosis—a dangerous condition where ketones spike and blood sugar increases to alarming rates.

This occurs primarily in diabetics type 1 (and sometimes 2) patients who are not receiving enough insulin to bring glucose into their cells. Regardless of how low carbohydrate intake is, a person with a normal pancreas cannot enter diabetic ketoacidosis because even a trace amount of insulin will keep ketone levels at a safe level.

Having said that, there are three groups of people that should NOT play around with nutritional ketosis unless under the care of a professional in a one-on-one setting—pregnant women, diabetics (type 1), and individuals with kidney disease or a kidney imbalance.

Clarification of "Being in Ketosis" and "Being Keto-Adapted"

Our bodies burn whatever fuel is available—glucose, fatty acids, ketones, alcohol. Whatever there is more of is what the body will burn for energy.

Following a ketogenic eating style puts you into a state of ketosis. What this means is that your body is breaking down enough fat so that there are ketones in your bloodstream. This happens either by fasting or with the support of a low-carb, high-fat, moderate protein eating style. Being "in ketosis" is a normal metabolic state.

One of the goals of the ketogenic eating style is becoming "keto-adapted." Being keto-adapted means that your body is primed for functioning with very little glucose. This is the END goal of The Keto Beginning.

When you first enter ketosis (a result of following a ketogenic eating style for a couple of days), you are using fat for energy, but it's in limited amounts at first because you don't have as many fat-converting enzymes in your body. Different enzymes are involved in breaking down fat than breaking down glucose. And, up until now, you've been breaking down excess glucose more so than fats, so it takes the body a bit of time to "catch up" and store these enzymes when you first get started. This is one of the reasons many people feel tired at the beginning of following a ketogenic eating style. Once the enzymes are built up, your cells change the way they acquire energy and you become fully keto-adapted.

The process of becoming keto-adapted can take a few weeks to a month, depending on the person. Once you're keto-adapted, fatty acids and their substrates, ketone bodies, become your body's pre-ferred fuel. Hormone levels change, the energy stores in liver and muscle (glycogen) are depleted, your body carries around less water, and your energy is boosted to normal levels again.

This is why this ebook outlines sticking with the plan for thirty days before deviation, so that one can become fully keto-adapted.

When the body is keto-adapted and gets an overdose of carbohydrates, the process of getting back into ketosis doesn't take as long as the initial keto-adaptation because the body is primed to use fat as energy. When too many carbohydrates are consumed, the carbohydrates (glucose) still takes precedence over fat for fuel because excess blood sugar is fatal and so your body needs to handle the sugar first.

When the overdose occurs, a couple of things happen: glycogen (the way glucose is stored in the liver and muscles) gets replenished, leading to water retention, insulin rises, and hormone levels being boosted. While this is occurring, you are not burning ketones. Once the glucose is depleted, the body will go back into ketosis.

As you begin your keto journey, the more often you have sugar (or, an abundance of carbohydrates past what your body can manage on a daily basis without spiking insulin release), the longer it takes to become keto-adapted.

Your Goal for this BOOK

Become Keto-Adapted. This simply means that your body becomes efficient at being able to burn fat... and functions very well even in the presence of very little glucose.

By becoming keto-adapted, your body literally will become a fat-burning machine!

Following Keto

What to Eat on a Keto Diet?

When it comes to keto food choices, choosing nutrient-dense foods is key to maintaining good health—it's not all bacon and butter! What you eat matters and can directly affect your overall health, well-being and how successful you are on any type of diet.

What Foods are Keto?

Foods that fit into a keto diet are typically high-fat low-carb foods, and non-starchy veggies. Protein sources can also be included. Here is a rough list of the most nutritious foods that fit into a keto meal plan.

Healthy Keto Fats

- Nuts and nut butters made without added sugar
- Seeds
- Plant-based oils
- Avocado
- Olives
- Cacao

Low Carb Fruits and Vegetables

- Non-starchy veggies: leafy greens, radishes, cauliflower, broccoli, tomato, eggplant, zucchini, cucumber, peppers, green beans, celery, bok choy, jicama, mushrooms, artichokes, cabbage, beets, onions and carrots.
- Melon and strawberries (one serving provides half of the recommended 20g of carbs).
- All fresh herbs.

Keto Proteins

- Eggs
- Fatty fish like salmon, mackerel, and herring
- Bison, beef, pork, goat, and lamb
- Chicken with skin
- Shellfish
- Cottage cheese, cheese, and unsweetened yogurt
- Organ meats

Keto Sweeteners

- Erythritol
- Monk Fruit

- Stevia
- Other artificial sweeteners

What Foods to Avoid?

Since a keto meal plan is all about hitting your macros, just about any food can fit into this eating plan except carb-containing foods. Many carb sources will put you over your daily limit in a single serving or less. Here are some of the top foods/types of foods that you'll want to avoid on a keto diet.

High-Carb Foods

- All grains, pastas, and breads
- Beans, lentils, and other legumes
- Corn
- Potatoes
- Most fruits and dried fruits
- Juice and soda
- Milk
- Desserts
- Breaded meats and other breaded fried foods
- Sugars: maple, honey, agave, table sugar, etc.

Keto Beverages

Many beverages are loaded with added sugar or made from juice blends that are naturally higher in carbs. When looking for drinks that fit into a keto plan, it's always best to check the nutrition facts label.

Keto Drinks

- Water
- Sparkling water/club soda
- Tea and coffee, unsweetened
- Flavored water with no added sugar
- Wheat grass or other green vegetable juices made without fruit
- Artificially sweetened beverages

Low-Carb Alcohol

- Clear liquor: vodka, gin, rum
- Scotch and bourbon
- Light beers
- Champagne and some wine

RECIPES

BREAKFAST

COCONUT MILK PANCAKES

Nutrition: Cal 442;Fat 35 g;Carb 15 g;Protein 16,2 g
Serving 4; Cook time 15min

Dry Ingredients
6 tablespoons coconut flour
4 tablespoons granulated sweetener
1 teaspoon baking powder

Wet Ingredients
•6 tablespoons unsweetened coconut milk
•4 large eggs
•2 teaspoons vanilla extract

Instructions
1. In a mixing bowl add all of the dry ingredients.
2. In a separate bowl mix together coconut milk, eggs, and vanilla extract. Be sure to shake can before opening.
3. Preheat skillet or pan on medium heat for cooking and add coconut oil or butter.
4. Combine dry and wet and beat well with a whisk until batter is smooth and free of lumps.
5. Add to pan and cook each side evenly. If cooking too fast, pull off heat and lower temperature. Pancakes should be fluffy and not runny on the inside but golden brown on the outside.

KETO BREAKFAST CASSEROLE

Nutrition: Cal 200;Fat 15 g ;Carb 4g;Protein 13 g
Serving 10; Cook time 70min

Ingredients
• Drizzle of oil
• ½ cup onion
• 1 tablespoon garlic, minced
• 1 pound breakfast sausage
• 12 eggs
• ½ cup almond milk
• 2 teaspoons mustard powder
• 1 teaspoon oregano
• ¼ teaspoon salt
• Pepper, to taste
• 1½ cups broccoli florets
• 1 zucchini, diced
• 1 red bell pepper, diced (or 3–4 cups veggies of choice)

Instructions
1. Preheat oven to 375°F (190°C).
2. In a skillet over medium heat, add a drizzle of oil and sauté onion and garlic.
3. Once transparent, add sausage and cook until browned, 7–10 minutes.
4. Add to a 13×9-inch casserole or baking dish and set aside.
5. In a large bowl, whisk together eggs, milk of choice, and seasonings. Stir in chopped veggies.
6. Pour mixture over sausage.
7. Bake until firm and cooked through, 30–40 minutes.
8. Allow to cool slightly before slicing into squares, serving, and enjoying!
9. Store leftovers in the fridge for up to 5 days, and reheat individual portions in the microwave.

AVOCADO OMELETTE

Nutrition: Cal 310;Fat 23 g;Carb 11 g;Protein 16 g
Serving 2; Cook time 5min

Ingredients
3 eggs, lightly beaten
3 tablespoons almond milk
Nonstick cooking spray, as needed
1/2 cup tofu cheese
1 tablespoon sliced green onion

1/4 cup chopped red bell pepper
1 ripe, fresh California avocado; seeded, peeled, and cubed

Instructions
1. Mix eggs and milk.
2. Spray a large skillet with nonstick cooking spray and heat over medium low heat. Pour egg mixture into skillet. Cook eggs until top is almost set.
3. Sprinkle with cheese and green onion. Cook, about 2 minutes.
4. Top with red pepper and avocado, fold over, and serve immediately.

KETO BREAKFAST DAIRY-FREE SMOOTHIE BOWL

Nutrition: Cal 642;Fat 45 g;Carb 10 g;Protein 22,2 g
Serving 3; Cook time 10min

Ingredients
• 1 ½ cups (350 ml) full-fat coconut milk
• 1 cup (110 g) frozen raspberries
• ¼ cup (60 ml) MCT oil or melted coconut oil, or ¼ cup (40 g) unflavored MCT oil powder
• ¼ cup (40 g) collagen peptides or protein powder
• 2 tablespoons chia seeds
• 1 tablespoon apple cider vinegar
• 1 teaspoon vanilla extract
• 1 tablespoon erythritol, or 4 drops liquid stevia

Instructions
1. Place all the pudding ingredients in a blender or food processor and blend until smooth. Serve in bowls with your favorite toppings, if desired.

CRISPY KETO CORNED BEEF & RADISH HASH

Nutrition: Cal 252;Fat 16 g;Carb 1,5 g;Protein 23 g
Serving 2; Cook time 10min

Ingredients
• 2 tablespoons olive oil
• 1/2 cup diced onions
• 2 cups radishes, diced to about 1/2 inch
• 1 teaspoon kosher salt
• 1/2 teaspoon ground black pepper
• 1 teaspoon dried oregano (Mexican if you have it)
• 1/2 teaspoon garlic powder
• 2 twelve-ounce cans corned beef or 2 cups finely chopped corned beef, packed

Instructions
1. Heat the olive oil in a large saute pan and add the onions, radishes, salt, and pepper.
2. Saute the onions and radishes on medium heat for 5 minutes or until softened.
3. Add the oregano, garlic powder, and corned beef to the pan and stir well until combined.
4. Cook over low to medium heat, stirring occasionally for 10 minutes or until the radishes are soft and starting to brown.
5. Press the mixture into the bottom of the pan and cook on high heat for 2–3 minutes or until the bottom is crisp and brown.
6. Serve hot.

COCONUT FLOUR PORRIDGE

Nutrition: Cal 345;Fat 28,5 g;Carb 11 g;Protein 13 g
Serving 1; Cook time 7min

Ingredients
•2 tablespoons coconut flour
• 2 tablespoons golden flax meal
• 3/4 cup water
• Pinch of salt
• 1 large egg, beaten
• 2 teaspoons butter or ghee

- 1 tablespoon heavy cream or coconut milk
- 1 tablespoon low-carb brown sugar (or your favorite sweetener)

Instructions

1. Measure the first four ingredients into a small pot over medium heat and stir. When it begins to simmer, turn it down to medium-low and whisk until it begins to thicken.
2. Remove the coconut flour porridge from heat and add the beaten egg, a half at a time, while whisking continuously. Place back on the heat and continue to whisk until the porridge thickens. Remove from the heat and continue to whisk for about 30 seconds before adding the butter, cream, and sweetener.
3. Garnish with your favorite toppings (4 grams net carbs).

EASY SHAKSHUKA

Nutrition: Cal 216;Fat 12,8 g;Carb 16,6 g;Protein 112 g
Serving 6; Cook time 35min

Ingredients
- 2 tablespoons olive oil
- 1 large yellow onion, chopped
- 1 large red bell pepper or roasted red bell pepper, chopped
- 1/4 teaspoon fine sea salt
- 3 cloves garlic, pressed or minced
- 2 tablespoons tomato paste
- 1 teaspoon ground cumin
- 1/2 teaspoon smoked paprika
- 1/4 teaspoon red pepper flakes (reduce or omit if sensitive to spice)
- 1 large can (28 ounces) crushed tomatoes, preferably fire-roasted
- 2 tablespoons chopped fresh cilantro or flat-leaf parsley, plus addition cilantro or parsley leaves for garnish
- Freshly ground black pepper, to taste
- 5 to 6 large eggs

Instructions

1. Preheat the oven to 375°F. Warm the oil in a large, oven-safe skillet (preferably stainless steel) over medium heat. Once shimmering, add the onion, bell pepper, and salt. Cook, stirring often, until the onions are tender and turning translucent, about 4 to 6 minutes.
2. Add the garlic, tomato paste, cumin, paprika, and red pepper flakes. Cook, stirring constantly, until nice and fragrant, 1 to 2 minutes.
3. Pour in the crushed tomatoes with their juices and add the cilantro. Stir, and let the mixture come to a simmer. Reduce the heat as necessary to maintain a gentle simmer and cook for 5 minutes to give the flavors time to meld.
4. Turn off the heat. Taste (careful, it's hot!), and add salt and pepper as necessary. Use the back of a spoon to make a well near the perimeter and crack the egg directly into it. Gently spoon a bit of the tomato mixture over the whites to help contain the egg. Repeat with the remaining 4 to 5 eggs, depending on how many you can fit. Sprinkle a little salt and pepper over the eggs.
5. Carefully transfer the skillet to the oven (it's heavy) and bake for 8 to 12 minutes, checking often once you reach 8 minutes. They're done when the egg whites are an opaque white and the yolks have risen a bit but are still soft. They should still jiggle in the centers when you shimmy the pan (keep in mind that they'll continue cooking after you pull the dish out of the oven).

STEAK AND EGGS

Nutrition: Cal 210;Fat 36 g;Carb 3 g;Protein 44 g
Serving 1; Cook time 15min

Ingredients
- 1 tablespoon butter
- 3 eggs
- 4 ounces sirloin
- 1/4 avocado
- Salt
- Pepper

Instructions

1. Melt your butter in a pan and fry 2–3 eggs until the whites are set and yolk is to desired doneness. Season with salt and pepper.
2. In another pan, cook your sirloin (or favorite cut of steak) until desired doneness. Then slice into bite-sized strips and season with salt and pepper.

3. Slice up some avocado and serve together!

FARMER CHEESE PANCAKES

Nutrition: Cal 200;Fat 12 g;Carb 2,5 g;Protein 18 g
Serving 5; Cook time 20min

Ingredients
- 1 lb Farmer Cheese
- 1 cup coconut flour
- 2 eggs
- Pinch of salt, to taste (optional)
- 1 tsp Stevia, to taste (optional)

Instructions

1. Mix farmer cheese, coconut flour, salt, and 2 eggs. Mixture should be like paste texture.
2. Form pancakes into round shape. Dust it just a bit with coconut flour.
3. Fry till both sides are golden brown.

FRENCH OMELET

Nutrition: Cal 186;Fat 9 g;Carb 4 g;Protein 22 g
Serving 2; Cook time 10min

Ingredients
- 2 large eggs
- 4 large egg whites
- 1/4 cup fat-free milk
- 1/8 teaspoon salt
- 1/8 teaspoon pepper
- 1/4 cup cubed fully cooked ham
- 1 tablespoon chopped onion
- 1 tablespoon chopped green pepper
- 1/4 cup shredded reduced-fat cheddar cheese

Instructions

1. Whisk together first five ingredients.
2. Place a 10-in. skillet coated with cooking spray over medium heat. Pour in egg mixture. Mixture should set immediately at edges. As eggs set, push cooked portions toward the center, letting uncooked eggs flow underneath.
3. When eggs are thickened and no liquid egg remains, top one half with remaining ingredients. Fold omelet in half. Cut in half to serve.

CORNED BEEF AND RADISH HASH

Nutrition: Cal 252;Fat 16 g;Carb 2 g;Protein 23 g
Serving 4; Cook time 20min

Ingredients
- 1 tablespoon olive oil
- 1/4 cup diced onions
- 1 cup radishes, diced to about 1/4 inch
- 1/2 teaspoon kosher salt
- 1/4 teaspoon ground black pepper
- 1/2 teaspoon dried oregano (Mexican if you have it)
- 1/4 teaspoon garlic powder
- 1 - 12 ounce can corned beef or 1 cup finely chopped corned beef, packed

Instructions

1. Heat the olive oil in a large saute pan and add the onions, radishes, salt, and pepper.
2. Saute the onions and radishes on medium heat for 5 minutes or until softened.
3. Add the oregano, garlic powder, and corned beef to the pan and stir well until combined.
4. Cook over low to medium heat, stirring occasionally for 10 minutes or until the radishes are soft and starting to brown.
5. Press the mixture into the bottom of the pan and cook on high heat for 2-3 minutes or until the bottom is crisp and brown.

SHEET PAN EGGS WITH VEGGIES AND PARMESAN

Nutrition: Cal 215;Fat 14 g;Carb 5 g;Protein 18,5 g
Serving 6; Cook time 20min

Ingredients

- 12 large eggs, whisked
- Salt and pepper
- 1 small red pepper, diced
- 1 small yellow onion, chopped
- 1 cup diced mushrooms
- 1 cup diced zucchini
- 1 cup freshly grated parmesan cheese

Instructions

1. Preheat the oven to 350°F and grease a rimmed baking sheet with cooking spray.
2. Whisk the eggs in a bowl with salt and pepper until frothy.
3. Stir in the peppers, onions, mushrooms, and zucchini until well combined.
4. Pour the mixture in the baking sheet and spread into an even layer.
5. Sprinkle with parmesan and bake for 12 to 15 minutes until the egg is set.
6. Let cool slightly, then cut into squares to serve.

BEETS AND BLUEBERRY SMOOTHIE

Nutrition: Cal 215;Fat 17 g;Carb 15 g;Protein 2,5 g
Serving 1; Cook time 5 min

Ingredients

- 1 cup unsweetened coconut milk
- ¼ cup heavy cream
- ¼ cup frozen blueberries
- 1 small beet, peeled and chopped
- 1 teaspoon chia seeds
- Liquid stevia extract, to taste

Instructions

1. Combine the blueberries, beets, and coconut milk in a blender.
2. Pulse the ingredients several times.
3. Add the remaining ingredients and blend until smooth.
4. Pour into a large glass and enjoy immediately.

CINNAMON PROTEIN PANCAKES

Nutrition: Cal 440;Fat 38 g;Carb 5,5 g;Protein 22 g
Serving 4; Cook time 20 min

Ingredients

- 1 cup canned coconut milk
- ¼ cup coconut oil
- 8 large eggs
- 2 scoops (40g) egg white protein powder
- 1 teaspoon vanilla extract
- ½ teaspoon ground cinnamon
- Pinch ground nutmeg
- Liquid stevia extract, to taste

Instructions

1. Combine the coconut milk, coconut oil, and eggs in a food processor.
2. Pulse the mixture several times then add the remaining ingredients.
3. Blend until smooth and well combined – adjust sweetness to taste.
4. Heat a nonstick skillet over medium heat.
5. Spoon in the batter, using about ¼ cup per pancake.
6. Cook until bubbles form on the surface of the batter then carefully flip.
7. Let the pancake cook until the underside is browned.
8. Transfer to a plate to keep warm and repeat with the remaining batter.

SHEET PAN EGGS WITH HAM AND PEPPER JACK

Nutrition: Cal 235;Fat 15 g;Carb 2,5 g;Protein 21 g
Serving 6; Cook time 20 min

Ingredients

12 large eggs, whisked

Salt and pepper
2 cups diced ham
1 cup shredded pepper jack cheese

Instructions

1. Preheat the oven to 350°F and grease a rimmed baking sheet with cooking spray.
2. Whisk the eggs in a bowl with salt and pepper until frothy.
3. Stir in the ham and cheese until well combined.
4. Pour the mixture in the baking sheet and spread into an even layer.
5. Bake for 12 to 15 minutes until the egg is set.
6. Let cool slightly then cut into squares to serve.

DETOXIFYING GREEN SMOOTHIE

Nutrition: Cal 160;Fat 14 g;Carb 8 g;Protein 2,5 g
Serving 1; Cook time 3 min

Ingredients

- 1 cup fresh chopped kale
- ½ cup fresh baby spinach
- ¼ cup sliced celery
- 1 cup water
- 3 to 4 ice cubes
- 2 tablespoons fresh lemon juice
- 1 tablespoon fresh lime juice
- 1 tablespoon coconut oil
- Liquid stevia extract, to taste

Instructions

1. Combine the kale, spinach, and celery in a blender.
2. Pulse the ingredients several times.
3. Add the remaining ingredients and blend until smooth.
4. Pour into a large glass and enjoy immediately.

NUTTY PUMPKIN SMOOTHIE

Nutrition: Cal 205;Fat 16,5 g;Carb 13 g;Protein 3 g
Serving 1; Cook time 5 min

Ingredients

- 1 cup unsweetened cashew milk
- ½ cup pumpkin puree
- ¼ cup heavy cream
- 1 tablespoon raw almonds
- ¼ teaspoon pumpkin pie spice
- Liquid stevia extract, to taste

Instructions

1. Combine all of the ingredients in a blender.
2. Pulse the ingredients several times, then blend until smooth.
3. Pour into a large glass and enjoy immediately

MATCHA BREAKFAST BOWL

Nutrition: Cal 150;Fat 10 g;Carb 5 g;Protein 13 g
Serving 1; Cook time 10min

Ingredients
Matcha Chia Bowl

- 1 cup plant-based milk such as coconut, almond, or macadamia
- 2 tablespoons chia seeds
- 1-2 teaspoons matcha to taste (we use 2 teaspoons)
- Vanilla stevia drops or preferred sweetener, to taste
- Pinch of pink Himalayan salt

For the Smooth Version (optional)

- 1/4-1/2 avocado, to taste
- Mint extract or fresh mint leaves

Serving Suggestions (optional)

- Shredded coconut, lightly toasted
- Almonds, lightly toasted
- Fresh strawberries

Instructions

1. Mix chia seeds with your chosen milk, matcha, sweetener, and salt. Cover and refrigerate overnight. For the milk, I like to mix 1-2 tablespoons of full-fat coconut milk (the canned stuff) with 1 cup of water.

2.Add more liquid as needed to reach desired consistency (optional). Sweeten to taste and serve with toppings of choice.

3.To make the smooth version, simply blend in a high-speed blender. You can add some avocado for added creaminess, mint leaves (or extract) for a fresh touch, and a handful of ice.

4.Chia pudding (without the avocado) can be kept refrigerated in an airtight container for up to a week (it's ideal for meal prepping!)

SOUTHWESTERN OMELET

Nutrition: Cal 390;Fat 31 g;Carb 7 g;Protein 22 g
Serving 4; Cook time 10min

Ingredients
- 1/2 cup chopped onion
- 1 jalapeno pepper, minced
- 1 tablespoon canola oil
- 6 large eggs, lightly beaten
- 6 bacon strips, cooked and crumbled
- 1 small tomato, chopped
- 1 ripe avocado, cut into 1-inch slices
- 1 cup shredded Monterey Jack cheese, divided
- Salt and pepper, to taste
- Salsa (optional)

Instructions
1.In a large skillet, saute onion and jalapeno in oil until tender; remove with a slotted spoon and set aside. Pour eggs into the same skillet; cover and cook over low heat for 3-4 minutes.

2.Sprinkle with the onion mixture, bacon, tomato, avocado, and 1/2 cup cheese. Season with salt and pepper.

3.Fold omelet in half over filling. Cover and cook for 3-4 minutes or until eggs are set. Sprinkle with remaining cheese. Serve with salsa if desired.

PULLED PORK HASH

Nutrition: Cal 354;Fat 22 g;Carb 8 g;Protein 21 g
Serving 2; Cook time 20min

- 2 tablespoons FOC (fat of choice, I use lard)
- 1 turnip, diced (115 g)
- 1/2 teaspoon paprika
- 1/4 teaspoon salt
- 1/4 teaspoon garlic powder
- 1/4 teaspoon black pepper
- 3 Brussels sprouts, halved (50 g)
- 1 cup chopped lacinato kale, about 2 leaves (45 g)
- 2 tablespoons diced red onion (30 g)
- 3 ounces pulled pork
- 2 eggs

1.Heat the oil in a large cast iron skillet over medium-high heat. Add the diced turnip and the spices to the skillet. Cook 5 minutes, stirring occasionally.

2.Add the remaining vegetables to the skillet and cook another 2-3 minutes until they start to soften. Add in the pork and cook 2 minutes.

3.Make 2 divots in the hash and crack in two eggs. Cover and cook 3-5 minutes, just until the whites are set.

HAM & FETA OMELET

Nutrition: Cal 290;Fat 20 g;Carb 5 g;Protein 21 g
Serving 2; Cook time 15min

Ingredients
- 4 large eggs
- 1 green onion, chopped
- 1 tablespoon 2% milk
- 1/4 teaspoon dried basil
- 1/4 teaspoon dried oregano
- Dash of garlic powder
- Dash of salt
- Dash of pepper
- 1 tablespoon butter
- 1/4 cup crumbled feta cheese
- 3 slices deli ham, chopped
- 1 plum tomato, chopped
- 2 teaspoons balsamic vinaigrette

Instructions
1.In a small bowl, whisk eggs, green onion, milk, and seasonings until blended. In a large nonstick skillet, heat butter over medium-high heat. Pour in egg mixture. Mixture should set immediately at edge.

2.As eggs set, push cooked portions toward the center, letting uncooked eggs flow underneath. When eggs are thickened and no liquid egg remains, top one side with cheese and ham.

3.Fold omelet in half; cut into two portions. Slide onto plates; top with tomato. Drizzle with vinaigrette before serving.

HAM STEAKS WITH GRUYERE, BACON & MUSHROOMS

Nutrition: Cal 352;Fat 22 g;Carb 5 g;Protein 34 g
Serving 14; Cook time 15min

Ingredients
- 2 tablespoons butter
- 1/2 pound sliced fresh mushrooms
- 1 shallot, finely chopped
- 2 garlic cloves, minced
- 1/8 teaspoon coarsely ground pepper
- 1 fully cooked boneless ham steak (about 1 pound), cut into four pieces
- 1 cup shredded Gruyere cheese
- 4 bacon strips, cooked and crumbled
- 1 tablespoon minced fresh parsley (optional)

Instructions
1.In a large nonstick skillet, heat butter over medium-high heat. Add mushrooms and shallot; cook and stir 4-6 minutes or until tender. Add garlic and pepper; cook 1 minute longer. Remove from pan; keep warm. Wipe skillet clean.

2.In same skillet, cook ham over medium heat 3 minutes. Turn; sprinkle with cheese and bacon. Cook, covered, 2-4 minutes longer or until cheese is melted and ham is heated through. Serve with mushroom mixture. If desired, sprinkle with parsley.

BROCCOLI QUICHE CUPS

Nutrition: Cal 291;Fat 24 g;Carb 4 g;Protein 17 g
Serving 12; Cook time 20min

Ingredients
- 1 cup chopped fresh broccoli
- 1 cup pepper jack cheese
- 6 large eggs, lightly beaten
- 3/4 cup heavy whipping cream
- 1/2 cup bacon bits
- 1 shallot, minced
- 1/4 teaspoon salt
- 1/4 teaspoon pepper

Instructions
1.Preheat oven to 350°. Divide broccoli and cheese among 12 greased muffin cups.

2.Whisk together remaining ingredients; pour into cups. Bake until set, 15-20 minutes.

BROCCOLI & CHEESE OMELET

Nutrition: Cal 230;Fat 17 g;Carb 5 g;Protein 15 g
Serving 4; Cook time 15min

Ingredients
- 2-1/2 cups fresh broccoli florets
- 6 large eggs
- 1/4 cup 2% milk
- 1/2 teaspoon salt
- 1/4 teaspoon pepper
- 1/3 cup grated Romano cheese
- 1/3 cup sliced pitted Greek olives
- 1 tablespoon olive oil
- Shaved Romano cheese and minced fresh parsley

Instructions

1.Preheat broiler. In a large saucepan, place steamer basket over 1 inch of water. Place broccoli in basket. Bring water to a boil. Reduce heat to a simmer; steam, covered, 4-6 minutes or until crisp-tender.

2.In a large bowl, whisk eggs, milk, salt, and pepper. Stir in cooked broccoli, grated cheese, and olives. In a 10-inch ovenproof skillet, heat oil over medium heat; pour in egg mixture. Cook, uncovered, 4-6 minutes or until nearly set.

3.Broil 3-4 inches from heat 2-4 minutes or until eggs are completely set. Let stand 5 minutes. Cut into wedges. Sprinkle with shaved cheese and parsley

DENVER OMELET SALAD

Nutrition: Cal 230;Fat 14 g;Carb 7 g;Protein 17 g
Serving 4; Cook time 10min

Ingredients
•8 cups fresh baby spinach
•1 cup chopped tomatoes
•2 tablespoons olive oil, divided
•1-1/2 cups chopped fully cooked ham
•1 small onion, chopped
•1 small green pepper, chopped
•4 large eggs
•Salt and pepper, to taste

Instructions
1.Arrange spinach and tomatoes on a platter; set aside. In a large skillet, heat 1 tablespoon olive oil over medium-high heat. Add ham, onion, and green pepper; saute until ham is heated through and vegetables are tender, 5-7 minutes. Spoon over spinach and tomatoes.

2.In same skillet, heat remaining olive oil over medium heat. Break eggs one at a time into a small cup, then gently slide into skillet.

3.Immediately reduce heat to low; season with salt and pepper. To prepare sunny-side-up eggs, cover pan and cook until whites are completely set and yolks thicken but are not hard. Top salad with fried eggs.

TURKEY BREAKFAST SAUSAGE

Nutrition: Cal 85;Fat 5 g;Carb 2 g;Protein 10 g
Serving 8; Cook time 10min

Ingredients
•1 pound lean ground turkey
•3/4 teaspoon salt
•1/2 teaspoon rubbed sage
•1/2 teaspoon pepper
•1/4 teaspoon ground ginger

Instructions
1.Crumble turkey into a large bowl. Add the salt, sage, pepper, and ginger. Shape into eight 2-inch patties.

2.In a nonstick skillet coated with cooking spray, cook patties over medium heat for 4-6 minutes on each side or until a thermometer reads 165° and juices run clear.

AVOCADO BACON AND EGGS

Nutrition: Cal 125;Fat 9 g;Carb 2 g;Protein 8 g
Serving 2; Cook time 15min

Ingredients
•1 medium avocado
•2 eggs
•1 piece bacon, cooked and crumbled
•1 tablespoon low-fat cheese
•Pinch of salt

Instructions
1.Preheat oven to 425°F.

2.Begin by cutting the avocado in half and removing the pit.

3.With a spoon, scoop out some of the avocado so it's a tad bigger than your egg and yolk. Place in a muffin pan to keep the avocado stable while cooking.

4.Crack your egg and add it to the inside of your avocado. Sprinkle a little cheese on top with a pinch of salt. Top with cooked bacon.

5.Cook for 14-16 minutes. Serve warm.

PEANUT BUTTER GRANOLA

Nutrition:Cal 338;Fat 30 g;Carb 9 g;Protein 10 g
Serving 12; Cook time 30min

Ingredients
•1 1/2 cups almonds
•1 1/2 cups pecans
•1 cup shredded coconut or almond flour
•1/4 cup sunflower seeds
•1/3 cup Swerve sweetener
•1/3 cup vanilla whey protein powder OR collagen protein powder
•1/3 cup peanut butter
•1/4 cup butter
•1/4 cup water

Instructions
1.Preheat oven to 300°F and line a large rimmed baking sheet with parchment paper.

2.In a food processor, process almonds and pecans until they resemble coarse crumbs with some larger pieces. Transfer to a large bowl and stir in shredded coconut, sunflower seeds, sweetener, and vanilla protein powder.

3.In a microwave-safe bowl, melt the peanut butter and butter together.

4.Pour melted peanut butter mixture over nut mixture and stir well, tossing lightly. Stir in water. Mixture will clump together.

5.Spread mixture evenly on prepared baking sheet and bake 30 minutes, stirring halfway through. Remove and let cool completely

SPINACH-MUSHROOM SCRAMBLED EGGS

Nutrition: Cal 200;Fat 11 g;Carb 2 g;Protein 14 g
Serving 2; Cook time 10min

Ingredients
•2 large eggs
•2 large egg whites
•1/8 teaspoon salt
•1/8 teaspoon pepper
•1 teaspoon butter
•1/2 cup thinly sliced fresh mushrooms
•1/2 cup fresh baby spinach, chopped
•2 tablespoons shredded provolone cheese

Instructions
1.In a small bowl, whisk eggs, egg whites, salt, and pepper until blended. In a small nonstick skillet, heat butter over medium-high heat.

2.Add mushrooms; cook and stir 3-4 minutes or until tender. Add spinach; cook and stir until wilted. Reduce heat to medium.

3.Add egg mixture; cook and stir just until eggs are thickened and no liquid egg remains. Stir in cheese.

EGGS FLORENTINE CASSEROLE

Nutrition: Cal 271;Fat 20 g;Carb 7 g;Protein 17 g
Serving 12; Cook time 30min

Ingredients
•1 pound bulk pork sausage
•2 tablespoons butter
•1 large onion, chopped
•1 cup sliced fresh mushrooms
•1 package (10 ounces) frozen chopped spinach, thawed and squeezed dry
•12 large eggs
•2 cups 2% milk
•1 cup shredded Swiss cheese
•1 cup shredded sharp cheddar cheese
•1/4 teaspoon paprika

Instructions
1.Preheat oven to 350°. In a large skillet, cook sausage over medium heat 6-8 minutes or until no longer pink, breaking into crumbles; drain and transfer to a greased 13 x 9-inch baking dish.

2.In same skillet, heat butter over medium-high heat. Add onion and mushrooms; cook and stir 3-5 minutes, or until tender. Stir in spinach. Spoon vegetable mixture over sausage.

3.In a large bowl, whisk eggs and milk until blended; pour egg mixture over vegetables. Sprinkle with cheeses and paprika. Bake, uncovered, 30-35 minutes or until the center is set and a thermometer inserted in center reads 165°. Let stand 10 minutes before serving.

TACO BREAKFAST SKILLET
Nutrition: Cal 523;Fat 44 g;Carb 9 g;Protein 22 g
Serving 6; Cook time 45min

Ingredients
•1 pound ground beef
•4 tablespoons taco seasoning
•2/3 cup water
•10 large eggs
•1 1/2 cups shredded sharp cheddar cheese, divided
•1/4 cup heavy cream
•1 roma tomato, diced
•1 medium avocado, peeled, pitted, and cubed
•1/4 cup sliced black olives
•2 green onions, sliced
•1/4 cup sour cream
•1/4 cup salsa
•1 jalapeno, sliced (optional)
•2 tablespoons torn fresh cilantro (optional)

Instructions
1.Brown the ground beef in a large skillet over medium-high heat. drain the excess fat.
2.To the skillet, stir in the taco seasoning and water. Reduce the heat to low and let simmer until the sauce has thickened and coats the meat. About 5 minutes. Remove half of the seasoned beef from the skillet and set aside.
3.Crack the eggs into a large mixing bowl and whisk. Add 1 cup of the cheddar cheese and the heavy cream to the eggs and whisk to combine.
4.Preheat the oven to 375°F.
5.Pour the egg mixture over top of the meat retained in the skillet and stir to mix the meat into the eggs. Bake for 30 minutes, or until the egg bake is cooked all the way through and fluffy.
6.Top with remaining ground beef, the remaining ½ cup of cheddar cheese, tomato, avocado, olives, green onion, sour cream, and salsa.
7.Garnish with jalapeno and cilantro, if using

KETO CACAO COCONUT GRANOLA
Nutrition: Cal 112;Fat 6g;Carb 7 g;Protein 7 g
Serving 3; Cook time 30min

Ingredients
•1/2 cup chopped raw pecans
•1/2 cup flax seeds
•1/2 cup superfine blanched almond flour
•1/2 cup unsweetened dried coconut
•1/4 cup cacao nibs
•1/4 cup chopped raw walnuts
•1/4 cup sesame seeds
•1/4 cup sugar-free vanilla-flavored protein powder
•3 tablespoons granulated erythritol
•1 teaspoon ground cinnamon
•1/8 teaspoon kosher salt
•1/3 cup coconut oil
•1 large egg white, beaten

Instructions
1.Preheat the oven to 300°F.
2.Line a 15x10-inch sheet pan with parchment paper.
3.Stir all of the ingredients until the mixture is crumbly and holds together in small clumps.
4.Spread out on the parchment-lined pan.
5.Bake for approximately 30 minutes or until golden brown and fragrant (oven times may vary).
6.Let the granola cool completely in the pan before removing.
7.Store in an airtight container in the refrigerator for up to 2 weeks.

CHORIZO BREAKFAST BAKE
Nutrition:Cal 212;Fat 11 g;Carb 11 g;Protein 9 g
Serving 4; Cook time 50min

Ingredients
•2 tablespoon olive oil
•1 red bell pepper
•1 yellow bell pepper
•200 grams (7 ounces) chorizo sausage
•6 large eggs
•2 large red onion (cut into wedges)
•2 cloves garlic (minced)
•½ cup coconut milk
•Salt and pepper

Instructions
1.Preheat the oven to 425 degrees Fahrenheit (220 degrees Celsius).
2.Cut the bell peppers in half, remove the seeds and stem and place the halves on a baking tray. Drizzle with 1 tbsp olive oil and put in the oven to roast for 20 minutes. After 10 minutes of baking, place the red onion wedges on the tray, drizzle with a splash of olive oil and return to the oven to cook for another 10 minutes. The peppers are done when they are soft and have a slightly charred skin. When the peppers are done, place them on a cutting board and place a bowl overtop to trap the steam. Leave them to rest for 5 minutes (this will make it easier to peel off the skin).
3.In a cast iron skillet heat 1 tbsp olive oil on medium high heat. Stir in the minced garlic and cook for 20 seconds until fragrant and then add in the chopped chorizo and cook for 5 minutes until the chorizo is cooked through and then remove from the heat.
4.While the chorizo is cooking peel the skin off of the roasted bell peppers. Cut the peeled peppers into thin strips.
5.In a bowl whisk together the eggs, coconut milk, paprika, cayenne, salt and pepper.
6.Add the sliced peppers and red onion to the cast iron skillet and pour the egg mixture overtop. Transfer to the oven to bake for 20-25 minutes until the egg has set and the top of the frittata is firm to the touch. Serve sprinkled with chopped parsley.

BAKED EGGS IN AVOCADO
Nutrition: Cal 125;Fat 10 g;Carb 3 g;Protein 8 g
Serving 2; Cook time 15min

Ingredients
•1 medium avocado
•2 tablespoons lime juice
•2 large eggs
•Salt and pepper
•2 tablespoons shredded cheddar cheese

Instructions
1.Preheat the oven to 450°F and cut the avocado in half.
2.Scoop out some of the flesh from the middle of each avocado half.
3.Place the avocado halves upright in a baking dish and brush with lime juice.
4.Crack an egg into each and season with salt and pepper.
5.Bake for 10 minutes, then sprinkle with cheese.
6.Let the eggs bake for another 2 to 3 minutes until the cheese is melted. Serve hot.

BREAKFAST EGG MUFFINS FILLED WITH SAUSAGE GRAVY
Nutrition: Cal 607;Fat 46 g;Carb 6 g;Protein 42 g
Serving 6; Cook time 35min

Ingredients
For the muffins:
•12 large eggs
•Sea salt
•Black pepper
•1 pound thin shaved deli ham
•4 ounces shredded mozzarella cheese
•4 ounces grated parmesan cheese
•Low-carb sausage gravy   For the gravy:
•1/2 ground pork sausage
•8 ounces softened cream cheese
•3/4 cups beef broth

•Sea salt
Black pepper
Instructions
1.Prepare the eggs and gravy.
2.Whisk eggs together with salt and pepper to taste.
3.Cook the sausage over medium heat until thoroughly cooked through.
4.Add in the cream cheese and the broth and stirring constantly, cook until the mixture comes to a soft simmer and thickens.
5.Then reduce the heat to medium-low, still stirring constantly and simmer for 2 more minutes.
6.Season to taste with salt and pepper.
7.Set mixture aside.
8.Preheat oven to 325°F.
Assemble the muffins:
1.Place two pieces of ham in the bottom of each muffin cup, careful to overlap and try and cover the whole surface.
2.Evenly divide sausage gravy between each muffin.
3.Pour eggs into each muffin, dividing the mixture evenly.
4.Top each muffin with equal parts of the two types of cheeses.
5.Bake for approximately 30-40 minutes or until muffin is firm and cheese is melted.

LEMON POPPY RICOTTA PANCAKES
Nutrition: Cal 370;Fat 26 g;Carb 6,5 g;Protein 29 g
Serving 2; Cook time 20min
Ingredients
•1 large lemon, juiced and zested
•6 ounces whole milk ricotta
•3 large eggs
•10 to 12 drops liquid stevia
•¼ cup almond flour
•1 scoop egg white protein powder
•1 tablespoon poppy seeds
•¾ teaspoons baking powder
•¼ cup powdered erythritol
•1 tablespoon heavy cream
Instructions
1.Combine the ricotta, eggs, and liquid stevia in a food processor with half the lemon juice and the lemon zest—blend well, then pour into a bowl.
2.Whisk in the almond flour, protein powder, poppy seeds, baking powder, and a pinch of salt.
3.Heat a large nonstick pan over medium heat.
4.Spoon the batter into the pan, using about ¼ cup per pancake.
5.Cook the pancakes until bubbles form on the surface of the batter, then flip them.
6.Let the pancakes cook until the bottom is browned, then remove to a plate.
7.Repeat with the remaining batter.
8.Whisk together the heavy cream, powdered erythritol, and reserved lemon juice and zest.
Serve the pancakes hot, drizzled with the lemon glaze.

EGG STRATA WITH BLUEBERRIES AND CIN-NAMON
Nutrition: Cal 188;Fat 15 g;Carb 4 g;Protein 8 g
Serving 4; Cook time 20min
Ingredients
•6 large eggs
•2 tbsp softened butter
•1 tsp vanilla
•1/2 cup blueberries (or 1/4 cup, depending upon taste)
•1/2 tsp cinnamon (you could probably double this if you like cinnamon)
•1 tbsp coconut oil
Instructions
1.Preheat oven to 375°F.
2.In an 8" - 9" cast iron skillet (or any oven-proof skillet), heat coconut oil over medium heat.
3.In a medium bowl beat eggs, butter, cinnamon, and vanilla together with a hand mixer until combined and fluffy (about 1-2 minutes).

4.Pour egg mixture into heated pan and allow bottom to cook slightly (about 2 minutes). Gently drop blueberries into egg mixture and place pan in oven. Cook for 15-20 or until cooked through and browned on top (but not burned).
5.Remove from oven and allow to cool slightly.

SWEET BLUEBERRY COCONUT PORRIDGE
Nutrition: Cal 390;Fat 22 g;Carb 12 g;Protein 10 g
Serving 2; Cook time 15min
Ingredients
•1 cup unsweetened almond milk
•¼ cup canned coconut milk
•¼ cup coconut flour
•¼ cup ground flaxseed
•1 teaspoon ground cinnamon
•¼ teaspoon ground nutmeg
•Pinch salt
•60 grams fresh blueberries
•¼ cup shaved coconut
Instructions
1.Warm the almond milk and coconut milk in a saucepan over low heat.
2.Whisk in the coconut flour, flaxseed, cinnamon, nutmeg, and salt.
3.Turn up the heat and cook until the mixture bubbles.
4.Stir in the sweetener and vanilla extract, then cook until thickened to the desired level.
5.Spoon into two bowls and top with blueberries and shaved coconut.

LOW-CARB BREAKFAST QUICHE
Nutrition: Cal 450;Fat 36 g;Carb 6 g;Protein 24 g
Serving 4; Cook time 55min
Ingredients
•1 lb ground Italian sausage
•1.5 cups shredded cheddar cheese
•8 large eggs
•1 tbsp ranch seasoning
•1 cup sour cream
Instructions
1.Preheat oven to 350°F.
2.In an oven-safe skillet, brown ground sausage and drain the grease.
3.In a large bowl, whisk together egg, sour cream, and ranch seasoning. You may want to use a hand mixer.
4.Mix in cheddar cheese.
5.Pour egg mixture into pan and stir until everything is fully blended.
6.Cover with foil and bake for 30 minutes.
7.Remove foil and bake for another 25 minutes or until golden brown.

FAT-BUSTING VANILLA PROTEIN SMOOTHIE
Nutrition: Cal 540;Fat 46 g;Carb 8 g;Protein 25 g
Serving 2; Cook time 5min
Ingredients
•11 scoop (20g) vanilla egg white protein powder
•½ cup heavy cream
•¼ cup vanilla almond milk
•4 ice cubes
•1 tablespoon coconut oil
•1 tablespoon powdered erythritol
•½ teaspoon vanilla extract
•¼ cup whipped cream
Instructions
1.Combine all of the ingredients, except the whipped cream, in a blender.
2.Blend on high speed for 30 to 60 seconds until smooth.
3.Pour into a glass and top with whipped cream.

SAVORY HAM AND CHEESE WAFFLES
Nutrition: Cal 575;Fat 45 g;Carb 5g;Protein 35g
Serving 2; Cook time 25min

Ingredients
- 4 large eggs, divided
- 2 scoops (40 g) egg white protein powder
- 1 teaspoon baking powder
- 1/3 cup melted butter
- ½ teaspoon salt
- 1 ounce diced ham
- ¼ cup shredded cheddar cheese

Instructions
1. Separate two of the eggs and set the other two aside.
2. Beat 2 of the egg yolks with the protein powder, baking powder, butter, and salt in a mixing bowl.
3. Fold in the chopped ham and grated cheddar cheese.
4. Whisk the egg whites in a separate bowl with a pinch of salt until stiff peaks form.
5. Fold the beaten egg whites into the egg yolk mixture in two batches.
6. Grease a preheated waffle maker then spoon ¼ cup of the batter into it and close it.
7. Cook until the waffle is golden brown, about 3 to 4 minutes, then remove.
8. Reheat the waffle iron and repeat with the remaining batter.
9. Meanwhile, heat the oil in a skillet and fry the eggs with salt and pepper.
10. Serve the waffles hot, topped with a fried egg.

AVOCADO SMOOTHIE WITH COCONUT MILK
Nutrition: Cal 283;Fat 25g;Carb 14g;Protein 3,2 g
Serving 15; Cook time 5min

Ingredients
- 1 cup coconut milk, unsweetened
- 1 tsp ginger, fresh and grounded
- 1/2 avocado
- 5 leaves spinach
- 1 tsp lime juice (optional)
- 1 tsp Stevia (optional)
- 1 tsp chia seeds

Instructions
1. Wash your ginger and spinach thoroughly.
2. Peel the ginger and avocado. Slice them into pieces.
3. Using a blender, mix all of the ingredients (except chia seeds and stevia) for a minute to obtain a smooth and uniform mixture. Optionally, pour some water and lime juice into the blender to produce the desired thickness.
4. Include some ice cubes and the sweetener into the mix just to flavor it up. Transfer to a glass and garnish with a teaspoon of chia seeds on top. Serve immediately.

COCONUT FLOUR PANCAKES
Nutrition: Cal 274;Fat 23g;Carb 8g;Protein 8g
Serving 2; Cook time 20min

Ingredients
Main Ingredients:
- 2 tbsp coconut flour
- 2 eggs
- ½ tbsp So Nourished Erythritol or a dash of stevia extract
- ¼ tsp baking powder
- 2 tbsp sour cream
- 2 tbsp melted butter
- ½ tsp vanilla extract

For the topping:
- 50 g strawberries
- 1 tbsp shredded coconut
- 1 tbsp almond slices
- 1 tbsp maple syrup (optional)

Instructions
1. Put the eggs, sour cream, 1 ½ tbsp. of melted butter (you'll need the rest for frying the pancakes), vanilla extract, and mix well.

2. Add the coconut flour, baking powder, erythritol to the mixture and mix again. Let the mixture sit for about 15 minutes. If the mixture is too thick, add a little bit of water (20-30 ml) and mix again until the consistency is right.
3. In a pan on medium heat, add butter in and fry the pancakes in butter. The number of pancakes you make will depend on the size you want. We made 6 pancakes with this recipe.

SOUTHWESTERN OMELET
Nutrition: Cal 390;Fat 31 g;Carb 7 g;Protein 22 g
Serving 4; Cook time 10min

Ingredients
- 1/2 cup chopped onion
- 1 jalapeno pepper, minced
- 1 tablespoon canola oil
- 6 large eggs, lightly beaten
- 6 bacon strips, cooked and crumbled
- 1 small tomato, chopped
- 1 ripe avocado, cut into 1-inch slices
- 1 cup shredded Monterey Jack cheese, divided
- Salt and pepper, to taste
- Salsa (optional)

Instructions
1. In a large skillet, saute onion and jalapeno in oil until tender; remove with a slotted spoon and set aside. Pour eggs into the same skillet; cover and cook over low heat for 3-4 minutes.
2. Sprinkle with the onion mixture, bacon, tomato, avocado, and 1/2 cup cheese. Season with salt and pepper.
3. Fold omelet in half over filling. Cover and cook for 3-4 minutes or until eggs are set.
4. Sprinkle with remaining cheese. Serve with salsa if desired.

EASY CLOUD BUNS
Nutrition: Cal 50;Fat 5 g;Carb 1 g;Protein 2.5 g
Serving 10; Cook time 40 min

Ingredients
3 large eggs, separated
1/8 teaspoon cream of tartar
3 ounces cream cheese, chopped

Instructions
1. Preheat the oven to 300°F and line a baking sheet with parchment.
2. Beat the egg whites until foamy then beat in the cream of tartar until the whites are shiny and opaque with soft peaks.
3. In a separate bowl, beat the cream cheese and egg yolks until well combined then fold in the egg white mixture.
4. Spoon the batter onto the baking sheet in ¼-cup circles about 2 inches apart.
5. Bake for 30 minutes until the buns are firm to the touch.

PEPPERONI, HAM & CHEDDAR STROMBOLI
Nutrition: Cal 525;Fat 37 g;Carb 16 g;Protein 32 g
Serving 3; Cook time 40min

Ingredients
- 1 ¼ cups shredded mozzarella cheese
- ¼ cup almond flour
- 3 tablespoons coconut flour
- 1 teaspoon dried Italian seasoning
- Salt and pepper
- 1 large egg, whisked
- 6 ounces sliced deli ham
- 2 ounces sliced pepperoni
- 4 ounces sliced cheddar cheese
- 1 tablespoon melted butter
- 6 cups fresh salad greens

Instructions
1. Preheat the oven to 400°F and line a baking sheet with parchment.
2. Melt the mozzarella cheese in a microwave-safe bowl until it can be stirred smooth.
3. In a separate bowl, stir together the almond flour, coconut flour, and dried Italian seasoning.

4.Pour the melted cheese into the flour mixture and mix it with some salt and pepper.

5.Add the egg and work it into a dough then put it onto a piece of parchment.

6.Lay a piece of parchment on top and roll the dough out into an oval.

7.Use a knife to cut diagonal slits along the edges, leaving the middle 4 inches untouched.

8.Layer the ham and cheese slices in the middle of the dough then fold the strips over the top.

9.Brush the top with butter, then bake for 15 to 20 minutes until the dough is browned. Slice the Stromboli and serve with a small salad.

EGGS AND ASPARAGUS BREAKFAST BITES
Nutrition: Cal 426;Fat 35 g;Carb 6 g;Protein 20 g
Serving 2; Cook time 25 min

Ingredients
•4 medium eggs
•100 g asparagus, fresh or canned
•1 tbsp butter, melted
•¼ tsp baking powder
•1 tbsp coconut flour
•80 g cream cheese
•40 g shredded cheddar cheese
•Salt, to taste

Instructions
1.For fresh asparagus, chop them into about 2-cm long pieces. Pan fry for around 5 minutes in melted butter. For canned asparagus, simply chop them into pieces. Reserve.

2.Combine the rest of the ingredients in a bowl. Stir well to mix together. Put aside for 10 minutes.

3.Brush a decent amount of oil in the baking molds. Place some pieces of asparagus in the molds then add the combined mixture you reserved earlier. Avoid filling up to the brim.

4.Place in the oven set at 350°F for 20 minutes, checking occasionally if the bites are cooked thoroughly.

5.Serve on a plate and enjoy.

AVOCADO BREAKFAST MUFFINS
Nutrition: Cal 250;Fat 19 g;Carb 2,5 g;Protein 17 g
Serving 20; Cook time 30min

Ingredients
•20 beef patties (small size, about 50 g each)
•10 eggs, medium-sized
•1/2 cup heavy cream
•2 avocados, cubed
•10 oz cheddar cheese, cubed
•Black pepper, to taste
1.Preheat oven to 350°F.
2.Take a large muffin tin and put one sausage patty in each cup, shaping with a shot glass to line the entire inside.
3.Evenly divide the avocado and cheese in the cups.
4.Beat eggs and heavy cream together in a bowl, then pour into each cup until cheese and avocado are covered. Top with black pepper to taste.
5.Bake for 20 minutes at 350°; if desired, broil for an additional 1-2 minutes until top is browned. Enjoy!

CHEDDAR BISCUITS
Nutrition: Cal 284;Fat 25 g;Carb 2 g;Protein 20 g
Serving 4; Cook time 20 min

Ingredients
•1 cup cheddar cheese, shredded
•1/4 cup butter melted and slightly cooled
•4 eggs
•1/3 cup coconut flour
•1/4 teaspoon baking powder
•1/4 teaspoon garlic powder
•1 teaspoon dried parsley (optional)
•1/4 teaspoon Old Bay Seasoning (optional)
•1/4 teaspoon salt
Instructions

1.Set the oven to 400°F to preheat.

2.Crack the eggs in a bowl. Add the garlic powder, melted butter, dried parsley, and seasoning powder if you have some. Salt to taste.

3.Combine the cheese into the mixture together with the baking powder and coconut flour. Fold until you obtain a lump-free mixture.

4.Grease a cookie sheet before adding the batter into it. Place ice cream-size scoops on the sheet.

5.Lightly brown the biscuits in the oven for 15 minutes.

6.Serve with any meal or eat them alone.

7.If you like to keep them for later, allow them to cool completely before storing in a jar to preserve the crispness.

BACON AND MUSHROOM OMELETTE
Nutrition: Cal 313;Fat 24 g;Carb 1,5 g;Protein 23 g
Serving 2; Cook time 10min

Ingredients
•3 medium mushrooms, raw
•2 slices bacon
•3 eggs
•2 tbsp onion, chopped
•2 slices cheddar cheese
•Lettuce or watercress, to taste (optional)
•Pinch salt
•Pinch pepper

Instructions
1.Brunoise cut the onion. Slice the mushrooms and bacon into small chunks as well.

2.Heat an 8-inch non-stick skillet coated with cooking spray over medium-high heat. Cook the onion and bacon in the pan. Once the bacon is toasted enough, toss in the mushrooms and remove from the heat.

3.Beat the eggs in a mixing bowl. Flavor with sea salt and black pepper then add the cooked bacon, mushroom, and onion.

4.Gently pour the egg mixture into the pan. Once the omelette starts to firm up, ease around the edges with a spatula. Lay the slices of cheddar cheese on one half of the omelette. Fold the other half onto the cheese.

5.Leave in the pan for another 2 minutes, then let the cooked omelette slide onto a plate.

6.Fill the inside of the omelette with lettuce leaves if preferred. Serve immediately while still crispy and warm.

SCRAMBLED EGGS WITH MUSHROOMS AND COTTAGE CHEESE
Nutrition: Cal 210;Fat 19 g;Carb 3 g;Protein 9 g
Serving 3; Cook time 20min

Ingredients
•3 eggs
•1 cup button mushrooms, rinsed and sliced
•1/2 medium-sized onion, finely chopped
•3 tbsp olive oil
•1/4 tsp oregano
•1/4 cup cottage cheese
•1/2 tsp sea salt
•1/4 tsp black pepper

Instructions
1.Place a large skillet over medium-high heat. Let the olive oil heat in the pan. Sauté the finely chopped onions in the oil until they become translucent. Drop in the sliced mushrooms and let it simmer until the liquid in the pan evaporates. Stir well with oregano, pepper, and salt. Put aside.

2.Beat the eggs in a bowl. Flavor with a dash of salt and pepper enough to taste. Fry in the skillet and fold with a wooden spoon for a minute until slightly underdone.

VEGETABLE TART
Nutrition: Cal 250;Fat 22 g;Carb 5.5 g;Protein 10 g
Serving 8; Cook time 70 min

Ingredients
•6 eggs
•½ cup heavy cream
•8 oz cream cheese

- ½ cup shredded cheese
- ½ cup almond milk (or coconut milk)
- 12 oz zucchini
- 4 oz cauliflower
- 2 oz broccoli
- 8 oz red pepper
- 3 oz jalapeno
- 3 oz onion
- 3 cloves garlic
- Seasoning of your choice

Instructions

1. Mince the cauliflower, broccoli, garlic, onion, red pepper, and jalapeño into small cubes. Dice the zucchini as well.
2. Sauté the diced vegetables in a heated oil on a large skillet. Remove from the heat when they become soft enough but not mushy.
3. Crack the eggs in another bowl. Combine the almond milk, softened cream cheese, and heavy cream in the bowl. Mix everything to combine well.
4. Mix the vegetables into the cream cheese bowl. Stir with the cheese and seasonings of choice. Fold together until uniform.
5. Lay a foil on the base of the springform you will use to avoid seeping the mixture through the bottom. Cover with parchment paper and brush some oil on the sides and on the base. Pour the batter into the form. Bake for one hour or up till the surface of the tart is golden brown in color. The oven must be preheated to 350°F.
6. Generously dust with cheese on top after baking. Slice into wedges and serve.

ZUCCHINI BREAKFAST MUFFINS

Nutrition: Cal 185;Fat 16 g;Carb 2 g;Protein 9 g
Serving 12; Cook time 35min

Ingredients

- 6 eggs
- 1 zucchini, medium-sized
- 5 slices bacon
- 2 tbsp sour cream
- 1 cup heavy cream
- 1 cup shredded cheddar cheese
- 1 tbsp mayonnaise
- 1 tbsp mustard
- 1/2 cup coconut milk
- 1 oz dill
- 1 jalapeno small size
- 4 oz red pepper
- Salt and pepper, to taste

Instructions

1. Shred your zucchini into thin pieces and dust with some salt. Put aside for a few minutes to release the moisture.
2. Chop the dill into fine pieces, then mince your jalapeno and red pepper.
3. Crispy fry the bacon slices for around 5 minutes or simply heat them in the microwave. Cut into bits.
4. Strain all the unnecessary liquids from the grated zucchini. Press it with your hands to squeeze out the extracts. Alternatively, use a cheesecloth to do this. Transfer all of the chopped vegetables in a bowl and toss to mix well. Add in the cheese and bacon bits.
5. Crack the eggs in a separate bowl. Blend together with the sour cream, mustard, heavy cream, and mayo. Include the coconut milk as well. Adjust the flavor with salt and pepper.
6. Transfer the vegetable mix into 12 muffin forms. Distribute evenly. Gently add in the egg mixture into the cups. Remember to fill only ⅔ of the cup. Combine the two mixture with a spoon. Stir well.
7. Bake in the oven preheated at 370°F for 20-25 minutes. Make sure the muffins are golden and firm before removing from the oven.
8. Unmold from the cups and serve on a plate

KETO CEREAL

Nutrition: Cal 250;Fat 10 g;Carb 15 g;Protein 10 g
Serving 3; Cook time 45 min

Ingredients

- Cooking spray

- 1 c. almonds, chopped
- 1 c. walnuts, chopped
- 1 c. unsweetened coconut flakes
- 1/4 c. sesame seeds
- 2 tbsp. flax seeds
- 2 tbsp. chia seeds
- 1/2 tsp. ground clove
- 1 1/2 tsp. ground cinnamon
- 1 tsp. pure vanilla extract
- 1/2 tsp. kosher salt
- 1 large egg white
- 1/4 c. melted coconut oil

Instructions

1. Preheat oven to 350° and grease a baking sheet with cooking spray. In a large bowl, mix together almonds, walnuts, coconut flakes, sesame seeds, flax seeds, and chia seeds. Stir in cloves, cinnamon, vanilla, and salt.
2. Beat egg white until foamy then stir into granola. Add coconut oil and stir until everything is well coated. Pour onto prepared baking sheet and spread into an even layer. Bake for 20 to 25 minutes, or until golden, gently stirring halfway through. Let cool completely.

KETO SAUSAGE BREAKFAST SANDWICH

Nutrition: Cal 350;Fat 25 g;Carb 2 g;Protein 12 g
Serving 3; Cook time 20 min

Ingredients

- 6 large eggs
- 2 tbsp. heavy cream
- Pinch red pepper flakes
- Kosher salt
- Freshly ground black pepper
- 1 tbsp. butter
- 3 slices cheddar
- 6 frozen sausage patties, heated according to package instructions
- 1 Avocado, sliced

Instructions

1. In a small bowl beat eggs, heavy cream, and red pepper flakes together. Season generously with salt and pepper. In a nonstick skillet over medium heat, melt butter. Pour about ⅓ of the eggs into the skillet. Place a slice of cheese in the middle and let sit about 1 minute. Fold the sides of the egg into the middle, covering the cheese. Remove from pan and repeat with remaining eggs.

2. Serve eggs between two sausage patties with avocado.

CABBAGE HASH BROWNS

Nutrition: Cal 250;Fat 22 g;Carb 5.5 g;Protein 10 g
Serving 2; Cook time 35 min

Ingredients

2 large eggs
1/2 tsp. garlic powder
1/2 tsp. kosher salt
Freshly ground black pepper
2 c. shredded cabbage
1/4 small yellow onion, thinly sliced
1 tbsp. vegetable oil

Instructions

1. In a large bowl, whisk together eggs, garlic powder, and salt. Season with black pepper. Add cabbage and onion to egg mixture and toss to combine.
2. In a large skillet over medium-high heat, heat oil. Divide mixture into 4 patties in the pan and press with spatula to flatten. Cook until golden and tender, about 3 minutes per side.

OMELET-STUFFED PEPPERS

Nutrition: Cal 280;Fat 12 g;Carb 8 g;Protein 25 g

Serving 4; Cook time 60 min

Ingredients
- 2 bell peppers, halved and seeds removed
- 8 eggs, lightly beaten
- 1/4 c. milk
- 4 slices bacon, cooked and crumbled
- 1 c. shredded cheddar
- 2 tbsp. finely chopped chives, plus more for garnish
- Kosher salt
- Freshly cracked black pepper

Instructions
1. Preheat oven to 400°. Place peppers cut side up in a large baking dish. Add a little water to the dish and bake peppers for 5 minutes.
2. Meanwhile, beat together eggs and milk. Stir in bacon, cheese, and chives and season with salt and pepper.
3. When peppers are done baking, pour egg mixture into peppers. Place back in the oven and bake 35 to 40 minutes more, until eggs are set. Garnish with more chives and serve.

ZUCCHINI EGG CUPS
Nutrition: Cal 280;Fat 12g;Carb 8g;Protein 25 g
Serving 12; Cook time 50 min

Ingredients
- Cooking spray, for pan
- 2 zucchini, peeled into strips
- 1/4 lb. ham, chopped
- 1/2 c. cherry tomatoes, quartered
- 8 eggs
- 1/2 c. heavy cream
- Kosher salt
- Freshly ground black pepper
- 1/2 tsp. dried oregano
- 1 c. Pinch red pepper flakes
- 1 c. shredded cheddar

Instructions
1. Preheat oven to 400° and grease a muffin tin with cooking spray. Line the inside and bottom of the muffin tin with zucchini strips, to form a crust. Sprinkle ham and cherry tomatoes inside each crust.
2. In a medium bowl whisk together eggs, heavy, cream, oregano, and red pepper flakes then season with salt and pepper. Pour egg mixture over ham and tomatoes then top with cheese.
3. Bake until eggs are set, 30 minutes.

BACON AVOCADO BOMBS
Nutrition: Cal 250;Fat 19 g;Carb 2,5 g;Protein 17 g
Serving 4; Cook time 30min

Ingredients
- 2 avocados
- 1/3 c. shredded Cheddar
- 8 slices bacon

Instructions
1. Heat broiler and line a small baking sheet with foil.
2. Slice each avocado in half and remove the pits. Peel the skin off of each avocado.
3. Fill two of the halves with cheese, then replace with the other avocado halves. Wrap each avocado with 4 slices of bacon.
4. Place bacon-wrapped avocados on the prepared baking sheet and broil until the bacon is crispy on top, about 5 minutes. Very carefully, flip the avocado using tongs and continue to cook until crispy all over, about 5 minutes per side.
5. Cut in half crosswise and serve immediately.

HAM & CHEESE EGG CUPS
Nutrition: Cal 340;Fat 30 g;Carb 10 g;Protein 12 g

Serving 12; Cook time 30min

Ingredients
- Cooking spray, for pan
- 12 slices ham
- 1 c. shredded cheddar
- 12 large eggs
- Kosher salt
- Freshly ground black pepper
- Chopped fresh parsley, for garnish

Instructions
1. Preheat oven to 400° and grease a 12-cup muffin tin with cooking spray. Line each cup with a slice of ham and sprinkle with cheddar. Crack an egg into each ham cup and season with salt and pepper.
2. Bake until eggs are cooked through, 12 to 15 minutes (depending on how runny you like your yolks).
3. Garnish with parsley and serve.

KETO FAT BOMBS
Nutrition: Cal 290;Fat 28 g;Carb 5 g;Protein 5 g
Serving 16; Cook time 35 min

Ingredients
- 8 oz. cream cheese, softened to room temperature
- 1/2 c. keto-friendly peanut butter
- 1/4 c. coconut oil, plus 2 tbsp.
- 1/4 tsp. kosher salt
- 1/2 c. keto-friendly dark chocolate chips (such as Lily's)

Instructions
1. Line a small baking sheet with parchment paper. In a medium bowl, combine cream cheese, peanut butter, ¼ cup coconut oil, and salt. Using a hand mixer, beat mixture until fully combined, about 2 minutes. Place bowl in freezer to firm up slightly, 10 to 15 minutes.
2. When peanut butter mixture has hardened, use a small cookie scoop or spoon to create tablespoon-sized balls. Place in refrigerator to harden, 5 minutes.
3. Meanwhile, make chocolate drizzle: combine chocolate chips and remaining coconut oil in a microwave safe bowl and microwave in 30 second intervals until fully melted. Drizzle over peanut butter balls and place back in refrigerator to harden, 5 minutes.
4. To store, keep covered in refrigerator.

KETO PIZZA EGG WRAP
Nutrition: Cal 350;Fat 10 g;Carb 2 g;Protein 25 g
Serving 1; Cook time 15 min

Ingredients
- 2 large eggs
- ½ tbsp butter
- ½ tbsp tomato sauce
- ½ oz. (2 tbsp) mozzarella cheese, shredded
- 1½ oz. salami, sliced

Instructions
1. Heat a large, non-stick frying pan to medium heat. Add the butter.
2. Crack the eggs into a bowl, and whisk until smooth in color.
3. Slowly pour the eggs into the pan, allowing the mixture to go right to the edges.
4. Cook until the edges begin to lift off the side of the frying pan. Using a spatula all around the edge, lift the egg from the pan.
5. Flip and cook on the other side for 30 seconds.
6. Remove from the pan. Layer tomato sauce, mozzarella cheese, and salami in the middle. Roll it together into a wrap.

GREEN EGGS
Nutrition: Cal 300;Fat 20 g;Carb 8 g;Protein 18 g
Serving 2; Cook time 20 min

Ingredients
- 1½ tbsp rapeseed oil , plus a splash extra
- 2 trimmed leeks , sliced
- 2 garlic cloves , sliced
- ½ tsp coriander seeds

- ½ tsp fennel seeds
- pinch of chilli flakes , plus extra to serve
- 200g spinach
- 2 large eggs
- 2 tbsp Greek yogurt
- squeeze of lemon

Instructions
1. Heat the oil in a large frying pan. Add the leeks and a pinch of salt, then cook until soft. Add the garlic, coriander, fennel and chilli flakes. Once the seeds begin to crackle, tip in the spinach and turn down the heat. Stir everything together until the spinach has wilted and reduced, then scrape it over to one side of the pan. Pour a little oil into the pan, then crack in the eggs and fry until cooked to your liking.
2. Stir the yogurt through the spinach mix and season. Pile onto two plates, top with the fried egg, squeeze over a little lemon and season with black pepper and chilli flakes to serve.

MASALA FRITTATA WITH AVOCADO SALSA

Nutrition: Cal 350;Fat 25 g;Carb 12 g;Protein 16 g
Serving 4; Cook time 40 min

Ingredients
- 2 tbsp rapeseed oil
- 3 onions, 2½ thinly sliced, ½ finely chopped
- 1 tbsp Madras curry paste
- 500g cherry tomatoes, halved
- 1 red chilli, deseeded and finely chopped
- small pack coriander, roughly chopped
- 8 large eggs, beaten
- 1 avocado, stoned, peeled and cubed
- juice 1 lemon

Instructions
1. Heat the oil in a medium non-stick, ovenproof frying pan. Tip in the sliced onions and cook over a medium heat for about 10 mins until soft and golden. Add the Madras paste and fry for 1 min more, then tip in half the tomatoes and half the chilli. Cook until the mixture is thick and the tomatoes have all burst.
2. Heat the grill to high. Add half the coriander to the eggs and season, then pour over the spicy onion mixture. Stir gently once or twice, then cook over a low heat for 8-10 mins until almost set. Transfer to the grill for 3-5 mins until set.
3. To make the salsa, mix the avocado, remaining chilli and tomatoes, chopped onion, remaining coriander and the lemon juice together, then season and serve with the frittata.

TARRAGON, MUSHROOM & SAUSAGE FRIT-TATA

Nutrition: Cal 433;Fat 32g;Protein 25 g
Serving 2; Cook time 20 min

Ingredients
- 1 tbsp olive oil
- 200g chestnut mushrooms , sliced
- 2 pork sausages
- 1 garlic clove , crushed
- 100g fine asparagus
- 3 large eggs
- 2 tbsp half-fat soured cream
- 1 tbsp wholegrain mustard
- 1 tbsp chopped tarragon
- mixed rocket salad , to serve (optional)

Instructions
1. Heat the grill to high. Heat the oil in a medium-sized, non-stick frying pan, add the mushrooms and fry over a high heat for 3 mins. Squeeze the sausagemeat out of their skins into nuggets, add to the pan and fry for a further 5 mins until golden brown. Add the garlic and asparagus and cook for another 1 min.

2. Whisk the eggs, soured cream, mustard and tarragon in a jug. Season well, then pour the egg mixture in to the pan. Cook for 3-4 mins, then grill for a further 1-2 mins or until the top has just set with a slight wobble in the middle. Serve with the salad leaves, if you like.

KETO CHIA PUDDING

Nutrition: Cal 336;Fat 27 g;Carb 16 g;Protein 8 g
Serving 2; Cook time 35 min

Ingredients
- 2 tbsp low carb sugar (Sukrin:1, Swerve, Lakanto, Truvia, or Besti)
- 1 tbsp Cocoa Powder (sift before measuring)
- 1 tsp Vanilla Extract
- 1 cup Coconut Milk (from a can) (or Almond Milk for less calories)
- 1/4 cup Chia Seeds

Instructions
1. Add the cocoa powder and sweetener to a mason jar. Close the lid and shake well to remove any lumps.
2. Add the coconut milk and vanilla extract to the mason jar. Close the lid and shake to combine.
3. Add the chia seeds to the jar and shake again. Once the mixture is well combined, transfer the jar to the fridge.
4. Chill for at least 30 minutes.
5. Serve the chocolate chia pudding in your favourite jars, with coconut yogurt and seasonal fruit. Enjoy!

KETO BREAKFAST PARFAIT

Nutrition: Cal 335;Fat 29 g;Carb 10 g;Protein 11 g
Serving 2; Cook time 10 min

Ingredients
- ½ cup Greek Yogurt full fat
- ¼ cup Heavy Cream
- 1 teaspoon Vanilla Essence
- ½ cup Keto Chocolate Almond Clusters
- 2 Strawberries diced
- 8 Blueberries

Instructions
1. In a mixing bowl, add together the yogurt, cream and vanilla. Whisk together until thick and smooth.
2. Spoon half the yogurt between two glasses, then sprinkle over half the granola.
3. Add the remaining yogurt, followed by the remaining granola.
4. Top with the berries and enjoy!

KETO SAUSAGE & EGG BOWLS

Nutrition: Cal 435;Fat 29 g;Carb 8 g;Protein 27 g
Serving 2; Cook time 10 min

Ingredients
- 1/4 cup sausage – cooked and crumbled
- 2 whole eggs
- sprinkle of cheddar cheese
- salt & pepper to taste
- 1 tbs butter

Instructions
1. Start by cracking two eggs into a bowl and scramble with a fork until all mixed together
2. Add butter to skillet over medium high heat
3. Once melted, add eggs to pan – stirring around often – careful not to over cook
4. Once the eggs are mostly set but still glossy, add the sausage and cheese.
5. Remove from heat and mix in well.
6. Add salt and pepper to taste.

CHEESE AND EGG STUFFED PEPPERS

Nutrition: Cal 285;Fat 7 g;Carb 7g;Protein 14 g
Serving 8; Cook time 50 min

Ingredients
- •4 large bell peppers, cut in half lengthwise and remove inner seeds and stems
- •1 tablespoon olive oil
- •1 cup white onion
- •1 pound gluten free pork sausage, casing removed
- •2 cups spinach
- •4 large eggs
- •1/4 teaspoon salt & pepper, each
- •3/4 cup shredded mozzarella

Instructions
1. Preheat oven to 350°F/180°C. Lightly grease a 9x13 baking dish.
2. Arrange the bell peppers side-by-side in the greased baking dish - cut side up. Set aside
3. Warm the olive oil to a large skillet over a medium heat. Add the onions and cook about 5 minutes to soften. Add the sausage and cook until no longer pink. Stir in the spinach and cook an addition 1-2 minutes until wilted. Remove from the heat.
4. In a medium sized mixing bowl whisk together the eggs, salt and pepper. Stir in 1/2 cup of the cheese.
5. Spoon the sausage mixture evenly into your prepared peppers. Pour the egg mixture over the top of the sausage. Top with the remaining 1/4 cup cheese.
6. Return to the oven and bake an additional 35-40 minutes until the cheese has goldened.

KETO CROQUE MADAME
Nutrition: Cal 566;Fat 46.7g;Carb 3.1g;Protein 33 g
Serving 4; Cook time 30 min

Ingredients
Chaffles:
- •2 large egg
- •1 cup cheddar cheese, grated

Sandwich:
- •4 slice deli-sliced black forest ham
- •2/3 cup gruyere cheesc, shredded
- •2 tablespoon butter
- •4 large egg

Bechemel Sauce:
- •1/2 cup heavy cream
- •1/4 cup parmesan cheese
- •1/3 cup gruyere cheese, shredded

Instructions
1. Measure out and prepare the ingredients. Preheat oven to 425F.
2. In a bowl, make the chaffles by whisking together the eggs and grated cheese.
3. Using a small waffle iron that is greased, make the chaffles.
4. On a parchment lined baking sheet, add the chaffles, topped with the deli sliced ham, and the shredded gruyere cheese. Bake in the oven for 10-15 minutes or until cheese is melted.
5. While the chaffles are in the oven, fry up the eggs in a frying pan with butter. Then top the baked chaffle with the fried eggs.
6. In a saucepan on medium heat, make the bechemel sauce by adding the heavy cream. Slowly add in the parmesan cheese and gruyere cheese a small handful at a time and wait until it is melted before adding in more.
7. Drizzle the bechemel sauce on top of the chaffles, serve with a small side salad and enjoy!

KETO SPINACH SHAKSHUKA
Nutrition: Cal 318;Fat 23 g;Carb 5 g;Protein 19 g
Serving 4; Cook time 25 min

Ingredients
- •3 tablespoon olive oil
- •1/2 medium onion, minced
- •2 teaspoon fresh garlic, minced
- •1 medium jalapeno pepper, seeded + minced
- •16 ounce frozen spinach, thawed
- •1 teaspoon cumin
- •3/4 teaspoon ground coriander
- •2 tablespoon harissa
- •Salt and pepper to taste
- •1/2 cup vegetable broth
- •8 large eggs
- •1/4 cup fresh parsley, chopped, for garnish
- •1 teaspoon crushed red pepper flakes, for garnish

Instructions
1. Measure out and prepare all the ingredients. Preheat oven to 350F.
2. In a skillet, add the olive oil to the skillet over medium heat. Saute the minced onion in until fragrant.
3. Add the thawed spinach into the skillet and let it cook until it's wilted.
4. Add the cumin, coriander, harissa, and salt and pepper. Stir together well and let cook for another 1-2 minutes.
5. Transfer the seasoned spinach mixture to a food processor. Pulse until coarse. Then, add the vegetable broth and pulse until smooth. Wipe out your skillet.
6. Drizzle oil in the bottom of the skillet or spray some cooking spray. Pour the smooth spinach mixture into the skillet. Using a spoon, press the back of the spoon into parts of the spinach mixture.
7. Gently crack the eggs into these parts of the mixture. Cook in the oven until the egg whites are set and the yolk is a little runny. This should take about 20-25 minutes.

KETO SAUSAGE CREAM CHEESE ROLLS
Nutrition: Cal 203;Fat 16 g;Carb 3 g;Protein 12 g
Serving 10; Cook time 25 min

Ingredients
For the Rolls:
- •2 cups shredded mozzarealla cheese
- •2 ounces cream cheese
- •3/4 cup almond flour
- •2 tablespoons ground flax meal

For the Filling:
- •1/2 pound cooked breakfast sausage, drained
- •3 ounces of cream cheese

Instructions
Preheat oven to 400F.
For the Rolls:
1. In a microwave-safe mixing bowl, combine the shredded mozzarella cheese and cream cheese. Heat in 30 second increments, stirring in between until completely melted.
2. Add the almond flour and ground flax meal.
3. Mix the dough well until you have a soft ball
4. Between two silicone baking mats or parchment paper roll the dough into a rectangle roughly 12x9 inches.

For the filling:
1. Combine the sausage and cream cheese.
2. Spread the sausage cream cheese mixture evenly on the dough.
3. Starting at one end roll the dough as tightly as you can into a log.
4. Slice into rolls about the width of two fingers, be careful not to slice them too thick because it will be difficult for the dough in the center to cook through.
5. Place the rolls on a greased baking sheet.
6. Bake 12-15 minutes until golden brown.

PREHEAT OVEN TO 400F.
Nutrition: Cal 353;Fat 23 g;Carb 4 g;Protein 18 g
Serving 12; Cook time 25 min

Ingredients
For the Keto Almond Flour Biscuits
- •3 ounces cream cheese,softened
- •1 cup shredded cheddar cheese
- •2 eggs
- •2 cups almond flour
- •1 teaspoon baking powder
- •1/4 teaspoon salt

- 1/4 cup heavy cream (scrape the measuring cup out since it is thick, make sure you get ALL of the liquid)
- 1 tablespoon melted butter

Sausage Patties
- 1 1/2 pounds breakfast sausage, formed into 12 patties

Instructions
1. Preheat the oven to 350 degrees.
2. In a mixing bowl combine the softened cream cheese, cheddar cheese and eggs. Stir until cream cheese is smooth with no clumps.
3. Add almond flour, baking powder, salt, heavy cream and melted butter.
4. Stir until combined. Do not overmix or biscuits will be tough.
5. Chill the dough 10-15 minutes.
6. Lightly sprinkle almond flour onto a cutting board and turn the dough onto the floured surface. Pat the biscuits to about 1/2 inch thick and use a biscuit cutter or the top of a mason jar to cut out your biscuits.
7. Place the biscuits onto a greased or silicone lined baking sheet.
8. Bake 15-18 minutes until golden.
9. Cook the sausage patties in a skillet over medium heat until cooked through.
10. To assemble slice the warm biscuits in half and add the sausage patty.

KETO BISCUITS AND GRAVY
Nutrition: Cal 203;Fat 16g;Carb 3g;Protein 12 g
Serving 6; Cook time 40 min

Ingredients
Keto Biscuits
- ¼ cup unsalted butter melted
- 4 large eggs
- ⅓ cup coconut flour
- 1 cup cheddar cheese shredded
- 1 tbsp cream cheese
- ¼ tsp salt
- ¼ tsp baking powder

Keto Sausage Gravy
- 1 lb ground sausage
- ½ cup chicken broth
- 1 cup heavy cream
- salt & pepper to taste
- 4 tbsp cream cheese
- ½ tsp chili flakes optional
- ¼ tsp xanthan gum optional

Instructions
To make the keto biscuits
1. Preheat the oven to 350°F / 180°C and line a baking sheet with parchment paper.
2. In a large bowl add the eggs, one tablespoon cream cheese, and salt. Whisk for 30 seconds.
3. Pour the melted butter over the egg mixture and continue whisking.
4. Add the shredded cheddar cheese, coconut flour, and baking powder and combine well. Let the biscuits dough sit for about 5 minutes so the coconut flour can absorb the liquid and make the dough thick.
5. Divide the dough into 9 equal biscuits. Place them 2 inches apart on the baking sheet.
6. Bake in the preheated oven for about 15 minutes or until they get a beautiful golden color.

To make the sausage gravy
1. In a large skillet add the ground sausage. Brown and crumble the meat into smaller pieces over medium heat until fully cooked.
2. Add the chicken broth, cream cheese and whipping cream. Stir to combine well and let it simmer until it becomes thicker. Season with salt and pepper to taste (if necessary).
3. Serve one or two keto biscuits with 1/2 cup of gravy. Enjoy!

KETO PROTEIN BREAKFAST SCRAMBLE
Nutrition: Cal 511;Fat 41g;Carb 6g;Protein 28 g
Serving 4; Cook time 20 min

Ingredients

- 6 links breakfast sausage sliced
- 6 slices bacon chopped
- 4 oz hard salami (such as Genoa) cubed
- 1 small onion sliced
- 1 medium bell pepper sliced
- 6 large eggs
- ¼ cup sour cream
- ½ cup cheddar cheese grated
- 2 stalks green onion (scallion) sliced
- salt and pepper

Instructions
1. Place a frying pan over medium-high heat. Once hot add raw sliced bacon and sausage. Fry until cooked through, and just starting to brown and crisp. (5 - 8 minutes)
2. 6 slices bacon
3. Add chopped salami and continue to fry until the salami, bacon, and sausage have reached a level of crispness you are satisfied with. If the pan contains a lot of rendered fat, drain off a portion now to avoid greasy eggs (2 - 3 minutes)
4. 6 links breakfast sausage,4 oz hard salami (such as Genoa)
5. Next add the sliced onions and pepper to fry until softened. (1 minute)
6. 1 small onion,1 medium bell pepper
7. Stir in egg mixture, and using a spatula begin to combine and scramble everything in the pan. Cook eggs to desired doneness. (3-5 minutes)
8. Stir in grated cheese, top with sliced green onion, and season to taste with salt and pepper.
9. 2 stalks green onion (scallion),salt and pepper

EGG WRAPS WITH HAM AND GREENS
Nutrition: Cal 371;Fat 26 g;Carb 5 g;Protein 28 g
Serving 6; Cook time 20 min

Ingredients
- 8 large eggs
- 4 teaspoons water
- 2 teaspoons all-purpose flour or cornstarch
- 1/2 teaspoon fine salt
- 4 teaspoons vegetable or coconut oil
- 1 1/3 cups shredded Swiss cheese
- 4 ounces very thinly sliced ham
- 1 1/3 cups loosely packed watercress

Instructions
1. Place the eggs, water, flour or cornstarch, and salt in a medium bowl and whisk until broken up and the flour or cornstarch is completely dissolved.
2. Heat 1 teaspoon of the oil in a 12-inch nonstick frying pan over medium heat until shimmering. Swirl the pan to coat the bottom with the oil. Add 1/2 cup of the egg mixture and swirl to coat the bottom of the pan in a thin layer. Cook until the wrap is completely set on the edges and on the bottom (the top can be a little wet, but should be mostly set), 3 to 6 minutes.
3. Using a flat spatula, loosen the edges of the wrap and slide it underneath the wrap, making sure it can slide easily around the pan. Flip the wrap with the spatula. Immediately sprinkle 1/3 cup of the cheese over the wrap and cook until the second side is set, about 1 minute. Slide it onto a work surface or cutting board (the cheese might not be fully melted yet). While still warm, place a single layer of ham over the egg. Place 1/3 cup of the watercress across the center of the wrap. Roll it up tightly.
4. Repeat with cooking and filling the remaining wraps. Using a serrated knife, cut each wrap crosswise into 6 (1-inch) pieces.

BACON GRUYÈRE EGG BITES
Nutrition: Cal 208;Fat 17,5 g;Carb 1 g;Protein 11 g
Serving 9; Cook time 60 min

Ingredients
- Bacon fat or butter, for coating the pan
- 9 large eggs
- 3/4 cup grated Gruyère cheese (2 1/4 ounces)
- 1/3 cup cream cheese (about 2 1/2 ounces)
- 1/2 teaspoon kosher salt

•6 slices thick-cut bacon, cooked and crumbled

Instructions

1. Arrange a rack in the middle of the oven and heat to 350°F. Coat an 8x8-inch (broiler-safe if you want a browned top) baking dish generously with bacon fat or butter.
2. Place the eggs, Gruyère, cream cheese, and salt in a blender and blend on medium-high speed until very smooth, about 1 minute. Pour into the baking dish. Sprinkle with the bacon. Cover tightly with aluminum foil.
3. Pull the oven rack halfway out of the oven. Place a roasting pan on the oven rack. Pour in 6 cups of very hot tap water. Set the baking dish of eggs into the roasting pan. Bake until just set in the middle, 55 minutes to 1 hour.
4. Carefully remove the roasting pan from the oven. Remove the baking dish from the roasting pan and uncover. (For a browned top: Heat the oven to broil. Broil until the top is golde- brown, 4 to 5 minutes.) Cut into 9 squares and serve.

RADISH AND TURNIP HASH WITH FRIED EGGS

Nutrition: Cal 391;Fat 33,9 g;Carb 10 g;Protein 12 g
Serving 2; Cook time 20 min

Ingredients

•2 to 3 small turnips, trimmed, peeled, and cut into 3/4-inch cubes (about 1 1/2 cups cubed)
•4 to 5 small radishes, scrubbed and trimmed, and cut into 3/4-inch cubes (about 1 1/2 cups cubed)
•Coarse sea salt
•Freshly ground pepper
•2 tablespoons grapeseed oil, or other neutral, heat-tolerant oil
•1 stalk green garlic, trimmed and chopped (white and light green parts only)
•2 tablespoons unsalted butter
•4 eggs
•1 tablespoon minced parsley

Instructions

1. Fill a large saucepan with water and bring to a boil. Add 2 teaspoons sea salt. Boil turnip cubes just until tender, 3 to 4 minutes; remove to a bowl with a slotted spoon, pour off any excess water, and set aside. Next, boil radishes briefly, 30 to 60 seconds; remove to a bowl with a slotted spoon, pour off any excess water, and set aside.

2. Set a large cast iron skillet over medium-high heat. Add grapeseed oil and when hot, add turnips and radishes, and a pinch each sea salt and pepper. Turning vegetables only once or twice, cook 8 minutes or until golden-brown. Turn heat to medium and fold in green garlic, cooking for about a minute. Push vegetables to the sides, melt butter in the center of pan, and add the eggs, salting each individually. For over-easy eggs, cook uncovered 4 to 6 minutes; for over-medium eggs, cover pan for 3 minutes, then uncover and continue cooking just until whites are set, 2 to 3 minutes longer. Finish with minced parsley and sea salt and pepper to taste. Serve immediately.

KETO LOAF BREAD

Nutrition: Cal 239;Fat 22 g;Carb 4 g;Protein 8 g
Serving 1; Cook time 60 min

Ingredients

•2 cups finely ground almond flour, such as Bob's Red Mill or King Arthur brands
•1 teaspoon baking powder
•1/2 teaspoon xanthan gum
•1/2 teaspoon kosher salt
•7 large eggs, at room temperature
•8 tablespoons (1 stick) unsalted butter, melted and cooled
•2 tablespoons refined coconut oil, melted and cooled

Instructions

1. Arrange a rack in the middle of the oven and heat to 350°F. Line the bottom and sides of a 9x5-inch metal loaf pan with parchment paper, letting the excess hang over the long sides to form a sling. Set aside.

2. Whisk together the almond flour, baking powder, xanthan gum, and salt in a medium bowl. Set aside.
3. Place the eggs in the bowl of a stand mixer fitted with the whisk attachment. Beat on medium-high speed until light and frothy. Reduce the speed to medium, slowly add the melted butter and coconut oil, and beat until until fully combined. Reduce the speed to low, slowly add the almond flour mixture, and beat until combined. Increase the speed to medium high and beat until mixture thickens, about 1 minute.
4. Pour into the prepared pan and smooth the top. Bake until a knife inserted in the center comes out clean, 45 to 55 minutes. Let cool in the pan for about 10 minutes. Grasping the parchment paper, remove the loaf from the pan and transfer to a wire rack. Cool completely before slicing.

KALE AND GOAT CHEESE FRITTATA CUPS

Nutrition: Cal 179;Fat 14,7 g;Carb 1 g;Protein 10 g
Serving 8; Cook time 40 min

Ingredients

2 cups chopped lacinato kale
1 garlic clove, thinly sliced
3 tablespoons olive oil
1/4 teaspoon red pepper flakes
8 large eggs
1/4 teaspoon salt
Dash ground black pepper
1/2 teaspoon dried thyme
1/4 cup goat cheese, crumbled

Instructions

1. Preheat the oven to 350°F. To get 2 cups kale, remove the leaves from the kale ribs. Wash and dry the leaves and cut them into 1/2-inch-wide strips.
2. In a 10-inch nonstick skillet, cook the garlic in 1 tablespoon of oil over medium-high heat for 30 seconds. Add the kale and red pepper flakes and cook until wilted, 1 to 2 minutes.
3. In a medium bowl, beat the eggs with the salt and pepper. Add the kale and thyme to the egg mixture.
4. Using a 12-cup muffin tin, use the remaining 2 tablespoons of oil to grease 8 of the cups (you may also use butter or nonstick spray if you'd prefer). Sprinkle the tops with goat cheese. Bake until they are set in the center, about 25 to 30 minutes.
5. Frittata is best eaten warm from the oven or within the next day, but leftovers can be kept refrigerated and reheated for up to a week.

ROASTED RADISH AND HERBED RICOTTA OMELET

Nutrition: Cal 350;Fat 27 g;Carb 5,3 g;Protein 20 g
Serving 2; Cook time 15 min

Ingredients

For the roasted radishes:
•1 cup thinly-sliced French Breakfast radishes, or other radish variety
•2 teaspoons olive oil
•1/4 teaspoon sea salt

For the ricotta:
•1/4 cup plus 2 tablespoons fresh whole milk ricotta
•2 teaspoons minced fresh chives
•1 teaspoon minced fresh thyme
•1 teaspoon minced fresh flat leaf parsley, plus extra for topping

For the eggs:
•4 large or extra-large eggs
•2 tablespoons whole milk
•1/2 teaspoon sea salt
•1/4 teaspoon black pepper
•1 tablespoon butter

Instructions

1. To make the radishes, preheat the oven to 400°F. Toss the radishes with the olive oil and salt. Spread in a thin layer in a roasting dish and bake until soft and tender, 10 to 12 minutes (any longer and you may end up with radish chips).
2. In a small bowl, combine the ricotta with the minced herbs.

3. To make the omelet, whisk together the eggs, milk, salt, and pepper. Heat 1/2 tablespoon of butter in an 8-inch non-stick skillet over medium-low heat. Pour in half the egg mixture and cook for 1 to 2 minutes, allowing the bottom to set slightly. Run a spatula under the edges, lifting up and tilting the pan to allow uncooked eggs to run under the cooked part. Continue to do this until the majority of the egg is set. Carefully flip the omelet and remove from heat.
4. Spread half the ricotta mixture over half of the omelet and sprinkle with half of the radishes. Fold the omelet over over the filling and sprinkle with a few more roasted radish slices and minced parsley.
5. Repeat to make the second omelet. Serve both omelets immediately.

MIXED MUSHROOM EGG BAKES
Nutrition: Cal 287;Fat 21 g;Carb 8,3 g;Protein 16 g
Serving 4; Cook time 35 min

Ingredients
- Butter or cooking spray
- 2 tablespoons extra-virgin olive oil
- 1/3 cup minced shallot (from about 2 small shallots)
- 8 ounces sliced mixed fresh mushrooms (cremini, oyster or shiitake, stems removed before slicing)
- 2 tablespoons chopped fresh thyme
- 6 large eggs
- 3/4 cup whole milk
- 1/2 teaspoon kosher salt
- 1/2 teaspoon ground black pepper
- 1/2 cup shredded mozzarella cheese

Instructions
1. Arrange a rack in the middle of the oven and heat to 400°F. Coat 4 (8-ounce) ramekins with a little butter, or use cooking spray instead. Place the ramekins on a rimmed baking sheet so they'll be easier to move to and from the oven; set aside.
2. Heat the olive oil in a medium saucepan over medium-high heat until shimmering. Add the shallot and sauté until soft and translucent, about 3 minutes. Add the mushrooms and a pinch of salt and cook until softened and fragrant, about 5 minutes. Stir in the thyme and remove from the heat.
3. Whisk the eggs, milk, salt, and pepper together in a medium bowl. Divide the mushroom mixture evenly between the ramekins. Divide the cheese over the mushrooms. Pour the egg mixture over the top, stopping just below the top of the ramekin.
4. Place the baking sheet in the oven and bake until the tops are golden and have puffed slightly and the eggs are completely set, 20 to 25 minutes.

3-INGREDIENT PESTO ZOODLE BOWL
Nutrition: Cal 400;Fat 38 g;Carb 8,3 g;Protein 10 g
Serving 1; Cook time 10 min

Ingredients
- 2 tablespoons olive oil, divided
- 1 medium zucchini (about 6 ounces), ends trimmed and spiralized, or 1 heaping cup of store-bought zucchini noodles
- 1 tablespoon basil pesto
- 1 large egg
- Kosher salt
- Freshly ground black pepper
- Red pepper flakes or hot sauce, for serving (optional)

Instructions
1. Heat 1 tablespoon of the oil in a medium nonstick skillet over medium heat until shimmering. Add the zucchini noodles and sauté until just tender, about 2 minutes. Add the pesto and toss until the noodles are well-coated. Transfer the noodles to a plate or shallow bowl.
2. Heat the remaining 1 tablespoon oil in the skillet until shimmering. Add the egg, season with salt and pepper, and cook undisturbed until the outer white edges are opaque, about 1 minute. Cover and cook until the yolk is set but still runny, 2 to 3 minutes.
3. Gently slide a spatula under the egg and place it on top of the zoodles. Sprinkle with a pinch of red pepper flakes or finish with a little hot sauce, if using.

CHOCOLATE PROTEIN PANCAKES
Nutrition: Cal 380;Fat 31 g;Carb 5.4 g;Protein 19 g
Serving 2; Cook time 20 min

Ingredients
Dry ingredients
- 1scoop vanilla protein powder
- 1 tablespoon cocoa powder
- 2 teaspoon baking powder
- 1 tablespoon coconut flour
- 1 tablespoon granulated sweetener
- 1 pinch salt

Wet ingredients
- 2 eggs
- 4 tablespoon unsalted butter (softened)
- 1 tablespoon cream cheese
- 1/4 teaspoon vanilla extract

Instructions
1. Whisk together all of the dry ingredients in a mixing bowl until no lumps remain.
2. Make a well in the middle of the dry ingredients and add the eggs, butter, cream cheese, and vanilla extract into the middle.
3. Fold the batter together gently and set aside for 5 minutes.
4. Heat a non-stick frying pan over medium to high heat.
5. Add 1/4 cup of the batter to the pan at a time. Cook until bubbles form on the top surface, then flip over to cook on the other side, cooking for about 3 – 4 minutes per side.

KETO BREAKFAST SANDWICH
Nutrition: Cal 603;Fat 54 g;Carb 4 g;Protein 22 g
Serving 2; Cook time 35 min

Ingredients
- 4 sausage patties
- 2 egg
- 2 tbsp cream cheese
- 4 tbsp sharp cheddar
- 1/2 medium avocado, sliced
- 1/2–1 tsp sriracha (to taste)
- Salt, pepper to taste

Instructions
1. In skillet over medium heat, cook sausages per package instructions and set aside
2. In small bowl place cream cheese and sharp cheddar. Microwave for 20-30 seconds until melted
3. Mix cheese with sriracha, set aside
4. Mix egg with seasoning and make small omelette
5. Fill omelette with cheese sriracha mixture and assemble sandwich

POACHED EGGS MYTILENE
Nutrition: Cal 275;Fat 23.6 g;Carb 6 g;Protein 13 g
Serving 1; Cook time 20 min

Ingredients
- 4 sausage patties
- 2 egg
- 2 tbsp cream cheese
- 4 tbsp sharp cheddar
- 1/2 medium avocado, sliced
- 1/2–1 tsp sriracha (to taste)
- Salt, pepper to taste
- Instructions
- In skillet over medium heat, cook sausages per package instructions and set aside

Instructions
1. Combine lemon juice and oil in a small serving bowl; whisk to combine.

2. Add water and vinegar to a medium saute pan or small saucepan and bring to a slow boil. Reduce the heat to medium-low. Crack 1 egg into a small bowl, being careful not to break the yolk. Gently slip egg into the simmering water, holding the bowl just above the surface of water. Repeat with the remaining egg. Cook eggs until the whites are firm and the yolks are lightly cooked outside, but liquid inside, 2 to 3 minutes. Remove the eggs from the water with a slotted spoon, and place into a serving bowl.
3. Break the yolks with a fork and drizzle with lemon juice mixture. Stir yolks twice; season with salt and pepper.

HEALTHY BREAKFAST CHEESECAKE
Nutrition: Cal 152;Fat 12.6 g;Carb 3 g;Protein 6 g
Serving 1; Cook time 1 hour 5 min
Ingredients
• Crust Ingredients:
• 2 cups whole almonds
• 2 tablespoon Joy Filled Eats Sweetener (or see alternatives in recipe notes)
• 4 tablespoon salted butter
Filling Ingredients:
• 16 oz 4% fat cottage cheese
• 8 oz cream cheese
• 6 eggs
• ¾ cup Joy Filled Eats Sweetener (or see alternatives in recipe notes)
• ½ teaspoon almond extract
• ½ teaspoon vanilla extract
Topping when serving:
• ¼ cup frozen mixed berries per cheesecake thawed
Instructions
1. Preheat the oven to 350. In a large food processor pulse the almonds, 2 tablespoon sweetener, and 4 tablespoon butter until a coarse dough forms. Grease two twelve hole standard silicone muffin pans or line metal tins with paper or foil cupcake liners. I used a silicone muffin pan for this and the cheesecakes popped out really easily. Divide the dough between the 24 holes and press into the bottom to form a crust. Bake for 8 minutes.
2. Meanwhile, combine the Friendship Dairies 4% cottage cheese and the cream cheese in the food processor (you don't need to wash the bowl). Pulse the cheeses until smooth. Add the sweetener and extracts. Mix until combined.
3. Add the eggs. Blend until smooth. You will need to scrape down the sides. Divide the batter between the muffin cups.
4. Bake for 30-40 minutes until the centers no longer jiggly when the pan is lightly shaken. Cool completely. Refrigerate for at least 2 hours before trying to remove them if you didn't use paper or foil liners. Serve with thawed frozen berries.

BLUEBERRY PANCAKES
Nutrition: Cal 202;Fat 16 g;Carb 9 g;Protein 10 g
Serving 3; Cook time 10 min
Ingredients
• 2 eggs
• 2/3 cup almond flour
• 1 tsp baking powder
• 1/2 tsp vanilla
• 1 tsp Swerve sweetener
• 3 tbsp milk or almond milk
• 1/4 cup blueberries
• Keto pancake syrup for serving, optional
Instructions
1. Whisk the eggs in a bowl, then add vanilla, Swerve and milk and mix until combined. Add almond flour and baking powder and mix until combined. Stir in the blueberries.
2. Spray a non-stick frying pan or pancake griddle with a non-stick cooking spray and heat over medium-high heat. Laddle the pancake batter on a frying pan, making 6 small pancakes.

3. Cook for 3-4 minutes (or until the bottom is golden-brown and bubbles begin to form on top of the pancakes), then flip the pancakes over with a spatula and cook for another 2 minutes, or until the other side is golden-brown.

LOW CARB PUMPKIN CHEESECAKE PANCAKES
Nutrition: Cal 202;Fat 16 g;Carb 9 g;Protein 10 g
Serving 16; Cook time 10 min
Ingredients
• 4 ounces Cream Cheese
• 4 large Eggs
• 2 Tablespoons Pure Pumpkin Puree
• 1 teaspoon Pure Vanilla Extract
• 1 teaspoon Pyure Sugar Substitute (or your choice)
• 1/2 teaspoon Baking Powder
• 1/4 teaspoon Pumpkin Pie Spice
• 1/8 teaspoon Ground Cinnamon
• 2 teaspoons Butter
Instructions
1. Add all ingredients except butter to blender and process until smooth. Let sit while the skillet is heating.
2. Heat a cast iron skillet or griddle with a medium flame until hot and then add 1 teaspoon of butter.
3. Slowly pour pancake mix into skillet to make 3 inch pancakes. When bubbles begin to form, flip pancakes. Continue until all batter has been used. Use the second teaspoon of butter, half way through, to grease pan.
4. Serve with butter and maple syrup.

MEDITERRANEAN KETO QUICHE
Nutrition: Cal 133;Fat 8 g;Carb 9 g;Protein 7 g
Serving 8; Cook time 50 min
Ingredients
1 tsp olive oil or butter
1/2 cup red onion, chopped
2 tsp (1 large clove) garlic, minced
2/3 to 3/4 cup unsweetened almond or coconut milk
4 eggs
2 tbsp grated Parmesan cheese + extra for topping
3 tbsp coconut flour, sifted
3 tbsp tapioca starch or non-GMO cornstarch
1 tsp baking powder
1/4 tsp kosher salt or fine sea salt
1 tsp smoked paprika
1 cup chopped/sliced zucchini, divided
1/2 to 2/3 cup crumbled feta cheese, divided
1 red bell pepper, roasted and diced (fresh and roasted in oven or roasted red bell peppers from a jar both work)
Fresh basil for garnish.
Optional black pepper, to season.
Instructions
1. Grease or line a 9-inch pie or cake pan with parchment paper.
2. Coat small skillet with 1 tsp butter or oil. Add onion and garlic to the pan and cook over medium to medium high for 5 minutes (or until fragrant). Set aside.
3. To a large mixing bowl or bowl of stand mixer, add milk, eggs, and Parmesan cheese. Whisk/blend until smooth.
4. In a separate bowl, sift the coconut flour, then add tapioca flour, spices, salt, baking powder. Mix together.
5. Mix the dry ingredients with the blended egg/milk batter. Whisk together until smooth.
6. Layer your onion and garlic at the bottom of the pie pan.
7. Layer 2/3 cup zucchini on top, roasted pepper slices, and 1/3 cup feta crumbles.
8. Evenly pour the egg/flour mixture into your prepared pie or cake pan. Add remaining zucchini slices and cheese on top (Parmesan and/or feta)
9. Bake at 400F for 35 -45 minutes. Check at 25 minutes for doneness. The edges will be crispy brown and a knife or toothpick inserted into the center of the quiche will come out clean. Check the middle to make sure it's no longer soft.

10. When the crustless quiche is finished cooking, remove it from the oven and garnish with fresh basil before serving.

KETO SAUSAGE BALLS
Nutrition: Cal 363;Fat 8 g;Carb 9 g;Protein 7 g
Serving 6; Cook time 30 min

Ingredients
FATHEAD DOUGH
• cups mozzarella cheese
• 1 oz cream cheese
• 3/4 cup almond flour
• 1 large egg
SAUSAGE
• 12 oz ground breakfast sausage

Instructions
1. Preheat your oven to 400 degrees F and line a baking sheet with parchment paper.
SAUSAGE BALLS
2. Preheat a medium skillet to medium high heat.
3. Divide the sausage into 6 and roll into balls. Add to the hot skillet and cook through. Set aside on a plate to cool.
FATHEAD DOUGH
1. Add the mozzarella cheese and cream cheese to a microwave safe mixing bowl and microwave on high for 30 seconds. Combine using a fork until evenly mixed.
2. Add the almond flour and egg and combine as thoroughly as possible. If it does not combine well microwave for another 20 seconds.
3. Switch to a spatula if necessary and combine. Pour the dough onto a piece of parchment paper. If it is not evenly combined use your hands to incorporate everything.
4. Portion the dough out into 6 even balls.
5. Flatten out each ball using your hands or roll it out with another piece of parchment on top (so there is no sticking) and place the cooked sausage in the center. Pull up the side and place the sausage ball, seam side down, on a lined baking sheet.
6. Repeat until all 6 sausage balls are complete and on the baking sheet.
7. Bake for 10-15 minutes, until browned on top.
8. Best stored in a air tight sealed container in the fridge up to 5 days.

TURKISH-STYLE BREAKFAST RECIPE
Nutrition: Cal 359;Fat 27 g;Carb 7 g;Protein 17 g
Serving 4; Cook time 25 min

Ingredients
• 4 eggs
• 250g halloumi, sliced thickly into 8 pieces
• 250g yogurt
• 400g tomatoes, roughly chopped
• 400g cucumber, sliced
For The Zhoug:
• 1 bunch parsley
• ½ bunch coriander
• 2 green chillies
• 2 cloves garlic
• 200ml olive oil
• Pinch of sugar
• ½ tsp ground cumin
• ¼ tsp cardamom

Instructions
1. To make the zhoug blitz all the ingredients in a food processor until finely chopped, adding water to get the consistency of a loose pesto. Season to taste.
2. Bring a pan of water to a rolling boil. Add the eggs and cook for 6 mins for soft boiled. Immediately plunge in cool water and peel.
3. Bring a griddle pan to a high heat. Add the halloumi and fry on each side for 2 mins, until golden and slightly charred.
4. Swirl the zhoug into the yogurt and spoon onto plates. Top with the tomatoes, cucumber and halloumi.

POACHED EGG AND BACON SALAD
Nutrition: Cal 311;Fat 22 g;Carb 12 g;Protein 15 g
Serving 2; Cook time 20 min

Ingredients
• 100g (3½oz) unsmoked bacon lardons
• 1 slice bread, cut into small cubes
• 2 medium or large eggs
• 2 good handfuls of mixed salad leaves (we used rocket and chard)
• 10 baby plum tomatoes, halved
• 1 stick celery, chopped
• **For The Dressing:**
• 1tbsp olive oil
• 1tsp white wine vinegar
• ½tsp Dijon mustard
• Salt and ground black pepper

Instructions
1. Heat a frying pan, add the bacon and fry until golden and crispy. Take out of the pan with a draining spoon and set aside. Add the bread cubes to the pan, and fry in the bacon fat until browned and crispy.

2. Meanwhile poach the eggs, pour boiling water, 10cm (4in) in depth, into a small pan, over a high heat. Add a dash of white wine vinegar. When water boils again, break egg into pan.

3. As water comes back to the boil, gather egg white round yolk, using a draining spoon. Turn down heat. Simmer for a minute for a soft egg, longer for a firmer one.

4. Lift the egg out of the pan with the draining spoonand put into a bowl of warm water if cooking more than one or two eggs. Add another egg to the pan. How to poach an egg video

5. Mix together the dressing ingredients. Put a good handful of salad leaves on to 2 plates. Divide the bacon, croutons, tomatoes and celery between them. Spoon drained eggs on top, drizzle the salad with dressing and sprinkle with salt and pepper.

CHICKEN LIVER SALAD
Nutrition: Cal 450;Fat 33 g;Carb 9 g;Protein 28 g
Serving 4; Cook time 25 min

Ingredients
• 400g (14oz) fresh chicken livers
• Salt and ground black pepper
• 2 thick slices white bread
• 3 tbsp clarified butter
• 4-6 rashers streaky bacon, chopped
• 4 good handfuls of salad leaves
For The Dressing
• 1 tbsp cider vinegar
• 1 tsp Dijon mustard
• Pinch of sugar
• 2 tbsp light olive oil
• 1 tbsp walnut oil

Instructions
1. Remove sinews from the livers and, if large, cut livers into bite-sized pieces. Season well.
2. Cut the crusts off the bread and cut the bread into 1cm (½in) cubes.
3. Heat 2 tablespoons of butter in a frying pan over a medium heat. Add the bread, stir well to coat in butter and fry for a few mins until crisp and golden. Drain them on kitchen paper and keep them warm in the oven.
4. Add the chopped bacon to the hot pan and fry until crispy. Put on the baking tray with the fried bread. Heat the rest of the butter in the pan with any fat from the bacon, add the chicken livers in one layer and fry for a couple of mins each side. Take the frying pan off the heat.
5. Mix the dressing ingredients in a small bowl or jug and season. Put a handful of leaves on each plate, then divide the chicken livers, bacon and croutons between the plates. Drizzle with the dressing and serve warm.

SPINACH PANCAKES

Nutrition: Cal 186;Fat 15 g;Carb 5 g;Protein 7 g
Serving 4; Cook time 15 min

Ingredients
For The Batter:
- 30g or ⅓ cup gram (chickpea) flour
- 85ml/⅓ cup water
- A pinch of sea salt
- 1 garlic clove
- 2 handfuls of spinach
- 2 tbsp olive oil
- 1 tbsp no-taste coconut oil or unrefined rapeseed oil

For The Filling:
- 50g Parmesan cheese, grated
- ½ avocado, sliced lengthways
- 1 tbsp chopped chives
- Chopped chillies (if liked)

Instructions
1. Add all of the batter ingredients to a blender and mix until smooth. Heat the coconut oil or rapeseed oil in a frying pan.
2. Pour a thin layer of the mixture into the pan. Top with most of the avocado slices, chives and most of the grated cheese – leaving some to decorate with later.
3. Cook a few minutes, loosen edges with a spatula then flip over.
4. Top with the remaining cheese, chives and avocados – plus a few slices of red chilli, if preferred

HALLOUMI SALAD WITH ROASTED PLUMS

Nutrition: Cal 382;Fat 32 g;Carb 11 g;Protein 28 g
Serving 4; Cook time 30 min

Ingredients
- 4 whole plums, quartered and de-stoned
- 1tbsp olive oil
- 2tsp butter
- 1 pack halloumi cheese, sliced into 8 pieces

For The Dressing
- 4tbsp olive oil
- Zest and juice of 1 lime, plus 1 lime cut into wedges to serve
- 1tsp sugar
- 1tsp Dijon mustard
- Small bunch of each mint and coriander, finely chopped

Instructions
1. Preheat the oven to 220C. Place the plums on a baking tray, drizzle with olive oil and season well with salt and pepper. Roast in the oven for 15-18 mins until they are slightly charred and just beginning to soften.
2. Mix the dressing ingredients together in a small bowl and season well. Heat the butter in a frying pan and pan-fry the halloumi slices for a few mins on each side until golden brown and starting to melt slightly.
3. Plate up the halloumi slices with the roasted plums, and drizzle over the dressing. Serve with lime wedges on the side.

GRIDDLED HALLOUMI AND WATERMELON SALAD

Nutrition: Cal 386;Fat 30 g;Carb 16 g;Protein 16 g
Serving 4; Cook time 20 min

Ingredients
- ½ x 1.5kg watermelon
- 4tbsp extra virgin olive oil
- 1tbsp balsamic vinegar
- 250g halloumi
- 150g Mixed baby leaf salad leaves
- 1tbsp fresh basil, finely sliced
- Edible flowers, optional

Instructions
1. Remove the rind and pips from the watermelon, and cut into 2.5cm cubes. Mix 3tbsp of olive oil and the balsamic vinegar together and season with salt and pepper.
2. Cut the halloumi lengthways into eight slices and toss in the remaining 1tbsp olive oil. Place a griddle pan over a medium heat and cook each slice for 30-60 seconds on each side, or until there are golden brown griddle marks on each side.
3. To serve divide the salad leave between four plates, scatter with watermelon cubes and top each salad with 2 slices of halloumi. Drizzle over the dressing, add a few slices of basil leaves and some edible flowers.

LUNCH

CHICKEN EGG SALAD WRAPS

Nutrition: Cal 545;Fat 38 g;Carb 23 g;Protein33 g
Serving 3; Cook time 10 min

Ingredients
- 2 romaine lettuce heads, chopped
- 2 cups chopped Baked Boneless Chicken Thighs
- 1 cup grape tomatoes
- 2 cucumbers, diced
- ½ cup chopped red onion
- 4 slices Perfectly Cooked Bacon , chopped
- ½ cup crumbled blue cheese
- 4 Hard-boiled Eggs , sliced
- ½ cup Dairy-Free Ranch Dressing

Instructions
1 Evenly divide the lettuce between 4 storage containers.
2 Evenly distribute and arrange the chicken, tomatoes, cucumbers, onion, bacon, blue cheese, and eggs over the lettuce.
3 Divide the dressing into 2-tablespoon servings and store on the side.

COBB SALAD

Nutrition: Cal 545;Fat 38 g;Carb 23 g;Protein33 g
Serving 4; Cook time 20 min

Ingredients
- 1½ cups chopped Baked Boneless Chicken Thighs
- 6 Hard-boiled Eggs , chopped
- 3 celery stalks, minced
- 2 tablespoons minced red onion
- 1 tablespoon Dijon mustard
- 2 cups Mayonnaise
- Salt
- Freshly ground black pepper
- 8 leaves butter or romaine lettuce

Instructions
1. In a large bowl, combine the chicken, eggs, celery, onion, and mustard. Add the Mayonnaise and stir until mixed. Season with salt and pepper.
2. Divide the egg salad and lettuce between 3 storage containers. To serve, make egg salad wraps by filling the lettuce leaves with the salad and wrapping the lettuce around it.

BLUE CHEESE BACON BURGERS

Nutrition: Cal 772;Fat 54 g;Carb 6 g;Protein61 g
Serving 4; Cook time 20 min

Ingredients
- 1½ pounds ground beef
- 4 slices Perfectly Cooked Bacon , crumbled
- ½ cup crumbled blue cheese
- 1 tablespoon Worcestershire sauce
- 2 large eggs
- Salt
- Freshly ground black pepper
- 1 romaine lettuce head, chopped
- 1 avocado, chopped
- 1 cup grape tomatoes

Instructions
1. In a large mixing bowl, combine the beef, bacon, blue cheese, Worcestershire sauce, and eggs. Season with salt and pepper. Use your hands to shape 4 patties. Cover with plastic and refrigerate for 30 minutes to 2 hours.
2. Heat the grill or broiler on high and cook for 4 to 5 minutes on each side, or until the burgers are cooked to your liking. Remove from the grill and let cool.
3. Into each of 4 storage containers, divide the lettuce, avocado, and tomatoes, and top with a burger patty.

FAJITA SALAD

Nutrition: Cal 893;Fat 60 g;Carb 17 g;Protein70 g
Serving 4; Cook time 30 min

Ingredients
FOR THE STEAK
- 1 (2-pound) flank steak
- ¼ cup extra-virgin olive oil
- 1 teaspoon garlic powder
- 1 teaspoon onion powder
- 1 teaspoon ground cumin
- Juice of 1 lime
- 1 bunch cilantro, leaves chopped
- Salt
- Freshly ground black pepper

FOR THE SALAD
- 2 tablespoons extra-virgin olive oil or coconut oil
- 1 yellow onion, sliced
- 1 green bell pepper, sliced
- 1 red bell pepper, sliced
- 6 cups chopped romaine lettuce
- ½ cup sour cream
- ½ cup shredded Cheddar cheese
- 2 limes, quartered
- 1 avocado

Instructions
1. In a large resealable bag, add the flank steak, oil, garlic powder, onion powder, cumin, lime juice, cilantro, salt, and pepper. Marinate for 30 minutes to 24 hours.
2. When ready to cook, turn the broiler on high and remove the flank steak from the marinade, discarding the remaining marinade. Place the steak on a baking sheet and bake for 3 to 5 minutes on each side. Let rest for 10 minutes before thinly slicing against the grain.

TO MAKE THE SALAD
1. Heat a large skillet over medium heat and combine the oil, onion, and peppers. Stir often and cook until the onion becomes translucent, 8 to 10 minutes.
2. Into each of 4 divided storage containers, place the steak, peppers, and onions in one side, and the lettuce, sour cream, cheese, and lime wedges in the other side. Before enjoying an individual serving, halve, pit, and chop an avocado. Top the steak with ¼ of the chopped avocado, along with the lettuce, sour cream, and cheese. Squeeze the lime juice over everything and mix.
3. the lettuce around it.

ITALIAN ZUCCHINI BOATS

Nutrition: Cal 458;Fat 33 g;Carb 12 g;Protein42 g
Serving 3; Cook time 50 min

Ingredients
- 3 zucchini, halved lengthwise
- 1 tablespoon avocado oil
- 1 medium onion, diced
- 2 tablespoons minced garlic
- 1 pound ground Italian sausage
- 2 teaspoons paprika
- 1 teaspoon red pepper flakes
- 2 teaspoons dried oregano
- 1 cup chicken broth
- ¾ cup grated Parmesan cheese
- Salt
- Freshly ground black pepper

Instructions
1. Preheat the oven to 350°F.
2. Using a spoon, scoop out the flesh of each zucchini half and chop it up.
3. In a large skillet, heat the oil over medium heat. Sauté the onion, garlic, and sausage, cooking until browned, 6 to 8 minutes. Add the chopped zucchini flesh, paprika, red pepper flakes, and oregano.
4. Fill the prepped zucchini shells with equal portions of the sausage mixture. Place them in a 9-by-13-inch baking dish and pour the broth into the bottom of the dish.

5. Top with the Parmesan cheese and season with salt and pepper. Cook for 30 to 35 minutes, until the cheese is bubbling.

GROUND BEEF AND CABBAGE STIR-FRY
Nutrition: Cal 550;Fat 33 g;Carb 13 g;Protein 49 g
Serving 4; Cook time 35 min

Ingredients
- 1 tablespoon coconut oil
- 1½ pounds ground beef
- 2 garlic cloves, minced
- 1 green cabbage head, cored and chopped
- 2 tablespoons coconut aminos
- 2 tablespoons apple cider vinegar
- Salt
- Freshly ground black pepper
- 4 scallions, both white and green parts, chopped
- Sesame seeds (optional)
- Sriracha (optional)
- Toasted sesame oil (optional)

Instructions
1. In a large skillet, heat the oil over medium heat. Cook the beef and garlic until the beef is browned, 5 to 7 minutes.
2. Add the cabbage to the skillet and continue to cook until the cabbage becomes slightly wilted, 8 to 10 minutes.
3. Add the coconut aminos and vinegar and season with salt and pepper.

BAKED CAULIFLOWER TORTILLAS
Nutrition: Cal 150;Fat 12 g;Carb 7 g;Protein18 g
Serving 4; Cook time 35 min

Ingredients
- 1 Large Head of Cauliflower (Cut into florets)
- 4 Large Eggs
- 2 Garlic Cloves (Minced)
- 1 1/2 tsp. Herbs (Whatever your favorite is - basil, oregano, thyme)
- 1 tsp. salt

Instructions
1. Preheat oven to 375 degrees.
2. Cover two baking sheets with parchment paper.
3. Rice cauliflower in a food processor.
4. Add to saucepan 1/4 cup water and riced cauliflower.
5. Cook on medium high heat until tender 8-10 minutes.
6. Drain.
7. Wring out with clean kitchen towel.
8. Mix cauliflower, eggs, garlic, herbs and salt.
9. Form 4 thin circles on parchment paper.
10. Bake until dry and pliable 15-20 minutes.
11. Let cool on wire rack.

MASHED CAULIFLOWER
Nutrition: Cal 180;Fat 14 g;Carb 7 g;Protein21 g
Serving 26; Cook time 35 min

Ingredients
- 1 head of cauliflower
- 3 tbsp. milk
- 1 tbsp. butter
- 2 tbsp. sour cream
- ¼ tsp. garlic salt
- 1 pinch freshly ground black pepper
- Optional
- Chives
- Cheese
- Bacon bits

Instructions
1. Over medium heat bring to a simmer 1 cup water.
2. Separate florets while saving the core.
1. Dice core.
2. Add all cauliflower to pot.
3. Cover.

4. Cook 12-15 minutes.
5. Drain.
6. Add milk, butter, sour cream, salt and pepper.
7. Mash together.

KETO GRILLED VEGETABLES
Nutrition: Cal 135;Fat 3 g;Carb 22 g;Protein4 g
Serving 2; Cook time 15 min

Ingredients
- 1 small eggplant, cut into 3/4 inch thick slices
- 2 small red bell peppers, seeded and cut into wide strips
- 3 zucchinis, sliced
- 6 fresh mushrooms, stems removed
- 1/4 cup olive oil
- 1/4 cup lemon juice
- 1/4 cup coarsely chopped fresh basil
- 2 cloves garlic, peeled and minced

Instructions
1. Put vegetables, in a medium sized bowl.
2. In another bowl, whisk olive oil, lemon juice basil and garlic.
3. Pour over vegetables.
4. Cover and refrigerate for 1 hour.
5. Preheat BBQ to high heat.
6. Cook 2-3 minutes per side.
7. Frequently brush with marinade.

QUICK & EASY KETO TUNA FISH SALAD
Nutrition: Cal 430;Fat 3 g;Carb 22 g;Protein 18 g
Serving 2; Cook time 15 min

Ingredients
2 cups mixed greens
1 large tomato, diced
¼ cup fresh parsley, chopped
¼ cup fresh mint, chopped
10 large kalamata olives, pitted
1 small zucchini, sliced lengthwise
½ avocado, diced
1 green onion, sliced
1 can chunk light tuna in water, drained
1 tablespoon extra-virgin olive oil
1 tablespoon balsamic vinegar
¼ teaspoon Himalayan or fine sea salt
¾ teaspoon freshly cracked black peper

Instructions
1. In a sizzling hot cast iron skillet grill pan, grill the zucchini slices on both sides (or on a very hot grill).
2. •Remove from pan and let cool for a few minutes.
3. •Slice into bite size pieces.
4. •Add all the ingredients in a large mixing bowl and mix until well combined

CUCUMBER AVOCADO SALAD WITH BACON
Nutrition: Cal 365;Fat 24 g;Carb 13 g;Protein 7 g
Serving 2; Cook time 10 min

Ingredients
- 2 cups fresh baby spinach, chopped
- ½ English cucumber, sliced thin
- 1 small avocado, pitted and chopped
- 1 ½ tablespoons olive oil
- 1 ½ tablespoons lemon juice
- Salt and pepper
- 2 slices cooked bacon, chopped

Instructions:
1. Combine the spinach, cucumber, and avocado in a salad bowl.
2. Toss with the olive oil, lemon juice, salt and pepper.
3. Top with chopped bacon to serve

BACON CHEESEBURGER SOUP

Nutrition: Cal 315;Fat 20 g;Carb 6 g;Protein 27 g
Serving 4; Cook time 25 min

Ingredients:
- 4 slices uncooked bacon
- 8 ounces ground beef (80% lean)
- 1 medium yellow onion, chopped
- 1 clove garlic, minced
- 3 cups beef broth
- 2 tablespoons tomato paste
- 2 teaspoons Dijon mustard
- Salt and pepper
- 1 cup shredded lettuce
- ½ cup shredded cheddar cheese

Instructions:
1. Cook the bacon in a saucepan until crisp then drain on paper towels and chop.
2. Reheat the bacon fat in the saucepan and add the beef.
3. Cook until the beef is browned, then drain away half the fat.
4. Reheat the saucepan and add the onion and garlic – cook for 6 minutes.
5. Stir in the broth, tomato paste, and mustard then season with salt and pepper.
6. Add the beef and simmer on medium-low for 15 minutes, covered.
7. Spoon into bowls and top with shredded lettuce, cheddar cheese and bacon.

HAM AND PROVOLONE SANDWICH

Nutrition: Cal 425;Fat 31 g;Carb 5 g;Protein 31 g
Serving 1; Cook time 35 min

Ingredients:
- 1 large egg, separated
- Pinch cream of tartar
- Pinch salt
- 1 ounce cream cheese, softened
- ¼ cup shredded provolone cheese
- 3 ounces sliced ham

Instructions:
1. For the bread, preheat the oven to 300°F and line a baking sheet with parchment.
2. Beat the egg whites with the cream of tartar and salt until soft peaks form.
3. Whisk the cream cheese and egg yolk until smooth and pale yellow.
4. Fold in the egg whites a little at a time until smooth and well combined.
5. Spoon the batter onto the baking sheet into two even circles.
6. Bake for 25 minutes until firm and lightly browned.
7. Spread the butter on one side of each bread circle then place one in a preheated skillet over medium heat.
8. Sprinkle with cheese and add the sliced ham then top with the other bread circle, butter-side-up.
9. Cook the sandwich for a minute or two then carefully flip it over.
10. Let it cook until the cheese is melted then serve.

EGG SALAD OVER LETTUCE

Nutrition: Cal 260;Fat 32 g;Carb 5 g;Protein 10 g
Serving 2; Cook time 10 min

Ingredients:
- 3 large hardboiled eggs, cooled
- 1 small stalk celery, diced
- 3 tablespoons mayonnaise
- 1 tablespoon fresh chopped parsley
- 1 teaspoon fresh lemon juice
- Salt and pepper
- 4 cups fresh chopped lettuce

Instructions:
1. Peel and dice the eggs into a mixing bowl.
2. Stir in the celery, mayonnaise, parsley, lemon juice, salt and pepper.
3. Serve spooned over fresh chopped lettuce.

BAKED CHICKEN NUGGETS

Nutrition: Cal 400;Fat 26 g;Carb 2 g;Protein 43 g
Serving 4; Cook time 30 min

Ingredients:
- ¼ cup almond flour
- 1 teaspoon chili powder
- ½ teaspoon paprika
- 2 pounds boneless chicken thighs, cut into 2-inch chunks
- Salt and pepper
- 2 large eggs, whisked well

Instructions:
1. Preheat the oven to 400°F and line a baking sheet with parchment.
2. Stir together the almond flour, chili powder, and paprika in a shallow dish.
3. Season the chicken with salt and pepper, then dip in the beaten eggs.
4. Dredge the chicken pieces in the almond flour mixture, then arrange on the baking sheet.
5. Bake for 20 minutes until browned and crisp. Serve hot.

TACO SALAD WITH CREAMY DRESSING

Nutrition: Cal 470;Fat 36 g;Carb 7 g;Protein 28 g
Serving 2; Cook time 20 min

Ingredients:
- 6 ounces ground beef (80% lean)
- Salt and pepper
- 1 tablespoon ground cumin
- 1 tablespoon chili powder
- 4 cups fresh chopped lettuce
- ½ cup diced tomatoes
- ¼ cup diced red onion
- ¼ cup shredded cheddar cheese
- 3 tablespoons mayonnaise
- 1 teaspoon apple cider vinegar
- Pinch paprika

Instructions:
1. Cook the ground beef in a skillet over medium-high heat until browned.
2. Drain half the fat, then season with salt and pepper and stir in the taco seasoning.
3. Simmer for 5 minutes, then remove from heat.
4. Divide the lettuce between two salad bowls, then top with ground beef.
5. Add the diced tomatoes, red onion, and cheddar cheese.
6. Whisk together the remaining ingredients, then drizzle over the salads to serve.

EGG DROP SOUP

Nutrition: Cal 165;Fat 9.5 g;Carb 3 g;Protein 16 g
Serving 4; Cook time 15 min

Ingredients:
- 5 cups chicken broth
- 4 chicken bouillon cubes
- 1 ½ tablespoons chili garlic paste
- 6 large eggs, whisked
- ½ green onion, sliced

Instructions:
1. Crush the bouillon cubes and stir into the broth in a saucepan.
2. Bring it to a boil, then stir in the chili garlic paste.
3. Cook until steaming, then remove from heat.
4. While whisking, drizzle in the beaten eggs.
5. Let sit for 2 minutes then serve with sliced green onion.

FRIED SALMON CAKES

Nutrition: Cal 505;Fat 37.5 g;Carb 14.5 g;Protein 31 g
Serving 2; Cook time 25 min

Ingredients:
- 1 tablespoon butter
- 1 cup riced cauliflower
- Salt and pepper
- 8 ounces boneless salmon fillet
- ¼ cup almond flour
- 2 tablespoons coconut flour
- 1 large egg
- 2 tablespoons minced red onion
- 1 tablespoon fresh chopped parsley
- 2 tablespoons coconut oil

Instructions:
1. Melt the butter in a skillet over medium heat, then cook the cauliflower for 5 minutes until tender season with salt and pepper.
2. Spoon the cauliflower into a bowl and reheat the skillet.
3. Add the salmon and season with salt and pepper.
4. Cook the salmon until just opaque, then remove and flake the fish into a bowl.
5. Stir in the cauliflower along with the almond flour, coconut flour, egg, red onion, and parsley.
6. Shape into 6 patties then fry in coconut oil until both sides are browned.

SPRING SALAD WITH SHAVED PARMESAN

Nutrition: Cal 295;Fat 25.5 g;Carb 3 g;Protein 6.5 g
Serving 2; Cook time 15 min

Ingredients:
- 3 slices uncooked bacon
- 2 tablespoons red wine vinegar
- 1 tablespoon Dijon mustard
- Salt and pepper
- Liquid stevia extract, to taste
- 4 ounces mixed spring greens
- ½ small red onion, sliced thinly
- ⅓ cup roasted pine nuts
- ¼ cup shaved parmesan

Instructions:
1. Cook the bacon in a skillet until crisp then remove to paper towels.
2. Reserve ¼ cup of bacon fat in the skillet, discarding the rest, then chop the bacon.
3. Whisk the red wine vinegar and mustard into the bacon fat in the skillet.
4. Season with salt and pepper, then sweeten with stevia to taste and let cool slightly.
5. Combine the spring greens, red onion, pine nuts, and parmesan in a salad bowl.
6. Toss with the dressing, then top with chopped bacon to serve.

COCONUT CHICKEN TENDERS

Nutrition: Cal 325;Fat 95 g;Carb 2 g;Protein 45 g
Serving 4; Cook time 40 min

Ingredients:
- ¼ cup almond flour
- 2 tablespoons shredded unsweetened coconut
- ½ teaspoon garlic powder
- 2 pounds boneless chicken tenders
- Salt and pepper
- 2 large eggs, whisked well

Instructions:
1. Preheat the oven to 400°F and line a baking sheet with parchment.
2. Stir together the almond flour, coconut, and garlic powder in a shallow dish.
3. Season the chicken with salt and pepper, then dip into the beaten eggs.
4. Dredge the chicken tenders in the almond flour mixture, then arrange on the baking sheet.
5. Bake for 25 to 30 minutes until browned and cooked through. Serve hot.

SESAME CHICKEN AVOCADO SALAD

Nutrition: Cal 540;Fat 47 g;Carb 10.5 g;Protein 23 g
Serving 2; Cook time 10 min

Ingredients:
- 1 tablespoon sesame oil
- 8 ounces boneless chicken thighs, chopped
- Salt and pepper
- 4 cups fresh spring greens
- 1 cup sliced avocado
- 2 tablespoons olive oil
- 2 tablespoons rice wine vinegar
- 1 tablespoon sesame seeds

Instructions:
1. Heat the sesame oil in a skillet over medium-high heat.
2. Season the chicken with salt and pepper, then add to the skillet.
3. Cook the chicken until browned and cooked through, stirring often.
4. Remove the chicken from the heat and cool slightly.
5. Divide the spring greens onto two salad plates and top with avocado.
6. Drizzle the salads with olive oil and rice wine vinegar.
7. Top with cooked chicken and sprinkle with sesame seeds to serve.

SPINACH CAULIFLOWER SOUP

Nutrition: Cal 165;Fat 12.5 g;Carb 3 g;Protein 9 g
Serving 4; Cook time 20 min

Ingredients:
- 1 tablespoon coconut oil
- 1 small yellow onion, chopped
- 2 cloves garlic, minced
- 2 cups chopped cauliflower
- 8 ounces fresh baby spinach, chopped
- 3 cups vegetable broth
- ½ cup canned coconut milk
- Salt and pepper

Instructions:
1. Heat the oil in a saucepan over medium-high heat – add the onion and garlic.
2. Sauté for 4 to 5 minutes until browned, then stir in the cauliflower.
3. Cook for 5 minutes until browned, then stir in the spinach.
4. Let it cook for 2 minutes until wilted, then stir in the broth and bring to boil.
5. Remove from heat and puree the soup with an immersion blender.
6. Stir in the coconut milk and season with salt and pepper to taste. Serve hot.

CHEESY BUFFALO CHICKEN SANDWICH

Nutrition: Cal 555;Fat 33 g;Carb 3.5 g;Protein 55 g
Serving 1; Cook time 30 min

Ingredients:
- 1 large egg, separated into white and yolk
- Pinch cream of tartar
- Pinch salt
- 1 ounce cream cheese, softened
- 1 cup cooked chicken breast, shredded
- 2 tablespoons hot sauce
- 1 slice Swiss cheese

Instructions:
1. For the bread, preheat the oven to 300°F and line a baking sheet with parchment.
2. Beat the egg whites with the cream of tartar and salt until soft peaks form.
3. Whisk the cream cheese and egg yolk until smooth and pale yellow.
4. Fold in the egg whites a little at a time until smooth and well combined.
5. Spoon the batter onto the baking sheet into two even circles.
6. Bake for 25 minutes until firm and lightly browned.
7. Shred the chicken into a bowl and toss with the hot sauce.
8. Spoon the chicken onto one of the bread circles and top with cheese.
9. Top with the other bread circle and enjoy.

AVOCADO SPINACH SALAD WITH ALMONDS
Nutrition: Cal 415;Fat 40 g;Carb 14 g;Protein 6.5 g
Serving 2; Cook time 10 min

Ingredients:
- 4 cups fresh baby spinach
- 2 tablespoons olive oil
- 1 ½ tablespoons balsamic vinegar
- ½ tablespoon Dijon mustard
- Salt and pepper
- 1 medium avocado, sliced thinly
- ¼ cup sliced almonds, toasted

Instructions:
1. Toss the spinach with the olive oil, balsamic vinegar, Dijon mustard, salt and pepper.
2. Divide the spinach between two salad plates.
3. Top the salads with sliced avocado and toasted almonds to serve.

CAULIFLOWER LEEK SOUP WITH PANCETTA
Nutrition: Cal 200;Fat 13 g;Carb 8 g;Protein 12 g
Serving 4; Cook time 60 min

Ingredients:
- 4 cups chicken broth
- ½ medium head cauliflower, chopped
- 1 cup sliced leeks
- ½ cup heavy cream
- Salt and pepper
- 2 ounces diced pancetta

Instructions:
1. Combine the broth and cauliflower in a saucepan over medium-high heat.
2. Bring the chicken broth to a boil then add the sliced leeks.
3. Boil on medium heat, covered, for 1 hour until the cauliflower is tender.
4. Remove from heat and puree the soup with an immersion blender.
5. Stir in the cream, then season with salt and pepper.
6. Fry the chopped pancetta in a skillet over medium-high heat until crisp.
7. Spoon the soup into bowls and sprinkle with pancetta to serve.

BEEF AND PEPPER KEBABS
Nutrition: Cal 365;Fat 21 g;Carb 6.5 g;Protein 35.5 g
Serving 2; Cook time40 min

Ingredients:
- 2 tablespoons olive oil
- 1 ½ tablespoons balsamic vinegar
- 2 teaspoons Dijon mustard
- Salt and pepper
- 8 ounces beef sirloin, cut into 2-inch pieces
- 1 small red pepper, cut into chunks
- 1 small green pepper, cut into chunks

Instructions:
1. Whisk together the olive oil, balsamic vinegar, and mustard in a shallow dish.
2. Season the steak with salt and pepper, then toss in the marinade.
3. Let marinate for 30 minutes, then slide onto skewers with the peppers.
4. Preheat a grill pan to high heat and grease with cooking spray.
5. Cook the kebabs for 2 to 3 minutes on each side until the beef is done.

THREE MEAT AND CHEESE SANDWICH
Nutrition: Cal 610;Fat 48 g;Carb 3 g;Protein 40 g
Serving 1; Cook time35 min

Ingredients:
- 1 large egg, separated
- Pinch cream of tartar
- Pinch salt
- 1 ounce cream cheese, softened
- 1 ounce sliced ham
- 1 ounce sliced hard salami
- 1 ounce sliced turkey
- 2 slices cheddar cheese

Instructions:
1. For the bread, preheat the oven to 300°F and line a baking sheet with parchment.
2. Beat the egg whites with the cream of tartar and salt until soft peaks form.
3. Whisk the cream cheese and egg yolk until smooth and pale yellow.
4. Fold in the egg whites a little at a time until smooth and well combined.
5. Spoon the batter onto the baking sheet into two even circles.
6. Bake for 25 minutes until firm and lightly browned.
7. To complete the sandwich, layer the sliced meats and cheeses between the two bread circles.
8. Grease a skillet with cooking spray and heat over medium heat.
9. Add the sandwich and cook until browned underneath, then flip and cook until the cheese is just melted.

SIMPLE TUNA SALAD ON LETTUCE
Nutrition: Cal 550;Fat 35 g;Carb 8 g;Protein 38 g
Serving 2; Cook time 10 min

Ingredients:
- ¼ cup mayonnaise
- 1 tablespoon fresh lemon juice
- 1 tablespoon pickle relish
- 2 (6-ounce) cans tuna in oil, drained and flaked
- ½ cup cherry tomatoes, halved
- ¼ cup diced cucumber
- Salt and pepper
- 4 cups chopped romaine lettuce

Instructions:
1. Whisk together the mayonnaise, lemon juice, and relish in a bowl.
2. Toss in the flaked tuna, tomatoes, and cucumber – season with salt and
pepper.
3. Spoon over chopped lettuce to serve.

HAM, EGG, AND CHEESE SANDWICH
Nutrition: Cal 365;Fat 21 g;Carb 6.5 g;Protein 35.5 g
Serving 1; Cook time35 min

Ingredients:
- 1 large egg, separated
- Pinch cream of tartar
- Pinch salt
- 1 ounce cream cheese, softened
- 1 large egg
- 1 teaspoon butter
- 3 ounces sliced ham
- 1 slice cheddar cheese

Instructions:
1. For the bread, preheat the oven to 300°F and line a baking sheet with parchment.
2. Beat the egg whites with the cream of tartar and salt until soft peaks form.
3. Whisk the cream cheese and egg yolk until smooth and pale yellow.
4. Fold in the egg whites a little at a time until smooth and well combined.
5. Spoon the batter onto the baking sheet into two even circles.
6. Bake for 25 minutes until firm and lightly browned.
7. To complete the sandwich, fry the egg in butter until done to your preference.
8. Arrange the sliced ham on top of one bread circle.
9. Top with the fried egg and the sliced cheese then the second bread circle.
10. Serve immediately or cook in a greased skillet to melt the cheese first.

BACON-WRAPPED HOT DOGS
Nutrition: Cal 500;Fat 4 g;Carb 3 g;Protein 24 g
Serving 2; Cook time40 min

Ingredients:
- 4 all-beef hot dogs
- 2 slices cheddar cheese
- 4 slices uncooked bacon

Instructions:
1. Slice the hotdogs lengthwise, cutting halfway through the thickness.
2. Cut the cheese slices in half and stuff one half into each hot dog.
3. Wrap the hotdogs in bacon then place them on a foil-lined roasting pan.
4. Bake for 30 minutes or until the bacon is crisp.

FRIED TUNA AVOCADO BALLS
Nutrition: Cal 455;Fat 38 g;Carb 8 g;Protein 23 g
Serving 4; Cook time 20 min

Ingredients:
- ¼ cup canned coconut milk
- 1 teaspoon onion powder
- 1 clove garlic, minced
- Salt and pepper
- 10 ounces canned tuna, drained
- 1 medium avocado, diced finely
- ½ cup almond flour
- ¼ cup olive oil

Instructions:
1. Whisk together the coconut milk, onion powder, garlic, salt and pepper in a bowl.
2. Flake the tuna into the bowl and stir in the avocado.
3. Divide the mixture into 10 to 12 balls and roll in the almond flour.
4. Heat the oil in a large skillet over medium-high heat.
5. Add the tuna avocado balls and fry until golden brown then drain on paper towels.

CURRIED CHICKEN SOUP
Nutrition: Cal 390;Fat 22 g;Carb 14 g;Protein 34 g
Serving 4; Cook time 30 min

Ingredients:
- 2 tablespoons olive oil, divided
- 4 boneless chicken thighs (about 12 ounces)
- 1 small yellow onion, chopped
- 2 teaspoons curry powder
- 2 teaspoons ground cumin
- Pinch cayenne
- 4 cups chopped cauliflower
- 4 cups chicken broth
- 1 cup water
- 2 cloves minced garlic
- ½ cup canned coconut milk
- 2 cups chopped kale
- Fresh chopped cilantro

Instructions:
1. Chop the chicken into bite-sized pieces then set aside.
2. Heat 1 tablespoon oil in a saucepan over medium heat.
3. Add the onions and cook for 4 minutes then stir in half of the spices.
4. Stir in the cauliflower and sauté for another 4 minutes.
5. Pour in the broth then add the water and garlic and bring to a boil.
6. Reduce heat and simmer for 10 minutes until the cauliflower is softened.
7. Remove from heat and stir in the coconut milk and kale.
8. Heat the remaining oil in a skillet and add the chicken – cook until browned.
9. Stir in the rest of the spices then cook until the chicken is done.
10. Stir the chicken into the soup and serve hot, garnished with fresh cilantro.

CHOPPED KALE SALAD WITH BACON DRESSING
Nutrition: Cal 230;Fat 12 g;Carb 14 g;Protein 16 g
Serving 2; Cook time 15 min

Ingredients:
- 6 slices uncooked bacon
- 2 tablespoons apple cider vinegar
- 1 teaspoon Dijon mustard
- Liquid stevia, to taste
- Salt and pepper
- 4 cups fresh chopped kale
- ¼ cup thinly sliced red onion

Instructions:
1. Cook the bacon in a skillet until crisp then remove to paper towels and chop.
2. Reserve ¼ cup of the bacon grease in the skillet and warm over low heat.
3. Whisk in the apple cider vinegar, mustard, and stevia then season with salt and pepper.
4. Toss in the kale and cook for 1 minute then divide between two plates.
5. Top the salads with red onion and chopped bacon to serve.

KALE CAESAR SALAD WITH CHICKEN
Nutrition: Cal 390;Fat 30 g;Carb 13 g;Protein 15 g
Serving 2; Cook time 20 min

Ingredients:
- 1 tablespoon olive oil
- 6 ounces boneless chicken thigh, chopped
- Salt and pepper
- 3 tablespoons mayonnaise
- 1 tablespoon lemon juice
- 1 anchovy, chopped
- 1 teaspoon Dijon mustard
- 1 clove garlic, minced
- 4 cups fresh chopped kale

Instructions:
1. Heat the oil in a skillet over medium-high heat.
2. Season the chicken with salt and pepper, then add to the skillet.
3. Cook until the chicken is no longer pink, then remove from heat.
4. Combine the mayonnaise, lemon juice, anchovies, mustard, and garlic in a blender.
5. Blend smooth, then season with salt and pepper.
6. Toss the kale with the dressing, then divide in half and top with chicken to serve.

CHICKEN ENCHILADA SOUP
Nutrition: Cal 390;Fat 27 g;Carb 12 g;Protein 24 g
Serving 4; Cook time 60 min

Ingredients:
- 2 tablespoons coconut oil
- 2 medium stalks celery, sliced
- 1 small yellow onion, chopped
- 1 small red pepper, chopped
- 2 cloves garlic, minced
- 1 cup diced tomatoes
- 2 teaspoons ground cumin
- 1 teaspoon chili powder
- ½ teaspoon dried oregano
- 4 cups chicken broth
- 1 cup canned coconut milk
- 8 ounces cooked chicken thighs, chopped
- 2 tablespoons fresh lime juice
- ¼ cup fresh chopped cilantro

Instructions:
1. Heat the oil in a saucepan over medium-high heat then add the celery, onion, peppers, and garlic – sauté for 4 to 5 minutes.
2. Stir in the garlic and cook for a minute until fragrant.
3. Add the tomatoes and spices then cook for 3 minutes, stirring often.
4. Add the broth and bring the soup to a boil, then reduce heat and simmer for about 20 minutes.

5. Stir in the coconut milk and simmer for another 20 minutes, then add the chicken.
6. Cook until the chicken is heated through, then stir in the lime juice and cilantro.

BACON-WRAPPED CHICKEN ROLLS
Nutrition: Cal 350;Fat 16 g;Carb 0,5 g;Protein 46 g
Serving 2; Cook time 40 min

Ingredients:
• 6 boneless, skinless, chicken breast halves
• 6 slices uncooked bacon

Instructions:
1. Preheat the oven to 350°F.
2. Pound the chicken breast halves with a meat mallet to flatten.
3. Roll the chicken breast halves up then wrap each one with bacon.
4. Place the rolls on a foil-lined baking sheet.
5. Bake for 30 to 35 minutes until the chicken is done and the bacon crisp.

THAI COCONUT SHRIMP SOUP
Nutrition: Cal 375;Fat 29 g; Carb 13 g;Protein 18 g
Serving 4; Cook time 40 min

Ingredients:
• 1 tablespoon coconut oil
• 1 small yellow onion, diced
• 4 cups chicken broth
• 1 (14-ounce) can coconut milk
• 1 cup fresh chopped cilantro
• 1 jalapeno, seeded and chopped
• 1 tablespoon grated ginger
• 2 cloves garlic, minced
• 1 lime, zested and juiced
• 6 ounces uncooked shrimp, peeled and deveined
• 1 cup sliced mushrooms
• 1 small red onion, sliced thinly
• 1 tablespoon fish sauce

Instructions:
1. Heat the coconut oil in a saucepan over medium heat.
2. Add the yellow onions and sauté until translucent, about 6 to 7 minutes.
3. Stir in the chicken broth, coconut milk, cilantro, and jalapeno.
4. Add the ginger, garlic, and lime zest then bring to boil.
5. Reduce heat and simmer for 20 minutes - strain the mixture and discard the solids.
6. Return the remaining liquid to the saucepan and add the shrimp, mushrooms, and red onion.
7. Stir in the lime juice and fish sauce then simmer for 10 minutes. Serve hot.

MUSHROOM AND ASPARAGUS SOUP
Nutrition: Cal 170; Fat 10 g; Carb 4 g; Protein 18 g
Serving 4; Cook time 40 min

Ingredients:
• 1 tablespoon butter
• 1 small yellow onion, chopped
• 3 cloves garlic, minced
• 1 pound asparagus, trimmed and chopped
• 2 cups sliced mushrooms
• 4 cups vegetable broth
• 4 cups fresh baby spinach
• 1 teaspoon fresh chopped tarragon
• ½ cup heavy cream
• ¼ cup fresh lemon juice
• ¼ cup fresh chopped parsley
• Salt and pepper

Instructions:
1. Melt the butter in a stockpot and add the onion.
2. Sauté the onion until browned, then stir in the garlic and cook 1 minute more.
3. Stir in the asparagus and mushrooms, then sauté for 4 minutes.

4. Pour in the vegetable broth along with the spinach and tarragon.
5. Bring to a boil, then reduce heat and simmer for 30 minutes on medium low heat.
6. Remove from heat, then stir in the cream, lemon juice, and parsley.
7. Cover and let rest for 20 minutes, then season with salt and pepper to taste.

SLOW-COOKER CHICKEN FAJITA SOUP
Nutrition: Cal 325;Fat 17 g; Carb 17 g;Protein 28 g
Serving 4; Cook time 60 hours

Ingredients:
• 12 ounces chicken thighs
• 1 cup diced tomatoes
• 2 cups chicken stock
• ½ cup enchilada sauce
• 2 ounces chopped green chiles
• 1 tablespoon minced garlic
• 1 medium yellow onion, chopped
• 1 small red pepper, chopped
• 1 jalapeno, seeded and minced
• 2 teaspoons chili powder
• ¾ teaspoon paprika
• ½ teaspoon ground cumin
• Salt and pepper
• 1 small avocado, sliced thinly
• ¼ cup chopped cilantro
• 1 lime, cut into wedges

Instructions:
1. Combine the chicken, tomatoes, chicken stock, enchilada sauce, chiles, and garlic in the slow cooker and stir well.
2. Add the onion, bell peppers, and jalapeno.
3. Stir in the seasonings then cover and cook on low for 5 to 6 hours.
4. Remove the chicken and chop or shred then stir it back into the soup.
5. Spoon into bowls and serve with sliced avocado, cilantro, and lime wedges.

AVOCADO EGG SALAD ON LETTUCE
Nutrition: Cal 375; Fat 30 g; Carb 8 g; Protein 15 g
Serving 2; Cook time 10 min

Ingredients:
• 4 large hardboiled eggs, cooled and peeled
• 1 small avocado, pitted and chopped
• 1 medium stalk celery, diced
• ¼ cup diced red onion
• 2 tablespoons fresh lemon juice
• Salt and pepper
• 4 cups chopped romaine lettuce

Instructions:
1. Coarsely chop the eggs into a bowl.
2. Toss in the avocado, celery, red onion, and lemon juice.
3. Season with salt and pepper then serve over chopped lettuce.

SLOW-COOKER BEEF CHILI
Nutrition: Cal 395; Fat 20 g; Carb 12 g; Protein 42 g
Serving 4; Cook time 6 hours

Ingredients:
• 1 tablespoon coconut oil
• 1 medium yellow onion, chopped
• 3 cloves garlic, minced
• 1 pound ground beef (80% lean)
• 1 small red pepper, chopped
• 1 small green pepper, chopped
• 1 cup diced tomatoes
• 1 cup low-carb tomato sauce
• 1 tablespoon chili powder
• 2 teaspoons dried oregano
• 1 ½ teaspoons dried basil
• Salt and pepper
• ¾ cup shredded cheddar cheese
• ½ cup diced red onion

Instructions:
1. Heat the oil in a skillet over medium-high heat.
2. Add the onions and sauté for 4 minutes, then stir in the garlic and cook 1 minute.
3. Stir in the beef and cook until it is browned, then drain some of the fat.
4. Spoon the mixture into a slow cooker and add the spices.
5. Cover and cook on low heat for 5 to 6 hours, then spoon into bowls.
6. Serve with shredded cheddar and diced red onion.

ZUCCHINI CRUST GRILLED CHEESE
Nutrition: Cal 155;Fat 10 g; Carb 5 g;Protein 10 g
Serving 4; Cook time 30 min

Ingredients
Zucchini Crust "Bread" Slices
•4 cups shredded zucchini
•1 egg
•½ cup shredded mozzarella cheese
•4 tablespoons grated Parmesan cheese
•1 teaspoon dried oregano
•½ teaspoon salt
•Pinch of ground black pepper
Grilled Cheese
•1 tablespoon butter, room temperature
•⅓ cup / 3 ounces / 85 g sharp cheddar cheese, grated/shredded, at room temperature

Instructions
Zucchini Crust "Bread" Slices
1.Preheat oven to 450°F (220°C) and place a rack in the middle.
2.Line a baking sheet with parchment paper and liberally grease it (alternatively use a silicone baking mat). Set aside.
3.Place shredded zucchini in a microwave-safe dish and microwave on high for 6 minutes. Transfer to a dishcloth (or tea towel) and twist it to squeeze as much moisture as you can. This is very important. The zucchini needs to be dry, otherwise you'll end up with mushy dough, impossible to use as slices of bread.
4.In a bowl mix zucchini, egg, mozzarella cheese, Parmesan cheese, oregano, salt, and pepper.
5.Spread zucchini mixture onto the lined baking sheet and shape into 4 squares.
6.Bake for about 15 to 20 minutes until lightly golden-brown.
7.Remove from the oven and let cool 10 minutes before peeling them off the parchment paper (be careful not to break them!).
Assemble Grilled Cheese
8.Heat a pan over medium heat.
9.Butter one side of each slice of zucchini crust bread (preferably the top part).
10.Place one slice of bread in the pan, buttered side down, sprinkle with the cheese and top with the remaining slice of zucchini crust bread, buttered side up.
11.Turn the heat down a notch and cook until golden-brown, about 2 to 4 minutes.
12.Gently flip and cook until golden-brown on the other side, about 2 to 4 minutes.

SHRIMP AVOCADO SALAD
Nutrition: Cal 340;Fat 33 g; Carb 12 g;Protein 24 g
Serving 2; Cook time 10 min

Ingredients
•8 ounces shrimp peeled, deveined, patted dry
•1 large avocado, diced
•1 small beefsteak tomato, diced and drained
•1/3 cup crumbled feta cheese
•1/3 cup freshly chopped cilantro or parsley
•2 tablespoons salted butter, melted
•1 tablespoon lemon juice
•1 tablespoon olive oil
•1/4 teaspoon salt
•1/4 teaspoon black pepper
Instructions
1.Toss shrimp with melted butter in a bowl until well-coated.

2.Heat a pan over medium-high heat for a few minutes until hot. Add shrimp to the pan in a single layer, searing for a minute or until it starts to become pink around the edges, then flip and cook until shrimp are cooked through, less than a minute.
3.Transfer the shrimp to a plate as they finish cooking. Let them cool while you prepare the other ingredients.
4.Add all other ingredients to a large mixing bowl -- diced avocado, diced tomato, feta cheese, cilantro, lemon juice, olive oil, salt, and pepper -- and toss to mix.
5.Add shrimp and stir to mix together. Add additional salt and pepper, to taste.

CAPRESE TUNA SALAD STUFFED TOMATOES
Nutrition: Cal 196;Fat 5 g; Carb 5 g;Protein 30 g
Serving 2; Cook time 10 min

Ingredients
•1 medium tomato
•1 (5 ounce) can tuna, very well drained
•2 teaspoons balsamic vinegar
•1 tablespoon chopped mozzarella (1/4 ounce)
•1 tablespoon chopped fresh basil
•1 tablespoon chopped green onion
Instructions
1.Cut the top 1/4-inch off the tomato. Use a spoon to scoop out the insides of the tomato. Set aside while you make the tuna salad.

2.Stir together the drained tuna, balsamic vinegar, mozzarella, basil, and green onion. Put the tuna salad in the hollowed out tomato, and enjoy!

CHICKEN ENCHILADA BOWL
Nutrition: Cal 356;Fat 35 g; Carb 6 g;Protein 28 g
Serving 4; Cook time 30 min

Ingredients
•2 tablespoons coconut oil (for searing chicken)
•1 pound of boneless skinless chicken thighs
•3/4 cup red enchilada sauce
•1/4 cup water
•1/4 cup chopped onion
•1 4 ounce can diced green chiles
•**Toppings (feel free to customize)**
•1 whole avocado, diced
•1 cup shredded cheese (I used mild cheddar)
•1/4 cup chopped pickled jalapenos
•1/2 cup sour cream
•1 roma tomato, chopped
Instructions
1.In a pot or dutch oven over medium heat melt the coconut oil. Once hot, sear chicken thighs until lightly brown.
2.Pour in enchilada sauce and water, then add onion and green chiles. Reduce heat to a simmer and cover. Cook chicken for 17-25 minutes or until chicken is tender and fully cooked through to at least 165° internal temperature.
3.Carefully remove the chicken and place onto a work surface. Chop or shred chicken (your preference), then add it back into the pot. Let the chicken simmer uncovered for an additional 10 minutes to absorb flavor and allow the sauce to reduce a little.
4.To serve, top with avocado, cheese, jalapeno, sour cream, tomato, and any other desired toppings. Feel free to customize these to your preference. Serve alone or over cauliflower rice if desired, just be sure to update your personal nutrition info as needed.

CAPRESE EGGPLANT PANINI WITH LEMON BASIL AIOLI
Nutrition: Cal 196;Fat 5 g; Carb 5 g;Protein 35 g
Serving 4; Cook time 10 min

Ingredients
•2 small eggplants, ends removed
•2 cloves garlic, peeled
•2 tablespoons mayonnaise

•8-10 lemon basil leaves, chopped
•½ cup mozzarella, shredded
•2 small tomatoes, campari, or other petite variety
•1 cup spinach leaves
•**Instructions**
1.Heat a panini press (or countertop grill with closable lid) to medium.
2.Remove ends of each small (baby) eggplant and slice in half, cutting end to end. Slice the remaining eggplant in ½ inch pieces and discard any pieces that are mostly skin.
3.In a hot skillet, brown garlic cloves until fragrant and soft. Once cool, mince garlic and add to mayonnaise. Stir in chopped lemon basil to finish the aioli.
5.Spread aioli onto an eggplant slice and top with spinach leaves, tomato slices, fresh mozzarella and pine nuts. Spread more aioli on another eggplant slice and place on top. Grill until cheese is melted. Serve hot!2 tablespoons toasted pine nuts

SPICY KIMCHI AHI POKE
Nutrition: Cal 300;Fat 18 g; Carb 5 g;Protein 5 g
Serving 4; Cook time 10 min
Ingredients
•1 lb sushi-grade ahi tuna, diced to roughly 1 inch
•1 tablespoon soy sauce (or coconut aminos for paleo)
•1/2 teaspoon sesame oil
•1/4 cup mayo
•2 tablespoons Sriracha
•1 ripe avocado, diced
•1/2 cup kimchi
•Chopped green onion
•Sesame seeds
Instructions
1.In a medium mixing bowl, add diced tuna.
2.Add soy sauce, sesame oil, mayo, Sriracha to the bowl and toss to combine.
3.Add diced avocado and kimchi to the bowl and gently combine.
4.Serve on top of salad greens, cauli rice, or traditional rice and top with a sprinkle of chopped green onion and sesame seeds if desired.

SPINACH MOZZARELLA STUFFED BURGERS
Nutrition: Cal 414;Fat 30 g; Carb 2 g;Protein 35 g
Serving 4; Cook time 20 min
Ingredients
•1½ lbs ground chuck
•1 teaspoon salt
•¾ teaspoon ground black pepper
•2 cups fresh spinach, firmly packed
•½ cup shredded mozzarella cheese (about 4 ounces)
•2 tablespoons grated Parmesan cheese
Instructions
1.In a medium bowl, combine ground beef, salt, and pepper.
2.Scoop about ⅓ cup of mixture and with dampened hands shape into 8 patties about ½-inch thick. Place in the refrigerator.
3.Place spinach in saucepan over medium-high heat. Cover and cook for 2 minutes, until wilted.
4.Drain and let cool. With your hands squeeze the spinach to extract as much liquid as possible.
5.Transfer to a cutting board, chop the spinach, and place in a bowl.
6.Stir in mozzarella cheese and Parmesan.
7.Scoop about ¼ cup of stuffing and mound in the center of 4 patties.
8.Cover with remaining 4 patties, and seal the edges by pressing firmly together.
9.Cup each patty with your hands to round out the edges, and press on the top to flatten slightly into a single thick patty.
10.Heat a grill or a grill pan to medium-high (if you're using an outdoor grill lightly oil the grill grates).
11.Grill burgers for 5 to 6 minutes on each side.
12.Serve!

MEXICAN MEATZA
Nutrition: Cal 414;Fat 30 g; Carb 2 g;Protein 35 g
Serving 4; Cook time 25 min
Ingredients
•1 lb ground beef, lean
•1/2 onion
•1 egg
•1 cup cauliflower, riced
•2 teaspoons chili powder
•1 teaspoon cumin
•1 teaspoon salt
•1/2 teaspoon pepper
•1 teaspoon garlic powder
•1/4 red onion, sliced thin
•1 cup cheddar cheese, shredded
•1/4 cup sweet pepper slices
Cilantro Crema (optional)
•1/3 cup cilantro leaves, loosely packed
•1/2 cup sour cream
•1 tablespoon lime juice
•1 clove garlic
Instructions
1.Preheat oven to 350°F.
2.Add onion to a food processor and pulse until finely chopped.
3.Place in a large bowl and then add cauliflower to food processor and pulse until it looks like grains of rice.
4.Add that to the large bowl along with meat, a beaten egg, chili powder, cumin, salt, pepper, and garlic powder.
5.Mix well and split meat into 4.
6.Take each piece and make into a very thin, round pizza-looking shell. Place on a sprayed cookie sheet. Continue with the rest of the meat mixture. May take 2 cookie sheets.
7.Bake for 20 minutes or until meat is cooked. (thickness of meat will affect cooking times. Try not to overcook.)
8.Take out of the oven, sprinkle cheese, and add onions and peppers on top.
9.Broil for 3 minutes or until cheese is melted.
10.Add avocado pieces onto each meatza, slice, and enjoy.
11.Note: You can use any topping you like such as tomatoes, lettuce, black olives, green onions, sour cream, hot sauce, etc.
12.Make crema.

CHICKEN PHILLY CHEESESTEAK
Nutrition: Cal 263;Fat 12 g; Carb 5 g;Protein 27 g
Serving 3; Cook time 15 min
Ingredients
•10 ounces boneless chicken breasts (about 2)
•2 tablespoons worcestershire sauce
•1/2 teaspoon onion powder
•1/2 teaspoon garlic powder
•1 dash of ground pepper
•2 teaspoons olive oil, divided
•1/2 cup diced onion, fresh or frozen
•1/2 cup diced bell pepper, fresh or frozen
•1/2 teaspoon minced garlic
•3 slices provolone cheese or queso melting cheese
Instructions
1.Slice chicken breasts into very thin pieces (freeze slightly, if desired, to make this easier) and place in a medium bowl. Add next 4 ingredients (worcestershire through ground pepper) and stir to coat chicken.
2.Heat 1 teaspoon olive oil in a large (9") ovenproof skillet. Add chicken pieces and cook until browned - about 5 minutes. Turn pieces over and cook about 2-3 minutes more or until brown. Remove from skillet.
3.Add remaining 1 teaspoon olive oil to warm skillet. Then add onions, bell pepper, and garlic. Cook and stir to heated and tender, 2-3 minutes.
4.Turn heat off and add chicken back to skillet and stir with veggies to combine. Place sliced cheese over all and cover 2-3 minutes to melt.

CREAMY CAULIFLOWER CHOWDER

Nutrition: Cal144;Fat 18 g; Carb 12 g;Protein 8 g
Serving 2; Cook time 20 min

Ingredients
- 1 tablespoon butter
- 1/2 cup diced onion
- 5 garlic cloves, minced
- 1/2 cup diced carrots
- 1 whole head of cauliflower, cut into small florets
- 1 1/2 cups vegetable broth
- 1 teaspoon freshly ground pepper
- 1/2 teaspoon dried oregano
- 1/4 cup cream cheese
- Salt, to taste
- Olive oil and cooked bacon for topping

Instructions
1. In a dutch oven or soup pot, heat butter and add onions and garlic. Saute for a few minutes till the onions are soft.
2. Add carrots, cauliflower, vegetable broth, pepper, oregano, and salt to the pot. Bring this to a boil, and slow the heat down to a simmer. Cook for 15 minutes or so till the cauliflower is tender.
3. Switch off the flame and using a blender, blend the soup partly in the soup pot. If you don't have a hand blender, pour half the soup into a blender and pulse a few times till creamy.
4. Switch the flame back on and add a cup of water or broth along with the cream cheese. Simmer for 5-10 minutes and switch off the flame. Feel free to thin the soup further, if you like, with some more broth or milk. Top with olive oil and bacon and serve hot.

RICH AND CHEESY BRUSSELS SPROUTS

Nutrition: Cal270;Fat 24 g; Carb 18 g;Protein 22 g
Serving 2; Cook time 15 min

Ingredients
- 1.5lbs (24oz) fresh Brussels sprouts
- 8oz cream cheese
- 1/2c full fat mayonnaise
- 3/4c shredded parmesan cheese
- 1/2c yellow onion, diced
- To taste:salt, pepper

Instructions
1. Preheat oven to 350 degrees.
2. Wash brussels sprouts and remove stems.
3. Chop brussel sprouts into bite sized pieces.
4. Dice onion.
5. Soften cream cheese for 40 seconds in the microwave.
6. Add mayo, Parmesan, onion, salt and pepper.
7. Spray baking dish and evenly spread mixture into dish.
8. Bake uncovered, 45 minutes.
9. Broil 3 minutes.

CHEESY VEGETABLE MACARONI

Nutrition: Cal144;Fat 18 g; Carb 12 g;Protein 8 g
Serving 2; Cook time 20 min

Ingredients
- 2.5 cups of Heavy Whipping Cream
- 1 tbsp. butter
- Head of cauliflower, cut up
- 1.5 cup chopped red bell pepper
- 8oz Mushrooms, sliced
- 3.5 cups of eggplant, cubed
- 7oz cheddar cheese
- 4oz Pepper Jack Cheese
- 2oz Swiss cheese
- 1oz Monterey Jack Cheese
- 1/2 package of Monterey Jack, Mozzarella and Cheddar cheese blend
- To taste:salt, pepper, paprika

Instructions
1. Preheat oven to 400 degrees.
2. In a large pot, bring to a simmer the heavy whipping cream. Do not boil.
3. Add cauliflower and let cook for 6-7 minutes.
4. Add mushrooms and cook for 2-3 minutes.
5. Add peppers and cook 2-3 minutes.
6. Add eggplant and cook until vegetables are soft.
7. Reduce to low heat and your cheese a little bit at a time, letting it melt bedding more.
8. Season with paprika, cayenne pepper, and salt and pepper.
9. Place in baking dish and bake for 10 minutes at 400 degrees.

PROSCIUTTO BLACKBERRY SHRIMP

Nutrition: Cal220;Fat 11 g; Carb 6 g;Protein 21 g
Serving 2; Cook time 20 min

Ingredients
- 10 Oz Pre-Cooked Shrimp
- 11 Slices Prosciutto
- 1/3 cup Blackberries, Ground
- 1/3 cup Red Wine
- 2 tbsp. Olive Oil
- 1 tbsp. Mint Leaves, Chopped
- 1-2 Tbsp. Erythritol (to taste)

Instructions
1. Preheat oven to 425 degrees.
2. Slice each piece of prosciutto in half depending on size of shrimp.
3. Wrap prosciutto around shrimp starting from tale up.
4. Place on baking sheet and drizzle with olive oil.
5. Bake for 15 minutes.
6. In a pan, add ground blackberries, mint leaves and erythritol.
7. Cook for 2-3 minutes.
8. Mix in red wine and reduce while shrimp cooks.
9. Strain if desired.

KETO BARBEQUE CHICKEN SOUP

Nutrition: Cal270;Fat 24 g; Carb 18 g;Protein 22 g
Serving 2; Cook time 60 min

Ingredients
The Base:
- 3 medium Chicken Thighs
- 2 teaspoon Chili Seasoning
- Salt and Pepper to Taste
- 2 tablespoon Chicken Fat or Olive Oil
- 1 1/2 cup Chicken Broth
- 1 1/2 cup Beef Broth
- Salt and Pepper to Taste
BBQ Sauce:
- 1/4 Cup Reduced Sugar Ketchup
- 1/4 cup Tomato Paste
- 2 tablespoon Dijon Mustard
- 1 tablespoon Soy Sauce
- 1 tablespoon hot sauce
- 2 1/2 teaspoon Liquid Smoke
- 1 teaspoon Worcestershire Sauce
- 1 1/2 teaspoon Garlic Powder
- 1 teaspoon Onion Powder
- 1 teaspoon Chili Powder
- 1 teaspoon Red Chili Flakes
- 1 teaspoon Cumin
- 1/4 cup Butter

Instructions
1. Preheat oven to 400F.
2. De-bone chicken thighs, set bones aside, and season well with your favorite chili seasoning.
3. Line a cookie sheet with foil and bake for 50 minutes.
4. While that is cooking, add 2 tablespoons of Chicken Fat or Olive Oil in a pot.
5. Heat this to a medium high heat and once hot, add chicken bones.
6. Let these cook for at least 5 minutes and then add broths.
7. Season with salt and pepper to taste.

8. Once the chicken is done, remove the skins and set aside.
9. Add all of the fat from the chicken thighs into the broth and stir.
10. Make the BBQ sauce by combining all ingredients above.
11. Add barbeque sauce to the pot and stir together.
12. Let this simmer in a pot for 20-30 minutes.
13. Use an immersion blender to emulsify all of the fats and liquids together.
14. Then, shred chicken thighs and add to the soup. You can optionally add spring onion or bell pepper here.
15. Simmer for another 10-20 minutes.
16. Serve with yellow bell pepper, spring onion, or cheddar cheese and the crispy chicken skins

KETO LUNCH JAMBALAYA
Nutrition: Cal 144;Fat 18 g; Carb 12 g;Protein 8 g
Serving 2; Cook time 20 min

Ingredients
- 1 medium cauliflower
- 1 green pepper, coarsely chopped
- 2 stalks celery, coarsely chopped
- 1 small onion, diced
- 2 cloves garlic, minced
- 2-3 boneless chicken breasts, cubed
- 8 ounces smoked sausage, sliced
- 8 ounces ham, cubed
- 14.5 ounce can diced tomatoes, undrained
- 8 ounce can tomato sauce
- 3 teaspoons Cajun Seasoning
- Salt and pepper, to taste
- Cooking oil

Instructions
1. In a 8-quart Dutch oven or pot, heat 2 tablespoons oil.
2. Sauté the peppers, celery, onion, garlic, chicken and Cajun seasoning, on medium-high heat, until the chicken is nearly done.
3. Add the sausage, ham and cauliflower. Mix well.
4. Mix in the tomatoes and tomato sauce. Bring to a boil, turn down to low.
5. Cover and simmer about 20 minutes until the cauliflower is tender, but not mushy.
6. Season to taste with salt and pepper.

EASY KETO EGG SALAD
Nutrition: Cal362;Fat 33 g; Carb 2.5 g;Protein 13 g
Serving 2; Cook time 10 min

Ingredients
- 1/2 cup Mayonnaise
- 1 tbsp Dijon mustard
- 1 tbsp Lemon juice
- 8 large Hard boiled eggs (diced)
- 1/4 cup Celery (finely chopped)
- 2 tbsp White onion (minced)
- 2 tbsp Chives (chopped)
- 1/2 tsp Sea salt (to taste)
- 1/8 tsp Black pepper (to taste)
- Paprika (optional, for garnish)

Instructions
1. In a medium bowl, whisk together the mayo, mustard, and lemon juice, until smooth.

2. Gently fold in the eggs, celery, onions, and chives. Season with salt and pepper to taste. Garnish with paprika on top, if desired.

KETO COBB SALAD
Nutrition: Cal 374;Fat 27 g; Carb 8 g;Protein 24 g
Serving 2; Cook time 10 min

Ingredients
- 1 ¼ cups Romaine lettuce (chopped)
- 1 ¼ cups Watercress (chopped)
- 2 slices Cooked bacon (cut into small pieces or crumbled)
- 3 oz Cooked chicken breast (cut into cubes or shredded)
- ½ cups Grape tomatoes (halved)
- ½ medium Avocados
- 1 large Hard boiled eggs (diced or sliced)
- ⅛ cup Roquefort cheese (crumbled)
- ½ tbsp Chives (finely chopped)
- ⅛ cup Ranch dressing
- Sea salt, Black pepper (to taste)

Instructions
1. In a large bowl, combine all ingredients except dressing, salt and pepper.
2. Add dressing and toss to combine. Season to taste with salt and pepper.

ZUCCHINI NOODLES WITH GARLIC, BUTTER, PARMESAN
Nutrition: Cal 283;Fat 21 g; Carb 7 g;Protein 16 g
Serving 2; Cook time 25 min

Ingredients
- 2 medium zucchini
- 2 Tablespoons (30 g) butter
- 3 large cloves garlic , minced (or to taste)
- 3/4 cup (75 g) parmesan cheese (approximately)
- kosher salt , to taste
- black pepper , to taste
- 1/4 teaspoon (1.25 ml) red chili flakes

Instructions
1. Cut zucchini into spirals or noodle strands using the vegetable spiralizer or julienne peeler. Set aside noodles.
2. Heat large pan on medium-high heat. Melt butter, then add garlic. Cook garlic until fragrant and translucent, about 30 seconds. Don't let the garlic burn.
3. Add zucchini noodles and cook until tender, about 3-5 minutes. Zucchini noodles cook really fast, so taste a strand as you cook and decide how firm or "al-dente" you want the zucchini. Don't overcook the zucchini noodles or else they'll become mush.
4. Remove the pan from the heat, add parmesan cheese and season generously with salt and pepper to taste. Add chili flakes then serve warm.

SPICY SHRIMP TACO LETTUCE WRAPS
Nutrition: Cal 186;Fat 17 g; Carb 8 g;Protein 2 g
Serving 4; Cook time 20 min

Ingredients
- 20 medium shrimp peeled and deveined (about 1 pound)
- 1 tablespoon oil of choice
- 1 clove garlic minced
- 1/2 teaspoon
- 1/2 teaspoon ground cumin
- 1/4 teaspoon kosher salt
- 1 tablespoon olive oil
- squeeze of lime optional

Avocado Salsa
- 1 avocado cut into chunks
- 1 tomato, chopped
- 1/4 cup loosely packed fresh cilantro leaves coarsely chopped
- 1 tablespoon fresh lime juice from half a lime
- 1/2 teaspoon salt
- 1/4 teaspoon black pepper

Cilantro Sauce
- 1/4 cup sour cream
- 1/4 cup cilantro
- 1 clove garlic

- 1 tablespoon fresh lime juice
- salt and pepper, to taste
- 8-12 lettuce leaves

Instructions

To cook the shrimp

1. In a medium bowl whisk together olive oil, garlic, cumin, chili, and salt. Add shrimp and mix until shrimp is covered in seasoning. Heat a large heavy-duty or cast iron skillet on high heat for 2 minutes. Add the olive oil and shrimp. Cook 2-3 minutes per side or until shrimp is cooked through. Turn off heat and finish with a squeeze of lime (optional).

To make avocado tomato salsa

2. In a medium bowl, gently combine tomato, avocado, cilantro, lime juice and a sprinkle of salt and pepper and mixed through. Set aside.

To make the Jalapeno Cilantro Sauce

3. Add the sour cream, jalapeno, garlic, cilantro, lime and salt and pepper to a food processor. Blend for 30 seconds or until creamy.

To assemble:

4. Plac two romaine or butter lettuce leaves on top of each-other for each lettuce wraps. Top with 4-5 pieces of shrimp, a few tablespoons of avocado salsa and a genros drizzle of the spicy jalapeno cilantro sauce. Enjoy hot or cold!

KETO BURRITO BOWL

Nutrition: Cal 374;Fat 25 g; Carb 15 g;Protein 27 g
Serving 4; Cook time 20 min

Ingredients

- 1 cup Mexican Cauliflower Rice
- 1/2 cup Mexican Shredded Beef
- 1/4 cup Keto Guacamole
- 1/4 cup Pico de Gallo
- 1/4 cup shredded cheddar cheese
- 1 tablespoon chopped cilantro

Instructions

1. Arrange all of the ingredients in a shallow bowl and taste for seasoning.
2. Add salt and pepper or hot sauce, if desired.
3. Serve immediately.

EGG ROLL IN A BOWL

Nutrition: Cal 331;Fat 23.5 g; Carb 5 g;Protein 25 g
Serving 4; Cook time 15 min

Ingredients

- 1 lb (16 ounces) ground pork or beef
- 1 teaspoon minced garlic
- 14 ounces shredded cabbage or coleslaw mix
- 1/4 cup low-sodium soy sauce (or liquid aminos)
- 1 teaspoon ground ginger
- 1 whole egg
- 2 teaspoons sriracha
- 1 tablespoon sesame oil
- 2 tablespoons sliced green onions

Instructions

1. In a large skillet, brown the pork or beef until no longer pink. Drain the meat if it's really wet. Add the garlic and sautee for 30 seconds. Add the cabbage/coleslaw, soy sauce, ginger, and sautee until desired tenderness. You can add a little water if you need more liquid to sautee the coleslaw down.
2. Make a well in the center of the skillet and add the egg. Scramble until done over low heat.
3. Stir in sriracha. Drizzle with sesame oil and sprinkle with green onions. Add additional soy sauce and sriracha if desired.

CHICKEN QUESADILLA

Nutrition: Cal 600;Fat 40 g; Carb 6 g;Protein 52 g
Serving 1; Cook time 15 min

Ingredients

1 1/2 Cups Mozzarella Cheese
1 1/2 Cups Cheddar Cheese
1 Cup Cooked Chicken
1/4 Cup Bell Pepper
1/4 Cup Diced Tomato
1/8 Cup Green Onion

Instructions

1. Preheat oven to 400 F. Cover a pizza pan with Parchment Paper (NOT wax paper). Mix the Cheeses together, then evenly spread them over the parchment paper (in a circle shape). Bake the cheese shell for 5 minutes. Pour off any extra oil as soon as it comes out of the oven.
2. Place the chicken over half of the cheese shell. Then add the sliced peppers, diced tomato and the chopped green onion. Fold the Cheese shell in half over the chicken and veggies. Press it firmly, then return it to the oven for another 4- 5 minutes.
3. Serve with sour cream, salsa and guacamole. Garnish with Chopped Fresh Basil, Parsley or Cilantro.

AVOCADO CHICKEN SALAD

Nutrition: Cal 267;Fat 20 g; Carb 4 g;Protein 19 g
Serving 3; Cook time 30 min

Ingredients

- 2 cups poached chicken finely diced (10 oz)
- 1 medium Hass Avocado, mashed
- 1/3 cup celery, finely diced (1 large rib)
- 2 tbsp red onion or scallion, minced
- 2 tbsp cilantro, finely chopped
- 2 tbsp avocado oil (or your favorite)
- 1 tbsp fresh lemon juice (or lime juice)
- salt and pepper to taste

Instructions

1. Prepare the celery, onion, and cilantro, placing in a medium bowl. Dice the chicken and add it to the bowl with the vegetables.
2. Cut into the avocado with a chef's knife until the blade hits the pit. Slide the knife around the pit, cutting the avocado in half. Twist the halves to separate. Remove the pit by tapping the knife into the pit until it sticks, make sure the avocado half is held steadily on a cutting board before attempting. Scoop out the avocado flesh with a spoon and place into a small bowl. Mash with a fork until smooth and creamy. Stir in the lemon juice and oil.
3. Add the mashed avocado to the to the chicken and vegetables and stir to mix. Serve over lettuce or enjoy on a low carb bagel.
4. Makes 3, 3/4-1 cup servings.

KETO BACON CHEESEBURGER WRAPS

Nutrition: Cal 267;Fat 20 g; Carb 4 g;Protein 19 g
Serving 4; Cook time 30 min

Ingredients

- 7 oz. bacon
- 4 oz. mushrooms, sliced
- 1½ lbs ground beef or ground turkey
- ½ tsp salt
- ¼ tsp pepper
- 1 cup (4 oz.) shredded cheddar cheese
- 1 butterhead lettuce, leaves separated and washed
- 8 (5 oz.) cherry tomatoes, sliced

Instructions

1. Add the bacon to a large skillet and cook over medium heat for about 15 minutes, or until crispy. Remove the bacon from the pan and set aside.
2. Over medium-high heat, sauté the mushrooms in the bacon fat, for about 5 to 7 minutes, or until browned and tender. Set aside.

3. Add the ground beef, salt, and pepper. Sauté the beef (breaking up any chunks with the back of a wooden spoon) for about 10 minutes, or until evenly browned.
4. For serving, spoon the ground beef onto the lettuce leaves and layer the cheddar cheese, bacon, mushrooms, and tomatoes on top.

KETO CHICKEN SOUP

Nutrition: Cal 267;Fat 20 g; Carb 9 g;Protein 22 g
Serving 4; Cook time 60 min

Ingredients
- 2 tbsp. vegetable oil
- 1 medium onion, chopped
- 5 cloves garlic, smashed
- 2" piece fresh ginger, sliced
- 1 small cauliflower, cut into florets
- 3/4 tsp. crushed red pepper flakes
- 1 medium carrot, peeled and thinly sliced on a bias
- 6 c. low-sodium chicken broth
- 1 stalk celery, thinly sliced
- 2 boneless skinless chicken breasts
- Freshly chopped parsley, for garnish

Instructions
1. In a large pot over medium heat, heat oil. Add onion, garlic and ginger. Cook until beginning to brown.
2. Meanwhile, pulse cauliflower in a food processor until broken down into rice-sized granules. Add cauliflower to pot with onion mixture and cook over medium high heat until beginning to brown, about 8 minutes.
3. Add pepper flakes, carrots, celery and chicken broth and bring to a simmer. Add chicken breasts and let cook gently until they reach an internal temperature of 165°, about 15 minutes. Remove from pan, let cool until cool enough to handle, and shred. Meanwhile, continue simmering until vegetables are tender, 3 to 5 minutes more.
4. Remove ginger from pot, and add shredded chicken back to soup. Season to taste with salt and pepper, then garnish with parsley before serving.

KETO VEGETABLE SOUP

Nutrition: Cal 180;Fat 10 g; Carb 9 g;Protein 8 g
Serving 4; Cook time 35 min

Ingredients
- ⅔ tbsp Olive oil
- ⅓ large Onion (diced)
- ⅔ large Bell peppers (diced, the same size as onions)
- 1 ⅓ cloves Garlic (minced)
- ⅓ medium head Cauliflower (cut into 1-inch florets)
- ⅔ cups Green beans (trimmed, cut into 1-inch pieces)
- ⅔ 14.5-oz cans Diced tomatoes
- 2 ⅔ cups Chicken broth (or vegetable broth for vegetarian/vegan)
- ⅓ tbsp Italian seasoning
- ⅔ Dried bay leaves (optional)
- Sea salt (optional, to taste)
- Black pepper (optional, to taste)

Instructions
1. Heat olive oil in a pot or dutch oven over medium heat.

2. Add the onions and bell peppers. Saute for 7 to 10 minutes, until onions are translucent and browned.

3. Add the minced garlic. Saute for about a minute, until fragrant.

4. Add the cauliflower, green beans, diced tomatoes, broth, and Italian seasoning. Adjust sea salt and black pepper to taste. Add the bay leaves, if using.

5. Bring the soup to a boil. Cover, reduce heat to medium low, and cook for about 10 to 20 minutes, until veggies are soft.

CREAMY TACO SOUP

Nutrition: Cal 347;Fat 24 g; Carb 9 g;Protein 22 g
Serving 4; Cook time 25 min

Ingredients
- 1 lb ground beef or turkey or chicken
- 1 tbsp oil of choice
- 1 small onion diced
- 2-3 cloves garlic minced
- 1 small green bell pepper diced (optional)
- 1 (10 oz) can Rotel tomatoes or 1 large tomato, chopped
- 1 (8 oz) pkg cream cheese OR 1 cup heavy cream
- 2 tablespoons homemade or 1 packet
- Salt and pepper to taste
- 1 (14.5) oz can beef broth 1.5 cups

Instructions
1. Add 1 tablespoon oil to a pot or large pot or dutch oven, brown beef, onion, and garlic over medium-high heat for 7-8 minutes or until the ground beef is browned through.
2. Add the bell pepper, Rotel diced tomatoes, cream cheese, and spices. Stir for 4-5 minutes or until tomatoes are soft and tender and cream cheese is mixed through.
3. Pour in beef broth and reduce heat to low-medium. Simmer 15-20 minutes or until desired thickness is achieved.
4. Serve in small soup bowls. Top with freshly sliced avocado, sour cream, shredded cheese, freshly minced cilantro, jalapeno, and a drizzle of lime.

KETO WHITE CHICKEN CHILI

Nutrition: Cal 480;Fat 30 g; Carb 5 g;Protein 38 g
Serving 4; Cook time 45 min

Ingredients
- 1 lb chicken breast
- cups chicken broth
- 2 garlic cloves, finely minced
- 1 4.5oz can chopped green chiles
- 1 diced jalapeno
- 1 diced green pepper
- 1/4 cup diced onion
- 4 tbsp butter
- 1/4 cup heavy whipping cream
- 4 oz cream cheese
- 2 tsp cumin
- 1 tsp oregano
- 1/4 tsp cayenne (optional)
- Salt and Pepper to taste

Instructions
1. In large pot, season chicken with cumin, oregano, cayenne, salt and pepper
2. Sear both sides over medium heat until golden
3. Add broth to pot, cover and cook chicken for 15-20 minutes or until fully cooked
4. While chicken is cooking, melt butter in medium skillet
5. Add chiles, diced jalapeno, green pepper and onion to skillet and saute until veggies soften
6. Add minced garlic and saute additional 30 seconds and turn off heat, set aside
7. Once chicken is fully cooked, shred with fork and add back into broth
8. Add sauteed veggies to pot with chicken and broth and simmer for 10 minutes
9. In medium bowl, soften cream cheese in microwave until you can stir it (~20 sec)
10. Mix cream cheese with heavy whipping cream
11. Stirring quickly, add mixture into pot with chicken and veggies
12. Simmer additional 15 minutes
13. Serve with favorite toppings such as: pepper jack cheese, avocado slices, cilantro, sour cream

CHICKEN WITH SPINACH AND FETA
Nutrition: Cal 300;Fat 12 g; Carb 2 g;Protein 40 g
Serving 4; Cook time 30 min

Ingredients
- Chicken breasts (no bones and skin, 4 pieces)
- Spinach (half cup)
- Coconut oil (2 tbsp)
- Feta cheese (1/3 cup)
- Garlic powder (¼ teaspoon)
- Salt (¼ teaspoon)
- Dry oregano (¼ teaspoon)
- Parsley (¼ teaspoon, dry or fresh)
- Water (1 cup)

Instructions
1. Pound the chicken breasts but don't make these to thin; cut "pockets" inside meat.
2. In a bowl mix the feta along with the spinach and add the salt. Put this mix inside the "pockets" and after that close it with toothpicks.
3. Add the remainder in the seasoning all on the meat.
4. Set the pressure cooker to "Sauté" and squeeze coconut oil inside; fry the chicken breasts till they have a golden color. When the meat is cooked, press "Cancel."
5. Put the chicken breasts over a plate and pour water inside the pressure cooker; place the steaming rack inside and put the meat onto it. Steam the meat for fifteen minutes.
6. Release the stress naturally for fifteen minutes.
7. Serve while still warm.

MEATBALLS IN TOMATO SAUCE
Nutrition: Cal 388;Fat 27 g; Carb 11 g;Protein 23 g
Serving 8; Cook time 25 min

Ingredients
For meatballs
- Ground beef (2 lbs)
- Eggs (2)
- Garlic (3 cloves)
- Oregano (dry, 2 teaspoons)
- Salt (1 along with a half teaspoon)
- Pepper (1 teaspoon)
- Onion powder (2 teaspoons)

For the tomato sauce
- Coconut oil (2 teaspoons)
- Garlic (2 cloves)
- Tomatoes (grated or blended, around 30 oz.)
- Onion (1, chopped)
- Water (¼ cup)
- Tomato paste (2 tbsp)
- Salt (2 teaspoons)

Instructions
1. Mix the meatball
2. Ingredients and roll the meat in small balls.
3. Set the pressure cooker to "Sauté" and pour inside the coconut oil (it's ok to make use of avocado oil at the same time).
4. The garlic and onion come next and must be cooked for 5 minutes with occasional stirring (before the onion is tender).
5. Press Cancel and adding the lake, grated tomatoes, tomato paste, and salt. Put within the meatballs, stir everything together (the meatballs ought to be well covered with tomato sauce).
6. Close pressure cooker and seal the pressure valve; place it to "Manual" and cook the meatballs for 7 minutes.
7. When the cooking is complete, release pressure naturally for 10 minutes.
8. Serve the meatballs with pasta, vegetables, or alone.

CARNITAS FOR PRESSURE COOKER
Nutrition: Cal 377;Fat 13 g; Carb 16 g;Protein 40 g
Serving 6; Cook time 60 min

Ingredients
- Pork shoulder (4-5 lb, chopped in big pieces)
- Half onion (chopped)
- Grapefruit zest and juice
- Garlic (4 cloves, minced)
- Dry oregano (1 teaspoon)
- Cumin (2 teaspoons)
- Chili powder (1 teaspoon)
- Bay leaf (one)
- Salt (3 teaspoons)
- Cilantro
- Lime juice

Instructions
1. First, pour the grapefruit juice within the pressure cooker.
2. In a bowl put the grapefruit zest, pork chunks, oregano, cumin, garlic, salt, and chili powder, and mix all this up.
3. Put the seasoned meat bay leaf and onion in the Pressure cooker; close and seal the lead and hang up the cooking for 35 minutes.
4. Release pressure naturally if the timer is off; let the pressure release naturally (around 20 min).
5. Remove the meat and put it on baking paper. With forks shred the meat and take off any fat pieces.
6. Pre-heat the grill and once it's hot enough, position the meat on it so that it can get a brown color and turn into crispy.
7. Pour the lime juice on the meat and sprinkle with cilantro.

BEEF STEW
Nutrition: Cal 310;Fat 14 g; Carb 26 g;Protein 3.8 g
Serving 6; Cook time 45 min

Ingredients
- Beef (16 oz)
- Beef broth (2 cups)
- Worchester Sauce (4 teaspoons)
- Butter (2 tbsp, unsalted)
- Brown sugar (2 teaspoons)
- Garlic (2 cloves)
- Soy sauce (1 tbsp)
- Onion (chopped, 1 cup)
- Carrots (chopped, 1 cup)
- Rosemary (1 teaspoon)
- Potatoes (2, chopped)

Instructions
1. Season the beef with salt and pepper.
2. Put the butter within the pressure cooker and set it to "Sauté" and permit the butter fully melt. Put the meat in the pot and cook on each side until it gets brown color.
3. Pour the beef broth and stir well; add the Worchester sauce, brown sugar, soy sauce, garlic, and rosemary.
4. Add the chopped potatoes and carrots in cubes. Add them along while using onion inside Pressure cooker and stir all the ingredients
5. Close the lid along with the steam valve. Set to "Meat/Stew" and let it cook for 35 minutes. Once the cooking is complete, release pressure to succeed naturally and allow it to cool.
6. Open the pot, stir the components, add salt and pepper by taste and serve hot.

RIBS IN WHITE SAUCE
Nutrition: Cal 645;Fat 42 g; Carb 2.3 g;Protein 57 g
Serving 5; Cook time 50 min

Ingredients
For ribs
- Ribs (pork or lamb, 3-4 lb.)
- Water (1 cup)

- Apple cider vinegar (¼ cup)
- Garlic powder (half teaspoon)
- Onion powder (half teaspoon)
- Salt, Pepper

For white sauce
- Full-fat coconut milk (2 cans, 13.5 oz.)
- Lemon juice (2 tbsp)
- Mustard (2 tbsp)
- Apple cider vinegar (2 tbsp)
- Garlic (4 cloves, minced)
- Honey (1 teaspoon)
- Salt (1 teaspoon), Pepper (1 teaspoon)

Instructions
1. Pour water and apple cider vinegar in the pressure cooker and add the steam rack around the bottom.
2. Make sure the ribs are dry; season all of them with salt, pepper, garlic, and onion.
3. The ribs should be placed vertically in the pressure cooker and on the top with the rack.
4. Close and secure the duvet. Set the cooking to 25 minutes to "Manual" and under ruthless. The pressure must be naturally released for fifteen minutes once cooking ends.
5. To prepare the white sauce pour the coconut milk in a pan as well as heat it on medium heat. It should simmer for fifteen minutes; it must be thick enough (milk and oil must separate from one another).

The sauce
1. Ingredients go within the pan; whisk until things are all smooth.
2. Prepare the oven; take away the ribs through the Pot and set them in a baking pan covered with baking paper.
3. Add white sauce all on the ribs. Let them bake shortly for 5 minutes (the ribs should form a crust).
4. You can trim the ribs in pieces or serve them whole.

SALSA CHICKEN
Nutrition: Cal 244;Fat 10 g; Carb 4.2 g;Protein 30 g
Serving 6; Cook time 35 min

Ingredients
- Chicken thighs without bones (2 lbs)
- Chicken broth (1/4 cup)
- Cream cheese (4 oz.)
- Salsa (1 cup)
- Taco seasoning (3 tbsp)
- Salt, Pepper

Instructions
1. Put the chicken thighs inside pressure cooker and add the taco seasoning, salt, and pepper.
2. Add the salsa, chicken broth and cream cheese, close and seal the lead. Press "Manual" and set it to prepare for 20 mins on questionable.
3. When it's over, release pressure naturally for quarter-hour.
4. Put the chicken thighs inside a plate; blend the sauce until it's smooth.
5. With a fork shred the meat and place it back inside the creamy sauce. Stir so the meat coats well inside the sauce.
6. Serve with lettuce and avocados and other

CHICKEN WINGETTES WITH CILANTRO DIP
Nutrition: Cal 296;Fat 22 g; Carb 11 g;Protein 10 g
Serving 6; Cook time 60 min

Ingredients
- 10 fresh cayenne peppers, trimmed and chopped
- 3 garlic cloves, minced
- 1 ½ cups white wine vinegar
- ½ teaspoon black pepper
- 1 teaspoon sea salt
- 1 teaspoon onion powder
- 12 chicken wingettes
- 2 tablespoons olive oil
- **DIPPING SAUCE:**

- ½ cup mayonnaise
- ½ cup sour cream
- ½ cup cilantro, chopped
- 2 cloves garlic, minced
- 1 teaspoon smoked paprika

Instructions
1. Place cayenne peppers, 3 garlic cloves, white vinegar, black pepper, salt, and onion powder in the container. Add chicken wingettes, and allow them marinate, covered, for one hour inside the refrigerator.
2. Add the chicken wingettes, along while using marinade and extra virgin olive oil on the Instant Pot.
3. Secure the lid. Choose the "Manual" setting and cook for 6 minutes. Once cooking is complete, use a quick pressure release; carefully take away the lid.
4. In a mixing bowl, thoroughly combine mayonnaise, sour cream, cilantro, garlic, and smoked paprika.
5. Serve warm chicken with all the dipping sauce privately.

TURKEY TACO BOWLS
Nutrition: Cal 366;Fat 10 g; Carb 42 g;Protein 23 g
Serving 4; Cook time 70 min

Ingredients
- cheese cheddar or mozzarella

Rice
- 3/4 cup uncooked brown rice
- 1/8 tsp salt
- Zest of 1 lime
- Turkey
- 3/4 lb lean ground turkey
- 2 tablespoons taco seasoning of choice

Salsa
- 1 pint cherry tomatoes quartered
- 1 jalapeno minced
- 1 1/4 cup red onion minced
- Juice from 1/2 a lime
- 1/8 tsp salt

OTHER:
- One 12 oz/341 mL can corn kernels drained & rinsed
- 1/4 cup shredded chee

Instructions
1. Cook brown rice according to package directions, adding the lime zest and salt to the cooking water.
2. Cook turkey over medium heat, tossing in the taco seasoning and breaking it up as you cook. Cook for 10 or so minutes, until cooked through.
3. Combine all salsa ingredients and toss together.
4. To assemble lunch bowls:
5. 1/4 portion of cooked rice (roughly ½ cup)
6. 1/2 cup corn kernels
7. 1/2 cup cooked taco meat
8. 1/4 portion of salsa (just over ½ cup)

TURKEY BREAST
Nutrition: Cal 268 ;Fat 10 g; Carb 8 g;Protein 30 g
Serving 2; Cook time 15 min

Ingredients
- 2 turkey breast fillets
- 1 cup water
- 1 tbsp. rosemary
- 1 tbsp. garlic powder
- 1 tbsp. sage
- ¼ tsp. pepper
- ½ tsp. salt
- ½ tsp. thyme

Instructions
1. Arrange the rack within the Instant Pot or just add the breast to the river for poaching.

2. Use the spices and herbs to rub the turkey and place them in to the pot. Secure the lid using the "Poultry" function (7-10 min).
3. Quick release pressure if the time is completed and eliminate the meat.
4. You can use the juices with all the meat or save it for the broth later.

TURKEY WITH BROCCOLI

Nutrition: Cal 268 ;Fat 10 g; Carb 8 g;Protein 30 g
Serving 2; Cook time 15 min

Ingredients
- ½ pound ground turkey
- 1 spring onion, finely chopped
- 1 cup broccoli, chopped
- 1 cup shredded mozzarella
- 3 tbsps. sour cream
- ¼ cup Parmesan cheese, grated
- 2 tbsps. essential olive oil
- ¼ cup chicken stock
- ¼ tsp. dried oregano
- ¼ tsp. white pepper, freshly ground
- ½ tsp. dried thyme
- ½ tsp. salt

Instructions
1. Plug inside the Instant Pot and press the "Sauté" button. Add organic olive oil and warm up.
2. Now add spring onions and cook for 1 minute, stirring constantly.
3. Add turkey and broccoli. Pour inside the stock and cook for 12 - quarter-hour, stirring occasionally. Season with salt, pepper, thyme, and oregano and stir in the cheese.
4. Press the "Cancel" button and remove from your pot. Transfer a combination to a small baking dish as well as set aside.
5. Preheat the oven to 3500 F and bake for 15 - 20 mins, or until lightly charred.
6. Remove through the oven and chill for a while. Top with sour cream and serve.

JALAPENO CHICKEN

Nutrition: Cal 358 ;Fat 12 g; Carb 3 g;Protein 55 g
Serving 4; Cook time 30 min

Ingredients
5 chicken thighs, skin on
1 large onion, chopped
3 jalapeno peppers, chopped
¾ cup cauliflower, chopped into florets
1 chili pepper, chopped
3 tbsps. fish sauce
1 tbsps. Swerve
5 cups chicken stock
2 tbsps. extra virgin olive oil
3 bay leaves
1 tsp peppercorn
1 tsp dried thyme
1½ tsp salt

Instructions
1. Combine all ingredients inside instant pot and stir well. Seal the lid and hang the steam release handle for the "Sealing" position.
2. Press the "Poultry" button and hang up the timer for twenty minutes on high heat.
3. When done, release the stress naturally and open the lid. Remove the meat in the bones and stir well again. Serve by incorporating grated Parmesan cheese.

TURKEY STEW RECIPE

Nutrition: Cal 386 ;Fat 20 g; Carb 12 g;Protein 36 g
Serving 5; Cook time 30 min

Ingredients

- 2 lbs turkey breast, chopped into smaller pieces
- 2 cups cherry tomatoes, chopped
- 1 onion, finely chopped
- 4 cups chicken broth
- ¾ cup heavy cream
- 2 celery stalks, chopped
- 4 tbsps. butter
- 1 tsp. dried thyme
- 1 tsp. peppercorn
- 2 tsps. Salt

Instructions
1. Combine the constituents in the instant pot and seal the lid
2. Set the steam release handle towards the "Sealing" position and press the "Stew" button. Set the timer for twenty minutes on high heat.
3. When done; release pressure to succeed naturally and open the lid. Chill for a while and stir in most sour cream. To enjoy, serve it immediately.

POMEGRANATE MOLASSES ROASTED CHUCK

Nutrition: Cal 466 ;Fat 32 g; Carb 3 g;Protein 37 g
Serving 10; Cook time 55 min

Ingredients
- 3 lbs chuck steak, boneless
- 2 tsp salt
- 1 ½ tsp freshly grounded black pepper
- 1 ¼ tsp garlic powder
- 1 tbsp pomegranate molasses
- 2 tbsp balsamic vinegar
- 1 onion, finely chopped
- 2 cups regular water
- ½ tsp xanthan gum (it is possible to use 1 tsp of Agar Agar if unavailable)
- 1/3 cup fresh parsley, finely chopped

Instructions
On a cutting board, slice the meat in two and season each half, on each party with salt, pepper and garlic powder.
Place the Instant Pot over heat and hang up on "Sauté" mode.
Place the seasoned meat into the pot and cook until browned on both sides.
Once the meat has browned, start adding the remaining with the
Add the pomegranate molasses, balsamic vinegar, onion and half the water.
Cover the pot and hang up the timer on 35 minutes.
When enough time is finished, manually release pressure to succeed by pressing "venting".
Remove the lid once all the pressure may be released. Transfer the meat to some cutting board and remove any fat or refuse. Cut the meat into large slices.
Simmer the sauce that was left within the pot by setting the pot on "sauté". Allow it to simmer for ten mins before the liquid has reduced.
Stir within the xanthan gum and return the meat into the pot and stir.
Turn over heat and transfer the meat onto serving plate. Drizzle the sauce on the meat and garnish with parsley. Serve hot.

SPICY MINCED LAMB WITH PEAS AND TOMATO SAUCE

Nutrition: Cal 242 ;Fat 12 g; Carb 10 g;Protein 24 g
Serving 6; Cook time 55 min

Ingredients
- 2 lbs ground lamb
- 3 tbsp ghee
- 1 onion, finely chopped
- 5 cloves garlic, crushed
- 1 tsp ground ginger
- 1 Serrano pepper, chopped
- 2 tsp ground coriander
- 1 tsp red pepper flakes

- 1 tsp Kosher salt
- ½ tsp turmeric powder
- ¾ tsp freshly ground black pepper
- ½ tsp chat masala
- ¾ tsp ground cumin
- ¼ tsp cayenne powder
- 2 cardamom pods, shell removed
- 1 can diced tomatoes
- 1 can peas
- Fresh cilantro, finely chopped

Instructions

1. Place the Instant Pot over medium heat and set on "Sauté". Add the ghee and onion. Stir before onion is tender.
2. Stir inside ginger, garlic along with the spices. Stir for 3 minutes and then add the minced meat.
3. Stir the meat until browned and covered well using the spices.
4. Add in the tomatoes and peas and cover the pot. Set on "Keep Warm" then choose "Bean/Chili" option.
5. When time is completed, release the pressure from your pot. Set back on 'Sauté' and allow the liquid to simmer for ten mins until reduced.
6. Transfer the meat into serving bowl and sprinkle fresh cilantro and serve hot.

ROASTED LAMB SHANKS WITH VEGETABLES

Nutrition: Cal 422 ;Fat 20 g; Carb 35 g;Protein 48 g
Serving 4; Cook time 65 min

Ingredients
- 4 lbs lamb shanks
- 2 tsp salt
- 1 tsp freshly ground black pepper
- 3 tbsp ghee
- 3 carrots, diced
- 3 celery stalks, sliced
- 1 large onion, diced
- 2 tbsp tomato paste
- 4 cloves garlic, minced
- 1 can diced tomatoes
- 1 1/3 cup bone broth
- 2 tsp fish sauce (optional)
- 1 ½ tbsp balsamic vinegar
- ½ cup fresh parsley, finely chopped

Instructions

1. Season the lamb with salt and pepper from either side.
2. Place the Instant Pot over medium heat and hang on "Sauté", stir within the ghee until melted and add the meat. Stir until browned for a few minutes.
3. Transfer the meat to your plate and add the vegetables to the pot and sauté for some minutes. Season with many salt and pepper.
4. Add the tomato paste and garlic and stir for any minute. Return the meat to the pot and add the diced tomatoes.
5. Pour within the broth, fish sauce and vinegar.
6. Cover the pot and press "Cancel/Keep Warm". Manually set the timer for 45 minutes. Lower the temperature after the first 5 minutes.
7. When some time ends, release pressure.
8. Transfer the meat onto serving platter and pour the rest of the sauce within the meat. Garnish with fresh parsley and serve hot.

CLASSIC MEATLOAF STUFFED WITH MOZZA-RELLA

Nutrition: Cal 537 ;Fat 17 g; Carb 30 g;Protein 63 g
Serving 8; Cook time 45 min

Ingredients
- 3 lbs minced beef
- 2 cups bread crumbs
- 4 eggs
- 1 tsp salt

- 1 tsp freshly ground black pepper
- 1 tsp garlic powder
- 4 oz mozzarella cheese, sliced
- ¼ cup fresh basil, finely chopped
- 1 cup beef broth
- ¼ cup light brown sugar
- ½ cup ketchup
- 2 tbsp Dijon mustard
- 1 tbsp Worcestershire sauce

Instructions

1. In a large bowl combine the meat with the breadcrumbs. Add the eggs and season with salt, pepper and garlic powder. It is best to use both your hands to mix the components to insure that they're fully incorporated.
2. In a another bowl, whisk together the brown sugar, ketchup, mustard and Worcestershire sauce.
3. Place Instant Pot over medium heat, position the rack provided with the pot inside and pour inside broth.
4. Cut a big part of aluminum foil and put half with the meatloaf mixture. Flatten it out just a little bit. Line the mozzarella slices over meatloaf, sprinkle the basil. Place the opposite half with the meatloaf and press the sides to seal.
5. Carefully place the wrapped meatloaf inside the pot, for the rack.
6. Using a spoon, spread half from the brown sugar mixture around the meatloaf.
7. Cover the pot and manually set the timer on 30 minutes. Once enough time is completed, manually release the pressure and remove the lid.
8. Take the meatloaf out with the pot and allow it to cool a little to start with serving.

BARACOA-STYLE SHREDDED BEEF

Nutrition: Cal 435 ;Fat 31 g; Carb 4.5 g;Protein 31 g
Serving 12; Cook time 75 min

Ingredients
- 3 lbs minced beef
- 2 cups bread crumbs
- 4 eggs
- 1 tsp salt
- 1 tsp freshly ground black pepper
- 1 tsp garlic powder
- 4 oz mozzarella cheese, sliced
- ¼ cup fresh basil, finely chopped
- 1 cup beef broth
- ¼ cup light brown sugar
- ½ cup ketchup
- 2 tbsp Dijon mustard
- 1 tbsp Worcestershire sauce

Instructions

1. Trim any body fat off the meat then cut into 4 large pieces. Season with salt and pepper on either side.
2. Place the Instant Pot over medium heat, then one tablespoon of olive oil. Cook the meat until browned for a couple minutes. You will add the meat in to the pot in two batches.
3. Meanwhile, inside a food processor, blend together the onion, vinegar, lime juice, garlic, peppers, broth, cumin, cloves and tomato paste until smooth no lumps are normally found.
4. Pour inside the blended mixture on the meet and add the bay leaves.
5. Cover the pot as well as set on "Beef/Stew" for an hour.
6. Once time is finished, manually release the pressure and uncover the pot.
7. Transfer the meat onto a cutting board, using two forks start shredding the meat.
8. Discard the bay leaves and return the shredded meat in to the pot. Cover the pot and enable the meat to take a seat for 10 mins.
9. Serve the shredded meat like a filling for tortilla wraps, tacos or sandwiches with your favorite sauce.

BEEF SHAWARMA WITH TAHINI SAUCE

Nutrition: Cal 787 ;Fat 23 g; Carb 90 g;Protein 63 g
Serving 8; Cook time 45 min

Ingredients
•2 lbs ground turkey
•5 cups baby spinach leaves
•1 cup ricotta
•1 cup mozzarella cheese, grated
•1 can crushed tomatoes
•3 tsp dried oregano
•2 tsp thyme
•3 tbsp fresh parsley, finely chopped
•1 tsp salt
•1 tsp freshly ground black pepper
•1 tsp onion powder
•1 tsp garlic powder
•8 lasagna sheets
•3 cups water

Instructions
1. Trim the extra fat off of the chuck roast and sear the meat lengthwise. Make about 4 cuts. Place the crushed garlic cloves into each cut.
2. In a bowl mix together every one of the spices together. Add the balsamic vinegar and one tablespoon in the extra virgin olive oil.
3. Rub the spices mixture on the meat, make certain you cover the whole surface area.
4. Place the meat in a shallow dish and cover with cling film. position the meat inside fridge for about 8 hours or overnight.
5. Once the meat has rested inside the fridge, squeeze Instant Pot over medium heat as well as set on "Sauté". Add the rest of the olive oil and grill the meat for 8 minutes until browned on either side. Pour inside broth and cover the pot.
6. Set on "Beef/Stew" and invite it in order to cook with an hour.
7. Once the time is fully gone, release pressure to succeed and get rid of the lid. Stir inside the onion rings. Allow the meat to sit down inside pot, while using lid off for 5 minutes.
8. Transfer the meat in to a cutting board or possibly a plate and initiate slicing or shredding it into small pieces.
9. To serve, spread some tahini sauce into each pita bread, fill with shawarma and wrap. Enjoy these Arabian wraps with many French fries or pickles.

TURKEY LASAGNA WITH RICOTTA

Nutrition: Cal 740 ;Fat 56 g; Carb 7.8 g;Protein 47 g
Serving 8; Cook time 60 min

Ingredients
•2 lbs ground turkey
•5 cups baby spinach leaves
•1 cup ricotta
•1 cup mozzarella cheese, grated
•1 can crushed tomatoes
•3 tsp dried oregano
•2 tsp thyme
•3 tbsp fresh parsley, finely chopped
•1 tsp salt
•1 tsp freshly ground black pepper
•1 tsp onion powder
•1 tsp garlic powder
•8 lasagna sheets
•3 cups water

Instructions
1. In a bowl mix together the ricotta and mozzarella and place aside.
2. In another bowl, mix the crushed tomatoes using the oregano, thyme, parsley, salt, pepper, onion and garlic powder.
3. Start layering the lasagna in a very heatproof dish that fits inside Instant Pot.
4. Spread one tablespoon of the tomatoes sauce and layer some with the lasagna sheets. Spread more of the tomatoes sauce around the sheets and top using a layer of each one in the following: cheese, minced meat and spinach. Top with more sauce and set the remainder in the lasagna. Repeat the layering process before you uses up lasagna sheets. Sprinkle with leftover cheese and cover tightly with aluminum foil.
5. Place the Instant Pot over medium heat, pour in water and punctiliously position the lasagna dish inside pot on the trivet.
6. Cover the pot and manually set the timer for a half-hour. When time is conducted, carefully release pressure.
7. Uncover the pot and eliminate the foil. To allow the lasagna to brown.
8. Carefully remove the lasagna dish out of the pot and serve hot.

AVOCADO BEEF CHILI WITH COCONUT YOGURT

Nutrition: Cal 366 ;Fat 8.5 g; Carb 90 g;Protein 55 g
Serving 8; Cook time 25 min

Ingredients
•2 tbsp avocado oil
•1 onion, finely chopped
•1 red bell pepper, diced
•1 tsp salt
•3 tbsp tomato paste
•5 garlic cloves, crushed
•3 lbs ground beef
•4 tsp chili powder
•2 tsp dried oregano
•2 tsp ground cumin
•½ tsp red pepper flakes
•1 can roasted diced tomatoes
•1/3 cup bone broth
•1 tbsp fish sauce
•2 tsp apple cider vinegar
•1 ripe avocado, cubed
•2 scallion, sliced
•1/3 cup fresh parsley
•½ cup coconut yogurt
•1 lime, cut into wedges

Instructions
1. Place the Instant Pot over medium heat and set on "Sauté". Heat the avocado oil and stir in the onions and pepper. Season with salt and stir for a couple of minutes until tender.
2. Add the tomato paste and crushed garlic.
3. Stir inside the ground beef, season with increased salt and mix using a wooden spoon for 6 minutes.
4. Season the meat with chili powder, oregano, cumin and red pepper flakes.
5. Drain the tomatoes and stir into the meat. Pour inside broth, fish sauce and vinegar.
6. Cover the pot as well as set "Pressure Cook" and manually set the time for quarter-hour.
7. When the time is fully gone, manually release the stress and get rid of the lid.
8. To serve, transfer the chili for a serving bowls, top with avocado, scallion and a dollop of coconut yogurt. Garnish with fresh parsley, serve with lime wedges.

SPARE RIBS WITH CURRY SAUCE

Nutrition: Cal 522 ;Fat 23 g; Carb 15 g;Protein 71 g
Serving 4; Cook time 45 min

Ingredients
•3 lbs lamb spare ribs
•2 tbsp salt, divided
•2 tbsp freshly ground black pepper
•2 tbsp curry powder, divided
•3 tsp coconut oil

- 1 onion, pureed
- 4 ripe tomatoes, pureed
- 5 cloves garlic, crushed
- Juice of 1 lemon
- 1 bunch fresh cilantro, finely chopped
- 5 scallion, finely chopped

Instructions

1. Start by seasoning the ribs with one tablespoon of salt, pepper and curry powder.
2. Place the ribs in a very shallow dish and cover. Refrigerate overnight.
3. To cook the ribs, put the Instant Pot over medium heat. Melt the oil inside the pot and add in half the ribs. You would want to prepare them by 50 % batches so that you can be certain they're cooked evenly.
4. When the ribs have browned on each side, transfer these phones a plate and repeat with all the remaining half.
5. When the subsequent batch of ribs are browned, transfer these to home plate and stir within the crushed garlic and stir for half a moment. Add the pureed tomato and onion. Add the remainder salt and pepper, lemon juice and half the cilantro.
6. Bring the sauce to your boil and add the ribs back into the pot. Cover the pot and turn heat. Set the timer on 20 minutes. Once the time is finished, allow pressure to be released naturally.
7. To serve, transfer the ribs onto serving platter and garnish with scallion and cilantro, serve hot.

RED PEPPER FLAKES BEEF RIBS WITH RICE

Nutrition: Cal 537 ;Fat 24 g; Carb 7g;Protein 67g
Serving 6; Cook time 45 min

Ingredients

- 3 lbs beef short ribs, boneless
- 2 tbsp red pepper flakes
- 2 tsp salt
- 2 tbsp butter
- 1 onion, finely chopped
- 2 tbsp tomato paste
- 5 garlic cloves, minced
- 2/3 cup roasted tomato salsa (accessible in supermarkets)
- 2/3 cup beef broth
- 1 tsp fish sauce
- ½ tsp freshly ground black pepper
- 1 small bunch fresh cilantro, finely chopped

Instructions

1. On a cutting board, cut the meat into cubes or slices. Place the meat right into a bowl and add inside the red pepper flakes and salt.
2. Place the Instant Pot over medium heat, set on "Sauté" and melt the butter. Stir inside onion, keep stirring until it will become translucent.
3. Add the tomato paste, garlic and salsa. Stir for any minute.
4. Drop the meat in the pot, and pour within the broth and fish sauce and stir.
5. Cover the pot and hang up on "Keep Warm" and "Meat/Stew". You only need in order to smoke it for a half-hour.
6. Once some time ends, allow the stress to be removed naturally.
7. Meanwhile cook the rice according to the instructions for the package.
8. To serve, put the rice into serving bowl and top with meat, drizzle using the meat sauce and garnish with fresh cilantro.

SIMPLE CORNED BEEF

Nutrition: Cal 251 ;Fat 3 g; Carb 1g;Protein 7g
Serving 6; Cook time 75 min

Ingredients

- 4 pounds beef brisket
- 2 oranges, sliced
- 2 garlic cloves, minced
- 2 yellow onions, thinly sliced
- 11 ounces celery, thinly sliced
- 1 tbsp dill, dried

- 3 bay leaves
- 4 cinnamon sticks, cut into halves
- Salt and black pepper to taste
- 17 ounces water

Instructions

1. Put the beef in the bowl, add some water to hide, leave aside to soak for a few hours, drain and transfer for a instant pot.
2. Add celery, orange slices, onions, garlic, bay leaves, dill, cinnamon, dill, salt and pepper and 17 ounces water.
3. Stir, cover and cook on High for 50 minutes.
4. Release the pressure, leave beef aside to chill down for 5 minutes, transfer to a cutting board, slice and divide among plates.
5. Drizzle the juice and veggies through the pot over beef and serve.

BEEF BOURGUIGNON

Nutrition: Cal 442 ;Fat 17 g; Carb 16 g;Protein 39 g
Serving 6; Cook time 45 min

Ingredients

- 5 pounds round steak, cut into small cubes
- 2 carrots, sliced
- ½ cup beef stock
- 1 cup dry burgandy or merlot wine
- 3 bacon slices, chopped
- 8 ounces mushrooms, cut into quarters
- 2 tbsp white flour
- 12 pearl onions
- 2 garlic cloves, minced
- ¼ tsp basil, dried
- Salt and black pepper to taste

Instructions

1. Set your instant pot on Sauté mode, add bacon and brown it for 2 minutes.
2. Add beef pieces, stir and brown for 5 minutes.
3. Add flour and stir well.
4. Add salt, pepper, wine, stock, onions, garlic and basil, stir, cover and cook on High for 20 minutes.
5. Release pressure to succeed quickly, uncover your pot, add mushrooms and carrots, cover again and cook on High for 5 minutes more.
6. Release pressure to succeed again, spoon beef bourguignon onto plates and serve.

ASIAN BEEF CURRY

Nutrition: Cal 434 ;Fat 20 g; Carb 14 g;Protein 27 g
Serving 4; Cook time 30 min

Ingredients

- 2 pounds beef steak, cubed
- 2 tbsp extra virgin olive oil
- 3 potatoes, diced
- 1 tbsp wine mustard
- 2 and ½ tbsp curry powder
- 2 yellow onions, chopped
- 2 garlic cloves, minced
- 10 ounces canned coconut milk
- 2 tbsp tomato sauce
- Salt and black pepper to taste

Instructions

1. Set your instant pot on Sauté mode, add the oil and heat
2. Add onions and garlic, stir and cook for 4 minutes.
3. Add potatoes and mustard, stir and cook for 1 minute.
4. Add beef, stir and brown on the sides.
5. Add curry powder, salt and pepper, stir and cook for just two minutes.
6. Add coconut milk and tomato sauce, cover and cook on High for ten mins.
7. Release the pressure, serve and luxuriate in.

BORDEAUX POT ROAST

Nutrition: Cal 290 ;Fat 20 g; Carb 2 g;Protein 25 g
Serving 6; Cook time 70 min

Ingredients
- 3 pounds beef roast
- Salt and black pepper to taste
- 17 ounces beef stock
- 3 ounces red
- ½ tsp chicken salt
- ½ tsp smoked paprika
- 1 yellow onion, chopped
- 4 garlic cloves, minced
- 3 carrots, chopped
- 5 potatoes, chopped

Instructions
1. In a bowl, mix salt, pepper, chicken salt and paprika and stir.
2. Rub beef using this type of mixture and put roast inside your instant pot.
3. Add onion, garlic, stock and wine, toss to coat, cover and cook on High for 50 minutes.
4. Release the stress quickly, uncover, add carrots and potatoes, cover again and cook on High for ten minutes.
5. Release pressure again, uncover, transfer roast to some platter, drizzle cooking juices all over and serve with veggies privately.

BEEF HOT POT

Nutrition: Cal 221 ;Fat 5.3 g; Carb 13 g;Protein 23 g
Serving 4; Cook time 40 min

Ingredients
- 2 tbsp extra virgin olive oil
- 1 ½ pounds beef stew meat, cubed
- 4 tbsp white flour
- 1 yellow onion, chopped
- 2 tbsp red wine
- 2 garlic cloves, minced
- 2 cups water
- 2 cups beef stock
- Salt and black pepper to taste
- 1 bay leaf
- ½ tsp thyme, dried
- 2 celery stalks, chopped
- 2 carrots, chopped
- 4 potatoes, chopped
- ½ bunch parsley, chopped

Instructions
1. Season beef with salt and pepper and mix with half of the flour.
2. Set your instant pot on Sauté mode, add oil and heat
3. Add beef, brown for just two minutes and transfer to a bowl.
4. Add onion in your pot, stir and fry for 3 minutes.
5. Add garlic, stir and cook for 1 minute.
6. Add wine, stir well and cook for 15 seconds.
7. Add the others from the flour and stir well for two main minutes to stop lumps forming.
8. Return meat to pot, add stock, water, bay leaf and thyme, stir, cover and cook on High for 12 minutes.
9. Release pressure quickly, add carrots, celery and potatoes, stir and cover pot again and cook on High for 5 minutes.
10. Release the pressure naturally for 10 minutes and serve with parsley sprinkled ahead.

VEAL AND MUSHROOM SYMPHONY

Nutrition: Cal 390 ;Fat 17 g; Carb 7 g;Protein 43 g
Serving 4; Cook time 45 min

Ingredients
- ounces button mushrooms, sliced
- ounces shiitake mushrooms, sliced
- 2 pounds veal shoulder, cut into medium chunks
- 17 ounces potatoes, chopped
- 16 ounces shallots, chopped
- 9 ounces beef stock
- 2 ounces white wine
- 1 tbsp white flour
- 2 garlic cloves, minced
- 2 tbsp chives, chopped
- 1 tsp sage, dried
- 1/8 tsp thyme, dried
- Salt and black pepper to taste
- 3 ½ tbsp extra virgin organic olive oil

Instructions
1. Set your instant pot on Sauté mode, add 1 ½ tbsp oil and heat
2. Add veal, season with salt and pepper, stir, brown for 5 minutes and transfer to your bowl.
3. Add the remaining with the oil for the pot as well as heat
4. Add all mushrooms and fry for 3 minutes.
5. Add garlic, stir for 1 minute and transfer everything to some bowl.
6. Add wine and flour on the pot, stir and cook for the further minute.
7. Add stock, sage, thyme and return meat to pot at the same time.
8. Stir, cover and cook on High for twenty minutes.
9. Release pressure, uncover, return mushrooms and garlic on the pot.
10. Also add potatoes and shallots, stir, cover and cook on High for 4 minutes.
11. Release the stress again, uncover your instant pot, combine salt and pepper if needed, divide in bowls and serve with chive garnish.

BEEF AND PASTA CASSEROLE

Nutrition: Cal 182 ;Fat 5.3 g; Carb 28 g;Protein 14 g
Serving 4; Cook time 30 min

Ingredients
- 17 ounces pasta
- 1 pound beef, ground
- 13 ounces mozzarella cheese, shredded
- 16 ounces tomato puree
- 1 celery stalk, chopped
- 1 yellow onion, chopped
- 1 carrot, chopped
- 1 tbsp dark wine
- 2 tbsp butter
- Salt and black pepper to taste

Instructions
1. Set your instant pot on Sauté mode, add the butter and melt.
2. Add carrot, onion and celery and fry for 5 minutes.
3. Add beef, salt and pepper and cook for 10 more minutes.
4. Add wine, while stirring and cook to get a further minute.
5. Add pasta, tomato puree and water to cover pasta, stir, cover and cook on High for 6 minutes.
6. Release the stress, uncover, add cheese, stir well to melt cheese and enjoy.

KOREAN HOT BEEF SALAD

Nutrition: Cal 310 ;Fat 9 g; Carb 18 g;Protein 35 g
Serving 4 Cook time 35 min

Ingredients
- ¼ cup Korean soybean paste
- 1 cup chicken stock
- 2 pounds beef steak, cut into thin strips
- ¼ tsp red pepper flakes
- Salt and black pepper to taste
- 1 yellow onion, thinly sliced
- 1 zucchini, cubed
- 1 ounce shiitake mushroom caps, cut into quarters
- 12 ounces extra firm tofu, cubed
- 1 chili pepper, sliced
- 1 scallion, chopped

Instructions
1. Set your instant pot on Sauté mode, add stock and soybean paste, stir and simmer for two minutes.
2. Add beef, salt, pepper and pepper flakes, stir, cover and cook on High for fifteen minutes.
3. Release pressure quickly, add tofu, onion, zucchini and mushrooms, stir, bring to your boil, cover and cook on High for 4 minutes more.
4. Release the stress again, increase the salt and pepper to taste, add chili and scallion, stir well and ladle into bowls and serve.

CHINESE BEEF AND BROCCOLI
Nutrition: Cal 310 ;Fat 9 g; Carb 18 g;Protein 35 g
Serving 4 Cook time 20 min

Ingredients
• 3 pounds chuck roast, cut into thin strips
• 1 tbsp peanut oil
• 1 yellow onion, chopped
• ½ cup beef stock
• 1 pound broccoli florets
• 2 tsp toasted sesame oil
• 2 tbsp potato starch
For the marinade:
• ½ cup soy sauce
• ½ cup black soy sauce
• 1 tbsp sesame oil
• 2 tbsp fish sauce
• 5 garlic cloves, minced
• 3 red peppers, dried and crushed
• ½ tsp Chinese five spice
• White rice, already cooked for servings
• Toasted sesame seeds for serving
Instructions
1. In a bowl, mix black soy sauce with soy sauce, fish sauce, 1 tbsp sesame oil, 5 garlic cloves, five spice and crushed red peppers and stir well.
2. Add beef strips, toss to coat and marinade for ten minutes.
3. Set your instant pot on Sauté mode, add peanut oil and also heat
4. Add onions, stir and fry for 4 minutes.
5. Add beef and marinade, stir and cook for 2 minutes.
6. Add stock, stir, cover and cook on High for 5 minutes.
7. Release the stress naturally for ten mins, uncover, add cornstarch after you've mixed it to a smooth paste with ¼ cup liquid from your pot, add broccoli on the steamer basket, cover pot again and cook for 3 minutes on High.
8. Release pressure again and dish up beef into bowls at the top of rice, add broccoli quietly, drizzle toasted sesame oil over items in bowls, sprinkle sesame seeds and enjoy this delicious Chinese meal.

BRISKET AND CABBAGE HODGEPODGE
Nutrition: Cal 340 ;Fat 24 g; Carb 14 g;Protein 26 g
Serving 6 Cook time 90 min

Ingredients
• 2 ½ pounds beef brisket
• 4 cups water
• 2 bay leaves
• 3 garlic cloves, chopped
• 4 carrots, chopped
• 1 cabbage heat, cut into 6 wedges
• 6 potatoes, cut into quarters
• Salt and black pepper to taste
• 3 turnips, cut into quarters
• Horseradish sauce for serving
Instructions
1. Put beef brisket and water with your instant pot, add salt, pepper, garlic and bay leaves, cover and cook on High for an hour and 15 minutes.
2. Release pressure quickly, uncover, add carrots, cabbage, potatoes and turnips, stir, cover again and cook on High for 6 minutes.

3. Release pressure naturally, uncover your pot and serve this delicious meal with horseradish sauce.

MERLOT LAMB SHANKS
Nutrition: Cal 430 ;Fat 17 g; Carb 11 g;Protein 50 g
Serving 4 Cook time 45 min

Ingredients
• 4 lamb shanks
• 2 tbsp extra virgin organic olive oil
• 2 tbsp white flour
• 1 yellow onion, finely chopped
• 3 carrots, roughly chopped
• 2 garlic cloves, minced
• 2 tbsp tomato paste
• 1 tsp oregano, dried
• 1 tomato, roughly chopped
• 2 tbsp water
• 4 ounces red Merlot wine
• Salt and black pepper to taste
• 1 beef bouillon cube
Instructions
1. In a bowl, mix flour with salt and pepper.
2. Add lamb shanks and toss to coat.
3. Set your instant pot on Sauté mode, add oil and warmth
4. Add lamb, brown on the sides and transfer with a bowl.
5. Add onion, oregano, carrots and garlic for the pot, stir and cook for 5 minutes.
6. Add tomato, tomato paste, water, wine and bouillon cube, stir and produce to your boil.
7. Return lamb to pot, cover and cook on High for 25 minutes.
8. Release pressure to succeed and set one shank on each plate, pour cooking sauce over and get with seasonal vegetables!

ROSEMARY LAMB RIBS
Nutrition: Cal 234 ;Fat 8.5 g; Carb 3 g;Protein 35 g
Serving 8 Cook time 35 min

Ingredients
• 8 lamb ribs
• 4 garlic cloves, minced
• 2 carrots, chopped
• 13 ounces veggie stock
• 4 rosemary springs
• 2 tbsp extra virgin organic olive oil
• Salt and black pepper to taste
• 3 tbsp white flour
Instructions
1. Set your instant pot on Sauté mode, add the oil as well as heat
2. Add lamb, garlic, salt and pepper and brown it on every side.
3. Add flour, stock, rosemary and carrots, stir well, cover and cook on High for 20 minutes.
4. Release pressure quickly and discard rosemary, divide lamb ribs onto plates and serve while using cooking liquid drizzled on the top.

MEDITERRANEAN LAMB
Nutrition: Cal 238 ;Fat 5 g; Carb 17 g;Protein 27 g
Serving 4 Cook time 75 min

Ingredients
• 6 pounds lamb leg, boneless
• 2 tbsp extra virgin organic olive oil
• Salt and black pepper to taste
• 1 bay leaf
• 1 tsp marjoram
• 1 tsp sage, dried
• 1 tsp ginger, grated
• 3 garlic cloves, minced

- 1 tsp thyme, dried
- 2 cups veggie stock
- 3 pounds potatoes, chopped
- 3 tbsp arrowroot powder blended with 1/3 cup water

Instructions
1. Set your instant pot on Sauté mode, add the oil and warmth
2. Add lamb leg and brown on all sides.
3. Add salt, pepper, bay leaf, marjoram, sage, ginger, garlic, thyme and stock, stir, cover and cook on High for 50 minutes.
4. Release pressure to succeed quickly and add potatoes, arrowroot mix, more salt and pepper if needed, stir, cover again and cook on High for ten minutes.
5. Release pressure to succeed again, uncover, divide Mediterranean lamb onto serving plates and revel in.

CREAMY LAMB CURRY
Nutrition: Cal 378 ;Fat 8 g; Carb 18 g;Protein 22 g
Serving 6 Cook time 35 min

Ingredients
- 1 ½ pounds lamb shoulder, cut into medium chunks
- 2 ounces coconut milk
- 3 ounces dry white wine
- 3 tbsp pure cream
- 3 tbsp curry powder
- 2 tbsp vegetable oil
- 3 tbsp water
- 1 yellow onion, chopped
- 1 tbsp parsley, chopped
- Salt and black pepper to taste

Instructions
1. In a bowl, mix half with the curry powder with salt, pepper and coconut milk and stir well.
2. Set your instant pot on Sauté mode, add oil and also heat
3. Add onion, stir and fry for 4 minutes.
4. Add the remaining of the curry powder, stir and cook for 1 minute.
5. Add lamb pieces, brown them for 3 minutes and mix with water, salt, pepper and wine.
6. Stir, cover and cook on High for 20 mins.
7. Release the stress quickly, set pot to Simmer mode, add coconut milk mixture, stir and boil for 5 minutes.
8. Divide among serving plates, sprinkle parsley at the top and serve.

LAMB AND VEGETABLE HOTPOT
Nutrition: Cal 435 ;Fat 31 g; Carb 6 g;Protein 22 g
Serving 6 Cook time 50 min

Ingredients
- 3 pounds lamb chops
- Salt and black pepper to taste
- 2 tbsp flour
- 2 tbsp extra virgin olive oil
- 2 yellow onions, chopped
- 3 ounces red
- 2 garlic cloves, crushed
- 2 carrots, sliced
- 2 celery sticks, chopped
- 2 tbsp tomato sauce
- 2 bay leaves
- 1 cup green peas
- 14 ounces canned tomatoes, chopped
- 4 ounces green beans
- 2 tbsp parsley, finely chopped
- Beef stock to the pot

Instructions
1. Put flour in a very bowl and mix with salt and pepper.
2. Add lamb chops and toss to coat.
3. Set your instant pot on Sauté mode, add the oil as well as heat

4. Add lamb, stir, brown for 3 minutes on the sides and transfer to a plate.
5. Add garlic and onion and stir for two main minutes.
6. Add wine and cook an extra 2 minutes.
7. Add bay leaves, carrots, celery and return lamb to pot.
8. Also add tomato sauce, tomatoes, green beans and peas and stir.
9. Add stock to hide
10. Ingredients, cover and cook on High for 20 mins.
11. Release pressure to succeed, uncover, add parsley, more salt and pepper if required.

MOROCCAN LAMB
Nutrition: Cal 434 ;Fat 21 g; Carb 41 g;Protein 20 g
Serving 6 Cook time 35 min

Ingredients
- 2 ½ pounds lamb shoulder, chopped
- 3 tbsp honey
- 3 ounces almonds, peeled and chopped
- 9 ounces prunes, pitted
- 8 ounces vegetable stock
- 2 yellow onions, chopped
- 2 garlic cloves, minced
- 1 bay leaf
- Salt and black pepper to tastes
- 1 cinnamon stick
- 1 tsp cumin powder
- 1 tsp turmeric powder
- 1 tsp ginger powder
- 1 tsp cinnamon powder
- Sesame seeds for servings
- 3 tbsp extra virgin organic olive oil

Instructions
1. In a bowl, mix cinnamon powder with ginger, cumin, turmeric, garlic and 2 tbsp extra virgin olive oil and stir well.
2. Add meat and toss to coat.
3. Put prunes in the bowl, cover them hot water and leave aside.
4. Set your instant pot on Sauté mode, add the remainder of the oil as well as heat
5. Add onions, stir, cook for 3 minutes, transfer to your bowl and then leave aside.
6. Add meat to your pot and brown it for 10 minutes.
7. Add stock, cinnamon stick, bay leaf and return onions, stir, cover and cook on High for 25 minutes.
8. Release pressure to succeed naturally, uncover, add drained prunes, salt, pepper, honey and stir.
9. Set the pot on Simmer mode, cook mixture for 5 minutes and discard bay leaf and cinnamon stick.
10. Divide among plates and scatter almonds and sesame seeds ahead.

LAMB RAGOUT
Nutrition: Cal 360 ;Fat 14 g; Carb 15 g;Protein 30 g
Serving 8 Cook time 75 min

Ingredients
- 1 ½ pounds mutton, bone-in
- 2 carrots, sliced
- ½ pound mushrooms, sliced
- 4 tomatoes, chopped
- 1 small yellow onion, chopped
- 6 garlic cloves, minced
- 2 tbsp tomato paste
- 1 tsp vegetable oil
- Salt and black pepper to taste
- 1 tsp oregano, dried
- A handful parsley, finely chopped

Instructions
1. Set your instant pot on Sauté mode, add oil and warmth
2. Add meat and brown it on the sides.

3. Add tomato paste, tomatoes, onion, garlic, mushrooms, oregano, carrots and water to pay for.
4. Add salt, pepper, stir, cover and cook on High for one hour.
5. Release the pressure, take meat out from the pot and discard bones before shredding.
6. Return meat to pot, add parsley and stir.
7. Add more salt and pepper as needed and serve right away.

LAMB AND BARLEY BOWLS
Nutrition: Cal 484 ;Fat 19 g; Carb 21 g;Protein 44 g
Serving 4 Cook time 60 min

Ingredients
• 6 ounces barley
• 5 ounces peas
• 1 lamb leg, already cooked, boneless and chopped
• 3 yellow onions, chopped
• 5 carrots, chopped
• 6 ounces beef stock
• 12 ounces water
• Salt and black pepper to taste

Instructions
1. In your instant pot, mix stock with water and barley, cover and cook on High for 20 minutes.
2. Release pressure to succeed, uncover, add onions, peas and carrots, stir, cover again and cook on High for ten mins.
3. Release pressure again, add meat, salt and pepper to taste, stir, dish into bowls and serve.

MEXICAN STYLE LAMB
Nutrition: Cal 324 ;Fat 9 g; Carb 19 g;Protein 15 g
Serving 4 Cook time 60 min

Ingredients
• 3 pounds lamb shoulder, cubed
• 19 ounces enchilada sauce
• 3 garlic cloves, minced
• 1 yellow onion, chopped
• 2 tbsp extra virgin olive oil
• Salt to taste
• ½ bunch cilantro, finely chopped
• Corn tortillas, warm for serving
• Lime wedges for serving
• Refried beans for serving

Instructions
1. Put enchilada sauce inside a bowl, add lamb meat and marinade for 24 hours.
2. Set your instant pot on Sauté mode, add the oil as well as heat
3. Add onions and garlic and fry for 5 minutes.
4. Add lamb, salt and its particular marinade, stir, bring to a boil, cover and cook on High for 45 minutes.
5. Release the stress, take meat and set on a cutting board and then leave for cooling down for a couple of minutes.
6. Shred meat and set inside a bowl.
7. Pour cooking sauce over it and stir.
8. Portion out meat onto tortillas, sprinkle cilantro on each, add beans, squeeze lime juice over, roll and serve.

GOAT AND TOMATO POT
Nutrition: Cal 340 ;Fat 4 g; Carb 12 g;Protein 12 g
Serving 4 Cook time 70 min

Ingredients
• 17 ounces goat meat, cubed
• 1 carrot, chopped
• 1 celery rib, chopped
• 4 ounces tomato paste
• 1 yellow onion, chopped
• 3 garlic cloves, crushed
• A dash of sherry wine
• ½ cup water
• Salt and black pepper to taste
• 1 cup chicken stock
• 2 tbsp extra virgin olive oil
• 1 tbsp cumin seeds, ground
• A pinch of rosemary, dried
• 2 roasted tomatoes, chopped

Instructions
1. Set your instant pot on Sauté mode, add 1 tbsp oil and also heat
2. Add goat meat, salt and pepper and brown for a few minutes on either side.
3. Add cumin seeds, rosemary, stir, cook for just two minutes and transfer to your bowl.
4. Add the remainder in the oil on the pot and warmth
5. Add onion, garlic, salt and pepper, stir and cook for 1 minute.
6. Add carrot and celery, stir and cook 2 minutes.
7. Add sherry wine, stock, water, goat meat, tomato paste, more salt and pepper, stir, cover and cook on High for 40 minutes.
8. Release pressure naturally, uncover, add tomatoes, stir, divide among plates and serve.

CORNED BEEF WITH VEGETABLE
Nutrition: Cal 434 ;Fat 22 g; Carb 21 g;Protein 28 g
Serving 8 Cook time 90 min

Ingredients
• 3 lbs corned beef brisket
• 10 peppercorns
• 4 garlic cloves, peeled
• 1 cup onion, minced
• 3 cups water
• 3 cups chicken broth
• 1 cabbage head, cut into wedges
• 4 carrots, peeled and cut into pieces
• 5 potatoes, cut into pieces
• 1/2 Tsp salt

Instructions
1. Place beef to the instant pot atart exercising . 1/2 cup onions, peppercorns, 2 garlic cloves, chicken stock, and water.
2. Seal pot with lid and select MANUAL and hang up the timer for one hour.
3. Once all pressure release its very own then open lid and take away corned beef from instant pot make on a dish.
4. Cover beef with foil and hang up aside.
5. Now add potatoes, salt, garlic, onions, carrots, and cabbage within the pot.
6. Seal pot with lid and select MANUAL button as well as set the timer for ten minutes.
7. Allow to releasing steam its very own then open.
8. Sliced cooked beef and serve with vegetables.

SPICY TACO MEAT
Nutrition: Cal 414 ;Fat 21 g; Carb 7 g;Protein 47 g
Serving 6 Cook time 45 min

Ingredients
• 2 lbs ground beef
• 1/2 tbsp chili powder
• 1/4 Tsp chipotle powder
• 1 tsp cayenne
• 1/2 Tsp cumin
• 1/2 Tsp smoked paprika
• 1/2 Tsp turmeric
• 2 tsp oregano
• 2 large sweet peppers, diced
• 1 large onion, diced
• 4 tbsp olive oil

•3 garlic cloves, minced
•1/4 Tsp black pepper
•1 tsp salt

Instructions
1. Add all ingredients except meat in to the instant pot.
2. Select sauté and stir fry for 5 minutes.
3. Add ground beef and stir until lightly brown.
4. Seal pot with lid and cook on HIGH pressure for half an hour.
5. Allow to releasing steam its then open.
6. Select sauté function and stir for 10 mins.
7. Garnish with fresh chopped cilantro and serve.

BEEF BEAN RICE
Nutrition: Cal 506 ;Fat 17 g; Carb 28 g;Protein 38 g
Serving 6 Cook time 25 min

Ingredients
•1 lb ground beef
•1 1/2 cup cheese, shredded
•3 tbsp fresh cilantro, chopped
•1 cup fresh corn
•14 oz can black beans, rinsed and drained
•16 oz salsa
•2 cups beef stock
•1 cup rice, rinsed and drained
•1/2 Tsp cumin
•1 1/2 Tsp chili powder
•1 onion, diced
•1 tbsp extra virgin olive oil
•1/2 Tsp salt

Instructions
1. Select sauté function with the instant pot.
2. Once the pot is hot then adds organic olive oil, ground beef, cumin, chili powder, onion, and salt and sauté for 5 minutes or until browned.
3. Add rice, corn, black beans, salsa, and stock in a very pot and stir well.
4. Seal pot with lid and select MANUAL HIGH pressure for 8 minutes.
5. Quick release steam then opens the lid and stir well.
6. Top with cilantro and cheese.
7. Serve and revel in.

GARLIC & GINGER ASIAN RIBS
Nutrition: Cal 440 ;Fat 29 g; Carb 11 g;Protein 27 g
Serving 9 Cook time 9 hours

Ingredients
•3 pounds country-style pork ribs
•1/4 cup sesame oil
•2 tbsp organic olive oil
•2 tbsp rice vinegar
•2 tbsp lemon juice
•1/4 cup brown sugar
•1 cup soy sauce
•2 tbsp garlic, minced
•2 tbsp fresh ginger, minced
•1/2 tsp hot pepper sauce
•Pinch of salt

Instructions
1. Stir together the brown sugar, soy sauce, sesame oil, extra virgin olive oil, rice vinegar, fresh lemon juice, garlic, ginger, and hot pepper sauce in the large zip-lock bag.
2. Add ribs into the zip-lock bag.
3. Seal zip-lock bag and shake well. Place in refrigerator for 8 hours or overnight.
4. Before cooking, drain marinade and discard.
5. Add marinated ribs within the instant pot.
6. Cover and turn the steam release handle towards the venting position.
7. Select the slow cooker setting and set to medium.
8. Cook for 9 hours.

CREAMY HONEY & MUSTARD PORK RIBS
Nutrition: Cal 385 ;Fat 17 g; Carb 16 g;Protein 39 g
Serving 6 Cook time 4 hours

Ingredients
•3 1/2 pounds country style pork ribs
•1/2 cup honey mustard
•1 cup BBQ sauce
•2 tsp Salt-Free Seasoning Blend

Instructions
1. Place ribs in instant pot.
2. In a tiny bowl, stir together barbecue sauce, honey mustard, and seasoning blend.
3. Pour over ribs in instant pot, stir to coat.
4. Cover and turn the steam release handle on the venting position.
5. Select the slow cooker setting and set to high. Cook for 4 hours.
6. Transfer ribs to a serving platter.
7. Strain sauce into a bowl, skim fat from sauce.
8. Drizzle some in the sauce in the ribs and pass the rest of the sauce in the table.

TENDER AND JUICY SHREDDED PORK
Nutrition: Cal 550 ;Fat41 g; Carb 2 g;Protein 38 g
Serving 8 Cook time 8 hours

Ingredients
•4 pounds pork shoulder roast
•4 ounces green chilies, diced
•1 cup using apple cider vinegar
•1 1/2 tsp garlic, minced
•1 cup onion, finely chopped
•1 tsp ground black pepper
•1 tsp salt

Instructions
1. Place roast in instant pot.
2. Combine remaining ingredients and pour over roast.
3. Cover and turn the steam release handle towards the venting position.
4. Select the slow cooker setting and hang to medium.
5. Cook for 8 hours.
6. Remove to some chopping board and shred with two forks, discarding fat and bones.

KETO SHRIMP THAI SALAD
Nutrition: Cal 380 ;Fat 9 g; Carb 14 g;Protein 25 g
Serving 4 Cook time 15 min

Ingredients
•6 Tablespoon extra-virgin olive oil, divided
•2 Tablespoon. soy sauce
•1 teaspoon fish sauce
•1 teaspoon sambal oelek
•1 Tablespoon brown sugar
•3 Tablespoon lime juice
•1 Tablespoon minced red pepper
•1/2 pound shrimp, peeled and deveined
•1 cup sugar snap peas, blanched and cooled in an ice bath
•2 bundles vermicelli noodles, boiled and rinsed under cool water (you can use the same water you boiled the snap peas in)
•4 cups shredded romaine lettuce
•1/2 cup cherry tomatoes, halved
•1/2 cup thinly sliced sweet peppers
•cilantro, mint leaves and crushed peanuts for garnish
•coarse salt and freshly ground peanuts to taste

Instructions
1. In a medium bowl, beat together 4 tablespoons of oil, soy sauce, fish sauce, sambal oelek, sugar, lime juice and the minced red pepper.
2. Heat the remaining oil in a large skillet over medium-high.
3. Add the shrimp, season with salt and pepper and sear on one side for 2 minutes.

4. Flip and sear another minute.
5. Salad Assembly:
6. In 2 bowls add romaine lettuce
7. Add some vermicelli noodles, the snow peas, peppers, tomatoes, shrimp, cilantro, mint, and some good crushed peanuts.
8. Shake up (or whisk) your dressing and then drizzle it over the salads.

SHRIMP AND NORI ROLLS
Nutrition: Cal 340 ;Fat 12 g; Carb 8 g;Protein 25 g
Serving 1 Cook time 10 min

Ingredients
- 1 cup shrimp
- 1 tbsp. Mayonnaise
- 1 thinly sliced green onion
- 2 sheets Nori
- ¼ cucumber diced and seeded
- 1 tbsp. toasted Sesame seeds

Instructions
1. Wash and drain shrimp.
2. Add together shrimp with Mayonnaise and green onions.
3. Place Nori on flat surface and spoon on the shrimp and green onion mixture.
4. Dust with cucumber and sesame seeds.
5. Roll tightly and cut into bite size pieces.

KETO MASHED GARLIC TURNIPS
Nutrition: Cal 280 ;Fat 17 g; Carb 14 g;Protein 12 g
Serving 2 Cook time 20 min

Ingredients
- 3 cups diced turnip
- 2 cloves garlic, minced
- 1/4 cup heavy cream
- 3 Tablespoon melted butter
- salt, pepper to taste

Instructions
1. Boil turnips until tender.
2. Drain and mash turnips as you would for mashed potatoes.
3. Add in heavy cream, butter, salt, pepper and garlic and mix well.

KETO TANDOORI CHICKEN WINGS
Nutrition: Cal 420 ;Fat 16 g; Carb 8 g;Protein 25 g
Serving 2 Cook time 2 hours 10 min

Ingredients
- 2-1/2 lbs. chicken wings, trimmed and separated
- 1 cup Homemade Yogurt*
- 2 tbsp. ginger
- 6 cloves garlic, minced
- 1-1/2 tsp. curry powder
- ¼ tsp. turmeric
- ½ tsp. cumin
- ½ tsp. dry mustard
- 2 tsp. red pepper flakes
- 1 lemon, juiced
- 3 tbsp. vegetable oil
- Salt, pepper

Instructions
1. Add all ingredients in a a bowl and mix well
2. Marinade for at least two hours at room temperature. (saving marinade)
3. Place wings on broiling rack and broil until browned, about 20 minutes
4. Baste wings with marinade about every 10 minutes.
5. Transfer to platter and serve.

KETO RICED CAULIFLOWER & CURRY CHICKEN
Nutrition: Cal 420 ;Fat 16 g; Carb 8 g;Protein 25 g
Serving 4 Cook time 30 min

Ingredients
1. 2 Lbs. of Chicken (4 breasts)
2. 1 packet of Curry Paste
3. 1 Cup Water
4. 3 Tablespoons Ghee (can substitute butter)
5. ½ Cup Heavy Cream
6. 1 Head Cauliflower (around 1 kg)

Instructions
1. In a large pot, melt the Ghee
2. Add the curry paste and mix to combine
3. Once combined, add the water and simmer for an additional 5 minutes
4. Add the chicken, cover, and simmer for 20 minutes.
5. Meanwhile, chop up a head of cauliflower into florets and pulse in the food processor to make riced cauliflower, (cauliflower doesn't need to be cooked)
6. Once the chicken is cooked, uncover, add the cream, and cook for an additional 5 minutes.

KETO PROSCIUTTO SPINACH SALAD
Nutrition: Cal 420 ;Fat 16 g; Carb 8 g;Protein 25 g
Serving 2 Cook time 10 min

Ingredients
- 2 cups baby spinach
- 1/3 lb. prosciutto
- 1 cantaloupe
- 1 avocado
- 1/4 cup diced red onion
- handful of raw, unsalted walnuts

Instructions
1. lace a cup of spinach on each plate.
2. Top with diced prosciutto, cubes of balls of melon, slices of avocado, a sprinkling of red onion, and a few walnuts.
3. Add some freshly ground pepper, if you like.

SUN-DRIED TOMATO AND GOAT CHEESE CHICKEN
Nutrition: Cal 460 ;Fat 17 g; Carb 14 g;Protein 22 g
Serving 4 Cook time 20 min

Ingredients
- 1/3 cup sun-dried tomatoes, packed without oil, finely chopped
- 2 tsp. olive oil, divided
- 1/2 cup chopped shallots, divided
- 1 tsp. Splenda
- 3 garlic cloves, minced
- 2 1/2 Tablespoon balsamic vinegar, divided
- 1/2 cup (2 oz.) crumbled goat cheese - to cut down on the fat, find the lowest-fat variety
- 2 Tablespoon chopped fresh basil
- 3/4 tsp. salt, divided
- 4 (6-oz) skinless, boneless chicken breast halves
- 1/8 tsp. freshly ground black pepper
- 3/4 cup fat-free, less-sodium chicken broth
- 1/4 tsp. dried thyme

Instructions
1. Heat 1 tsp. oil in a large non-stick skillet over medium heat.
2. Add 1/3 cup shallots, Splenda, and garlic.
3. Cook 4 minutes or until golden brown, stirring often.
4. Spoon into a mixing bowl and stir in 1 1/2 tsp. vinegar.
5. Incorporate chopped tomatoes, shallot mixture, cheese, basil, and 1/4 tsp. salt together and mix well.
6. Cut a horizontal slit through each chicken breast half.
7. Stuff 2 Tbsps. cheese mixture into each newly formed pocket.

8. Season with 1/2 tsp. salt and black pepper.
9. Heat 1 tsp. oil in pan over medium-high heat and add stuffed chicken.
10. Cook approximately 6 minutes on each side or until juices run clear.
11. Remove chicken from pan and add broth, remaining shallots, 2 Tbsps. vinegar, and thyme.
12. Bring to a boil and stir until thickened.
13. Serve over chicken.

ZOODLES AND TURKEY BALLS
Nutrition: Cal 360 ;Fat 14 g; Carb 12 g;Protein 25 g
Serving 2 Cook time 30 min

Ingredients
1 zucchini cut into spirals
1 can vodka pasta sauce
1 package of frozen Armour Turkey meatballs
Instructions
1. Cook meatballs and sauce on medium heat for 22-25 minutes and stir occasionally.
2. Clean zucchini and put through a vegetable spiral maker.
3. Boil water and blanch raw zoodles 45 seconds.
4. Remove and drain.
5. Combine zoodles and prepared saucy meatballs.

GLUTEN FREE CHEVRE LASAGNE
Nutrition: Cal 280 ;Fat 10 g; Carb 18 g;Protein 12 g
Serving 2 Cook time 1 hours 30 min

Ingredients
•1 head garlic
•1 teaspoon extra-virgin olive oil
•½ cup raw cashews pieces (2.25 ounces)
•¾ cup filtered water
•1 egg
•4 ounces chevre or fresh goat cheese
•1 tablespoon chopped mixed fresh herbs such as thyme, rosemary and sage
•¾ teaspoon salt
•¼ teaspoon Freshly ground pepper
•2 medium zucchini, stem cut off (1.5 pounds)
•1 small eggplant, stem cut off (1.25 pounds)
•1 small sweet onion, peeled and cored
•1 medium tomato, cored and thinly sliced
•½ cup shredded Parmesan Reggiano or Hard Aged Goat Cheese
•Fresh basil for garnish
Instructions
1. Preheat oven to 350 degrees.
2. Cut ends of garlic head off and place root-side down on a double layer of baking foil.
3. Drizzle olive oil over the exposed garlic clove ends and wrap foil into a packet.
4. Roast garlic packet in oven 45 minutes to 1 hour, until soft.
5. Remove from oven and open packet to allow steam to escape and garlic to cool.
6. Puree cashew pieces with water until completely smooth.
7. Squeeze garlic out of skins into the cashew mixture and discard skins.
8. Add egg, chevre or fresh goat cheese, chopped mixed herbs, salt and pepper.
9. Puree mixture until creamy.
10. Cut zucchini, eggplant and onion lengthwise as thinly as possible to resemble lasagna sheets.
11. Spoon about ¼ cup chevre sauce onto bottom of a lined 9x9 baking dish.
12. Layer 1/3 of the zucchini, eggplant and onion into the bottom of the dish.
13. Add a layer of ½ cup chevre sauce.
14. Top with layer of vegetables and sauce.
15. Top with a final layer of vegetables, tomatoes, and any remaining chevre sauce until all ingredients are exhausted.
16. Cover with a layer of parchment paper and foil.
17. Bake until completely vegetables are tender, approximately 1 hr.

18. Remove foil and top with the Parmesan or aged goat cheese.
19. Broil until cheese is melted, 8 to 10 minutes.
20. Remove from oven, rest to cool 15 minutes, dress with basil.

PULLED ADOBO CHICKEN
Nutrition: Cal 360 ;Fat 14 g; Carb 12 g;Protein 25 g
Serving 2 Cook time 30 min

Ingredients
•2-3lb chicken tenderloins
•1/2 stick of organic butter
•1 tablespoon lemon pepper
•1 tbsp. minced garlic cloves
•2 tablespoons grape seed / olive oil
•1 tablespoon Paleo adobo seasoned salt
•1 teaspoon dried thyme
•cheddar cheese slices
•Dijon mustard
•wrap of your choice
Instructions
1. In a crockpot add the butter, lemon pepper, garlic cloves, oil, seasoned salt and thyme and melt on high.
2. Add chicken and cook on low 6 hours until chicken falls apart easily.
3. Shred inside the crockpot and mix with the juice in the pot.
4. Let rest on low.

BRIGHT SALSA PORK CHOPS
Nutrition: Cal 460 ;Fat 22 g; Carb 8 g;Protein 25 g
Serving 2 Cook time 8 hours 20 min

Ingredients
•2 x Pork Loins
•75g Salsa
•3 Tablespoon Lime Juice
•½ tsp. Ground Cumin
•½ tsp. Garlic Powder
•½ tsp. Salt
•½ tsp. Ground Black Pepper
•Calorie Free Cooking Spray
Instructions
1. In a small bowl combine cumin, garlic powder, salt and pepper and rub the spice mixture into pork chops.
2. Brown chops 5 minutes each side on a medium heat.
3. Spray the insides of your slow cooker cooking spray and add the pork chops.
4. Add the salsa and lime mixture.
5. Slow cook on low for 8 hours.

CRISPY FISH STICKS WITH CAPER DILL SAUCE
Nutrition: Cal 360 ;Fat 14 g; Carb 12 g;Protein 25 g
Serving 1 Cook time 30 min

Ingredients
•1 lb. white fish fillets
•1 cup grated parmesan
•1 cup almond meal/flour
•1/4 tsp. chili powder
•1/2 tsp. dried parsley
•1/4 tsp. salt
•pinch of pepper
•2 tbsp. mayo
•1 egg
•coconut oil for frying
Caper Dill Tartar Sauce
•1/2 cup mayo
•1/2 cup sour cream
•1 1/2 tbsp. capers (including the caper juice)
•2 medium dill/garlic pickles, diced

- 2 tbsp. chopped fresh dill
- 2 tsp. lemon juice

Instructions
1. Combine the dry ingredients, put in shallow dish and set aside.
2. Whisk together the egg and mayo.
3. Prepare tartar sauce by combining all ingredients cover and refrigerate until the fish is ready.
4. Cut the fillets to desired size. Dip the fish into the egg mixture and dredge in the breading mixture.
5. Heat 1/2-inch oil in a medium skillet and drop 2 fish sticks at a time for consistent cooking.
6. Cook for 1-2 minutes on each side, until golden.
7. Remove and drain on paper-towel.
8. Serve with tartar sauce.

CREAMY ITALIAN CHICKEN SCAMPI
Nutrition: Cal 360 ;Fat 14 g; Carb 12 g;Protein 25 g
Serving 2 Cook time 30 min

Ingredients
- 1 1/2 lbs. Chicken Breast – Cut into tenders sized pieces
- 6 Large Cloves garlic – Minced
- 6 Tbsp. Butter – Divided
- 1 Cup Chicken Stock
- 1 Cup Heavy Cream
- 1/4 Cup Parmesan Cheese – Grated
- 6 oz. Mixed Bell Peppers – Sliced
- A Few Slices Red Onion
- 1 tsp. Italian Seasoning
- 1/2 tsp. Red Pepper Flakes
- Salt and Pepper – To Taste

Instructions
1. In a large sauté pan, over medium-high heat, pan-sear seasoned chicken in 4 Tbsp. butter.
2. Sear on both sides until golden brown approximately 3-4 minutes each side.
3. Remove chicken from pan and set aside.
4. Using the same pan, reduce heat to medium and brown remaining 2 Tbs. butter, and minced garlic about 1-2 minutes.
5. Add sliced red onion and sauté until transparent.
6. De-glaze the pan with chicken stock. And add Italian seasoning and red pepper flakes.
7. Bring to a boil over medium heat and reduce to low.
8. Let simmer 2-3 minutes.
9. Add heavy cream and continue to simmer and thicken 5-10 minutes.
10. Mix in Parmesan cheese and salt and pepper to taste.
11. Stir in peppers and add chicken.
12. Simmer on low until chicken is fully cooked.

CREAMY SHRIMP AND MUSHROOM SKILLET
Nutrition: Cal 400 ;Fat 12 g; Carb 6 g;Protein 20 g
Serving 2 Cook time 15 min

Ingredients
- 4 slices organic uncured bacon
- 1 cup sliced mushrooms
- 4 oz. smoked salmon
- 4 oz. raw shelled shrimp (I used TJ's Argentinian wild)
- 1/2 cup heavy whipping cream OR coconut cream for a dairy free option
- 1 pinch Celtic Sea Salt
- freshly ground black pepper

Instructions
1. Cut the bacon in 1 inch pieces and cook over medium heat.
2. Add sliced mushrooms and cook for 5 minutes.
3. Add strips of smoked salmon and cook for 2 to 3 minutes.
4. Add the shrimp and sauté on a high for 2 minutes.
5. Stir in cream and salt.
6. Lower heat and let cook for 1 minute until thick and creamy.

ROASTED TURKEY BREAST TENDERLOINS
Nutrition: Cal 255 ;Fat 7 g; Carb 1 g;Protein 45g
Serving 6 Cook time 40 min

Ingredients
- 6 turkey breast tenderloins
- 4 cloves garlic, halved
- 2 tablespoons grapeseed oil
- ½ teaspoon paprika
- ½ teaspoon dried basil
- ½ teaspoon dried oregano
- ½ teaspoon dried marjoram
- 1 cup water
- sea salt, to taste
- ¼ teaspoon ground black pepper

Instructions
1. Rub turkey fillets with garlic halves. Now, massage 1 tablespoon of oil to your turkey and season it with paprika, basil, oregano, marjoram, water, salt, and black pepper. Press the "Sauté" button and add another tablespoon of oil. Brown the turkey fillets for three or four minutes per side.
2. Add the rack on the Instant Pot; lower the turkey on the rack.
3. Secure the lid. Choose the "Manual" setting and cook for thirty minutes. Once cooking is complete, make use of a natural pressure release; carefully eliminate the lid.

BEEF STROGANOFF
Nutrition: Cal 317 ;Fat 19 g; Carb 8 g;Protein 29 g
Serving 4 Cook time 40 min

Ingredients
- Beef (1 pound, chopped in cubes)
- Bacon (2 slices, cut in cubes)
- Beef stock (250 ml)
- Mushrooms (9 oz.)
- Onion (1, chopped)
- Garlic (2 cloves, chopped)
- Tomato paste (3 tbsp)
- Smoked paprika (1 tbsp)
- Sour cream

Instructions
1. Add oil inside Pressure cooker dish, and hang up it to "Sauté"; add the onion, bacon, and garlic and cook shortly or before the onion is tender.
2. Put the beef and continue to cook prior to the meat is cooked on every side (it will get brown color).
3. Add the mushrooms, beef broth, tomato paste, and paprika and stir well; close the lid and set it to high-pressure cooking for 30 minutes.
4. Use the quick-release approach to release the stress.
5. Serve while hot and top it with sour cream.

CHICKEN MEATBALLS
Nutrition: Cal 357 ;Fat 28 g; Carb 3 g;Protein 23 g
Serving 6 Cook time 30 min

Ingredients
- Chicken (1.5 lb., grounded)
- Ghee (2 tbsp)
- Garlic (2 cloves, minced)
- Onion (2, thin sliced)
- Almond meal (¾ cup)
- Hot sauce (6 tbsp)
- Butter (4 tbsp)

Instructions
1. Mix the almond meal, chicken, salt, garlic, and onions in the bowl; put ghee on the hands and form the meatballs.

2. Set the stress cooker to "Sauté" and place two tablespoons of ghee inside; squeeze meatballs inside and fry until they turn brown (roll them every minute, so either side is well fried).
3. Mix 4 tablespoons of butter and hot sauce and heat this mixture within the microwave (this will likely serve like a buffalo sauce for the meatballs). Pour this sauce within the meatballs; secure the lid over pressure cooker and hang up it to "Poultry."
4. Once the cooking is conducted (within 20 minutes), the sound will inform you, and it is possible to press "Cancel." Release the stress valve (protect your hand having a towel or possibly a kitchen glove).
5. Serve with any food you want or take in the meatballs on their own.

COCONUT MILK CHICKEN CURRY
Nutrition: Cal 357 ;Fat 28 g; Carb 3 g;Protein 23 g
Serving 6 Cook time 4 hours 20 min

Ingredients
- Chicken breasts (1 lb.)
- Curry powder (3 tbsp)
- Ground coriander (half teaspoon)
- Turmeric powder (1 teaspoon)
- Butter (2 tbsp)
- Garlic (2 cloves)
- Sweet potatoes (4 pieces, chopped in cubes)
- Rice
- Onion (1, chopped)
- Sugar (1 teaspoon)
- Salt (1 teaspoon)
- Coconut milk (2 cans of 15 oz.)
- Water (1 cup)

Instructions

1. Put the spices (turmeric, coriander, sugar, salt and curry powder) in a bowl and mix them well.
2. Put the chicken breasts inside the pressure cooker and fry them, but ensure they don't burn. Add coconut milk (and a few water when the coconut milk is thick).
3. Add the butter and garlic and also the seasoning mix and stir well, and so the chicken breasts soak in everything.
4. Add the onion and sweet potatoes and stir.
5. Close the lid and set it to high pressure for 4-6 hours.
6. In the final half hour of cooking, receive the chicken out with the pressure cooker, cut it which has a fork and send it back prior to the cooking is complete.
7. Turn pressure cooker off and allow the meal to put for 25 minutes before eating. Serve it with rice.

CHICKEN WINGETTES WITH CILANTRO DIP
Nutrition: Cal 300 ;Fat 22 g; Carb 11 g;Protein 10 g
Serving 4 Cook time 65 min

Ingredients
- 10 fresh cayenne peppers, trimmed and chopped
- 3 garlic cloves, minced
- 1 ½ cups white wine vinegar
- ½ teaspoon black pepper
- 1 teaspoon sea salt
- 1 teaspoon onion powder
- 12 chicken wingettes
- 2 tablespoons olive oil

DIPPING SAUCE:
- ½ cup mayonnaise
- ½ cup sour cream
- ½ cup cilantro, chopped
- 2 cloves garlic, minced
- 1 teaspoon smoked paprika

Instructions

1. Place cayenne peppers, 3 garlic cloves, white vinegar, black pepper, salt, and onion powder in the container. Add chicken wingettes, and allow them marinate, covered, for one hour inside the refrigerator.
2. Add the chicken wingettes, along while using marinade and extra virgin olive oil on the Instant Pot.
3. Secure the lid. Choose the "Manual" setting and cook for 6 minutes. Once cooking is complete, use a quick pressure release; carefully take away the lid.
4. In a mixing bowl, thoroughly combine mayonnaise, sour cream, cilantro, garlic, and smoked paprika.
5. Serve warm chicken with all the dipping sauce privately.

CHICKEN LEGS WITH PIQUANT MAYO SAUCE
Nutrition: Cal 485 ;Fat 42 g; Carb 2.5 g;Protein 22 g
Serving 4 Cook time 25 min

Ingredients
- 4 chicken legs, bone-in, skinless
- 2 garlic cloves, peeled and halved
- ½ teaspoon coarse sea salt
- ¼ teaspoon ground black pepper, or maybe more to taste
- ½ teaspoon red pepper flakes, crushed
- 1 tablespoon essential olive oil
- ¼ cup chicken broth

DIPPING SAUCE:
- ¾ cup mayonnaise
- 2 tablespoons stone ground mustard
- 1 teaspoon fresh freshly squeezed lemon juice
- ½ teaspoon Sriracha

TOPPING:
- ¼ cup fresh cilantro, roughly chopped

Instructions

1. Rub the chicken legs with garlic halves; then, season with salt, black pepper, and red pepper flakes. Press the "Sauté" button.
2. Once hot, heat the oil and sauté chicken legs for four or five minutes, turning once during cooking time. Add a a little chicken broth to deglaze the bottom of the pan.
3. Secure the lid. Choose "Manual" mode and questionable; cook for 14 minutes. Once cooking is complete, work with a natural pressure release; carefully eliminate the lid.
4. Meanwhile, mix all
5. Ingredients for that dipping sauce; place inside the refrigerator until ready to offer.
6. Garnish chicken legs with cilantro. Serve with the piquant mayo sauce quietly.

CHICKEN SHAWARMA
Nutrition: Cal 267 ;Fat 15 g; Carb 5 g;Protein 28 g
Serving 4 Cook time 25 min

Ingredients
- 1-pound boneless, skinless chicken thighs or breasts, cut into large bite-size chunks
- 3 teaspoons extra-virgin essential olive oil, divided
- 3 tablespoons Shawarma Spice Mix
- 1 cup thinly sliced onions
- ¼ cup water
- 4 large lettuce leaves
- 1 cup Tzatziki Sauce

Instructions

1. Place the chicken inside a zip-top bag and add 1 teaspoon of extra virgin olive oil and the shawarma spice mix. Mash it all together, so the chicken is evenly coated within the oil and spices.
2. At this aspect, it is possible to freeze the chicken to get a meal later inside week, or you'll get forced out inside the refrigerator to marinate for about twenty four hours. (I like to create half the chicken now and freeze one other half for an additional meal. Clearly this "now and later" is one area beside me.)

3. Select "Sauté" to preheat the Instant Pot and conform to high heat. When the hot, add the remainder 2 teaspoons of oil and let it shimmer. Add the chicken in a very single layer. Let it sear, then flip the pieces to the other side, about 4 minutes in whole.
4. Add the onion.
5. Pour inside water and scrape up any browned bits from your bottom in the pot.
6. Latch the lid. Select "Pressure Cook" or "Manual" as well as set pressure to high and cook for ten minutes. After some time finishes, allow ten minutes to naturally release the pressure. For any remaining pressure, just quick-release it. Open the lid. To serve, wrap the chicken inside lettuce leaves and serve with all the tzatziki sauce.

THAI GREEN CURRY

Nutrition: Cal 290 ;Fat 20 g; Carb 12 g;Protein 17 g
Serving 6 Cook time 10 min

Ingredients
- 1 tablespoon coconut oil
- 2 tablespoons Thai green curry paste (adjust in your preferred spice level)
- 1 tablespoon minced fresh ginger
- 1 tablespoon minced garlic
- ½ cup sliced onion
- 1-pound boneless, skinless chicken thighs
- 2 cups peeled, chopped eggplant
- 1 cup chopped green, yellow, or orange bell pepper
- ½ cup fresh basil leaves, preferably Thai basil
- 1½ cups unsweetened coconut milk
- 1 tablespoon fish sauce
- 2 tablespoons soy sauce
- 2 teaspoons Truvia or Swerve
- salt, to taste

Instructions
1. Select "Sauté" to preheat the Instant Pot and adapt to high heat. When the hot, add coconut oil and let it shimmer. Add the curry paste and cook for one to two minutes, stirring occasionally.
2. Add the ginger and garlic and stir-fry for a few seconds. Add the onion and stir all of it together.
3. Add the chicken, eggplant, bell pepper, basil, coconut milk, fish sauce, soy sauce, and Truvia or Swerve. Stir to blend.
4. Press "Cancel" to make off "Sauté" mode, and switch to "Slow Cook" mode. Adjust to cook for 8 hours on medium (not low).
5. When the curry has finished cooking, add salt to taste.

SWEET AND SPICY CHICKEN TINGA

Nutrition: Cal 260 ;Fat 16 g; Carb 9 g;Protein 24 g
Serving 6 Cook time 40 min

Ingredients
- 4 teaspoons vegetable oil
- 2 tomatillos, cut into thin slices
- ½ onion, cut into thin slices
- 3 garlic cloves
- 1 (0.9 lb.) can fire-roasted tomatoes
- ⅓ cup chicken broth
- 1 chipotle chile with adobo sauce coming from a can, chopped
- ½ teaspoon ground cumin
- ¼ teaspoon ground cinnamon
- ½ teaspoon dried oregano
- 1 teaspoon Truvia or Swerve
- 1 tablespoon fish sauce or soy sauce
- 1 tablespoon cider vinegar
- 1½ pounds boneless, skinless chicken thighs
- ½ cup sour cream
- 2 teaspoons fresh lemon juice
- 1 avocado, sliced

Instructions
1. Select "Sauté" to preheat the Instant Pot and accommodate high heat. When the hot, add oil and allow it shimmer.
2. Add the tomatillo slices inside a single layer and atart exercising . the onions as being a flat layer between your tomatillo slices. Nestle inside garlic cloves. You're gonna let them char, so not stir them.
3. Once the thinner slices start to look somewhat burned, flip the vegetables. The bottom of the pot may have large black spots where the vegetables have charred, but this is a great sign.
4. Once the vegetables are very well charred, add the tomatoes and broth and deglaze the pan, scraping up all of the lovely brown bits from the bottom. Do this very well and make certain there isn't any burned bits remaining around the bottom. Otherwise, your Instant Pot will not arrive at pressure.
5. Add the chipotle, cumin, cinnamon, oregano, sweetener, fish sauce, and vinegar. Cook for one to two minutes allowing the spices to bloom. Add the chicken.
6. Latch the lid. Select "Pressure Cook" or "Manual" as well as set pressure to high and cook for fifteen minutes. After the time finishes, allow 10 mins to naturally release pressure to succeed. For any remaining pressure, just quick-release it. Open the lid.
7. Remove the chicken and shred it.
8. Tilting the pot, readily immersion blender to purée the sauce until the mixture is smooth.
9. Turn the pot to "Sauté" and adapt to high heat; then cook to thicken the sauce for approximately ten minutes. Once it's thickened a little, add inside chicken and also heat.
10. While the chicken heats, make a crema inside a small bowl by mixing together the sour cream and lemon juice.
11. Top the chicken while using crema and avocado slices. Serve over cauliflower rice or wrapped in lettuce leaves to get a low-carb option. You can also use low-carb corn tortillas.

CHICKEN FAJITAS

Nutrition: Cal 322 ;Fat 6 g; Carb 12 g;Protein 4 5g
Serving 4 Cook time 30 min

Ingredients
- 1 lb. chicken white meat, chopped into bite-sized pieces
- 1 onion, finely chopped
- 1 tbsp lime juice
- 6 large leaves Iceberg lettuce
- 2 tbsps. homemade taco seasoning
- 1 cup cherry tomatoes, chopped
- 3 garlic cloves, minced
- 1 bell pepper, cut into strips

TACO SEASONING:
- 1 tbsp. smoked paprika
- ½ tsp. coriander powder
- ½ tsp. black pepper, freshly ground
- 3 tbsps. chili powder
- 1 tsp onion powder
- 2 tbsps. pink Himalayan salt
- 2 tsps. garlic powder
- 2 tsps. Oregano

Instructions
1. Ingredients for taco seasoning in a jar and shake well. Set aside.
2. Rinse the meat well and place in a deep bowl. Generously sprinkle with taco seasoning. Place in the pot and add tomatoes, garlic, sliced peppers, onions, and lime juice
3. Seal the lid and press the "Poultry" button. Set the timer for 8 minutes on underhand.
4. When done, perform a quick release and open the lid. Remove a combination in the pot and set in a bowl. Cool completely.
5. Spread about 2 - 3 tablespoons with the mixture at the center of every lettuce leaf and wrap tightly. Secure each wrap with a toothpick and serve immediately.
6. Cut the chicken into bite-size pieces. Add it back to the sauce.
7. Preheat the Instant Pot by selecting "Sauté" and adjust to less for low heat. Let the chicken heat through. Break it up into smaller pieces if you like, but don't shred it.
8. Serve over cauliflower rice or raw cucumber noodles.

SHORTCUT DAN DAN–STYLE CHICKEN

Nutrition: Cal 300 ;Fat 17 g; Carb 10 g;Protein 26 g
Serving 4 Cook time 15 min

Ingredients
- 2 tablespoons extra virgin olive oil
- 1 tablespoon doubanjiang
- 2 teaspoons soy sauce
- 2 teaspoons rice wine vinegar
- ½ to 2 teaspoons red pepper flakes
- 1 teaspoon ground Sichuan peppercorns
- ¼ cup warm water
- 1-pound boneless, skinless chicken, cut into bite-size pieces
- ¼ cup room-temperature water
- 1 (½ pound) package shirataki noodles, rinsed
- 1 tablespoon sesame oil
- ¼ cup chopped fresh cilantro (optional) 2 tablespoons extra virgin olive oil
- 1 tablespoon doubanjiang
- 2 teaspoons soy sauce
- 2 teaspoons rice wine vinegar
- ½ to 2 teaspoons red pepper flakes
- 1 teaspoon ground Sichuan peppercorns
- ¼ cup warm water
- 1-pound boneless, skinless chicken, cut into bite-size pieces
- ¼ cup room-temperature water
- 1 (½ pound) package shirataki noodles, rinsed
- 1 tablespoon sesame oil
- ¼ cup chopped fresh cilantro (optional)

Instructions
1. In a medium bowl, mix together the olive oil, doubanjiang, soy sauce, vinegar, red pepper flakes, peppercorns, and hot water.
2. Put the chicken in the bowl and mix, so the chicken is well coated. For the best results, permit the chicken marinate for 30 minutes.
3. Put the chicken and marinade inside the inner cooking pot. Pour inside room-temperature water.
4. Latch the lid. Select "Pressure Cook" or "Manual" and set pressure to high and cook for 7 minutes. After the time finishes, allow 10 minutes to naturally release pressure. For any remaining pressure, just quick-release it. Open the lid. While the chicken is cooking, prepare the shirataki noodles as outlined by the package instructions.
5. Mix the chicken while using noodles. Just before serving, stir within the sesame oil. Serve garnished using the peanuts and cilantro (if using).

CHICKEN BRATWURST MEATBALLS WITH CABBAGE

Nutrition: Cal 338 ;Fat 23 g; Carb 10 g;Protein 23 g
Serving 4 Cook time 20 min

Ingredients
- 1-pound ground chicken
- ¼ cup heavy (whipping) cream
- 2 teaspoons salt, divided
- ½ teaspoon ground caraway seeds
- 1½ teaspoons freshly ground black pepper, divided
- ¼ teaspoon ground allspice
- 4 to 6 cups thickly chopped green cabbage
- 2 tablespoons unsalted butter

Instructions
1. To make meatballs, place the chicken in the bowl. Add the cream, 1 teaspoon of salt, the caraway, ½ teaspoon of pepper, as well as the allspice. Mix thoroughly. Refrigerate a combination for a half-hour. Once the amalgamation has cooled, it is simpler to make up the meatballs.

2. Using a tiny scoop, make up the chicken mixture into small-to medium-size meatballs. Place half the meatballs inside inner cooking pot of the Instant Pot and cover them half the cabbage. Place the remaining meatballs at the top from the cabbage, then cover them while using rest of the cabbage.
3. Place pats from the butter randomly and sprinkle with all the remaining 1 teaspoon of salt and 1 teaspoon of pepper.
4. Latch the lid. Select "Pressure Cook" or "Manual" as well as set pressure to high and cook for 4 minutes. After time finishes, allow 10 mins to naturally release the stress. For any remaining pressure, just quick-release it. Open the lid. Serve the meatballs ahead in the cabbage.

CHICKEN LIVER PTÉ

Nutrition: Cal 109 ;Fat 7 g; Carb 5 g;Protein 10 g
Serving 8 Cook time 15 min

Ingredients
- 1 lb. chicken liver
- ½ cup leeks, chopped
- 2 garlic cloves, crushed
- 2 tablespoons essential olive oil
- 1 tablespoon poultry seasonings
- 1 teaspoon dried rosemary
- ½ teaspoon dried marjoram
- ¼ teaspoon dried dill weed
- ½ teaspoon paprika
- ½ teaspoon red pepper flakes
- salt, to taste
- ½ teaspoon ground black pepper
- 1 cup water
- 1 tablespoon stone ground mustard

Instructions
1. Press the "Sauté" button to warm up the Instant Pot. Now, heat the oil. Once hot, sauté the chicken livers until no longer pink.
2. Add the rest of the
3. Ingredients, apart from the mustard, for a Instant Pot.
4. Secure the lid. Choose the "Manual" setting and cook for 10 minutes at High pressure. Once cooking is complete, work with a quick pressure ease; carefully remove the lid.
5. Transfer the cooked mixture to some blender; add stone ground mustard. Process until smooth and uniform.

DINNER

EASY CASHEW CHICKEN

Nutrition: Cal 330;Fat 24 g; Carb 8 g;Protein 22 g
Serving 3; Cook time 15 min

Ingredients
- 3 raw chicken thighs, boneless and skinless
- 2 tablespoons coconut oil (for cooking)
- 1/4 cup raw cashews
- 1/2 medium green bell pepper
- 1/2 teaspoon ground ginger
- 1 tablespoon rice wine vinegar
- 1 1/2 tablespoons liquid aminos
- 1/2 tablespoon chili garlic sauce
- 1 tablespoon minced garlic
- 1 tablespoon sesame oil
- 1 tablespoon sesame seeds
- 1 tablespoon green onions
- 1/4 medium white onion
- Salt and pepper, to taste

Instructions
1. Heat a pan over low heat and toast the cashews for 8 minutes, or until they start to lightly brown and become fragrant. Remove and set aside.
2. Dice chicken thighs into 1 inch chunks. Cut onion and pepper into equally large chunks.
3. Increase heat to high and add coconut oil to pan.
4. Once oil is up to temperature, add in the chicken thighs and allow them to cook through (about 5 minutes).
5. Once the chicken is fully cooked add in the pepper, onions, garlic, chili garlic sauce, and seasonings (ginger, salt, pepper). Allow to cook on high for 2-3 minutes.
6. Add liquid aminos, rice wine vinegar, and cashews. Cook on high and allow the liquid to reduce down until it is a sticky consistency. There should not be excess liquid in the pan upon completing cooking.

BUTTERED COD IN SKILLET

Nutrition: Cal 294;Fat 18 g; Carb 2 g;Protein 30 g
Serving 4; Cook time 15 min

Ingredients
Cod
- 1 1/2 lbs cod fillets
- 6 tablespoons unsalted butter, sliced
Seasoning
- ¼ teaspoon garlic powder
- ½ teaspoon table salt
- ¼ teaspoon ground pepper
- ¾ teaspoon ground paprika
- Few lemon slices
- Herbs, parsley, or cilantro

Instructions
1. Stir together ingredients for seasoning in a small bowl.
2. Cut cod into smaller pieces, if desired. Season all sides of the cod with the seasoning.
3. Heat 2 tablespoons butter in a large skillet over medium-high heat. Once butter melts, add cod to skillet. Cook 2 minutes.
4. Turn heat down to medium. Turn cod over, top with remaining butter and cook another 3-4 minutes.
5. Butter will completely melt and the fish will cook. (Don't overcook the cod, it will become mushy and completely fall apart.)
6. Drizzle cod with fresh lemon juice. Top with fresh herbs, if desired. Serve immediately.

ZUCCHINI PIZZA BOATS

Nutrition: Cal 390;Fat 26 g; Carb 12 g;Protein 32 g
Serving 4; Cook time 15 min

Ingredients
- 4 zucchini, sliced in half lengthwise
- 1 small can pizza sauce
- 1/2 8 ounce package button mushrooms, sliced
- 1 small red onion, diced
- 1/2 green pepper, diced
- 2 cups shredded mozzarella cheese
- 1 tablespoon fresh chopped basil (optional topping)
- 1 teaspoon red chili flakes (optional topping)
- Homemade quick turkey sausage (alternative option: use store-bought turkey/pork sausage, remove casings, and break up with spoon)
- 2 teaspoons olive oil
- 1/2 lb ground turkey
- 2 teaspoons fennel seeds
- 1 teaspoon garlic powder
- 1/2 teaspoon salt
- 1 teaspoon Italian seasoning (or 1/2 teaspoon oregano & 1/2 teaspoon basil)

Instructions
1. Preheat olive oil in a large skillet over med-high heat. Add turkey and seasonings, crushing up with a crushing spoon and mixing well. Cook for 5-6 minutes until turkey is browned and fully cooked. Remove from heat and set aside.
2. Preheat oven to 400°F. Cut zucchini in half lengthwise and scoop out flesh. On a baking sheet or in a 9 x 13 casserole dish, spread each zucchini boat with pizza sauce, then top with sausage, mushrooms, red onion, green pepper, and cheese.
3. Bake in the oven for 15 minutes or until cheese is melted. Remove from oven and sprinkle with fresh basil and chili flakes. Serve and enjoy!

CHILE LIME STEAK FAJITAS

Nutrition: Cal 230;Fat 30 g; Carb 13 g;Protein 25 g
Serving 4; Cook time 15 min

Ingredients
Marinade
- 2 tablespoons olive oil
- 1/3 cup freshly squeezed lime juice
- 2 tablespoons fresh chopped cilantro
- 2 cloves garlic , crushed
- 1 teaspoon brown sugar
- ¾ teaspoon red chilli flakes (adjust to your preference of spice)
- ½ teaspoon ground cumin
- 1 teaspoon salt
- 1 pound (500 g) steak (rump, skirt, or flank steak)
Fajitas
- 3 bell peppers (capsicums) of different colors: red, yellow, and green, deseeded and sliced
- 1 onion, sliced
- 1 avocado sliced

Optional Serving Suggestion:
- Flour tortillas
- Lettuce leaves for low-carb option
- Extra cilantro leaves to garnish
- Sour cream to serve

Instructions
1. Whisk marinade ingredients together to combine. Pour out half of the marinade into a shallow dish to marinade the steak for 30 minutes, if time allows. Alternatively, refrigerate for 2 hours or overnight. Remove from the refrigerator 30 minute prior to cooking.
Refrigerate the reserved untouched marinade to use later
For Skillet
2. Heat about one teaspoon of oil in a grill pan or cast iron skillet over medium-high heat and grill steak on each side until desired doneness (about 4 minutes each side for medium-rare, depending on thickness). Set aside and allow to rest for 5 minutes.
For Grilling
3. Heat barbecue (or grill) on high heat. Remove steak from the marinade. Grill for 5-7 minutes per side, or until desired doneness is reached. Transfer to a plate and allow to rest for 5-10 minutes.
For Vegetables
4. Wipe pan or grill plates over with paper towel; drizzle (or brush) with another teaspoon of oil and fry peppers (capsicums) and onion strips. Add half of the reserved marinade, salt and pepper; continue cooking until done.

Assemble

5.To serve steak, slice against the grain into thin strips. Pack into warmed tortillas, extra cilantro leaves, sour cream, sliced avocado (or your desired fillings), and drizzle over the remaining reserved untouched marinade.

THAI CHICKEN LETTUCE WRAPS

Nutrition: Cal 270;Fat 14 g; Carb 12 g;Protein 21 g
Serving 4; Cook time 10 min

Ingredients
•1 lb ground chicken
•1 tablespoon olive oil
•2 tablespoons red curry paste
•1 tablespoon ginger, minced
•4 cloves garlic, minced
•1 red bell pepper, sliced thinly
•4 green onions, chopped
•1 cup cabbage, shredded or coleslaw mix
•1/4 cup hoisin sauce
•1/4 teaspoon salt, or to taste
•1/4 teaspoon pepper, or to taste
•5 leaves basil, chopped
•1/2 head iceberg lettuce, cut into half

Instructions
1.Add olive oil to a large skillet and heat until oil is very hot. Add ground chicken and cook until no longer pink and starts to brown, break it up with a wooden spoon as necessary. Should take about 3 minutes.
2.Add red curry paste, ginger, garlic, peppers, coleslaw mix, and stir-fry for another 3 minutes. Add hoisin sauce and green onions, and toss. Remove from heat then add basil and toss. Transfer cooked chicken to a bowl.
3.Serve by placing spoonfuls of chicken into pieces of lettuce, fold lettuce over like small tacos, and eat.

SESAME TOFU WITH EGGPLANT

Nutrition: Cal 325;Fat 24 g; Carb 6 g;Protein 11 g
Serving 4; Cook time 20 min

Ingredients
•1 pound block firm tofu
•1 cup (31 g) chopped cilantro
•3 tablespoons rice vinegar
•4 tablespoons toasted sesame oil
•2 cloves garlic, finely minced
•1 teaspoon crushed red pepper flakes
•2 teaspoons Swerve confectioners
•1 whole (458 g) eggplant
•1 tablespoon olive oil
•Salt and pepper, to taste
•¼ cup sesame seeds
•¼ cup soy sauce

Instructions
1.Preheat oven to 200°F. Remove the block of tofu from it's packaging and wrap with some paper towels. Place a plate on top of it and weigh it down. I used a really large tin of vegetables in this picture, but you can use anything handy. Let the tofu sit for a while to press some of the water out.
2.Place about ¼ cup of cilantro, 3 tablespoons rice vinegar, 2 tablespoons toasted sesame oil, minced garlic, crushed red pepper flakes, and Swerve into a large mixing bowl. Whisk together.
3.Peel and julienne the eggplant. You can julienne roughly by hand like I did, or use a mandolin with a julienne attachment for more precise "noodles." Mix the eggplant with the marinade.
4.Add the tablespoon of olive oil to a skillet over medium-low heat. Cook the eggplant until it softens. The eggplant will soak up all of the liquids, so if you have issues with it sticking to the pan, feel free to add a little bit more sesame or olive oil. Just be sure to adjust your nutrition tracking.
5.Turn the oven off. Stir the remaining cilantro into the eggplant then transfer the noodles to an oven safe dish. Cover with a lid, or foil, and place into the oven to keep warm. Wipe out the skillet and return to the stovetop to heat up again.

6.Unwrap the tofu then cut into 8 slices. Spread the sesame seeds on a plate. Press both sides of each piece of tofu into the seeds.
7.Add 2 tablespoons of sesame oil to the skillet. Fry both sides of the tofu for 5 minutes each, or until they start to crisp up. Pour the ¼ cup of soy sauce into the pan and coat the pieces of tofu. Cook until the tofu slices look browned and caramelized with the soy sauce.
8.Remove the noodles from the oven and plate the tofu on top.

THAI BEEF SALAD

Nutrition: Cal 350;Fat 18 g; Carb 8 g;Protein 27 g
Serving 2; Cook time 15 min

Ingredients
Dressing
•1 clove garlic
•1 jalapeno, halved
•1 lime, juiced
•1 1/2 tablespoons fish sauce
•2 tablespoons minced lemongrass (remove the tough outer leaves and slice the tender white core)
•1 1/4 teaspoons brown sugar
•1/4 teaspoon red chile flakes
Steak
•1/2 tablespoon vegetable oil
•1 1-inch thick New York strip steak, 9 to 10 ounces
•2 medium shallots, thinly sliced
•1/4 cup fresh mint leaves loosely packed, roughly chopped
•3 tablespoons roughly chopped cilantro leaves and stems
Rice Powder
•2 tablespoons uncooked rice
For Serving
•Lettuce of your choosing
Cherry tomatoes, halved

Instructions
Dressing
1.Mince the garlic and one of the chile halves and place in a small bowl. Slice the remaining chile half into thin rings and add it to the bowl, along with the lime juice, fish sauce, lemongrass, brown sugar, and red chile flakes. Taste and adjust seasonings with additional lime juice, fish sauce, sugar, if needed. Stir well and set aside.
Rice Powder
2.Put rice in a small frying pan over medium heat. Cook, stirring frequently, until the grains are toasted and golden, about 10 minutes. Let cool for a few minutes and then grind into a coarse powder in a spice grinder or with a mortar and pestle.
Steak
3.Heat the oil in a skillet over medium high heat. Sear the steak until it is well browned on one side, 5 to 6 min. Flip and cook until the second side is dark brown and the meat is medium rare, another 5 to 6 min. Transfer to a cutting board and let rest for 5 min. Slice the steak thinly and then cut into bite-size pieces.
4.In a medium bowl, combine the beef (and any accumulated juices), shallots, mint, and cilantro. Stir the dressing and pour it on top. Toss gently. Add the ground toasted rice, and toss.

EASY PIZZA DIP

Nutrition: Cal 160;Fat 14 g; Carb 6 g;Protein 8 g
Serving 8; Cook time 25 min

Ingredients
•8 ounces cream cheese
•1/2 cup sour cream
•1/2 teaspoon onion powder
•1 teaspoon oregano
•1/4 teaspoon red pepper flakes
•1/4 teaspoon garlic powder
•1/2 cup tomato sauce
•2 ounces pepperoni
•2 ounces mozzarella cheese
•1/4 teaspoon Pink Himalayan salt
•1/8 teaspoon black pepper

Instructions
1.Preheat oven to 350°F.

2.Combine first six ingredients in a bowl and spread onto the bottom of a 9 inch baking pan.

3.Top with pizza sauce and season with salt and pepper.

4.Layer pepperoni on top of sauce whole or chopped up in pieces. Both work great!

5.Bake for 15 minutes.

6.Pull out of the oven and layer on the mozzarella cheese and bake for another 10 minutes or until cheese is fully melted.

7.Serve warm and enjoy!

CAPRESE MEATBALLS
Nutrition: Cal 311;Fat 22 g; Carb 2 g;Protein 26 g
Serving 16; Cook time 20 min

Ingredients
•1 lb ground turkey
•1 egg
•1/4 cup almond flour
•1/2 teaspoon salt
•1/4 teaspoon ground black pepper
•1/2 teaspoon garlic powder
•1/2 cup shredded whole milk mozzarella
•2 tablespoons sun dried tomatoes, chopped
•2 tablespoons fresh basil, chopped
•2 tablespoons olive oil for frying

Instructions
1.Combine all ingredients except the olive oil in a medium bowl, and mix thoroughly. Form into 16 meatballs. Heat the olive oil in a large nonstick saute pan.

2.Add the meatballs to the hot oil about 1 inch apart (you may have to do two batches) and cook over low-medium heat for about 3 minutes per side or until cooked through. Because the cheese melts out a bit, be careful that they don't burn – if they appear to be getting dark quickly, then turn down the heat and cook them at a lower temp.

3.Serve alone, with marinara sauce, or on skewers with fresh mozzarella, basil leaves, and cherry tomatoes.

CHEESY CHEDDAR BITES
Nutrition: Cal 222;Fat 17 g; Carb 2 g;Protein 8 g
Serving 8; Cook time 15 min

Ingredients
•½ cup shredded cheddar cheese
•¼ cup shredded mozzarella cheese
•¼ cup grated Parmesan cheese
•½ cup almond flour
•2 eggs
•¼ teaspoon garlic powder
•¼ teaspoon parsley flakes
•Salt and pepper, to taste

Instructions
1.Pre-heat the oven to 400°F.

2.Crack 2 eggs in a mixing bowl, season with salt and pepper, and beat with a whisk.

3.Add all three cheeses, almond flour, garlic powder, and parsley flakes to the eggs and stir until a dough forms.

4.Separate dough into 8 sections and roll each section into a ball.

5.Bake on a parchment-lined baking sheet for 14 minutes until golden-brown and slightly crispy.

LOADED CAULIFLOWER
Nutrition: Cal 200;Fat 17 g; Carb 8 g;Protein 12 g
Serving 6; Cook time 20 min

Ingredients
•1 pound cauliflower florettes
•4 ounces sour cream
•1 cup grated cheddar cheese
•2 slices cooked bacon, crumbled
•2 tablespoons snipped chives
•3 tablespoons butter
•1/4 teaspoon garlic powder

•Salt and pepper, to taste

Instructions
1.Cut the cauliflower into florettes and add them to a microwave-safe bowl. Add 2 tablespoons of water and cover with cling film. Microwave for 5-8 minutes, depending on your microwave, until completely cooked and tender. Drain the excess water and let sit uncovered for a minute or two. (alternately, steam your cauliflower the conventional way. You may need to squeeze a little water out of the cauliflower after cooking).

2.Add the cauliflower to a food processor and process until fluffy. Add the butter, garlic powder, and sour cream and process until it resembles the consistency of mashed potatoes. Remove the mashed cauliflower to a bowl and add most of the chives, saving some to add to the top later. Add half of the cheddar cheese and mix by hand. Season with salt and pepper.

3.Top the loaded cauliflower with the remaining cheese, remaining chives and bacon. Put back into the microwave to melt the cheese or place the cauliflower under the broiler for a few minutes.

4.I visually divide the cauliflower into sixths. Serving size is approximately 1/3-1/2 cup.

AVOCADO LIME SALMON
Nutrition: Cal 570;Fat 44 g; Carb 12 g;Protein 26 g
Serving 16; Cook time 20 min

Ingredients
•100 grams chopped cauliflower
•1 large avocado
•1 tablespoon fresh lime juice
•2 tablespoons diced red onion
•2 tablespoons olive oil
•2 (6-ounce) boneless salmon fillets
•Salt and pepper

Instructions
1.Melt your butter in a pan and fry 2-3 eggs until the whites are set and yolk is to desired doneness. Season Place the cauliflower in a food processor and pulse into rice-like grains.

2.Grease a skillet with cooking spray and heat over medium heat.

3.Add the cauliflower rice and cook, covered, for 8 minutes until tender. Set aside.

4.Combine the avocado, lime juice, and red onion in a food processor and blend smooth.

5.Heat the oil in a large skillet over medium-high heat.

6.Season the salmon with salt and pepper, then add to the skillet skin-side down.

7.Cook for 4 to 5 minutes until seared, then flip and cook for another 4 to 5 minutes.

8.Serve the salmon over a bed of cauliflower rice topped with the avocado cream.

BROCCOLI AND SHRIMP SAUTÉED IN BUTTER
Nutrition: Cal 277;Fat 14 g; Carb 5 g;Protein 30 g
Serving 2; Cook time 15 min

Ingredients
•1 cup broccoli, cut into small pieces
•1 clove garlic, crushed
•300 g shrimp, cleaned
•2 tbsp butter
•1 tsp lemon juice
•Salt, to taste

Instructions
1.Chop the broccoli into small portions or whichever size you prefer, but smaller pieces cook faster.

2.Melt the butter in a preheated pan. Gently toss in the chopped broccoli and crushed garlic when the butter becomes hot (but not smoking). Stir to cook.

3.Leave over the heat for 3-4 minutes. Stir from time to time.

4.Clean the shrimp before adding them to the pan. Let it cook for around 3-4 minutes.

5.Once the shrimp turns pink and opaque, drizzle the lemon juice all over.

KETO CALAMARI

Nutrition: Cal 286;Fat 15 g; Carb 11 g;Protein 22 g
Serving 4; Cook time 30 min

Ingredients
- 1 lb fresh squid cleaned
-
- 1 egg beaten
- 1/2 cup coconut flour
- 1 teaspoon salt
- 1 teaspoon paprika
- 1/2 teaspoon garlic powder
- 1/2 teaspoon onion powder
- Coconut oil for frying (about 1/4 cup)
- Minced cilantro optional
- Sliced Fresno chili optional
- Squeeze of lime optional
- Harissa Mayo
- 1/4 cup mayonnaise
- 1 tablespoon prepared hariss

Instructions
1. In a small bowl beat the egg. In another bowl combine the coconut flour and spices.
2. Pat the squid dry and dip into the beaten egg then dredge through the flour mixture.
3. Heat the oil in a 10" or larger cast-iron skillet over medium-high heat.
4. Frying in batches making sure to not overcrowd the skillet, fry 2 minutes per side until golden and crisp. Drain on paper towels
5. Either serve as is or toss with cilantro, chilis, and lime and serve with the harissa mayo

CALAMARI STUFFED WITH PANCETTA AND VEGETABLES

Nutrition: Cal 456;Fat 35 g; Carb 10 g;Protein 24 g
Serving 4; Cook time 20 min

Ingredients
- 500 g (8 large or 12 16 smaller) squid cleaned
- 82 g (1/2 cup) keto bun center only diced into very small pieces
- Stuffing
- 70 g (3 oz) pancetta or pork belly chopped into very small pieces
- 42 g (3 tbsp) of olive oil for grilling
- 68 g (5 tbsp) olive oil for stuffing
- 40 g (1/4 cup) carrots grated
- 8 g (1 tbsp) garlic grated
- 80 g (3/4 cup) celery diced into very small pieces
- 100 g (1 cup, or one bulb) fennel bulb diced into very small pieces
- 1/2 g (1/2 tsp) thyme powder
- 1-2 bunches fresh rosemary
- 6 g (1 tsp) salt
- 2 g (1 tsp) black pepper
- 14 g (1 tbsp) olive oil drizzling over prepared stuffed squid
- 15 g (1 tbsp) lemon juice freshly squeezed

Instructions
1. Clean your squid or purchase cleaned squid with tentacles. Rinse under cold running water and set aside
2. Prepare and weigh your vegetables: grate the carrots, onion and garlic. Chop the celery and fennel bulb into very small pieces
3. Cut the pancetta or pork belly and the squid arms into thin strips and then chop into very small pieces
4. Heat a grilling pan and add 3 tbsp of olive oil. When oil is sizzling add the pancetta/pork belly and squid arms, carrots, celery, fennel, onion and garlic. Place the fresh bunch of rosemary into the pan. Season with salt. Stir and cook on low heat until the vegetables are translucent, and the pancetta/pork belly is done (but not crispy). Remove the rosemary and discard
5. When stuffing is done, place into a mixing bowl and add 2 tbsp of olive oil and the pepper. Toss to combine
6. Use a teaspoon to insert the stuffing into each squid. Quantity of stuffing needed per squid will depend on the size of your squid. Do not overstuff as the squid will shrink as it cooks. Use a toothpick to seal the opening

7. Heat up the grill pan, and add the olive oil. Reduce heat to low and lay your stuffed squid perpendicular to the grill ridges. Cook for 5-6 minutes on the first side then flip and cook 5-6 minutes on the other side. Remove from heat and place on a platter
8. Finish by drizzling the tablespoon of fresh lemon juice on top and then the tablespoon of olive oil. Garnish with the fennel leaves and a wedge of lemon.

LOW CARB ALMOND CRUSTED COD

Nutrition: Cal 219;Fat 13 g; Carb 4 g;Protein 22 g
Serving 4; Cook time 25 min

Ingredients
- 1 4 filets cod or other white fish
- 1 med lemon zested and juiced
- 1/2 cup crushed almonds can use a food processor or blender to crush
- 1 Tbsp dill either fresh
- 1 Tbsp olive oil
- salt & pepper to taste
- 1 tsp mild to med. chili spice optional
- 4 tsp Dijon mustard more if you like mustard

Instructions
1. Preheat oven to 400 degrees F. Prepare a baking sheet with either parchment paper laid on top or spray with cooking spray
2. Place cod filets on paper towels to drain of water and pat dry. Place on baking sheet.
3. In a small bowl, combine the lemon zest, lemon juice, crushed almonds, dill, oil, salt and pepper and chili spice if using.
4. Spread each cod filet with a tsp or so of Dijon mustard,smoothing it over the entire top of the filet. Divide the almond mixture among the 4 filets, pressing it evely into the mustard with your hands.
5. Bake the fish until opaue at the thickest part, about 7 minutes for most.cod filets (less time for thin filets).
6. Serve with a green vegetable and lemon slices for a great low carb or keto fish dinner.

MEXICAN FISH STEW

Nutrition: Cal 196;Fat 7 g; Carb 8 g;Protein 19 g
Serving 6; Cook time 30 min

Ingredients
- 2 Tbsp olive oil
- 1 med onion chopped
- 1 large carrot sliced thinly
- 3 med celery stalks sliced thinly
- 3-6 cloves garlic smashed or minced
- 1 tsp smoky pepper blend
- 1/2 tsp dried thyme
- 1 cup white wine
- 4 cups chicken broth
- 1/2 cup chopped cilantro
- 2 14 oz cans Rotel diced tomatoes
- 1/2 tsp salt
- 3 leaves bay
- 6 oz scallops
- 7 oz walleye, coarsely chopped
- 1 lb mussels
- 3 oz white fish, coarsely chopped
- 2 med limes, cut into wedges optional
- 1 med lemon, sliced for garnish

Instructions
1. Heat oil over med-high heat in a dutch oven or large pot. Saute onion, carrot and celery in oil for 3-5 minutes until translucent. Add smashed garlic and cook for 1 more minute
2. Add spices and stir in to the onion mixture to coat. Add wine, broth, cilantro, and tomatoes to pot and simmer together for 15-20 minutes over medium heat. Add salt to taste.
3. Add all fish to the pot and cook, covered for about 5 minutes or until mussels open and white fish is opaque.
4. Add sliced lemons to the pot and serve.
5. Optional: serve with lime wedges that people can squeeze into the soup.

CREAMY KETO FISH CASSEROLE

Nutrition: Cal 221;Fat 15 g; Carb 9 g;Protein 27 g
Serving 4; Cook time 30 min

Ingredients
- 1 tbsp butter, for greasing baking dish
- 3 tbsp olive oil
- 1 lb broccoli, small florets
- 1 tsp salt
- ½ tsp ground black pepper
- 4 oz. (1¼ cups) scallions, finely chopped
- 2 tbsp small capers (non-pareils)
- 1½ lbs white fish (see tip), cut into serving-sized pieces
- 1 tbsp dried parsley
- 1¼ cups heavy whipping cream
- 1 tbsp Dijon mustard
- 3 oz. butter, cut into thin, equal slices

Instructions
1. Preheat oven to 400°F (200°C). Grease a 13" x 9" (33 x 23 cm) baking dish, set aside.
2. Heat the oil in a large frying pan, over medium-high heat. Add the broccoli, and stir-fry for 5 minutes, or until lightly browned and tender. Season with salt and pepper.
3. Add the scallions and capers, stir together, and fry for a couple of minutes. Spoon the broccoli mixture into the baking dish.
4. Place the fish amongst the vegetables.
5. In a medium-sized bowl, whisk together the parsley, whipping cream, and mustard. Pour over the fish and vegetables. Top with the sliced butter.
6. Bake on the middle rack, uncovered, for 20 minutes or until the fish is cooked through, and flakes easily with a fork.
7. Serve as is, or with leafy greens on the side

GRILLED SALMON WITH AVOCADO SALSA

Nutrition: Cal 528;Fat 43 g; Carb 13 g;Protein 25 g
Serving 2; Cook time 22 min

Ingredients
- 2 4-6 oz salmon fillets
- 2 tablespoons olive oil
- 1 clove garlic minced or crushed
- 1/2 teaspoon
- 1/2 teaspoon
- 1/2 teaspoon onion powder
- 1/4 teaspoon black pepper
- 1/4 teaspoon salt
- For the avocado salsa
- 1 ripe avocado pitted and diced
- 1/2 cup tomato diced (any type of tomato)
- 2 tablespoons onion diced
- 2 tablespoons cilantro minced
- 1 tablespoon olive oil
- 1 tablespoon lime juice
- salt and pepper to taste

Instructions
1. Stir the olive oil, garlic, and spices in a small bowl. Brush or rub salmon with the spice mixture.
2. Heat a large heavy-duty (preferably non-stick) pan or grill medium-high heat. Add salmon to the pan and cook for 5-6 minutes per side. Remove from pan, top with avocado salsa and serve immediately.
3. To make the avocado salsa: Add the avocado, tomato, onion, and cilantro to a large mixing bowl. Drizzle with olive oil, fresh lime juice and a pinch of salt and pepper. Gently mix with a spoon until fully combined. Cover with plastic wrap until ready to serve.

(INSTANT POT) COCONUT CURRY MUSSELS WITH ZUCCHINI NOODLES

Nutrition: Cal 269;Fat 20 g; Carb 11 g;Protein 10 g
Serving 4; Cook time 25 min

Ingredients
- tablespoons avocado oil
- 1 (10- to 12-ounce) package zucchini noodles or 2 large zucchini, zoodled
- ⅓ cup diced onion
- 2 tablespoons minced fresh ginger
- 4 cloves garlic, minced
- 1 tablespoon red curry paste
- 1 cup coconut milk
- 1 cup chicken broth
- ¾ pound (15 to 18) mussels, scrubbed, beards removed
- ½ medium red bell pepper, cut into strips
- 1 tablespoon fish sauce
- ½ teaspoon fine Himalayan pink salt
- ¼ teaspoon black pepper
- Juice of ½ lime
- ¼ cup chopped fresh cilantro, for serving

Instructions
1. Select SAUTÉ on the Instant Pot. When the pot is hot, add 1 table-spoon of the avocado oil. Add the zucchini noodles to the hot oil and cook, stirring frequently, until just tender, 3 to 4 minutes. Select CANCEL. Transfer the zoodles to a dish and cover to keep warm.
2. Select SAUTÉ again. Add the remaining 2 tablespoons avocado oil to the pot. When the oil is hot, add the onion, ginger, garlic, and curry paste. Cook, stirring frequently, until fragrant, about 1 minute. Select CANCEL. Add the coconut milk, broth, mussels, and bell pep-per to the pot.
3. Secure the lid and close the pressure-release valve. Set the pot to HIGH pressure for 3 minutes. At the end of the cooking time, quick-release the pressure. Discard any mussels that have not opened.
4. Divide the zucchini noodles and mussels among four shallow serving bowls. Stir the fish sauce, pink salt, pepper, and lime juice into the curry sauce, then pour over the mussels. Sprinkle with cilantro before serving

CRISPY CHIPOTLE CHICKEN THIGHS

Nutrition: Cal 400;Fat 20 g; Carb 8 g;Protein 25 g
Serving 2; Cook time 22 min

Ingredients
- ½ teaspoon chipotle chili powder
- ¼ teaspoon garlic powder
- ¼ teaspoon onion powder
- ¼ teaspoon ground coriander
- ¼ teaspoon smoked paprika
- 12 ounces boneless chicken thighs
- Salt and pepper
- 1 tablespoon olive oil
- 3 cups fresh baby spinach

Instructions
1. Combine the chipotle chili powder, garlic powder, onion powder, coriander, and smoked paprika in a small bowl.
2. Pound the chicken thighs out flat, then season with salt and pepper on both sides.
3. Cut the chicken thighs in half and heat the oil in a heavy skillet over medium-high heat.
4. Add the chicken thighs skin-side-down to the skillet and sprinkle with the spice mixture.
5. Cook the chicken thighs for 8 minutes then flip and cook on the other side for 3 to 5 minutes.
6. During the last 3 minutes, add the spinach to the skillet and cook until wilted. Serve the crispy chicken thighs on a bed of wilted spinach.

EASY CASHEW CHICKEN

Nutrition: Cal 330;Fat 24 g; Carb 8 g;Protein 22 g
Serving 3; Cook time 15 min

Ingredients
- 3 raw chicken thighs, boneless and skinless
- 2 tablespoons coconut oil (for cooking)
- 1/4 cup raw cashews
- 1/2 medium green bell pepper
- 1/2 teaspoon ground ginger
- 1 tablespoon rice wine vinegar
- 1 1/2 tablespoons liquid aminos

- 1/2 tablespoon chili garlic sauce
- 1 tablespoon minced garlic
- 1 tablespoon sesame oil
- 1 tablespoon sesame seeds
- 1 tablespoon green onions
- 1/4 medium white onion
- Salt and pepper, to taste

Instructions

1. Heat a pan over low heat and toast the cashews for 8 minutes, or until they start to lightly brown and become fragrant. Remove and set aside.
2. Dice chicken thighs into 1 inch chunks. Cut onion and pepper into equally large chunks.
3. Increase heat to high and add coconut oil to pan.
4. Once oil is up to temperature, add in the chicken thighs and allow them to cook through (about 5 minutes).
5. Once the chicken is fully cooked add in the pepper, onions, garlic, chili garlic sauce, and seasonings (ginger, salt, pepper). Allow to cook on high for 2-3 minutes.
6. Add liquid aminos, rice wine vinegar, and cashews. Cook on high and allow the liquid to reduce down until it is a sticky consistency. There should not be excess liquid in the pan upon completing cooking.
7. Serve in a bowl, top with sesame seeds, and drizzle with sesame oil.

ROASTED TURKEY BREAST WITH MUSH-ROOMS & BRUSSELS SPROUTS

Nutrition: Cal 210;Fat 9 g; Carb 6 g;Protein 27 g
Serving 4; Cook time 50 min

Ingredients
- 2 tbsp olive oil
- 1 tsp salt
- 1 tsp black pepper
- 1 tsp garlic powder
- 1 pound turkey breast raw, cut into 1 inch cubes
- 1/2 pound brussels sprouts cleaned, cut in half
- 1 cups mushrooms cleaned

Instructions

1. Preheat oven to 350 degrees Fahrenheit.
2. In a small mixing bowl, combine olive oil, salt, black pepper, and garlic powder.
3. In a 9 x 6-inch casserole dish, combine turkey, brussels sprouts, and mushrooms. Pour the olive oil mixture over the top.
4. Cover with foil and bake for 45 minutes or until the turkey is cooked through and no longer pink. An internal temperature of 165 degrees Fahrenheit is a safe bet.

TURKEY AND BACON LETTUCE WRAPS

Nutrition: Cal 305;Fat 20 g; Carb 22 g;Protein 11 g
Serving 4; Cook time 15 min

Ingredients
Wraps
- 1 head iceberg lettuce
- 4 slices deli turkey
- 4 slices bacon cooked
- 1 avocado thinly sliced
- 1 roma tomato thinly sliced
- 1 cucumber thinly sliced
- 1 carrot thinly sliced

Basil Mayo
- 1/2 cup mayo
- 6 basil leaves chopped
- 1 tsp lemon juice
- 1 garlic clove minced
- salt and pepper to taste

Instructions
Basil Mayo
1. Combine all of the ingredients in a food processor, blend until smooth
Wraps
1. Lay out two large lettuce leaves then layer on 1 slice of turkey and slather with Basil-Mayo.

2. Layer on a second slice of turkey followed by the bacon, and a few slices of avocado, tomato, cucumber and carrot.
3. Season lightly with salt and pepper then fold the bottom up, the sides in, and roll like a burrito.
4. Slice in half and serve cold.

CHIKEN STIR-FRY

Nutrition: Cal 312;Fat 14 g; Carb 11 g;Protein 31 g
Serving 4; Cook time 40 min

Ingredients
- 3 boneless, skinless chicken breasts, trimmed and cut into pieces at least 1 inch square
- 2 red bell peppers
- 2 cups sugar snap peas
- 1 1/2 T peanut oil
- 1-2 T sesame seeds, preferably black

Marinade ingredients:
- 1/3 cup soy sauce (gluten-free if needed)
- 2 T unseasoned (unsweetened) rice vinegar
- 2 T low-carb sweetener of your choice (see notes)
- 1 T sesame oil
- 1/2 tsp. garlic powder

Instructions

1. Trim the chicken breasts and cut into pieces at least 1 inch square.
2. Combine soy sauce, rice vinegar, Stevia, agave or maple syrup, sesame oil and garlic powder.
3. Put the chicken into a Ziploc bag and pour in HALF the marinade. Let chicken marinate in the fridge for at least 4 hours (or all day while you're at work would be even better.)
4. When you're ready to cook, cover a large baking sheet with foil, then put it in the oven and let the pan get hot while the oven heats to 425F/220C.
5. Drain the marinated chicken well in a colander placed in the sink.
6. Remove the hot baking sheet from the oven and spread the chicken out over the surface (so pieces are not touching). Put baking sheet into the oven and cook chicken 8 minutes.
7. While the chicken cooks, trim ends of the sugar snap peas. Cut out the core and seeds of the red bell peppers and discard; then cut peppers into strips about the same thickness as the sugar snap peas.
8. Put veggies into a bowl and toss with the peanut oil.
9. After 8 minutes, remove pan from the oven and arrange the veggies around the chicken, trying to have each vegetable piece touching the pan as much as you can.
10. Put back into the oven and cook about 11 minutes more, or until the chicken is cooked through and lightly browned.
11. Brush cooked chicken and vegetables with the remaining marinade and sprinkle with black sesame seeds. Serve hot.

PAN-SEARED PORK TENDERLOIN MEDAL-LIONS

Nutrition: Cal 150;Fat 7 g; Carb 3 g;Protein 18 g
Serving 4; Cook time 18 min

Ingredients
- 1 tablespoon canola oil 1 (1-lb.)
- pork tenderloin, trimmed and cut crosswise into 12 medallions
- 1/2 teaspoon kosher salt
- 1/4 teaspoon garlic powder
- 1/4 teaspoon black pepper Fresh thyme leaves (optional)

Instructions

1. Heat oil in a 12-inch skillet over medium-high. Arrange pork medallions in a single layer on a work surface, and press each with the palm of your hand to flatten to an even thickness.
2. Combine salt, garlic powder, and pepper; sprinkle evenly over pork. Add pork to skillet in a single layer; cook just until done, about 3 minutes per side
3. Remove from heat; let stand 5 minutes before serving. Garnish with thyme leaves, if desired.

COCONUT PORK CURRY

Nutrition: Cal 260;Fat 16 g; Carb 10 g;Protein 18 g
Serving 4; Cook time 60 min

Ingredients
- 1 teaspoon ground cumin
- 1 teaspoon ground coriander
- 1/2 teaspoon ground cinnamon
- 1/4 teaspoon ground chilli powder
- 800g diced pork
- 1 tablespoon vegetable oil
- 1 large (200g) brown onion, chopped
- 2 cloves garlic, chopped
- 4cm piece (20g) fresh ginger, grated
- 1 tablespoon water
- 400ml can coconut cream or coconut milk
- 2 tablespoons brown sugar
- 1 teaspoon salt
- 1 tablespoon lemon juice
- 1/4 cup fresh coriander leaves

Instructions
1. Combine the spices in a medium bowl; add pork, toss to coat.
2. Heat half the oil in a large frying pan. Cook the pork in 2 batches, using the remaining oil, until browned all over. Remove from pan.
3. Add onion to same pan with garlic, ginger and water; cook, stirring, over medium heat until softened. Return the pork to the pan with coconut cream, sugar and salt. Simmer, covered, stirring occasionally, for about 1 hour to 1 hour 30 minutes or until the pork is tender and the sauce is thickened.
4. Stir in juice; season to taste with salt and pepper. Sprinkle with coriander.

THE BEST BAKED GARLIC PORK TENDERLOIN

Nutrition: Cal 449;Fat 13 g; Carb 6 g;Protein 32 g
Serving 4; Cook time 60 min

Ingredients
- 2 tbsp extra virgin olive oil
- 1 tbsp celtic sea salt and fresh cracked pepper
- 2 lb pork tenderloin, optional: pre-marinate pork before cooking
- 4 tbsp butter, sliced into 4-6 pats
- 2 tbsp diced garlic
- 1 tsp dried basil*
- 1 tsp dried oregano*
- 1 tsp dried thyme*
- 1 tsp dried parsley*
- ½ tsp dried sage*
- 2 tbsp Italian Herb Seasoning Blend

Instructions
1. Preheat oven to 350 degrees.
2. Line baking sheet with aluminum foil.
3. In a small bowl, combine garlic, basil, oregano, thyme, parsley, and sage. Set aside.
4. Generously season meat with salt and pepper.
5. In a large pan, heat oil until shimmery.
6. Add to pan, and cook on all sides until dark golden brown.
7. Transfer to baking sheet.
8. Generously coat with herb mix.
9. Place pats of butter on top of the pork.
10. Wrap in foil, bake until meat is 150 degrees internally at the widest, thickest part of the tenderloin (about 25 minutes.)
11. When pork has come to temperature, remove and let rest, tented with foil, for at least five minutes to lock in juices.
12. Slice against the grain and serve immediately.
13. To store leftovers, place in an airtight container and keep in refrigerator for up to three days.
14. To freeze leftovers, place in a plastic bag or wrap in plastic wrap and keep in freezer for up to three months.
15. To reheat, let thaw naturally in the refrigerator overnight, and bake at 350, wrapped in foil, until piping hot when ready to serve.

PORK SKEWERS WITH CHIMICHURRI

Nutrition: Cal 450;Fat 36 g; Carb 6 g;Protein 30 g
Serving 2; Cook time 20 min

Ingredients
- 1/2 pound boneless pork shoulder
- 1/4 teaspoon ground cumin
- 1/4 teaspoon paprika
- 1 tablespoon coconut oil
- 1/4 cup olive oil
- 1/4 cup diced green peppers
- 3 tablespoons fresh chopped parsley
- 1 tablespoon fresh chopped cilantro
- 1 1/2 tablespoons fresh lemon juice
- 1 garlic clove (minced)
- salt and pepper

Instructions
1. Cut the pork into slices about 1-inch thick.
2. Season the pork with salt, pepper, cumin and paprika.
3. Slide the pork slices onto wooden skewers and heat the coconut oil in a skillet.
4. Fry the skewers until both sides are browned and the meat is cooked through.
5. Combine the remaining ingredients in a food processor.
6. Pulse several times to chop then blend until smooth.
7. Serve the pork skewers with the chimichurri spooned over them.

KETO ASIAN STEAK SALAD

Nutrition: Cal 350;Fat 22 g; Carb 6 g;Protein 27 g
Serving 2; Cook time 15 min

Ingredients
- 2 Ribeye Steaks
- 1/2 cup Soy sauce or coconut aminos divided
- For the asian sesame dressing
- 1/2 cup Olive oil
- 2 tbsp Soy sauce or coconut aminos
- 2 tbsp Apple Cider Vinegar
- 1 tsp Sesame Oil
- 1/8 tsp liquid stevia
- For assembling
- 4 cups Raw spinach
- 4 radishes sliced thin
- Sesame seeds for garnish

Instructions
1. Place each steak in a zip top bag with 1/4 cup of soy sauce. Zip up the bags and allow to marinate on the counter for 1 hour.
2. Remove the steaks from the bag and discard the marinade. In a cast iron skillet on high heat, cook the steaks to your desired doneness. I did 4 minutes on each side for medium.
3. Let the steaks rest for 10 minutes on a cutting board.
4. While the steaks are resting, make your dressing. Add all of the dressing ingredients to a jar with a lid and shake to combine.
5. Assemble the salads. Add 2 cups of spinach and half of the sliced radish to each of the 2 bowls. Slice the steaks into 1/2 in thick pieces and add those to the salads. Drizzle the dressing on top and garnish with sesame seeds.

KETO BEEF AND BROCCOLI

Nutrition: Cal 294;Fat 14 g; Carb 13 g;Protein 29 g
Serving 4; Cook time 35 min

Ingredients
- 1 pound flank steak sliced into 1/4 inch thick strips
- 5 cups small broccoli florets about 7 ounces
- 1 tablespoon avocado oil
- For the sauce:
- 1 yellow onion sliced
- 1 Tbs butter
- ½ tbs olive oil
- 1/3 cup low-sodium soy sauce
- ⅓ cup beef stock
- 1 tablespoon fresh ginger minced

•2 cloves garlic minced

Instructions

1. Heat avocado oil in a pan over medium heat for a few minutes or until hot.
2. Add sliced beef and cook until it browns, less than 5 minutes, don't stir too much, you want it to brown. Transfer to a plate and set aside.
3. Add onions to a skillet with butter and olive oil and cook 20 minutes until onions are caramelized and tender.
4. Add all other sauce ingredients into the skillet and stir the ingredients together over medium-low heat until it starts to simmer, about 5 minutes.
5. Use an immersion blender to blend sauce.
6. Keep the sauce warm over low heat, and add broccoli to the skillet.
7. Return beef to the pan and toss with broccoli and sauce top. Stir until everything is coated with the sauce.
8. Bring to a simmer and cook for another few minutes until broccoli is tender.
9. Season with salt and pepper to taste, if needed.
10. Serve immediately, optionally pairing with cooked cauliflower rice.

KETO MONGOLIAN BEEF

Nutrition: Cal 350;Fat 14 g; Carb 17 g;Protein 30 g
Serving 4; Cook time 25 min

Ingredients

•1 Tablespoon avocado oil
•2 teaspoons Minced ginger
•1 Tablespoon Minced garlic
•1/2 Cup Soy sauce or Coconut aminos
•1/2 cup Water
•3/4 cup Granulated sweetener
•1 1/2 pounds Flank steak or Flatiron steak
•1/4 teaspoon Red pepper flakes
•5 Stems Green onions-cut diagonal into 2 inch pieces
•1/4 teaspoon xanthan gum

Instructions

Making the sauce:

1. 1Heat 1 tablespoon Avocado Oil in a medium saucepan over medium heat.
2. Add ginger, garlic, red pepper flakes and stir for 30 seconds.
3. Add soy sauce, water and sweetener. Bring to a boil and simmer until thickened. Should take about 5 minutes.
4. Remove from skillet to a bowl and set aside.

For the Steak:

1. Slice flank steak against the grain into 1/4 inch slices with the knife held at a 45 degree angle. Some of the really long pieces I cut in half to make them more bite-sized.
2. Heat avocado oil in skillet over medium-high heat.
3. Add beef (may need to cook in 2 batches) and cook 2-3 minutes, until brown, flipping pieces over to cook both sides.
4. Add the sauce to the pan along with the xantham gum and cook over medium heat for a few minute, Stirring to coat meat.
5. Add green onions and remove from heat.

MEATLOAF RECIPE

Nutrition: Cal 575;Fat 44 g; Carb 10 g;Protein 35 g
Serving 4; Cook time 70 min

Ingredients

•1 tablespoon tallow
•1 small onion finely chopped
•2 cloves garlic crushed
•2 pounds ground beef
•2 large eggs
•2 tablespoons oregano dried
•1 1/2 teaspoon salt
•1/4 teaspoon pepper ground
•1/3 cup low carb marinara sauce
•1/3 cup almond flour
•2 tablespoons low carb marinara sauce extra

Instructions

1. Preheat your oven to 160C/320F and prepare a loaf tin by lining with baking paper.

2. Place a non-stick frying pan over high heat and saute the onion and garlic in the tallow, until the onion is turning translucent. Set aside to cool slightly.
3. In a large mixing bowl add the warm onion mixture and all remaining ingredients, except the extra marinara sauce.
4. Using clean hands, or wearing disposable gloves, mix the ingredients very well.
5. Press into the base of your prepared loaf tin, ensuring there are no air bubbles, and smooth the top.
6. Bake for 50 minutes.
7. Drain off some of the juices and top the meatloaf with the extra marinara sauce.
8. Bake for another 10 minutes.
9. Leave to sit for 10 minutes to rest, before slicing and serving.

MOROCCAN MEATBALLS

Nutrition: Cal 363;Fat 27 g; Carb 6 g;Protein 22 g
Serving 8; Cook time 6 hours

Ingredients

•2 pounds of Ground Beef
•1 small Onion, grated
•4 cloves of Garlic, crushed
•1 large Egg
•2 tablespoons of Cilantro, finely chopped
•1 tablespoon of Cumin, ground
•1 tablespoon of Coriander, ground
•1 tablespoon of Smoked Paprika, ground
•2 teaspoons of Ground Ginger
•1 teaspoon of Cinnamon, ground
•1 teaspoon of Salt
•2 tablespoon of Olive Oil
•2 tablespoons of Tomato Paste
•1 ½ cups of Tomato Passata
•½ cup of Beef Stock ro, to serve

Instructions

1. In a large bowl add the beef, half the grated onion, half the garlic, egg, cilantro, cumin, coriander, paprika, ginger, cinnamon, and salt. Mix well.
2. Roll into 2 tablespoon-sized meatballs and set aside. We got 40.
3. Place the oil, remaining onion, and garlic into a nonstick frying pan over high heat. Saute for 3-5 minutes, until fragrant.
4. Add the tomato paste and cook for another 3 minutes, then add to your slow cooker, followed by the passata and stock. Mix well.
5 Add the meatballs to the sauce.
6. Cook on low for 5 hours.

LOW CARB BEEF BOLOGNESE SAUCE

Nutrition: Cal 279;Fat 21 g; Carb 5 g;Protein 17 g
Serving 6; Cook time 75 min

Ingredients

•4 cups of Beef Stock or Broth
•2 ounces of Tallow
•1 medium Onion, diced
•6 cloves of Garlic, crushed
•1 tablespoon of Marjoram, dried
•1 teaspoon of Salt
•3 pounds of Ground Beef
•24 ounces of Tomato Puree
•1 teaspoon of Pepper
•2 tablespoons of Basil, chopped
•2 tablespoons of Oregano, chopped
•1 tablespoon of Parsley, chopped

Instructions

1. Place the beef stock into a small saucepan and simmer over medium-high heat until it reduces into 1 cup of liquid.
2. In a large saucepan over high heat, place the tallow and allow to melt and heat.
3. Add the diced onion, garlic, marjoram, and salt. Saute for 5 minutes, until the onions have softened and turned translucent.
4. Add the ground beef and saute until browned. Reduce the heat to low.

5.Pour in the tomato puree and reduced beef stock and simmer, uncovered, and stirring occasionally for 30-60 minutes. Until the liquid is mostly absorbed, leaving a thick and rich sauce.
6.Add the remaining ingredients, check the seasoning, and add more salt or pepper if desired.
7.Remove from the heat, serve, and enjoy.

KETO LAMB CHOPS ON THE GRILL
Nutrition: Cal 446;Fat 27 g; Carb 4 g;Protein 22 g
Serving 8; Cook time 30 min

Ingredients
•3 lbs of lamb loin chops (I had 8 6oz chops)
•1/4 cup of white wine vinegar
•1/2 cup of olive oil
•1 teaspoon of oregano
•1/2 teaspoon of salt
•1/4 teaspoon of pepper
•2 cloves of garlic, crushed
•zest of 1 lemon
•juice of 2 lemons (approx. 6 tablespoons)

Instructions
1.Whisk together all of the marinade ingredinets. Add the chops to a large baggie and pour the marinade over top.
2.Seal the bag and use your hands to mix the marinade through the chops and then place in the refrigerator for 8 hours or overnight.
3.Take out the lamb chops when ready to eat and let them sit on the ccounter for 15 minutes. Place them on a plate and discard the marinade.
4.Grill the lamb chops for about 5-6 minutes per side. The time will depend on the size and thickness of the chops. Mine were about 1 - 1.5 inches thick and too 6 minutes on each side and came out medium rare.

GARLIC, LEMON & THYME ROASTED CHICKEN BREASTS
Nutrition: Cal 230;Fat 27 g; Carb 4 g;Protein 26 g
Serving 4; Cook time 2 hours 45 min

Ingredients
•4 boneless skinless chicken breasts
•zest of 1 lemon
•juice of 1 lemon
•1/2 cup extra virgin olive oil
•4 cloves garlic minced
•1 tablespoon fresh thyme
•1 teaspoon salt
•1/2 teaspoon ground black pepper
•1 tablespoon olive oil for sauteing

Instructions
1.Create the marinade by mixing the lemon juice, zest, 1/2 cup of olive oil, garlic, thyme, salt, and pepper. Place the chicken breasts in a non-reactive glass dish, or plastic ziptop bag, and pour the marinade over the chicken. Make sure to evenly coat the chicken, then cover and refrigerate for 2 hours.
2.Preheat your oven to 400 degrees F. Remove the chicken from the marinade and wipe off the excess. Heat 1 tablespoon of olive oil, and sear the chicken breasts for 2 minutes on each side, until they're golden brown.
3.Place the chicken breasts on a baking sheet lined with a baking rack, and roast at 400 degrees F for 20-30 minutes depending on the thickness of the chicken breast, or until the internal temperature reads 165 degrees F.

GRILLED CHICKEN KABOBS
Nutrition: Cal 278;Fat 12 g; Carb 26 g;Protein 27 g
Serving 2; Cook time 30 min

Ingredients
•0.5 pound boneless skinless chicken breasts cut into 1 inch pieces
•0.13 cup olive oil
•0.17 cup soy sauce
•0.13 cup honey
•0.5 teaspoon minced garlic
•salt and pepper to taste
•0.5 red bell pepper cut into 1 inch pieces
•0.5 yellow bell pepper cut into 1 inch pieces
•1 small zucchini cut into 1 inch slices
•0.5 red onion cut into 1 inch pieces
•0.5 tablespoon chopped parsley

Instructions
1.Place the olive oil, soy sauce, honey, garlic and salt and pepper in a large bowl.
2.Whisk to combine.
3.Add the chicken, bell peppers, zucchini and red onion to the bowl. Toss to coat in the marinade.
4.Cover and refrigerate for at least 1 hour, or up to 8 hours.
5.Soak wooden skewers in cold water for at least 30 minutes. Preheat grill or grill pan to medium high heat.
6.Thread the chicken and vegetables onto the skewers.
7.Cook for 5-7 minutes on each side or until chicken is cooked through.
8.Sprinkle with parsley and serve.

BASIL TOMATO PORK CHOPS
Nutrition: Cal 210;Fat 10 g; Carb 9 g;Protein 21 g
Serving 4; Cook time 80 min

Ingredients
•2 tablespoons olive oil
•1 teaspoon finely chopped fresh garlic
•8 (1/2-inch thick) pork chops
•1 (28-ounce) can whole tomatoes, undrained, cut up
•1 teaspoon dried basil leaves
•1 teaspoon salt
•1/2 teaspoon pepper
•1/2 cup water
•3 tablespoons cornstarch
•1 medium green bell pepper, cut into rings
•1 medium onion, cut into rings

Instructions
1.Melt butter in 12-inch skillet until sizzling; stir in garlic. Add 4 pork chops. Cook over medium-high heat, turning occasionally,4-6 minutes or until browned on both sides. Remove from pan; set aside. Repeat with remaining pork chops.
2.Return pork chops to pan. Stir in tomatoes, basil, salt and pepper. Cook over medium-high heat 3-4 minutes or until mixture comes to a boil. Reduce heat to low. Cover; cook, stirring occasionally, 50-60 minutes or until pork chops are no longer pink. Remove pork chops; keep warm.
3.Stir together water and cornstarch in small bowl. Stir cornstarch mixture into hot cooking liquid with wire whisk; add green pepper and onion.
4.Increase heat to medium-high. Cook, stirring occasionally, 5-6 minutes or until mixture is thickened and vegetables are crisply tender. Serve sauce over pork chops.

SLOW-ROASTED PORK WITH CITRUS AND GARLIC
Nutrition: Cal 420;Fat 16 g; Carb 9 g;Protein 21 g
Serving 8; Cook time 2 hours 30 min

Ingredients
•10 cloves garlic
•2 tablespoons fresh oregano
•1 tablespoon fresh thyme
•2 tablespoons coriander seeds
•2 teaspoons cumin seeds
•4 bay leaves
•Kosher salt and freshly ground pepper
•1 6-to-8-pound Boston butt pork shoulder
•Juice of 6 oranges, peels reserved
•Juice of 4 lemons, peels reserved
•Juice of 4 limes
•1/4 cup Worcestershire sauce

• 3/4 cup extra-virgin olive oil
• 3 white onions, thinly sliced

Instructions

1. Pulse the garlic, oregano, thyme, coriander and cumin seeds, bay leaves, 2 tablespoons salt and 1 teaspoon pepper in a food processor to make a thick paste. Trim off all but a thin layer of fat from the pork, then make deep slits all over the roast (about every 2 inches) with a paring knife. Rub the spice paste over the pork and into the slits.
2. Mix the citrus juices, Worcestershire sauce and olive oil in a large glass bowl. Submerge the pork in the marinade and top with the onions and reserved orange and lemon peels. Cover with plastic wrap and refrigerate at least 8 hours or up to 2 days. Bring to room temperature 1 hour before roasting.
3. Preheat the oven to 450. Remove the citrus peels from the bowl and refrigerate. Place the pork on a rack in a large roasting pan (reserve the marinade and onions); roast, uncovered, about 1 hour. Add the marinade to the pan and pile the onions on top of the meat. Cover with foil, lower the oven temperature to 350 and roast 2 more hours. Uncover, place the citrus peels around the pork and continue to roast, basting occasionally, until the meat browns and a thermometer inserted into the bottom half registers 190, 1 hour 30 minutes to 2 hours.
4. Transfer the pork to a cutting board and let rest 10 minutes. Meanwhile, skim any excess fat from the pan juices. Slice the pork and serve with the onion and pan juices. Garnish with citrus peels.

KETO LAMB CURRY
Nutrition: Cal 480;Fat 17 g; Carb 2 g;Protein 30 g
Serving 8; Cook time 2 hours35 min

Ingredients
Marinade
• 2 teaspoons of Ginger, crushed
• 3 cloves of Garlic, crushed
• 2 teaspoons of Cumin, ground
• 2 teaspoons of Coriander, ground
• 1 teaspoon of Onion Powder
• 1 teaspoon of Cardamon, ground
• 1 teaspoon of Paprika, ground
• 1 teaspoon of Turmeric, ground
• 1 teaspoon of Kashmiri Chili Powder
• 2 tablespoons of Olive Oil
Curry
• 4 pounds of Lamb Shoulder, diced
• 3 tablespoons of Ghee
• 1 medium Onion, diced
• 1 teaspoon of Cinnamon, ground
• 1 teaspoon of Kashmiri Chili Powder
• 2 teaspoons of Salt
• 1 teaspoon of Pepper
• 1 cup of Heavy Cream
• ½ cup of Flaked Almonds
• 3 tablespoons of Cilantro, roughly chopped

Instructions
1. The Marinade: In a mixing bowl combine all marinade ingredients.
2. Add the diced lamb and mix well.
3. Store in the fridge to marinate for at least 1 hour, or overnight.
4. The Curry: In a large saucepan add the ghee and place over medium heat.
5. Add the onion, cinnamon & chili powder and saute for 3 minutes.
6. Add the marinated lamb, salt, and pepper and stir to ensure that lamb is browning.
7. Allow the lamb to cook for 10 minutes before adding the cream and reducing the heat to low.
8. Simmer the curry, partially covered, for 1 hour. Check the lamb for tenderness. If the lamb is tough, continue cooking until tender.
9. Remove the lid and simmer for another 10 minutes.
10. Add the flaked almonds and stir well. Add any extra seasoning.
11. Remove from the heat, garnish with coriander and serve.

ROSEMARY DIJON ROASTED LAMB CHOPS
Nutrition: Cal 446;Fat 40 g; Carb 2 g;Protein 18 g
Serving 4; Cook time 17 min

Ingredients
• 1 tbsp Dijon mustard
• 2 cloves garlic minced
• 3 tbsp olive oil
• 2 tsp fresh rosemary finely chopped
• 1/2 tsp salt
• 1/4 tsp pepper
• 4 lamb loin chops aprrox 2 lbs with bone-in

Instructions
1. Whisk together Dijon mustard, garlic, olive oil, rosemary, and salt and pepper in a bowl. Place lamb chops in a large zip-top bag or other air-tight container. Coat lamb with Dijon mixture on both sides. Let marinate in the fridge for at least 30 minutes, but up to 24 hours.
2. Position an oven rack to the highest position in the oven and line a broiler pan with aluminum foil.
3. Take lamb chops out of the bag and place onto prepared pan. Set oven to broil on high and place pan into the oven.
4. Cook lamb chops for 8 minutes, until brown, and then flip and cook for an additional 3-5 minutes depending on the doneness you like your meat. (3 minutes for medium rare, 4 for medium, 5 for well done)

KETO LAMB KOFTAS
Nutrition: Cal 330;Fat 26 g; Carb 3 g;Protein 22 g
Serving 4; Cook time 20 min

Ingredients
• 500 g minced (ground) lamb (1.1 lb)
• 1 garlic clove, minced
• 1/2 medium yellow onion, diced (50 g/ 1.8 oz)
• 1 tsp dried oregano
• 2 tbsp chopped fresh parsley
• 1/2 tsp sea salt
• 1/4 tsp ground black pepper
• 1 tbsp extra virgin olive oil (15 ml)

Instructions
1. Place your skewers in cold water for half and hour prior to starting (ideally leave them to soak for at least 30 minutes). Alternatively, you can use stainless steel skewers that don't require soaking.
2. Add minced lamb, diced onions, chopped garlic, finely chopped parsley and the herbs and seasonings into a large mixing bowl. Retain the olive oil.
3. Mix well with your hands until thoroughly combined.
4. Portion out into eight portions and place each one around a skewer. You need to gently squeeze and press your mixture around the skewer until you're happy with the result. If your skewers will fit in a pan, heat it on the stove top. Mine were too big so I cooked them on our barbeque instead.
5. Brush the surface with the retained olive oil before placing the koftas onto the hot pan.
6. Store the koftas in the refrigerator, covered for 4 days.

GREEK LAMB AND CABBAGE BOWLS
Nutrition: Cal 334;Fat 10 g; Carb 15 g;Protein 34 g
Serving 4; Cook time 24 min

Ingredients
• 1 tablespoon olive oil
• 1 large clove garlic, minced
• 1 small onion, diced
• 1 lb grass-fed ground lamb
• ¼ cup tomato paste
• 1 teaspoon ground cinnamon
• ½ teaspoon dried oregano
• ¼ teaspoon ground nutmeg
• ½ cup water (or broth), more or less as needed
• ½ large head green cabbage (or 1 small), cored and sliced
• 1 teaspoon sea salt and ½ teaspoon black pepper, or to taste

Instructions

1.In a large pan, dutch oven or skillet, heat the olive oil over medium-high heat. Add the onion, garlic and ground lamb. Sauté until the lamb is cooked about 5- 7 minutes.
2.Add in the tomato paste, cinnamon, oregano and nutmeg. Stir until well combined.
3.Add in the cabbage and continue to sauté. You want to cook until the cabbage is gently cooked with a little bite, not mushy.
4.Add a little water or broth, as needed if it's too dry.
5.Serve over cauli-rice or rice, zucchini noodles or pasta.

LAMB MEATBALLS WITH MINT GREMOLATA
Nutrition: Cal 306;Fat 17 g; Carb 4 g;Protein 34 g
Serving 4; Cook time 20 min
Ingredients
For the meatballs:
•2 lbs ground lamb
•2 eggs
•1/2 cup superfine almond flour **
•1/4 cup fresh parsley, chopped
•1 clove garlic, minced
•1 1/2 Tbsp Za'atar seasoning
•1 tsp kosher salt
•3 Tbsp water
•2 Tbsp olive oil for frying
•**For the gremolata:**
•2 Tbsp chopped fresh parsley
•2 Tbsp chopped fresh mint
•1 Tbsp lime zest
•2 cloves garlic, minced
Instructions
For the meatballs:
1.Combine the meatball ingredients (except olive oil) in a medium bowl and mix well.
2.Form into 24 one and a half inch (approximately) meatballs.
3.Heat the olive oil in a nonstick saute pan over medium heat.
4.Cook the meatballs in batches until brown on both sides and cooked through – about 2-3 minutes per side.
5.Remove cooked meatballs and place on a paper towel lined plate until ready to serve.
6.Serve warm, sprinkled generously with gremolata.
For the gremolata:
7.Combine the ingredients in a small bowl and mix well.

SMOKED SAUSAGE & GREEN BEANS
Nutrition: Cal 253;Fat 7 g; Carb 4 g;Protein 37 g
Serving 8; Cook time 3 hours 10 min
Ingredients
•1 pound smoked turkey sausage, sliced 1/2–inch thick
•1 pound green beans, frozen
•½ tsp garlic, minced
•1 tbsp dry mustard
•1 tsp ground ginger
•½ cup soy sauce
•½ cup sherry wine
•1 tsp thyme
•½ tsp ground black pepper
•½ tsp salt
Instructions
1.Place the pork roast in a very zip-lock bag, set in a very deep bowl.
2.Thoroughly blend together the soy sauce, sherry, garlic, mustard, ginger, thyme, and black pepper.
3.Pour marinade over meat in bag, seal bag.
4.Place the roast inside the refrigerator and marinate for just two to a few hours or overnight.
5.Transfer the pork roast and marinade to instant pot.
6.Cover and turn the steam release handle on the venting position.
7.Select the slow cooker setting as well as set to high.
8.Cook for 3 1/couple of hours.
9.Lift roast out onto a chopping board, let indicate ten minutes before slicing.

10.Serve with boiled potatoes.

APRICOT GLAZED PORK
Nutrition: Cal 315;Fat 10 g; Carb 20 g;Protein 35 g
Serving 12; Cook time 4 hours
Ingredients
•4 pounds boneless pork loin roast
•1 cup onion, chopped
•2 tbsp Dijon mustard
•2 cups beef broth
•1 cup apricot preserves
Instructions
1.Mix broth, preserves, onion, and mustard in instant pot.
2.Cut pork to match. Add to instant pot.
3.Cover and turn the steam release handle towards the venting position.
4.Select the slow cooker setting and set to high.
5.Cook for 4 hours.

EASY BBQ HAM
Nutrition: Cal 315;Fat 15 g; Carb 2 g;Protein 35 g
Serving 24; Cook time 14 hours
Ingredients
•3 pounds ham, boneless
•2 cups water
•2 cups onions, sliced
•6 whole cloves
•2 cups BBQ sauce
Instructions
1.Place half in the onions in bottom in the instant pot.
2.Stick cloves in ham and set it on top of onions in instant pot.
3.Put the others in the onions on top. Pour water.
4.Cover and turn the steam release handle for the venting position.
5.Select the slow cooker setting and hang up to medium.
6.Cook for 10 hours.
7.Shred or cut up meat and onion.
8.Put back to the instant pot.
9.Add barbecue sauce and cook 4 hours more.

CHEESY SCALLOPED POTATOES WITH HAM
Nutrition: Cal 435;Fat 15 g; Carb 23 g;Protein 23 g
Serving 24; Cook time 14 hours
Ingredients
•1 pound ham, sliced
•8 medium potatoes, peeled and sliced
•2 cups onions, sliced
•1 cup Cheddar cheese, grated
•½ tsp cream of tartar
•1 cup water
•10 ounces cream of mushroom soup
•Paprika
Instructions
1.Toss sliced potatoes in cream of tartar and water. Drain.
2.Put half ham, potatoes, and onions in instant pot.
3.Sprinkle with grated cheese.
4.Repeat with remaining half ham, potatoes, and onions.
5.Spoon undiluted soup over top.
6.Sprinkle with paprika.
7.Cover and turn the steam release handle to the venting position.
8.Select the slow cooker setting and hang to high.
9.Cook for 4 hours.

LAMB CASSOULET WITH BEANS
Nutrition: Cal 274;Fat 8 g; Carb 26 g;Protein 18 g
Serving 6; Cook time 5 hours
Ingredients
•2 cups can great northern beans
•1/2 tsp garlic, minced

- 1 tbsp fresh parsley
- 1/2 tsp thyme, crushed
- 2 tbsp organic olive oil
- 1 cup dry white wine
- 1 cup tomato sauce
- 2 bay leaves
- 8 ounces lean lamb, cut into 1/2-inch pieces
- 3/4 cup onion, chopped
- 1/4 cup water
- 2 tbsp flour

Instructions
1. In an immediate pot combine beans, wine, tomato sauce, bay leaves, garlic, parsley, and thyme.
2. Heat oil in a very saucepan over medium-high heat and cook lamb and onion until lamb is well browned on all sides, drain.
3. Stir lamb and onion into bean mixture in instant pot.
4. Cover and turn the steam release handle to the venting position.
5. Select the slow cooker setting and set to medium.
6. Cook for 5 hours.
7. Turn to high. Heat until bubbly (don't lift cover).
8. Slowly blend the cold water into flour, stir into meat-bean mixture.
9. Cover and cook until slightly thickened.
10. Before serving, remove bay leaves and discard.

ITALIAN RICE CASSEROLE
Nutrition: Cal 508;Fat 14 g; Carb 66 g;Protein 26 g
Serving 8; Cook time 6 hours

Ingredients
- 1 pound ground beef
- 3 cups rice, long grain and uncooked
- 3 cups tomato sauce
- 1 cup onion, chopped
- 1 tsp Italian seasoning
- 1/2 tsp garlic, minced
- 6 ounces mozzarella, shredded
- 1 cup cottage type cheese
- 4 cups water

Instructions
1. Place ground beef and chopped onion in the nonstick skillet.
2. Brown over medium-high heat and then drain.
3. Combine beef mixture and remaining
4. Ingredient in instant pot.
5. Cover and turn the steam release handle on the venting position.
6. Select the slow cooker setting and hang to high.
7. Cook for 6 hours.

SWISS CHEESE BEEF ZUCCHINI CASSEROLE
Nutrition: Cal 454;Fat 30 g; Carb 13 g;Protein 30 g
Serving 4; Cook time 2 hours

Ingredients
- 1 pound extra-lean ground beef
- 4 cups zucchini, sliced
- 10 ounces cream of mushroom soup
- 1/2 cup onion, chopped
- 1/4 tsp ground black pepper
- 1 cup Swiss cheese, shredded

Instructions
1. In a skillet over medium-high heat, brown ground beef with onions and pepper until don't pink. Drain.
2. Layer zucchini and beef mixture alternately in instant pot.
3. Top with soup. Sprinkle with cheese.
4. Cover and turn the steam release handle to the venting position.
5. Select the slow cooker setting and set to medium.
6. Cook for 120 minutes.

CHILI VERDE WITH POTATOES
Nutrition: Cal 414;Fat 20 g; Carb 40 g;Protein 21 g
Serving 8; Cook time 4 hours

Ingredients
- 1 pound extra-lean ground beef
- 1/2 pound ground pork
- 4 large potatoes, diced
- 10 ounces corn, frozen
- 3 cups chicken broth
- 2 cups water
- 8 ounces green chilies, diced
- 2 tbsp essential olive oil
- 1 cup onion, diced
- 1 tsp garlic, minced
- 1 tsp ground black pepper
- 1/2 tsp oregano
- 1 tsp cumin
- 1/2 tsp salt

Instructions
Heat oil inside a skillet over medium-high heat and after that brown onion, garlic, beef, and pork.
Cook until meat is no longer pink.
Combine meat mixture and remaining
Ingredients in instant pot.
Cover and turn the steam release handle for the venting position.
Select the slow cooker setting and hang up to medium.
Cook for 4 hours.

SIMPLE & CLASSIC GOULASH
Nutrition: Cal 167;Fat 10 g; Carb 8 g;Protein 11 g
Serving 8; Cook time 5 hours

Ingredients
- 1 pound ground beef, browned
- 1/2 cup ketchup
- 2 tbsp Worcestershire sauce
- 1 tbsp brown sugar
- 1 cup onion, chopped
- 1/2 tsp garlic, minced
- 2 tsp paprika
- 1/2 tsp dry mustard
- 1 cup water

Instructions
1. Place meat in instant pot. Cover with onions.
2. Combine remaining
3. Ingredients and pour over meat.
4. Cover and turn the steam release handle for the venting position.
5. Select the slow cooker setting and hang up to medium.
6. Cook for 5 hours.
7. Serve over rice or noodles.

SALAD WITH BROCCOLI, CAULIFLOWER AND BACON
Nutrition: Cal 164;Fat 14 g; Carb 8 g;Protein 5 g
Serving 4; Cook time 15 min

Ingredients
- Broccoli (3/4 cups, chopped)
- Cauliflower (3/4 cups, chopped)
- Bacon (3 slices, chopped)
- Onion (1, chopped)
- Vinegar (1 teaspoon)
- Sour cream (3/4 cups)
- Salt and Pepper

Instructions
1. Put the cauliflower and broccoli inside the pressure cooker as well as set it to "Steam" for the matter of minutes (they shouldn't be too tender). Take out your vegetables in the boiling water and hang up them aside.
2. Fry the bacon till it turns brown, set it up aside and allow it cool.
3. Mix the onion (you can use spring onion also) using the vinegar, salt, pepper, and sour cream.
4. Mix the sauce while using broccoli and cauliflower, serve with many more bacon pieces for decoration.

ASPARAGUS WRAPPED IN PROSCIUTTO
Nutrition: Cal 555;Fat 45 g; Carb 6.7 g;Protein 33 g
Serving 3; Cook time 25 min

Ingredients
- Mushrooms (3 cups)
- Rice (1 ½ cups)
- Chicken stock (4 cups)
- Olive oil (1/4 cup)
- Onion (1 cup, chopped)
- Butter (unsalted, ¼ cup)
- White wine (3/4 cup)
- Rosemary
- Parmesan (half cup, grated)
- Salt and pepper

Instructions
1. Set the Pressure cooker to "Sauté"; add the olive oil and butter and let it melt for any matter of minutes. Add the mushrooms and cook them about 3 minutes).
2. Put within the onion, stir and cook to get a couple of more minutes. Add the rosemary and cook it to get a minute.
3. Add the rice and stir until it coats inside the butter and olive oil mix; stir for a couple of minutes and after that pour the wine. Let it simmer for three more minutes.
4. Pour inside the chicken stock, stir for any minute.
5. Now close and secure the lid and select to "High pressure" as well as set the timer for 6 minutes.
6. Let the stress out naturally for 5 minutes.
7. Open the lid and stir the risotto (it ought to turn creamy); remove the rosemary (if you are using spring, if it's chopped, then get forced out as it really is).
8. Sprinkle salt, pepper, and parmesan, and stir till the cheese melts.
9. Serve while it's hot.

CREAMY CHILE SHRIMP
Nutrition: Cal 103;Fat 6 g; Carb 5g;Protein 7g
Serving 4; Cook time 30 min

Ingredients
- 1 lb. shrimp
- 1 chile pepper, cut into thin strips
- ½ cup bell pepper, cut into thin strips
- ½ cup white cabbage
- ½ tsp. cayenne powder
- ½ cup chicken stock
- ½ tsp. black pepper
- ½ cup heavy cream
- ½ tsp. hot sauce
- 1 tbsp. garlic, minced
- ½ tsp. lime juice
- ¼ cup canola oil

Instructions
1. Deseed and cut the green chile into thin strips lengthwise.
2. In the Instant Pot, sauté the bell pepper, cabbage and green chili with half oil for 3-4 minutes. Remove and warm by covering with foil.
3. Sauté ginger and garlic inside the Instant Pot with the rest in the oil and add shrimp. Turn off "Sauté" function. Add the spices, hot sauce, and lime juice.
4. Add chicken stock and cook on high pressure for 4 minutes. Quick pressure release, add the sautéed vegetables and mix well.
5. Add cream and sauté before sauce thickens slightly. Serve.

LEMON KALAMATA OLIVE SALMON
Nutrition: Cal 440;Fat 34 g; Carb 3g;Protein 30g
Serving 3; Cook time 25 min

Ingredients
- 4 x 0.3 lb. salmon filets
- 2 tbsps. fresh lemon juice
- ¼ tsp. black pepper
- ½ cup red onion, sliced
- 1 tsp. herbs de Provence
- 1 can pitted kalamata olives
- 1tsp. sea salt
- ½ lemon, thinly sliced
- 1 cup fish broth
- ½ tsp. cumin
- ½ cup essential olive oil

Instructions
1. Generously season salmon fillets with cumin, pepper, and salt; set your Instant Pot on "Sauté" mode as well as heat the essential olive oil; add fish and brown each side.
2. Stir the remainder
3. Ingredients to the pot and provide to your simmer; lock lid. Set your pot on manual high for ten minutes; when done, quick release pressure then serve.

SEAFOOD MEDLEY STEW
Nutrition: Cal 535;Fat 44 g; Carb 8g;Protein 27g
Serving 3; Cook time 25 min

Ingredients
- 2 cups chicken broth
- 2 tbsps. lemon juice
- ½ lb. shrimp
- ½ lb. mussels
- 2 cloves garlic, crushed
- ½ cup coconut cream
- ½ tsp. black pepper
- 100 g. halibut
- 1 dried whole star anise
- 1 bay leaf
- 1 cup light cream
- 3 tbsps. coconut oil

Instructions
1. In the Instant Pot, sauté the bay leaves, and star anise in coconut oil approximately 30 seconds.
2. Add garlic and attempt to sauté.
3. Add broth. Rub fresh lemon juice, salt, and pepper on fish fillets and put inside pot. Add shrimp and mussels too.
4. Cook for 10 mins. Release pressure naturally.
5. Add both creams and permit to simmer.
6. Remove bay leaves and star anise before serving.

FLAVORED OCTOPUS
Nutrition: Cal 180;Fat 3 g; Carb 1.5 g;Protein 30 g
Serving 4; Cook time 25 min

Ingredients
- 1 tsp chopped cilantro
- 2 tbsps. extra virgin olive oil
- 0.6 pounds octopus
- 2 tsps. garlic powder
- 3 tbsps. lime juice
- salt and pepper, to taste

Instructions
1. Place the octopus within the steaming basket. Season with garlic powder, salt, and pepper. Drizzle with olive and lime juice.
2. Pour water in the Instant Pot and lower the steaming basket. Close the lid and cook for 8 minutes on high.
3. Do a simple pressure release.

CARAMELIZED TILAPIA
Nutrition: Cal 150;Fat 4 g; Carb 3 g;Protein 21 g
Serving 4; Cook time 50 min

Ingredients
- 1-pound tilapia fillets
- 1 red chili, minced
- 3 tsp. minced garlic
- ¼ cup granulated sweetener
- 1 spring onion, minced

- ¾ cup coconut water
- 1/3 cup water
- 3 tbsp. fish sauce
- salt and pepper, to taste

Instructions
1. In a bowl, combine the fish sauce, garlic, salt, and pepper. Place the tilapia inside and mix to coat. Cover and let sit within the fridge for half an hour.
2. Meanwhile, combine the lake and sweetener inside Instant Pot. Cook on "Sauté" until caramelized.
3. Add fish and pour the coconut water over. Close the lid and cook on high for 10 minutes.
4. Do a fast pressure release. Top the fish with spring onion and chili.
5. Serve and enjoy!

CRUNCHY ALMOND TUNA
Nutrition: Cal 150;Fat 4 g; Carb 3 g;Protein 21 g
Serving 4; Cook time 15 min

Ingredients
- 2 cans of tuna, drained
- 1 cup shaved almond
- 2 tbsps. butter
- 1 tsp garlic powder
- 1 cup grated cheddar cheese

Instructions
1. Melt the butter in your Instant Pot on "Sauté." Add tuna, almonds, garlic powder, and cheddar. Cook on "Sauté" for 3 minutes.
2. Serve immediately over cauliflower, rice or on its own.
3. Side Dishes and Vegetables

EGG LOAF
Nutrition: Cal 150;Fat 4 g; Carb 3 g;Protein 21 g
Serving 6; Cook time 10 min

Ingredients
- unsalted butter, for greasing the bowl
- 6 eggs
- 2 cups water, for steaming

Instructions
1. Grease a heatproof bowl with the butter very well.
2. Crack the eggs in the greased bowl, keeping the yolks intact. Cover the bowl with aluminum foil and set aside briefly.
3. Pour the water to the inner cooking pot and put a trivet ahead. Place the foil-covered bowl of eggs for the trivet.
4. Close the lid, Select "Pressure Cook" or "Manual," and adjust pressure to succeed to high and cook for 4 minutes. Quick-release the pressure when the cooking is complete.
5. Carefully eliminate the bowl through the pot. Pop out the egg loaf through the bowl. You'll see mainly a loaf of egg white, with just several spots of egg yolk.
6. Chop the egg loaf as coarse or fine as you'd like. You can now mix it with a little mayonnaise for egg salad, stir it with a little butter, salt, and pepper for any quick snack or meal.

ARUGULA AND SALMON SALAD
Nutrition: Cal 390;Fat 31 g; Carb 6 g;Protein 26 g
Serving 3; Cook time 25 min

Ingredients
- 3 (4-ounce) salmon fillets
- 5 tablespoons extra-virgin olive oil, divided
- 1 teaspoon garlic salt
- Juice of 1 lemon
- 4½ cups arugula

Instructions
1. Preheat the oven to 450°F. Line a baking sheet with aluminum foil.
2. Rub the fillets with 2 tablespoons of oil and the garlic salt. Place them on the prepared sheet and drizzle the lemon juice over the top of the fillets.
3. Bake until the salmon is cooked through and flaky, 8 to 12 minutes. Let the fillets rest for 10 minutes.
4. Into each of 3 storage containers, place 1 cups of arugula and season with salt and pepper. Top the arugula with the salmon fillets.To serve, drizzle the arugula in each container with 1 tablespoon of oil and toss.

BEEF AND BROCCOLI STIR-FRY
Nutrition: Cal 588;Fat 38 g; Carb 6 g;Protein 54 g
Serving 4; Cook time 25 min

Ingredients
- 6 tablespoons coconut aminos
- ¼ cup avocado oil
- 2 tablespoons toasted sesame oil
- 1 teaspoon garlic powder
- 1 teaspoon onion powder
- Salt
- Freshly ground black pepper
- 1½ pounds sirloin steak, cut into ¼-inch-thick slices

FOR THE BEEF AND BROCCOLI
- 1 teaspoon salt, plus more for seasoning
- 2 broccoli crowns, florets separated and trimmed
- 2 tablespoons avocado oil
- 3 garlic cloves, minced
- 1 tablespoon finely minced ginger or ½ tablespoon ground ginger
- ¼ cup coconut aminos
- ¼ cup toasted sesame oil
- Freshly ground black pepper

Instructions
TO MAKE THE MARINADE
In a bowl, combine the coconut aminos, avocado oil, sesame oil, garlic powder, onion powder, salt, and pepper. Add the steak and toss to coat. Marinate for at least 30 minutes or up to 24 hours in the refrigerator.

TO MAKE THE BEEF AND BROCCOLI
1. Fill a large pot halfway with water and add 1 teaspoon of salt. Bring to a boil.
2. Add the broccoli and blanch for 1 to 3 minutes; drain in a colander. Rinse with cold water to prevent further cooking. Set aside.
3. Heat a large skillet over medium-high heat and combine the avocado oil, garlic, and ginger and cook for 30 seconds.
4. Add the sliced beef, discarding the marinade, and cook, stirring constantly, for 2 to 3 minutes. Add the broccoli, coconut aminos, and sesame oil to the skillet and season with salt and pepper. Continue to cook until the beef has reached your desired doneness (about 5 to 7 minutes for medium).
5. Divide the stir-fry evenly between 4 storage containers.

BRATWURSTS AND SAUERKRAUT
Nutrition: Cal 525;Fat 42 g; Carb 12 g;Protein 24 g
Serving 4; Cook time 50 min

Ingredients
- 2 tablespoons avocado oil
- 1 yellow onion, thinly sliced
- 1 pound bratwurst
- 1 (16-ounce) jar sauerkraut, drained
- 1½ cups chicken broth
- 1 teaspoon garlic powder
- Salt
- Freshly ground black pepper

Instructions
1. In large cast-iron skillet over medium heat, add the oil, onion, and bratwurst and cook for 6 to 8 minutes, or until they get some color.
2. Add the sauerkraut, broth, garlic powder, salt, and pepper and simmer for 30 to 40 minutes, or until the sausages are cooked through.
3. In each of 4 storage containers, place 1 cup of sauerkraut and 1 bratwurst.

ROASTED CHICKEN OVER PESTO SPAGHETTI SQUASH

Nutrition: Cal 361;Fat 30 g; Carb 6 g;Protein 18 g
Serving 4; Cook time 45 min

Ingredients

- 4 (3- to 4-ounce) bone-in chicken thighs
- ¼ cup extra-virgin olive oil
- 1 teaspoon garlic powder
- 1 teaspoon onion powder
- Salt
- Freshly ground black pepper
- 1 recipe Spaghetti Squash
- ¼ cup prepared pesto sauce (see Ingredient Tip)

Instructions

1. Preheat the oven to 375ºF.
2. Pat the chicken thighs dry with paper towels and place them in a shallow dish.
3. Add the oil, garlic powder, and onion powder. Season with salt and pepper. Mix until the chicken is coated evenly.
4. Place the seasoned chicken on a baking sheet, making sure the skin is wrapped around the thigh.
5. Bake for 30 to 40 minutes, or until the chicken has reached an internal temperature of 165ºF.
6. In a medium bowl, toss together the spaghetti squash and pesto sauce. Season with salt and pepper, and combine until the squash is evenly coated.
7. Divide the squash noodles between 4 storage containers and top each with a chicken thigh. Let cool and secure the lids.

GRILLED PESTO SALMON WITH ASPARAGUS

Nutrition: Cal 300;Fat 18 g; Carb 2.5 g;Protein 34 g
Serving 4; Cook time 20 min

Ingredients

- 4 (6-ounce) boneless salmon fillets
- Salt and pepper
- 1 bunch asparagus, ends trimmed
- 2 tablespoons olive oil
- ¼ cup basil pesto

Instructions

1. Preheat a grill to high heat and oil the grates.
2. Season the salmon with salt and pepper, then spray with cooking spray.
3. Grill the salmon for 4 to 5 minutes on each side until cooked through.
4. Toss the asparagus with oil and grill until tender, about 10 minutes.
5. Spoon the pesto over the salmon and serve with the asparagus

CHEDDAR-STUFFED BURGERS WITH ZUCCHINI

Nutrition: Cal 470;Fat 30 g; Carb 4,5 g;Protein 47 g
Serving 4; Cook time 25 min

Ingredients

- 1 pound ground beef (80% lean)
- 2 large eggs
- ¼ cup almond flour
- 1 cup shredded cheddar cheese
- Salt and pepper
- 2 tablespoons olive oil
- 1 large zucchini, halved and sliced

Instructions

1. Combine the beef, egg, almond flour, cheese, salt, and pepper in a bowl.
2. Mix well, then shape into four even-sized patties.
3. Heat the oil in a large skillet over medium-high heat.
4. Add the burger patties and cook for 5 minutes until browned.
5. Flip the patties and add the zucchini to the skillet, tossing to coat with oil.
6. Season with salt and pepper and cook for 5 minutes, stirring the zucchini occasionally.

7. Serve the burgers with your favorite toppings and the zucchini on the side.

CHICKEN CORDON BLEU WITH CAULIFLOWER

Nutrition: Cal 420;Fat 24 g; Carb 7 g;Protein 45 g
Serving 4; Cook time 55 min

Ingredients

- 4 boneless chicken breast halves (about 12 ounces)
- 4 slices deli ham
- 4 sliccs Swiss cheese
- 1 large egg, whisked well
- 2 ounces pork rinds
- ¼ cup almond flour
- ¼ cup grated parmesan cheese
- ½ teaspoon garlic powder
- Salt and pepper
- 2 cups cauliflower florets

Instructions

1. Preheat the oven to 350ºF and line a baking sheet with foil.
2. Sandwich the chicken breast halves between pieces of parchment and pound flat.
3. Lay the pieces out and top with sliced ham and cheese.
4. Roll the chicken up around the fillings then dip in the beaten egg.
5. Combine the pork rinds, almond flour, parmesan, garlic powder, salt and pepper in a food processor and pulse into fine crumbs.
6. Roll the chicken rolls in the pork rind mixture then place on the baking sheet.
7. Toss the cauliflower with melted butter then add to the baking sheet.
8. Bake for 45 minutes until the chicken is cooked through.

SESAME-CRUSTED TUNA WITH GREEN BEANS

Nutrition: Cal 380;Fat 19 g; Carb 8 g;Protein 44 g
Serving 4; Cook time 20 min

Ingredients

- ¼ cup white sesame seeds
- ¼ cup black sesame seeds
- 4 (6-ounce) ahi tuna steaks
- Salt and pepper
- 1 tablespoon olive oil
- 1 tablespoon coconut oil
- 2 cups green beans

Instructions

1. Combine the two types of sesame seeds in a shallow dish.
2. Season the tuna with salt and pepper.
3. Dredge the tuna in the sesame seed mixture.
4. Heat the olive oil in a skillet to high heat then add the tuna.
5. Cook for 1 to 2 minutes until seared then turn and sear on the other side.
6. Remove the tuna from the skillet and let the tuna rest while you reheat the skillet with the coconut oil.
7. Fry the green beans in the oil for 5 minutes then serve with sliced tuna.

ROSEMARY ROASTED PORK WITH CAULIFLOWER

Nutrition: Cal 300;Fat 17 g; Carb 3 g;Protein 37 g
Serving 4; Cook time 30 min

Ingredients

- 1 ½ pounds boneless pork tenderloin
- 1 tablespoon coconut oil
- 1 tablespoon fresh chopped rosemary
- Salt and pepper
- 1 tablespoon olive oil
- 2 cups cauliflower florets

Instructions

1. Rub the pork with coconut oil, then season with rosemary, salt, and pepper.
2. Heat the olive oil in a large skillet over medium-high heat.
3. Add the pork and cook for 2 to 3 minutes on each side until browned.

4. Sprinkle the cauliflower in the skillet around the pork.
5. Reduce the heat to low, then cover the skillet and cook for 8 to 10 minutes until the pork is cooked through.
6. Slice the pork and serve with the cauliflower.

CHICKEN TIKKA WITH CAULIFLOWER RICE
Nutrition: Cal 350;Fat 21 g; Carb 8 g;Protein 35 g
Serving 4; Cook time 15 min

Ingredients
- 2 pounds boneless chicken thighs, chopped
- 1 cup canned coconut milk
- 1 cup heavy cream
- 3 tablespoons tomato paste
- 2 tablespoons garam masala
- 1 tablespoon fresh grated ginger
- 1 tablespoon minced garlic
- 1 tablespoon smoked paprika
- 2 teaspoons onion powder
- 1 teaspoon guar gum
- 1 tablespoon butter
- 1 ½ cup riced cauliflower

Instructions
1. Spread the chicken in a slow cooker, then stir in the remaining ingredients except for the cauliflower and butter.
2. Cover and cook on low heat for 6 hours until the chicken is done and the sauce thickened.
3. Melt the butter in a saucepan over medium-high heat.
4. Add the riced cauliflower and cook for 6 to 8 minutes until tender.
5. Serve the chicken tikka with the cauliflower rice.

GRILLED SALMON AND ZUCCHINI WITH MANGO SAUCE
Nutrition: Cal 485;Fat 32 g; Carb 6,5 g;Protein 43 g
Serving 6; Cook time 6 hours 10 min

Ingredients
- 4 (6-ounce) boneless salmon fillets
- 1 tablespoon olive oil
- Salt and pepper
- 1 large zucchini, sliced in coins
- 2 tablespoons fresh lemon juice
- ½ cup chopped mango
- ¼ cup fresh chopped cilantro
- 1 teaspoon lemon zest
- ½ cup canned coconut milk

Instructions
1. Preheat a grill pan to high heat and spray liberally with cooking spray.
2. Brush the salmon with olive oil and season with salt and pepper.Toss the zucchini with lemon juice and season with salt and pepper.
3. Place the salmon fillets and zucchini on the grill pan.
4. Cook for 5 minutes then turn everything and cook 5 minutes more.
5. Combine the remaining ingredients in a blender and blend into a sauce.
6. Serve the salmon fillets drizzled with the mango sauce and zucchini on the side.

SLOW-COOKER POT ROAST WITH GREEN BEANS
Nutrition: Cal 375;Fat 13.5g; Carb 6 g;Protein 53 g
Serving 8; Cook time 8 hours 10 min

Ingredients
- 4 (6-ounce) boneless salmon fillets
- 1 tablespoon olive oil
- Salt and pepper
- 1 large zucchini, sliced in coins
- 2 tablespoons fresh lemon juice
- ½ cup chopped mango
- ¼ cup fresh chopped cilantro

Instructions
1. Combine the celery and onion in a slow cooker.
2. Place the roast on top and season liberally with salt and pepper.
3. Whisk together the beef broth and Worcestershire sauce then pour it in.
4. Cover and cook on low heat for 8 hours until the beef is very tender.
5. Remove the beef to a cutting board and cut into chunks.
6. Return the beef to the slow cooker and add the beans and chopped butter.
7. Cover and cook on high for 20 to 30 minutes until the beans are tender.

BEEF AND BROCCOLI STIR-FRY
Nutrition: Cal 350;Fat 19.5g; Carb 6,5 g;Protein 37 g
Serving 4; Cook time 35 min

Ingredients
- ¼ cup soy sauce
- 1 tablespoon sesame oil
- 1 teaspoon garlic chili paste
- 1 pound beef sirloin
- 2 tablespoons almond flour
- 2 tablespoons coconut oil
- 2 cups chopped broccoli florets
- 1 tablespoon grated ginger
- 3 cloves garlic, minced

Instructions
1. Whisk together the soy sauce, sesame oil, and chili paste in a small bowl.
2. Slice the beef and toss with almond flour, then place in a plastic freezer bag.
3. Pour in the sauce and toss to coat, then let rest for 20 minutes.
4. Heat the oil in a large skillet over medium-high heat.
5. Pour the beef and sauce into the skillet and cook until the beef is browned.
6. Push the beef to the sides of the skillet and add the broccoli, ginger, and garlic.
7. Sauté until the broccoli is tender-crisp, then toss it all together and serve hot.

PARMESAN-CRUSTED HALIBUT WITH ASPARAGUS
Nutrition: Cal 415;Fat 26 g; Carb 6 g;Protein 42 g
Serving 4; Cook time 25 min

Ingredients
- 1 pound asparagus, trimmed
- 2 tablespoons olive oil
- Salt and pepper
- ¼ cup butter, softened
- ¼ cup grated parmesan
- 2 tablespoons almond flour
- 1 teaspoon garlic powder
- 4 (6-ounce) boneless halibut fillets

Instructions
1. Preheat the oven to 400°F and line a baking sheet with foil.
2. Toss the asparagus with olive oil and spread on the baking sheet.
3. Combine the butter, parmesan cheese, almond flour, garlic powder, salt, and pepper in a blender and blend until smooth.
4. Place the fillets on the baking sheet with the asparagus and spoon the parmesan mixture over the fish.
5. Bake for 10 to 12 minutes, then broil for 2 to 3 minutes until browned.

HEARTY BEEF AND BACON CASSEROLE
Nutrition: Cal 410;Fat 26 g; Carb 8 g;Protein 37 g
Serving 8; Cook time 55 min

Ingredients
- 8 slices uncooked bacon

- 1 medium head cauliflower, chopped
- ¼ cup canned coconut milk
- Salt and pepper
- 2 pounds ground beef (80% lean)
- 8 ounces mushrooms, sliced
- 1 large yellow onion, chopped
- 2 cloves garlic, minced

Instructions

1. Preheat the oven to 375°F.
2. Cook the bacon in a skillet until crisp, then drain on paper towels and chop.
3. Bring a pot of salted water to boil, then add the cauliflower.
4. Boil for 6 to 8 minutes until tender, then drain and add to a food processor with the coconut milk.
5. Blend the mixture until smooth, then season with salt and pepper.
6. Cook the beef in a skillet until browned, then drain the fat.
7. Stir in the mushrooms, onion, and garlic, then transfer to a baking dish.
8. Spread the cauliflower mixture over top and bake for 30 minutes.
9. Broil on high heat for 5 minutes, then sprinkle with bacon to serve.

SESAME WINGS WITH CAULIFLOWER

Nutrition: Cal 400;Fat 28,5 g; Carb 4 g;Protein 31 g
Serving 4; Cook time 35 min

Ingredients

- 2 ½ tablespoons soy sauce
- 2 tablespoons sesame oil
- 1 ½ teaspoons balsamic vinegar
- 1 teaspoon minced garlic
- 1 teaspoon grated ginger
- Salt
- 1 pound chicken wing, the wings itself
- 2 cups cauliflower florets

Instructions

1. Combine the soy sauce, sesame oil, balsamic vinegar, garlic, ginger, and salt in a freezer bag, then add the chicken wings.
2. Toss to coat, then chill for 2 to 3 hours.
3. Preheat the oven to 400°F and line a baking sheet with foil.
4. Spread the wings on the baking sheet along with the cauliflower.
5. Bake for 35 minutes, then sprinkle with sesame seeds to serve.

FRIED COCONUT SHRIMP WITH ASPARAGUS

Nutrition: Cal 535;Fat 38,5 g; Carb 18 g;Protein 31 g
Serving 6; Cook time 25 min

Ingredients

- 1 ½ cups shredded unsweetened coconut
- 2 large eggs
- Salt and pepper
- 1 ½ pounds large shrimp, peeled and deveined
- ½ cup canned coconut milk
- 1 pound asparagus, cut into 2-inch pieces

Instructions

1. Pour the coconut into a shallow dish.
2. Beat the eggs with some salt and pepper in a bowl.
3. Dip the shrimp first in the egg, then dredge with coconut.
4. Heat the coconut oil in a large skillet over medium-high heat.
5. Add the shrimp and fry for 1 to 2 minutes on each side until browned.
6. Remove the shrimp to paper towels and reheat the skillet.
7. Add the asparagus and season with salt and pepper – sauté until tender-crisp, then serve with the shrimp

COCONUT CHICKEN CURRY WITH CAULI-FLOWER RICE

Nutrition: Cal 430;Fat 29 g; Carb 9 g;Protein 33,5 g
Serving 6; Cook time 45 min

Ingredients

- 1 tablespoon olive oil
- 1 medium yellow onion, chopped
- 1 ½ pounds boneless chicken thighs, chopped
- Salt and pepper
- 1 (14-ounce) can coconut milk
- 1 tablespoon curry powder
- 1 ¼ teaspoon ground turmeric
- 3 cups riced cauliflower

Instructions

1. Heat the oil in a large skillet over medium heat.
2. Add the onions and cook until translucent, about 5 minutes.
3. Stir in the chicken and season with salt and pepper – cook for 6 to 8 minutes, stirring often, until browned on all sides.
4. Pour the coconut milk into the skillet, then stir in the curry powder and turmeric.
5. Simmer for 15 to 20 minutes until hot and bubbling.
6. Meanwhile, steam the cauliflower rice with a few tablespoons of water until tender.
7. Serve the curry over the cauliflower rice.

SPICY CHICKEN ENCHILADA CASSEROLE

Nutrition: Cal 550;Fat 31 g; Carb 12 g;Protein 54 g
Serving 6; Cook time 1 hour 15 min

Ingredients

- 2 pounds boneless chicken thighs, chopped
- Salt and pepper
- 3 cups tomato salsa
- 1 ½ cups shredded cheddar cheese
- ¾ cup sour cream
- 1 cup diced avocado

Instructions

1. Preheat the oven to 375°F and grease a casserole dish.
2. Season the chicken with salt and pepper then spread into the dish.
3. Spread the salsa over the chicken and sprinkle with cheese.
4. Cover with foil, then bake for 60 minutes until the chicken is done.
5. Serve with sour cream and chopped avocado.

WHITE CHEDDAR BROCCOLI CHICKEN CASSE-ROLE

Nutrition: Cal 435;Fat 32 g; Carb 6 g;Protein 29 g
Serving 6; Cook time 45 min

Ingredients

- 2 tablespoons olive oil
- 1 pound boneless chicken thighs, chopped
- 1 medium yellow onion, chopped
- 1 clove garlic, minced
- 1 ½ cups chicken broth
- 8 ounces cream cheese, softened
- ¼ cup sour cream
- 2 ½ cups broccoli florets
- ¾ cup shredded white cheddar cheese

Instructions

1. Preheat the oven to 350°F and grease a casserole dish.
2. Heat the oil in a large skillet over medium-high heat.
3. Add the chicken and cook for 2 to 3 minutes on each side to brown.
4. Stir in the onion and garlic, and season with salt and pepper.
5. Sauté for 4 to 5 minutes until the chicken is cooked through.
6. Pour in the chicken broth, then add the cream cheese and sour cream.
7. Simmer until the cream cheese is melted, then stir in the broccoli.
8. Spread the mixture in the casserole dish and sprinkle with cheese.
9. Bake for 25 to 30 minutes until hot and bubbling

SAUSAGE STUFFED BELL PEPPERS

Nutrition: Cal 355;Fat 23,5 g; Carb 16,5 g;Protein 19 g
Serving 4; Cook time 55 min

Ingredients

- 1 medium head cauliflower, chopped
- 1 tablespoon olive oil

- 12 ounces ground Italian sausage
- 1 small yellow onion, chopped
- 1 teaspoon dried oregano
- Salt and pepper
- 4 medium bell peppers

Instructions
1. Preheat the oven to 350°F.
2. Pulse the cauliflower in a food processor into rice-like grains.
3. Heat the oil in a skillet over medium heat then add the cauliflower – cook for 6 to 8 minutes until tender.
4. Spoon the cauliflower rice into a bowl, then reheat the skillet.
5. Add the sausage and cook until browned, then drain the fat.
6. Stir the sausage into the cauliflower, then add the onion, oregano, salt and pepper.
7. Slice the tops off the peppers, remove the seeds and pith, then spoon the sausage mixture into them.
8. Place the peppers upright in a baking dish, then cover the dish with foil.
9. Bake for 30 minutes, then uncover and bake 15 minutes more. Serve hot.

CHEDDAR, SAUSAGE, AND MUSHROOM CAS-SEROLE
Nutrition: Cal 450;Fat 34 g; Carb 6 g;Protein 28 g
Serving 6; Cook time 45 min

Ingredients
- 1 pound ground Italian sausage
- 8 ounces mushrooms, diced
- 1 large yellow onion, chopped
- 1 cup shredded cheddar cheese
- 8 large eggs
- ½ cup heavy cream
- Salt and pepper

Instructions
1. Preheat the oven to 375°F and grease a baking dish.
2. Heat the sausage in a large skillet over medium-high heat.
3. Cook the sausage until browned then stir in the mushrooms and onions.
4. Cook for 4 to 5 minutes then spread in the baking dish.
5. Sprinkle the dish with cheese then whisk together the remaining ingredients in a separate bowl.
6. Pour the mixture into the dish then bake for 35 minutes until bubbling.

CAULIFLOWER CRUST MEAT LOVER'S PIZZA
Nutrition: Cal 560;Fat 40 g; Carb 11 g;Protein 41 g
Serving 2; Cook time 40 min

Ingredients
- 1 tablespoon butter
- 2 cups riced cauliflower
- Salt and pepper
- 1 ½ cups shredded mozzarella cheese, divided into 1 cup and ½ cup
- 1 cup fresh grated parmesan
- 1 teaspoon garlic powder
- 1 large egg white
- 1 teaspoon dried Italian seasoning
- ¼ cup low-carb tomato sauce
- 2 ounces sliced pepperoni
- 1 ounce diced ham
- 2 slices bacon, cooked and crumbled

Instructions
1. Preheat the oven to 400°F and line a baking sheet with parchment.
2. Heat the butter in a skillet over medium-high heat and add the cauliflower.
3. Season with salt and pepper, then cover and cook for 15 minutes, stirring occasionally, until very tender.
4. Spoon the cauliflower into a bowl and stir in ½ cup mozzarella along with the parmesan and garlic powder.

5. Stir in the egg white and Italian seasoning, then pour onto the baking sheet.
6. Shape the dough into a circle about ½-inch thick, then bake for 15 minutes.
7. Top with tomato sauce, along with the remaining mozzarella and the pepperoni, bacon, and ham.
8. Broil until the cheese is browned, then slice to serve.

SLOW COOKER BEEF BOURGUIGNON
Nutrition: Cal 335;Fat 12,5 g; Carb 6,5 g;Protein 37.5 g
Serving 8; Cook time 4 hours 55 min

Ingredients
- 2 tablespoons olive oil
- 2 pounds boneless beef chuck roast, cut into chunks
- Salt and pepper
- ¼ cup almond flour
- ½ cup beef broth
- 2 cups red wine (dry)
- 2 tablespoons tomato paste
- 1 pound mushrooms, sliced
- 1 large yellow onion, cut into chunks

Instructions
1. Heat the oil in a large skillet over medium-high heat.
2. Season the beef with salt and pepper, then toss with almond flour.
3. Add the beef to the skillet and cook until browned on all sides then transfer to a slow cooker.
4. Reheat the skillet over medium-high heat, then pour in the broth.
5. Scrape up the browned bits, then whisk in the wine and tomato paste.
6. Bring to a boil, then pour into the slow cooker.
7. Add the mushrooms and onion, then stir everything together.
8. Cover and cook on low heat for 4 hours until the meat is very tender. Serve hot.

PEPPER GRILLED RIBEYE WITH ASPARAGUS
Nutrition: Cal 380;Fat 25 g; Carb 4,5 g;Protein 35 g
Serving 4; Cook time 20 min

Ingredients
- 1 pound asparagus, trimmed
- 2 tablespoons olive oil
- Salt and pepper
- 1 pound ribeye steak
- 1 tablespoon coconut oil

Instructions
1. Preheat the oven to 400°F and line a small baking sheet with foil.
2. Toss the asparagus with olive oil and spread on the baking sheet.
3. Season with salt and pepper then place in the oven.
4. Rub the steak with the pepper and season with salt.
5. Melt the coconut oil in a cast-iron skillet and heat over high heat.
6. Add the steak and cook for 2 minutes then turn it.
7. Transfer the skillet to the oven and cook for 5 minutes or until the steak is done to the desired level.
8. Slice the steak and serve with the roasted asparagus.

BACON-WRAPPED PORK TENDERLOIN WITH CAULIFLOWER
Nutrition: Cal 330;Fat 18,5 g; Carb 3 g;Protein 38 g
Serving 4; Cook time 35 min

Ingredients
- 1 ¼ pounds boneless pork tenderloin
- Salt and pepper
- 8 slices uncooked bacon
- 1 tablespoon olive oil
- 2 cups cauliflower florets

Instructions
1. Preheat the oven to 425°F and season the pork with salt and pepper.
2. Wrap the pork in bacon and place on a foil-lined roasting pan.
3. Roast for 25 minutes until the internal temperature reaches 155°F.
4. Meanwhile, heat the oil in a skillet over medium heat.

5. Add the cauliflower and sauté until tender-crisp – about 8 to 10 minutes.
6. Turn on the broiler and place the pork under it to crisp the bacon.
7. Slice the pork to serve with the sautéed cauliflower

STEAK KEBABS WITH PEPPERS AND ONIONS
Nutrition: Cal 350;Fat 20 g; Carb 6,5 g;Protein 35 g
Serving 4; Cook time 40 min

Ingredients
- 1 pound beef sirloin, cut into 1-inch cubes
- ¼ cup olive oil
- 2 tablespoons balsamic vinegar
- Salt and pepper
- 1 medium yellow onion, cut into chunks
- 1 medium red pepper, cut into chunks
- 1 medium green pepper, cut into chunks

Instructions
1. Toss the steak cubes with the olive oil, balsamic vinegar, salt, and pepper.
2. Slide the cubes onto skewers with the peppers and onions.
3. Preheat a grill to high heat and oil the grates.
4. Grill the kebabs for 2 to 3 minutes on each side until done to your liking.

SEARED LAMB CHOPS WITH ASPARAGUS
Nutrition: Cal 380;Fat 18.5 g; Carb 4,5 g;Protein 48 g
Serving 4; Cook time 20 min

Ingredients
- 8 bone-in lamb chops
- Salt and pepper
- 1 tablespoon fresh chopped rosemary
- 1 tablespoon olive oil
- 1 tablespoon butter
- 16 spears asparagus, cut into 2-inch chunks

Instructions
1. Season the lamb with salt and pepper then sprinkle with rosemary.
2. Heat the oil in a large skillet over medium-high heat.
3. Add the lamb chops and cook for 2 to 3 minutes on each side until seared.
4. Remove the lamb chops to rest and reheat the skillet with the butter.
5. Add the asparagus and turn to coat then cover the skillet.
6. Cook for 4 to 6 minutes until tender-crisp and serve with the lamb.

LEMON CHICKEN KEBABS WITH VEGGIES
Nutrition: Cal 360;Fat 21,5 g; Carb 8 g;Protein 34 g
Serving 4; Cook time 25 min

Ingredients
- 1 pound boneless chicken thighs, cut into cubes
- ¼ cup olive oil
- 2 tablespoons lemon juice
- 1 teaspoon minced garlic
- Salt and pepper
- 1 large yellow onion, cut into 2-inch chunks
- 1 large red pepper, cut into 2-inch chunks
- 1 large green pepper, cut into 2-inch chunks

Instructions
1. Toss the chicken with the olive oil, lemon juice, garlic, salt, and pepper.
2. Slide the chicken onto skewers with the onion and peppers.
3. Preheat a grill to medium-high heat and oil the grates.
4. Grill the skewers for 2 to 3 minutes on each side until the chicken is done.

BALSAMIC SALMON WITH GREEN BEANS
Nutrition: Cal 320;Fat 18 g; Carb 6 g;Protein 35 g
Serving 4; Cook time 25 min

Ingredients

- ½ cup balsamic vinegar
- ¼ cup chicken broth
- 1 tablespoon Dijon mustard
- 2 cloves garlic, minced
- 2 tablespoons coconut oil
- 4 (6-ounce) salmon fillets
- Salt and pepper
- 2 cups trimmed green beans

Instructions
1. Combine the balsamic vinegar, chicken broth, mustard, and garlic in a small saucepan over medium-high heat.
2. Bring to a boil then reduce heat and simmer for 15 minutes to reduce by half.
3. Heat the coconut oil in a large skillet over medium-high heat.
4. Season the salmon with salt and pepper then add to the skillet.
5. Cook for 4 minutes until seared, then flip and add the green beans.
6. Pour the glaze into the skillet and simmer for 2 to 3 minutes until done.

SHRIMP AND SAUSAGE "BAKE"
Nutrition: Cal 323;Fat 24 g; Carb 8 g;Protein 20 g
Serving 4; Cook time 35 min

Ingredients
- 2 tablespoons olive oil
- 6 ounces chorizo sausage, diced
- ½ pound (16 to 20 count) shrimp, peeled and deveined
- 1 red bell pepper, chopped
- ½ small sweet onion, chopped
- 2 teaspoons minced garlic
- ¼ cup chicken stock
- Pinch red pepper flakes

Instructions
1. Place a large skillet over medium-high heat and add the olive oil.
2. Sauté the sausage until it is warmed through, about 6 minutes.
3. Add the shrimp and sauté until it is opaque and just cooked through, about 4 minutes.
4. Remove the sausage and shrimp to a bowl and set aside.
5. Add the red pepper, onion, and garlic to the skillet and sauté until tender, about 4 minutes.
6. Add the chicken stock to the skillet along with the cooked sausage and shrimp.
7. Bring the liquid to a simmer and simmer for 3 minutes.
8. Stir in the red pepper flakes and serve.

HERB BUTTER SCALLOPS
Nutrition: Cal 306;Fat 24 g; Carb 4,5 g;Protein 20 g
Serving 4; Cook time 20 min

Ingredients
- 1 pound sea scallops, cleaned
- Freshly ground black pepper
- 8 tablespoons butter, divided
- 2 teaspoons minced garlic
- Juice of 1 lemon
- 2 teaspoons chopped fresh basil
- 1 teaspoon chopped fresh thyme

Instructions
1. Pat the scallops dry with paper towels and season them lightly with pepper.
2. Place a large skillet over medium heat and add 2 tablespoons of buter.
3. Arrange the scallops in the skillet, evenly spaced but not too close together, and sear each side until they are golden brown, about 2½ minutes per side.
4. Remove the scallops to a plate and set aside.
5. Add the remaining 6 tablespoons of buter to the skillet and sauté the garlic until translucent, about 3 minutes.
6. Stir in the lemon juice, basil, and thyme and return the scallops to the skillet, turning to coat them in the sauce.
7. Serve immediately

PAN-SEARED HALIBUT WITH CITRUS BUTTER SAUCE

Nutrition: Cal 320;Fat 26 g; Carb 2 g;Protein 22 g
Serving 4; Cook time 25 min

Ingredients
- 4 (5-ounce) halibut fillets, each about 1 inch thick
- Sea salt
- Freshly ground black pepper
- ¼ cup butter
- 2 teaspoons minced garlic
- 1 shallot, minced
- 3 tablespoons dry white wine
- 1 tablespoon freshly squeezed lemon juice
- 1 tablespoon freshly squeezed orange juice
- 2 teaspoons chopped fresh parsley
- 2 tablespoons olive oil

Instructions
1. Pat the fish dry with paper towels and then lightly season the fillets with salt and pepper. Set aside on a paper towel–lined plate.
2. Place a small saucepan over medium heat and melt the buter.
3. Sauté the garlic and shallot until tender, about 3 minutes.
4. Whisk in the white wine, lemon juice, and orange juice and bring the sauce to a simmer, cooking until it thickens slightly, about 2 minutes.
5. Remove the sauce from the heat and stir in the parsley; set aside.
6. Place a large skillet over medium-high heat and add the olive oil.
7. Panfry the fish until lightly browned and just cooked through, turning them over once, about 10 minutes in total.
8. Serve the fish immediately with a spoonful of sauce for each.

FISH CURRY

Nutrition: Cal 416;Fat 31 g; Carb 5 g;Protein 26 g
Serving 4; Cook time 35 min

Ingredients
- 2 tablespoons coconut oil
- 1&½ tablespoons grated fresh ginger
- 2 teaspoons minced garlic
- 1 tablespoon curry powder
- ½ teaspoon ground cumin
- 2 cups coconut milk
- 16 ounces firm white fish, cut into 1-inch chunks
- 1 cup shredded kale
- 2 tablespoons chopped cilantro

Instructions
1. Place a large saucepan over medium heat and melt the coconut oil.
2. Sauté the ginger and garlic until lightly browned, about 2 minutes.
3. Stir in the curry powder and cumin and sauté until very fragrant,
4. about 2 minutes.
5. Stir in the coconut milk and bring the liquid to a boil.
6. Reduce the heat to low and simmer for about 5 minutes to infuse the milk with the spices.
7. Add the fish and cook until the fish is cooked through, about 10 minutes.
8. Stir in the kale and cilantro and simmer until wilted, about 2 minutes.

ROASTED SALMON WITH AVOCADO SALSA

Nutrition: Cal 320;Fat 26 g; Carb 2 g;Protein 22 g
Serving 4; Cook time 25 min

Ingredients
FOR THE SALSA
- 1 avocado, peeled, pitted,
- and diced
- 1 scallion, white and green parts,
- chopped
- ½ cup halved cherry tomatoes
- Juice of 1 lemon
- Zest of 1 lemon

FOR THE FISH
- 1 teaspoon ground cumin
- ½ teaspoon ground coriander
- ½ teaspoon onion powder
- ¼ teaspoon sea salt
- Pinch freshly ground black pepper
- Pinch cayenne pepper
- 4 (4-ounce) boneless, skinless
- salmon fillets
- 2 tablespoons olive oil

Instructions
TO MAKE THE SALSA
1. In a small bowl, stir together the avocado, scallion, tomatoes, lemon juice, and lemon zest until mixed.
2. Set aside.

TO MAKE THE FISH
1. Preheat the oven to 400°F. Line a baking sheet with aluminum foil and set aside.
2. In a small bowl, stir together the cumin, coriander, onion powder, salt, black pepper, and cayenne until well mixed.
3. Rub the salmon fillets with the spice mix and place them on the baking sheet.
4. Drizzle the fillets with the olive oil and roast the fish until it is just cooked through, about 15 minutes.
5. Serve the salmon topped with the avocado salsa

SOLE ASIAGO

Nutrition: Cal 300;Fat 24 g; Carb 4 g;Protein 20 g
Serving 4; Cook time 20 min

Ingredients
- 4 (4-ounce) sole fillets
- ¾ cup ground almonds
- ¼ cup Asiago cheese
- 2 eggs, beaten
- 2&½ tablespoons melted coconut oil

Instructions
1. Preheat the oven to 350°F. Line a baking sheet with parchment paper and set aside.
2. Pat the fish dry with paper towels.
3. Stir together the ground almonds and cheese in a small bowl.
4. Place the bowl with the beaten eggs in it next to the almond mixture.
5. Dredge a sole fillet in the beaten egg and then press the fish into the almond mixture so it is completely coated. Place on the baking sheet and repeat until all the fillets are breaded.
6. Brush both sides of each piece of fish with the coconut oil.
7. Bake the sole until it is cooked through, about 8 minutes in total.
8. Serve immediately

BAKED COCONUT HADDOCK

Nutrition: Cal 406;Fat 31 g; Carb 6 g;Protein 29 g
Serving 4; Cook time 22 min

Ingredients
- 4 (5-ounce) boneless haddock fillets
- Sea salt
- Freshly ground black pepper
- 1 cup shredded unsweetened coconut
- ¼ cup ground hazelnuts
- 2 tablespoons coconut oil, melted

Instructions
1. Preheat the oven to 400°F. Line a baking sheet with parchment paper and set aside.
2. Pat the fillets very dry with paper towels and lightly season them with salt and pepper.
3. Stir together the shredded coconut and hazelnuts in a small bowl.
4. Dredge the fish fillets in the coconut mixture so that both sides of each piece are thickly coated.
5. Place the fish on the baking sheet and lightly brush both sides of each piece with the coconut oil.
6. Bake the haddock until the topping is golden and the fish flakes easily with a fork, about 12 minutes total.

CHEESY GARLIC SALMON

Nutrition: Cal 356;Fat 28 g; Carb 2 g;Protein 24 g
Serving 4; Cook time 30 min

Ingredients
- ½ cup Asiago cheese
- 2 tablespoons freshly squeezed
- lemon juice
- 2 tablespoons butter, at room
- temperature
- 2 teaspoons minced garlic
- 1 teaspoon chopped fresh basil
- 1 teaspoon chopped fresh oregano
- 4 (5-ounce) salmon fillets
- 1 tablespoon olive oil

Instructions
1. Preheat the oven to 350°F. Line a baking sheet with parchment paper and set aside.
2. In a small bowl, stir together the Asiago cheese, lemon juice, buter, garlic, basil, and oregano.
3. Pat the salmon dry with paper towels and place the fillets on the baking sheet skin-side down. Divide the topping evenly between the fillets and spread it across the fish using a knife or the back of a spoon.
4. Drizzle the fish with the olive oil and bake until the topping is golden and the fish is just cooked through, about 12 minutes.

LEMON BUTTER CHICKEN

Nutrition: Cal 300;Fat 26 g; Carb 4 g;Protein 12 g
Serving 4; Cook time 50 min

Ingredients
- 4 bone-in, skin-on chicken thighs
- Sea salt
- Freshly ground black pepper
- 2 tablespoons butter, divided
- 2 teaspoons minced garlic
- ½ cup chicken stock
- ½ cup heavy (whipping) cream
- Juice of ½ lemon

Instructions
1. Preheat the oven to 400°F.
2. Lightly season the chicken thighs with salt and pepper.
3. Place a large ovenproof skillet over medium-high heat and add 1 tablespoon of buter.
4. Brown the chicken thighs until golden on both sides, about 6 minutes in total. Remove the thighs to a plate and set aside.
5. Add the remaining 1 tablespoon of buter and sauté the garlic until translucent, about 2 minutes.
6. Whisk in the chicken stock, heavy cream, and lemon juice.
7. Bring the sauce to a boil and then return the chicken to the skillet.
8. Place the skillet in the oven, covered, and braise until the chicken is cooked through, about 30 minutes

CHICKEN BACON BURGERS

Nutrition: Cal 375;Fat 33 g; Carb 3 g;Protein 18 g
Serving 6; Cook time 25 min

Ingredients
- 1 pound ground chicken
- 8 bacon slices, chopped
- ¼ cup ground almonds
- 1 teaspoon chopped fresh basil
- ¼ teaspoon sea salt
- Pinch freshly ground black pepper
- 2 tablespoons coconut oil
- 4 large lettuce leaves
- 1 avocado, peeled, pitted, and sliced

Instructions
1. Preheat the oven to 350°F. Line a baking sheet with parchment paper and set aside.
2. In a medium bowl, combine the chicken, bacon, ground almonds, basil, salt, and pepper until well mixed.

3. Form the mixture into 6 equal paties.
4. Place a large skillet over medium-high heat and add the coconut oil.
5. Pan sear the chicken paties until brown on both sides, about 6 minutes in total.
6. Place the browned paties on the baking sheet and bake until completely cooked through, about 15 minutes.
7. Serve on the letuce leaves, topped with the avocado slices.

PAPRIKA CHICKEN

Nutrition: Cal 390;Fat 30 g; Carb 4 g;Protein 25 g
Serving 4; Cook time 35 min

Ingredients
- 4 (4-ounce) chicken breasts, skin-on
- Sea salt
- Freshly ground black pepper
- 1 tablespoon olive oil
- ½ cup chopped sweet onion
- ½ cup heavy (whipping) cream
- 2 teaspoons smoked paprika
- ½ cup sour cream
- 2 tablespoons chopped fresh Parsley

Instructions
1. Lightly season the chicken with salt and pepper.
2. Place a large skillet over medium-high heat and add the olive oil.
3. Sear the chicken on both sides until almost cooked through, about 15 minutes in total. Remove the chicken to a plate.
4. Add the onion to the skillet and sauté until tender, about 4 minutes.
5. Stir in the cream and paprika and bring the liquid to a simmer.
6. Return the chicken and any accumulated juices to the skillet and simmer the chicken for 5 minutes until completely cooked.
7. Stir in the sour cream and remove the skillet from the heat.
8. Serve topped with the parsley

STUFFED CHICKEN BREASTS

Nutrition: Cal 390;Fat 30 g; Carb 3 g;Protein 25 g
Serving 4; Cook time 30 min

Ingredients
- 1 tablespoon butter
- ¼ cup chopped sweet onion
- ½ cup goat cheese, at room temperature
- ¼ cup Kalamata olives, chopped
- ¼ cup chopped roasted red pepper
- 2 tablespoons chopped fresh basil
- 4 (5-ounce) chicken breasts, skin-on
- 2 tablespoons extra-virgin olive oil

Instructions
1. Preheat the oven to 400°F.
2. In a small skillet over medium heat, melt the buter and add the onion. Sauté until tender, about 3 minutes.
3. Transfer the onion to a medium bowl and add the cheese, olives, red pepper, and basil. Stir until well blended, then refrigerate for about 30 minutes.
4. Cut horizontal pockets into each chicken breast, and stuf them evenly with the filling. Secure the two sides of each breast with toothpicks.
5. Place a large ovenproof skillet over medium-high heat and add the olive oil.
6. Brown the chicken on both sides, about 10 minutes in total.
7. Place the skillet in the oven and roast until the chicken is just cooked through, about 15 minutes. Remove the toothpicks and serve.

TURKEY MEATLOAF

Nutrition: Cal 216;Fat 20 g; Carb 1 g;Protein 15 g
Serving 6; Cook time 35 min

Ingredients
- 1 tablespoon olive oil
- ½ sweet onion, chopped
- 1&½ pounds ground turkey
- ⅓ cup heavy (whipping) cream

- ¼ cup freshly grated Parmesan cheese
- 1 tablespoon chopped fresh parsley
- Pinch sea salt
- Pinch freshly ground black pepper

Instructions

1. Heat the oven to 450°F.
2. Place a small skillet over medium heat and add the olive oil.
3. Sauté the onion until it is tender, about 4 minutes.
4. Transfer the onion to a large bowl and add the turkey, heavy cream,
5. Parmesan cheese, parsley, salt, and pepper.
6. Stir until the ingredients are combined and hold together. Press the mixture into a loaf pan.
7. Bake until cooked through, about 30 minutes.
8. Let the meatloaf rest for 10 minutes and serve.

TURKEY RISSOLES

Nutrition: Cal 440;Fat 34 g; Carb 7 g;Protein 27 g
Serving 4; Cook time 35 min

Ingredients

- 1 pound ground turkey
- 1 scallion, white and green parts,
- finely chopped
- 1 teaspoon minced garlic
- Pinch sea salt
- Pinch freshly ground black pepper
- 1 cup ground almonds
- 2 tablespoons olive oil

Instructions

1. Preheat the oven to 350°F. Line a baking sheet with aluminum foil and set aside.
2. In a medium bowl, mix together the turkey, scallion, garlic, salt, and pepper until well combined.
3. Shape the turkey mixture into 8 paties and flaten them out.
4. Place the ground almonds in a shallow bowl and dredge the turkey paties in the ground almonds to coat.
5. Place a large skillet over medium heat and add the olive oil.
6. Brown the turkey paties on both sides, about 10 minutes in total.
7. Transfer the paties to the baking sheet and bake them until cooked through, flipping them once, about 15 minutes in total.

ROASTED PORK LOIN WITH GRAINY MUSTARD SAUCE

Nutrition: Cal 368;Fat 29 g; Carb 2 g;Protein 25 g
Serving 8; Cook time 80 min

Ingredients

- 1 (2-pound) boneless pork loin roast
- Sea salt
- Freshly ground black pepper
- 3 tablespoons olive oil
- 1&½ cups heavy (whipping) cream
- 3 tablespoons grainy mustard, such as Pommery

Instructions

1. Preheat the oven to 375°F.
2. Season the pork roast all over with sea salt and pepper.
3. Place a large skillet over medium-high heat and add the olive oil.
4. Brown the roast on all sides in the skillet, about 6 minutes in total, and place the roast in a baking dish.
5. Roast until a meat thermometer inserted in the thickest part of the roast reads 155°F, about 1 hour.
6. When there is approximately 15 minutes of roasting time lef, place a small saucepan over medium heat and add the heavy cream and mustard.
7. Stir the sauce until it simmers, then reduce the heat to low. Simmer the sauce until it is very rich and thick, about 5 minutes. Remove the pan from the heat and set aside.
8. Let the pork rest for 10 minutes before slicing and serve with the sauce

LAMB CHOPS WITH KALAMATA TAPENADE

Nutrition: Cal 348;Fat 28 g; Carb 2 g;Protein 21 g
Serving 4; Cook time 40 min

Ingredients

FOR THE TAPENADE

- 1 cup pitted Kalamata olives
- 2 tablespoons chopped
- fresh parsley
- 2 tablespoons extra-virgin
- olive oil
- 2 teaspoons minced garlic
- 2 teaspoons freshly squeezed
- lemon juice

FOR THE LAMB CHOPS

- 2 (1-pound) racks French-cut
- lamb chops (8 bones each)
- Sea salt
- Freshly ground black pepper
- 1 tablespoon olive oil

Instructions

TO MAKE THE TAPENADE

1. Place the olives, parsley, olive oil, garlic, and lemon juice in a food processor and process until the mixture is puréed but still slightly chunky.
2. Transfer the tapenade to a container and store sealed in the refrigerator until needed.

TO MAKE THE LAMB CHOPS

1. Preheat the oven to 450°F.
2. Season the lamb racks with salt and pepper.
3. Place a large ovenproof skillet over medium-high heat and add the olive oil.
4. Pan sear the lamb racks on all sides until browned, about 5 minutes in total.
5. Arrange the racks upright in the skillet, with the bones interlaced, and roast them in the oven until they reach your desired doneness, about 20 minutes for medium-rare or until the internal temperature reaches 125°F.
6. Let the lamb rest for 10 minutes and then cut the lamb racks into chops. Arrange 4 chops per person on the plate and top with the Kalamata tapenade

ROSEMARY-GARLIC LAMB RACKS

Nutrition: Cal 354;Fat 30 g; Carb 1 g;Protein 21 g
Serving 4; Cook time 1 hours 35 min

Ingredients

- 4 tablespoons extra-virgin olive oil
- 2 tablespoons finely chopped
- fresh rosemary
- 2 teaspoons minced garlic
- Pinch sea salt
- 2 (1-pound) racks French-cut
- lamb chops (8 bones each)

Instructions

1. In a small bowl, whisk together the olive oil, rosemary, garlic, and salt.
2. Place the racks in a sealable freezer bag and pour the olive oil mixture into the bag. Massage the meat through the bag so it is coated with the marinade. Press the air out of the bag and seal it.
3. Marinate the lamb racks in the refrigerator for 1 to 2 hours.
4. Preheat the oven to 450°F.
5. Place a large ovenproof skillet over medium-high heat. Take the lamb racks out of the bag and sear them in the skillet on all sides, about 5 minutes in total.
6. Arrange the racks upright in the skillet, with the bones interlaced, and roast them in the oven until they reach your desired doneness, about 20 minutes for medium-rare or until the internal temperature reaches 125°F.
7. Let the lamb rest for 10 minutes and then cut the racks into chops.
8. Serve 4 chops per person.

LAMB LEG WITH SUN-DRIED TOMATO PESTO

Nutrition: Cal 352;Fat 29 g; Carb 5 g;Protein 17 g
Serving 8; Cook time 85 min

Ingredients
FOR THE PESTO
- 1 cup sun-dried tomatoes packed
- in oil, drained
- ¼ cup pine nuts
- 2 tablespoons extra-virgin olive oil
- 2 tablespoons chopped fresh basil
- 2 tcaspoons minced garlic

FOR THE LAMB LEG
- 1 (2-pound) lamb leg
- Sea salt
- Freshly ground black pepper
- 2 tablespoons olive oil

Instructions
TO MAKE THE PESTO
1. Place the sun-dried tomatoes, pine nuts, olive oil, basil, and garlic in a blender or food processor; process until smooth.
2. Set aside until needed.

TO MAKE THE LAMB LEG
1. Preheat the oven to 400°F.
2. Season the lamb leg all over with salt and pepper.
3. Place a large ovenproof skillet over medium-high heat and add the olive oil.
4. Sear the lamb on all sides until nicely browned, about 6 minutes in total.
5. Spread the sun-dried tomato pesto all over the lamb and place the lamb on a baking sheet. Roast until the meat reaches your desired doneness, about 1 hour for medium.
6. Let the lamb rest for 10 minutes before slicing and serving.

SIRLOIN WITH BLUE CHEESE COMPOUND BUTTER

Nutrition: Cal 544;Fat 44 g; Carb 1 g;Protein 35 g
Serving 4; Cook time 1 hours 22 min

Ingredients
- 6 tablespoons butter, at room
- temperature
- 4 ounces blue cheese, such
- as Stilton or Roquefort
- 4 (5-ounce) beef sirloin steaks
- 1 tablespoon olive oil
- Sea salt
- Freshly ground black pepper

Instructions
1. Place the buter in a blender and pulse until the buter is whipped, about 2 minutes.
2. Add the cheese and pulse until just incorporated.
3. Spoon the buter mixture onto a sheet of plastic wrap and roll it into a log about 1½ inches in diameter by twisting both ends of the plastic wrap in opposite directions.
4. Refrigerate the buter until completely set, about 1 hour.
5. Slice the buter into ½-inch disks and set them on aplate in the refrigerator until you are ready to serve the steaks. Store lefover buter in the refrigerator for up to 1 week.
6. Preheat a barbecue to medium-high heat.
7. Let the steaks come to room temperature.
8. Rub the steaks all over with the olive oil and season them with salt and pepper.
9. Grill the steaks until they reach your desired doneness, about 6 minutes per side for medium.
10. If you do not have a barbecue, broil the steaks in a preheated oven for 7 minutes per side for medium.
11. Let the steaks rest for 10 minutes. Serve each topped with a disk of the compound buter.

GARLIC-BRAISED SHORT RIBS

Nutrition: Cal 481;Fat 38 g; Carb 5 g;Protein 29 g
Serving 4; Cook time 2 hours 30 min

Ingredients
- 4 (4-ounce) beef short ribs
- Sea salt
- Freshly ground black pepper
- 1 tablespoon olive oil
- 2 teaspoons minced garlic
- ½ cup dry red wine
- 3 cups Beef Stock

Instructions
1. Preheat the oven to 325°F.
2. Season the beef ribs on all sides with salt and pepper.
3. Place a deep ovenproof skillet over medium-high heat and add the olive oil.
4. Sear the ribs on all sides until browned, about 6 minutes in total. Transfer the ribs to a plate.
5. Add the garlic to the skillet and sauté until translucent, about 3 minutes.
6. Whisk in the red wine to deglaze the pan. Be sure to scrape all the browned bits from the meat from the botom of the pan. Simmer the wine until it is slightly reduced, about 2 minutes.
7. Add the beef stock, ribs, and any accumulated juices on the plate back to the skillet and bring the liquid to a boil.
8. Cover the skillet and place it in the oven to braise the ribs until the meat is fall-of-the-bone tender, about 2 hours.
9. Serve the ribs with a spoonful of the cooking liquid drizzled over each serving.

BACON-WRAPPED BEEF TENDERLOIN

Nutrition: Cal 565;Fat 49 g; Carb 2g;Protein 28 g
Serving 4; Cook time 25 min

Ingredients
- 4 (4-ounce) beef tenderloin steaks
- Sea salt
- Freshly ground black pepper
- 8 bacon slices
- 1 tablespoon extra-virgin olive oil

Instructions
1. Preheat the oven to 450°F.
2. Season the steaks with salt and pepper.
3. Wrap each steak snugly around the edges with 2 slices of bacon and secure the bacon with toothpicks.
4. Place a large skillet over medium-high heat and add the olive oil.
5. Pan sear the steaks for 4 minutes per side and transfer them to a baking sheet.
6. Roast the steaks until they reach your desired doneness, about 6 minutes for medium.
7. Remove the steaks from the oven and let them rest for 10 minutes.
8. Remove the toothpicks and serve.

CHEESEBURGER CASSEROLE

Nutrition: Cal 410;Fat 33 g; Carb 3g;Protein 20 g
Serving 6; Cook time 40 min

Ingredients
- 1 pound 75% lean ground beef
- ½ cup chopped sweet onion
- 2 teaspoons minced garlic
- 1&½ cups shredded aged Cheddar, divided
- ½ cup heavy (whipping) cream
- 1 large tomato, chopped
- 1 teaspoon minced fresh basil
- ¼ teaspoon sea salt
- ⅛ teaspoon freshly ground black pepper

Instructions
1. Preheat the oven to 350°F.
2. Place a large skillet over medium-high heat and add the ground beef.

3. Brown the beef until cooked through, about 6 minutes, and spoon of any excess fat.
4. Stir in the onion and garlic and cook until the vegetables are tender, about 4 minutes.
5. Transfer the beef and vegetables to an 8-by-8-inch casserole dish.
6. In medium bowl, stir together 1 cup of shredded cheese and the heavy cream, tomato, basil, salt, and pepper until well combined.
7. Pour the cream mixture over the beef mixture and top the casserole with the remaining ½ cup of shredded cheese.
8. Bake until the casserole is bubbly and the cheese is melted and lightly browned, about 30 minutes.

ITALIAN BEEF BURGERS
Nutrition: Cal 440;Fat 37 g; Carb 4g;Protein 22 g
Serving 4; Cook time 22 min

Ingredients
- 1 pound 75% lean ground beef
- ¼ cup ground almonds
- 2 tablespoons chopped fresh basil
- 1 teaspoon minced garlic
- ¼ teaspoon sea salt
- 1 tablespoon olive oil
- 1 tomato, cut into 4 thick slices
- ¼ sweet onion, sliced thinly

Instructions
1. In a medium bowl, mix together the ground beef, ground almonds, basil, garlic, and salt until well mixed.
2. Form the beef mixture into four equal paties and flaten them to about ½ inch thick.
3. Place a large skillet on medium-high heat and add the olive oil.
4. Panfry the burgers until cooked through, flipping them once, about 12 minutes in total.
5. Pat away any excess grease with paper towels and serve the burgers with a slice of tomato and onion

VEGETABLE DISHES

SNAP PEA SALAD

Nutrition: Cal 212;Fat 20 g; Carb 6 g;Protein 4 g
Serving 4; Cook time 40 min

Ingredients
- 8 ounces cauliflower riced
- 1/4 cup lemon juice
- 1/4 cup olive oil
- 1 clove garlic crushed
- 1/2 teaspoon coarse grain dijon mustard
- 1 teaspoon granulated stevia/erythritol blend
- 1/4 teaspoon pepper
- 1/2 teaspoon sea salt
- 1/2 cup sugar snap peas ends removed and each pod cut into three pieces
- 1/4 cup chives
- 1/2 cup sliced almonds
- 1/4 cup red onions minced

Instructions

1. Pour 1 to 2 inches of water in a pot fitted with a steamer. Bring water to a simmer.
2. Place riced cauliflower in the steamer basket, sprinkle lightly with sea salt, cover, and place over the simmering water in the bottom of the steamer. Steam until tender, about 10-12 minutes.
3. When cauliflower is tender, remove the top of the steamer from the simmering water and place it over a bowl, so any excess water can drain out. Allow to cool, uncovered for about 10 minutes, then cover and place the steamer and the bowl in the refrigerator. Chill for at least 1/2 hour or until cool to the touch.
4. While cauliflower is cooling, make the dressing. Pour olive oil in a small mixing bowl. Gradually stream in the lemon juice while vigorously whisking. Whisk in the garlic, mustard, sweetener, pepper, and salt.
5. In a medium mixing bowl, combine chilled cauliflower, peas, chives, almonds, and red onions. Pour dressing over and stir to mix. Transfer to an airtight container and refrigerate until serving. This salad is best if it is allowed to sit for a few hours in the refrigerator so the flavors mingle.

GARLIC & CHIVE CAULIFLOWER MASH

Nutrition: Cal 178;Fat 18 g; Carb 3 g;Protein 2 g
Serving 2; Cook time 20 min

Ingredients
- 4 cups cauliflower florets
- 1/3 cup mayonnaise
- 1 clove garlic, peeled
- 1 Tbsp water
- 1/2 tsp Kosher salt
- 1/8 tsp black pepper
- 1/4 tsp lemon juice
- 1/2 tsp lemon (or lime) zest
- 1 Tbsp fresh chives, chopped

Instructions

1. Combine the cauliflower, mayonnaise, garlic, water, salt and pepper in a large microwave safe bowl, stirring to coat.
2. Microwave on high for 12-15 minutes (or longer), until completely softened.
3. Add the cooked mixture to a magic bullet or food processor and puree until smooth.
4. Add the lemon juice, zest and chives and pulse until combined.
5. Serve warm.

CREAMY CILANTRO LIME COLESLAW

Nutrition: Cal 119;Fat 9 g; Carb 9 g;Protein 3 g
Serving 5; Cook time 10 min

Ingredients
- 14 oz coleslaw, bagged
- 1 1/2 avocados
- 1/4 cup cilantro leaves
- 2 limes, juiced
- 1 garlic clove
- 1/4 cup water
- 1/2 teaspoon salt
- cilantro to garnish

Instructions

1. In a food processor add the garlic and cilantro and process until chopped.
2. Add the lime juice, avocados and water. Pulse until nice and creamy.
3. Take out the avocado mixture and in a large bowl mix it with the coleslaw. It will be a bit thick but it will cover the slaw nicely.
4. For best results, refrigerate for a few hours before eating to soften the cabbage.

CAULIFLOWER HUMMUS

Nutrition: Cal 119;Fat 14 g; Carb 4 g;Protein 2 g
Serving 1; Cook time 20 min

Ingredients
- 3 cups raw cauliflower florets
- 2 Tbsp water
- 2 Tbsp avocado or olive oil
- 1/2 tsp salt
- 3 whole garlic cloves
- Tbsp Tahini paste
- 3 Tbsp lemon juice
- 2 raw garlic cloves, crushed (in addition to above)
- 3 Tbsp extra virgin olive oil
- 3/4 tsp kosher salt
- smoked paprika and extra olive oil for serving

Instructions

1. Combine the cauliflower, water, 2 Tbsp avocado or olive oil, 1/2 tsp kosher salt, and 3 whole garlic cloves to a microwave safe dish. Microwave for about 15 minutes – or until softened and darkened in color.
2. Put the cauliflower mixture into a magic bullet, blender, or food processor and blend. Add the tahini paste, lemon juice, 2 raw garlic cloves, 3 Tbsp olive oil, and 3/4 tsp kosher salt. Blend until mostly smooth. Taste and adjust seasoning as necessary.
3. To serve, place the hummus in a bowl and drizzle with extra virgin olive oil and a sprinkle of paprika. Use thinly sliced tart apples, celery sticks, raw radish chips, or other vegges to dip with.

CRISPY TOFU AND BOK CHOY SALAD

Nutrition: Cal 398;Fat 6 g; Carb 9 g;Protein 24 g
Serving 3; Cook time 40 min

Ingredients
Oven Baked Tofu
- 15 ounces extra firm tofu
- 1 tablespoon soy sauce
- 1 tablespoon sesame oil
- 1 tablespoon water
- 2 teaspoons minced garlic
- 1 tablespoon rice wine vinegar
- Juice ½ lemon

Bok Choy Salad
- 9 ounces bok choy
- 1 stalk green onion
- 2 tablespoons chopped cilantro
- 3 tablespoons coconut oil
- 2 tablespoons soy sauce
- 1 tablespoon sambal olek
- 1 tablespoon peanut butter
- Juice ½ lime
- 7 drops liquid stevia

Instructions

1. Start by pressing the tofu. Lay the tofu in a kitchen towel and put something heavy over the top (like a cast iron skillet). It takes about 4-6 hours to dry out, and you may need to replace the kitchen towel half-way through.

2.Once the tofu is pressed, work on your marinade. Combine all of the ingredients for the marinade (soy sauce, sesame oil, water, garlic, vinegar, and lemon).

3.Chop the tofu into squares and place in a plastic bag along with the marinade. Let this marinate for at least 30 minutes, but preferably over night.

4.Pre-heat oven to 350°F. Place tofu on a baking sheet lined with parchment paper (or a silpat) and bake for 30-35 minutes.

5.As the tofu is cooked, get started on the bok choy salad. Chop cilantro and spring onion.

6.Mix all of the other ingredients together (except lime juice and bok choy) in a bowl. Then add cilantro and spring onion. Note: You can microwave coconut oil for 10-15 seconds to allow it it to melt.

7.Once the tofu is almost cooked, add lime juice into the salad dressing and mix together.

8.Chop the bok choy into small slices, like you would cabbage.

9.Remove the tofu from the oven and assemble your salad with tofu, bok choy, and sauce.

VEGAN KALE AND SPINACH SOUP
Nutrition: Cal 110;Fat 12 g; Carb 6 g;Protein 4 g
Serving 4; Cook time 15 min

Ingredients
•½ cup coconut oil, melted
•8 oz. kale
•8 oz. (7½ cups) fresh spinach
•2 (14 oz.) avocados
•3½ cups coconut milk or coconut cream
•1 cup water
•fresh mint or dried mint (optional)
•1 tsp salt
•¼ tsp ground black pepper
•1 tbsp lime juice

Fried kale
•3 oz. kale
•2 garlic cloves, chopped
•2 tbsp coconut oil
•½ tsp ground cardamom (green)
•salt and pepper

Instructions
1.Melt the coconut oil in a hot thick-bottomed pot or pan.

2.Sauté the spinach and kale briefly. The vegetable should just shrink and get a little color, but no more. Remove from the heat.

3.Add water, coconut milk, avocado and spices. Blend with a hand blender until creamy.

4.Add lime juice. Add more spices if you want.

5.Fry kale and garlic on high heat until the garlic turns golden. Garnish the soup and serve.

CARROT SALAD
Nutrition: Cal 110;Fat 12 g; Carb 6 g;Protein 4 g
Serving 5; Cook time 10 min

Ingredients
•1 pound carrots, julienned
•3 Medjool dates, pitted and diced
•¼ cup chopped pistachios
•⅓ cup finely chopped cilantro
•¼ cup mint leaves, optional

Dressing
•2 tablespoons extra-virgin olive oil
•2 tablespoons fresh lemon juice
•1 tablespoon tahini
•1 tablespoon honey
•1 small garlic clove, grated
•¼ teaspoon cumin
•¼ teaspoon sea salt

Instructions
1.Place the julienned carrots in a large bowl and sprinkle the dates on top.

2.Make the dressing: In a small bowl, whisk together the olive oil, lemon juice, tahini, honey, garlic, cumin, and salt.

3.Drizzle the dressing over the carrots and toss to coat. Sprinkle on the pistachios and cilantro and toss again. Sprinkle the mint leaves and serve.

CABBAGE SOUP
Nutrition: Cal 112;Fat 8 g; Carb 16 g;Protein 8g
Serving 6; Cook time 35 min

Ingredients
•2 tablespoons extra-virgin olive oil
•2 carrots, chopped
•1 medium yellow onion, diced
•1 celery rib, diced
•2 tablespoons white wine vinegar
•2 (14.5-ounce) cans fire roasted diced tomatoes
•4 cups vegetable broth
•1 (15.5-ounce) can cooked white beans, drained and rinsed
•4 garlic cloves, grated
•2 Yukon gold potatoes, diced
•1 small green cabbage, about 1 pound (9 cups chopped)
•1 teaspoon dried thyme
•¾ teaspoon sea salt
•Freshly ground black pepper
•Fresh parsley, for garnish

Instructions
1.Heat the oil in a large pot over medium heat. Add the carrots, onion, celery, salt, and several grinds of fresh pepper, and cook, stirring occasionally, for 8 minutes.

2.Add the vinegar, stir, and then add the tomatoes, broth, beans, garlic, potatoes, cabbage and thyme. Cover and simmer for 20 to 30 minutes, or until the potatoes and cabbage are tender.

3.Season to taste, garnish with fresh parsley, and serve.

CREAMY DAIRY FREE AVOCADO SAUCE
Nutrition: Cal 180;Fat 16 g; Carb 8 g;Protein 6 g
Serving 5; Cook time 10 min

Ingredients
•1 Avocado
•1 Tbspn lemon juice
•1 garlic clove
•3 Tbspn olive oil
•2 Tbspn fresh parsley
•3 Tbspn water
•Sea Salt and freshly ground black pepper to taste

Instructions
1.Add all ingredients into food processor or blender.

2.Blend until smooth.

3.Add more water to reach a thinner consistency if desired.

4.Taste and adjust seasoning if necessary.

EASY NO-CHURN AVOCADO ICE CREAM
Nutrition: Cal 274;Fat 17 g; Carb 29 g;Protein3 g
Serving 4; Cook time 5 hours

Ingredients
•1/4 cup hardened coconut cream (from 1 14-oz can full-fat coconut milk, refrigerated overnight — only the cream)
•2 ripe avocados, halved, pitted and peeled
•2 very ripe bananas, sliced and frozen
•3 tbsp pure maple syrup, plus more, to taste
•1 tbsp freshly squeezed lemon juice

Instructions

1.Add sliced, peeled fresh avocado to a food processor or high-speed blender, and blend until smooth.

2.Add hardened coconut cream from canned coconut milk, along with sliced frozen bananas, pure maple syrup, and lemon juice, and blend until smooth and creamy. If bananas are not fully ripe, you may need to add in additional maple syrup.

3.Taste, and add any more pure maple syrup, as needed, to reach the desired sweetness.

4.Transfer the mixture into a freezer-safe container, and place in freezer for at least 3-4 hours or overnight.

5.When ready to serve, let soften for 10-15 minutes at room temperature before scooping.

PORTOBELLO MUSHROOM PIZZA
Nutrition: Cal 274;Fat 17 g; Carb 29 g;Protein 3 g
Serving 4; Cook time 20 min

Ingredients
• 4 large portobello mushrooms, stems removed
• ¼ cup olive oil
• 1 teaspoon minced garlic
• 1 medium tomato, cut into 4 slices
• 2 teaspoons chopped fresh basil
• 1 cup shredded mozzarella cheese

Instructions
1.Preheat the oven to broil. Line a baking sheet with aluminum foil and set aside.

2.In a small bowl, toss the mushroom caps with the olive oil until well coated. Use your fingertips to rub the oil in withou breaking the mushrooms.

3.Place the mushrooms on the baking sheet gill-side down and broil the mushrooms until they are tender on the tops,about 2 minutes.

4.Flip the mushrooms over and broil 1 minute more.

5.Take the baking sheet out and spread the garlic over each mushroom, top each with a tomato slice, sprinkle with the basil,and top with the cheese.

6.Broil the mushrooms until the cheese is melted and bubbly, about 1 minute.

ARUGULA AVOCADO TOMATO SALAD
Nutrition: Cal 112;Fat 9 g; Carb 12 g;Protein 3 g
Serving 5; Cook time 10 min

Ingredients
• 5 oz baby arugula roughly chopped
• 6 large basil leaves thinly sliced
• 1 pint yellow grape tomatoes sliced in half
• 1 pint red grape tomatoes sliced in half
• 2 large avocados cut into chunks
• ½ cup red onion minced
• Balsamic Vinaigrette
• 2 tbsp balsamic vinegar
• 1 tbsp olive oil
• 1 tbsp maple syrup
• 1 tbsp lemon juice
• 1 small garlic clove minced
• ¼ tsp himalayan pink sea salt
• ¼ tsp black pepper

Instructions
1.Put the roughly chopped arugula and sliced basil leaves into a large mixing bowl. Add the sliced grape tomatoes, avocado chunks, and minced red onion to the bowl. Toss to combine.

2.In a small bowl, whisk together 2 tbsp balsamic vinegar, 1 tbsp olive oil, 1 tbsp maple syrup, 1 tbsp lemon juice, 1 garlic clove, ¼ tsp salt, and ¼ tsp black pepper until well combined.

3.Pour the balsamic dressing over the salad. Gently mix the salad until the dressing has been evenly distributed and then transfer the salad to a large platter.

RED CURRY CAULIFLOWER SOUP
Nutrition: Cal 274;Fat 16 g; Carb 18 g;Protein 6 g
Serving 6; Cook time 45 min

Ingredients
• 1 medium yellow onion sliced
• 3 medium garlic cloves sliced
• 4 ounces thai red curry paste (about 4 tbsp)
• 1 medium cauliflower (about 1 lb cauliflower florets)
• ½ cup red lentils
• 1 ½ cups water
• 4 cups low-sodium vegetable broth
• ½ tsp Himalayan pink sea salt
• ½ tsp black pepper
• 14 ounce can unsweetened coconut milk
• 3 tbsp lemon juice (1 large lemon)
• 1 tbsp chives sliced

Instructions
1.In a large pot, saute the sliced onions in 3-4 tbsp vegetable broth until soft. Add the sliced garlic and cook for 1-2 minutes until fragrant.

2.Add 4 tbsp red curry paste, cauliflower florets, ½ cup red lentils, 1 ½ cups water, 4 cups vegetable broth, ½ tsp salt, and ½ tsp black pepper to the pot. Bring the soup to a low simmer and then reduce the heat to medium. Let it cook for 15-20 minutes or until the cauliflower and red lentils are tender, stirring occasionally.

3.Transfer the soup to a large high-powered blender cup and then blend it on high until the soup is completely smooth. You may need to work in batches depending on how large your blender cup is.

4.Pour the blended soup back into the pot and stir in the coconut milk over medium heat. Add 3 tbsp lemon juice and stir it in. Garnish with chives before serving.

KETO OVEN ROASTED VEGETABLES
Nutrition: Cal 113;Fat 7 g; Carb 11 g;Protein 2 g
Serving 8; Cook time 40 min

Ingredients
• 2 cups Broccoli (cut into florets)
• 2 cups Cauliflower (cut into florets)
• 2 cups Zucchini (sliced into 1/4 inch thick circles)
• 2 cups Bell peppers (cut into 1.5 inch pieces)
• 2 cups Red onion (cut into 1.5 inch pieces)
• 1/4 cup Olive oil
• 2 tbsp Balsamic vinegar
• 1 tsp Garlic powder
• 1 tsp Italian seasoning
• 1 tsp Sea salt
• 1/2 tsp Black pepper

Instructions
1.Preheat the oven to 425 degrees F. Line an extra-large baking sheet with foil, if desired.

2.Combine the vegetables in a large bowl.

3.In a small bowl, whisk together the olive oil, balsamic vinegar, garlic powder, Italian seasoning, sea salt, and black pepper. Pour the mixture over the vegetables.

4.Arrange the vegetables in a single layer on the prepared baking sheet, making sure each piece is touching the pan. Do not overcrowd the pan - use multiple pans if needed.

5.Roast the vegetables in the oven for about 30 minutes, until they are golden brown.

VEGAN KETO COCONUT CURRY
Nutrition: Cal 425;Fat 33 g; Carb 10 g;Protein 18 g
Serving 4; Cook time 35 min

Ingredients
• ¼ cup vegan butter
• ½ green bell pepper, thinly sliced

- •2 scallions, thinly sliced, white and green parts kept separate
- •2 garlic cloves, thinly sliced
- •2½ tablespoons vegan red curry paste
- •1 medium zucchini, diced
- •1 medium carrot, diced
- •1½ cups unsweetened full-fat coconut milk
- •1 cup vegetable stock
- •2 tablespoons unflavored vegan protein powder
- •2 tablespoons natural unsweetened peanut butter
- •4 drops liquid stevia
- •1 teaspoon sea salt
- •Freshly ground black pepper
- •16 ounces extra-firm tofu, cut into medium dice
- •1 cup baby spinach
- •¼ cup chopped fresh cilantro, plus more for serving
- •4 tablespoons coconut oil, melted

Instructions

1. In a large pot, melt the butter over medium heat. Add the bell pepper, scallion whites and garlic; cook until fragrant, about 1 minute. Add the curry paste and cook, stirring constantly, until fragrant, about 1 minute.

2. Stir in the zucchini, carrot, coconut milk, vegetable stock, protein powder, peanut butter, stevia, salt and black pepper. Bring to a boil, then reduce the heat to medium-low and simmer uncovered until the vegetables are tender, 8 to 10 minutes. Taste and adjust the seasoning if necessary.

3. Add the tofu and simmer for 5 minutes to warm through. Add the spinach and cilantro to wilt. Taste and adjust the seasoning if necessary.

4. Divide the curry among four bowls. Drizzle 1 tablespoon melted coconut oil over each portion. Sprinkle with the scallion greens and more cilantro.

STUFFED BELL PEPPERS
Nutrition: Cal 202;Fat 16 g; Carb 7 g;Protein 8 g
Serving 3; Cook time 50 min

Ingredients
- •2 medium-sized yellow bell peppers, halved
- •½ cup mozzarella cheese
- •½ cup tomatoes, diced
- •2 medium-sized green bell pepper, halved
- •2 cups button mushrooms, diced
- •1 cup feta cheese, crumbled
- •2 tbsps. celery leaves, finely chopped
- •2 tbsps. extra virgin olive oil
- •½ tsp. black pepper, ground
- •½ tsp. smoked paprika, ground
- •¼ tsp. red pepper cayenne, ground
- •½ tsp. salt

Instructions

1. Cut the peppers in half and take away the stem and seeds. Set aside.
2. In a large mixing bowl, combine button mushrooms, feta cheese, mozzarella cheese, tomatoes, celery, and olive oil. Add all spices and mix until well incorporated. Stuff the bell pepper halves with this particular mixture. Use some additional oil to brush the peppers externally.
3. Line some parchment paper over a fitting springform pan and hang aside
4. Plug inside instant pot and pour 1 cup of water in the stainless insert. Set the trivet around the bottom and set the stuffed peppers on the top.
5. Close the lid and hang up the steam release handle. Press the "Manual" button and set the timer for a half-hour. Cook on underhand.
6. When done, perform a quick pressure release and open the pot.
7. Transfer the peppers to a serving plate and sprinkle by incorporating dried oregano or dried rosemary before serving. Optionally, top with Greek yogurt.

GARLICKY GREEN BEANS
Nutrition: Cal 104;Fat 9 g; Carb 2 g;Protein 4 g
Serving 4; Cook time 20 min

Ingredients
- •1 pound green beans, stemmed
- •2 tablespoons olive oil
- •1 teaspoon minced garlic
- •Sea salt
- •Freshly ground black pepper
- •¼ cup freshly grated Parmesan Cheese

Instructions

1. Preheat the oven to 425°F. Line a baking sheet with aluminum foil and set aside.
2. In a large bowl, toss together the green beans, olive oil, and garlic until well mixed.
3. Season the beans lightly with salt and pepper.
4. Spread the beans on the baking sheet and roast them until they are tender and lightly browned, stirring them once, about 10 minutes.
5. Serve topped with the Parmesan cheese

SAUTÉED ASPARAGUS WITH WALNUTS
Nutrition: Cal 124;Fat 12 g; Carb 4 g;Protein 3 g
Serving 4; Cook time 20 min

Ingredients
- •1&½ tablespoons olive oil
- •¾ pound asparagus, woody
- •ends trimmed
- •Sea salt
- •Freshly ground pepper
- •¼ cup chopped walnuts

Instructions

1. Place a large skillet over medium-high heat and add the olive oil.
2. Sauté the asparagus until the spears are tender and lightly browned, about 5 minutes.
3. Season the asparagus with salt and pepper.
4. Remove the skillet from the heat and toss the asparagus with the walnuts.

WHITE BEAN & SPINACH QUESADILLAS
Nutrition: Cal 500;Fat 20 g; Carb 35 g;Protein 19 g
Serving 5; Cook time 30 min

Ingredients
- •19 oz can of white beans navy, cannellini or white kidney beans are all fine, drained and rinsed
- •3 oz spinach chopped (roughly 3 cups chopped fresh spinach or 1 1/2cups frozen spinach)
- •1 teaspoon ground cumin
- •1 teaspoon ground coriander
- •1 1/8 teaspoon salt
- •3/4 cup feta cheese crumbled
- •1 1/4 cups shredded cheese
- •5 large 12 inch tortillas

Instructions

1. If spinach is frozen, thaw and press out extra moisture.
2. In a large bowl, mash the white beans using a fork or potato masher.
3. Stir in the spinach, cumin, coriander and salt. Stir/mash until the spinach is slightly wilted and fold in the feta cheese.
4. Heat a large pan over medium heat. Spray with oil, then assemble quesadillas in the pan (cooking 2 at a time).
5. Spoon out ½ cup of white bean/spinach filling, then sprinkle with ¼ cup cheese. Fold the tortilla over, then press down firmly.
6. Cook for 3 or so minutes per side, until golden and crispy.

BRUSSELS SPROUTS CASSEROLE
Nutrition: Cal 217;Fat 14 g; Carb 11 g;Protein 10 g
Serving 8; Cook time 45 min

Ingredients
- 8 bacon slices
- 1 pound Brussels sprouts, blanched for 10 minutes and cut into quarters
- 1 cup shredded Swiss cheese, divided
- ¾ cup heavy (whipping) cream

Instructions
1. Preheat the oven to 400°F.
2. Place a skillet over medium-high heat and cook the bacon until it is crispy, about 6 minutes.
3. Reserve 1 tablespoon of bacon fat to grease the casserole dish and roughly chop the cooked bacon.
4. Lightly oil a casserole dish with the reserved bacon fat and set aside.
5. In a medium bowl, toss the Brussels sprouts with the chopped bacon and ½ cup of cheese and transfer the mixture to the caserole dish.
6. Pour the heavy cream over the Brussels sprouts and top the casserole with the remaining ½ cup of cheese.
7. Bake until the cheese is melted and lightly browned and the vegetables are heated through, about 20 minutes

SAUTÉED VEGETABLES
Nutrition: Cal 171;Fat 12 g; Carb 9 g;Protein 5.3g
Serving 5; Cook time 10 min

Ingredients
- 1 red bell pepper, sliced
- 1 small onion, sliced
- 1 small zucchini, cut into cubes
- 1 green bell pepper, sliced
- ¼ cup dried porcini mushrooms
- ¼ cup Feta cheese
- ½ cup sour cream
- 2 tbsps. tamari sauce
- 2 tbsps. sesame oil
- ½ tsp. dried thyme
- ¼ tsp. dried oregano
- 1 tsp. pink Himalayan salt

Instructions
1. Plug in the instant pot and press the "Sauté" button. Heat up the sesame oil and add zucchini. Sprinkle with many salt and cook for 5 - 6 minutes, stirring constantly.
2. Now add bell peppers and onions. Sprinkle with tamari sauce and provides it a good stir. Optionally, drizzle with a few rice vinegar.
3. Season by incorporating more salt, thyme, and oregano. Continue in order to cook for two - 3 minutes and atart exercising . Feta cheese and mushrooms. Pour in about three tablespoons of water and cook for three or four minutes.
4. When done, press the "Cancel" button and stir inside sour cream. To enjoy, serve it immediately.

STEAMED BROCCOLI WITH BASIL
Nutrition: Cal 181;Fat 10 g; Carb 10 g;Protein 10 g
Serving 3; Cook time 20 min

Ingredients
- 1 lb. broccoli, chopped
- 2 garlic cloves, peeled
- ½ cup fresh basil, chopped
- ½ cup some kinds of cheese
- ½ cup avocado, chopped
- 1 tbsp. extra virgin olive oil
- 1 tbsp. fresh lemon juice, freshly squeezed
- ¼ tsp. dried oregano, ground
- ½ tsp. red pepper, ground
- ¼ tsp. dried parsley, ground
- 1 tsp. salt

Instructions
1. Plug in the Instant Pot and pour in 1 cup of water inside the stainless insert.
2. Place the trivet about the bottom of the pot as well as set the steam basket at the top. Place broccoli inside the steam basket and sprinkle with salt and pepper. Close the lid and set the steam release handle by moving the valve on the "Sealing" position. Press the "Steam" button as well as set the timer for ten mins.
3. Meanwhile, combine basil, cottage type cheese, avocado, garlic, olive oil, fresh lemon juice, red pepper, parsley, and oregano in a mixer. Pulse until smooth and totally incorporated.
4. When you hear the cooker's end signal, release pressure to succeed naturally. Open the pot and transfer the broccoli to a serving plate. Top with basil cream and serve immediately!

ONION CAULIFLOWER HASH
Nutrition: Cal 217;Fat 14 g; Carb 11 g;Protein 10 g
Serving 3; Cook time 20 min

Ingredients
- 1 lb. cauliflower, chopped
- 1 cup green cabbage, shredded
- 2 medium-sized onions, sliced
- ¼ cup parmesan cheese
- 1 cup vegetable stock
- 2 tbsps. olive oil
- ¼ tsp. black pepper, ground
- ½ tsp. dried thyme, ground
- ½ tsp. smoked paprika, ground
- 1 tsp. salt

Instructions
1. Plug in the Instant Pot and grease the stainless steel insert with essential olive oil. Press the "Sauté" button and add cauliflower and onions. Sprinkle with salt, pepper, and thyme. Stir well and cook for 5 minutes.
2. Add cabbage and pour inside vegetables stock. Stir again and securely lock the lid. Set the steam release handle and press the "Manual" button. Set the timer for 8 minutes and cook on questionable.
3. When you hear the cooker's end signal, perform a quick release of the pressure by moving the valve for the "Venting" position. Open the pot and stir inside thyme and smoked paprika.
4. Transfer all to a serving plate and sprinkle with parmesan cheese before serving.

PESTO ZUCCHINI NOODLES
Nutrition: Cal 93;Fat 8 g; Carb 2 g;Protein 4 g
Serving 4; Cook time 15 min

Ingredients
- 4 small zucchini, ends trimmed
- ¾ cup Herb Kale Pesto (page 133)
- ¼ cup grated or shredded
- Parmesan cheese

Instructions
1. Use a spiralizer or peeler to cut the zucchini into "noodles" and place them in a medium bowl.
2. Add the pesto and the Parmesan cheese and toss to coat.

TASTY CREAMY COLLARD GREENS
Nutrition: Cal 217;Fat 17 g; Carb 25 g;Protein 5.7 g
Serving 4; Cook time 25 min

Ingredients
- 1 lb. collard greens, chopped
- 1 medium-sized onion, chopped
- ½ cup bacon, cut into bite-sized pieces
- 2 garlic cloves, finely chopped
- 1 cup sour cream

- ½ tsp. balsamic vinegar
- 1 tbsp. essential olive oil
- ¼ tsp. black pepper, ground
- ½ tsp. Italian seasoning
- 1 tsp. red pepper flakes
- 1 tsp. sea salt

Instructions

1. Plug with your Instant Pot and add the bacon for the stainless-steel insert. Press the "Sauté" button and cook for three to four minutes, or until crisp. Remove the bacon through the pot and add olive oil. When hot, add onions and garlic. Stir-fry for 3 - 4 minutes, or until the onions translucent.
2. Add collard greens and cook for two main minutes. Sprinkle with salt, pepper, Italian seasoning, and red pepper flakes. Pour in 1 cup of water and securely lock the lid. Adjust the steam release handle and press the "Manual" button. Set the timer for 5 minutes and cook on underhand.
3. When done, perform a quick pressure release and open the pot.
4. Stir in the sour cream, balsamic vinegar, and bacon. Press the "Sauté" button and cook for 2 - 3 minutes more, or until heated through. Turn over pot and transfer all to a serving plate.

GOLDEN ROSTI
Nutrition: Cal 171;Fat 15 g; Carb 3 g;Protein 5 g
Serving 8; Cook time 30 min

Ingredients

- 8 bacon slices, chopped
- 1 cup shredded acorn squash
- 1 cup shredded raw celeriac
- 2 tablespoons grated or shredded
- Parmesan cheese
- 2 teaspoons minced garlic
- 1 teaspoon chopped fresh thyme
- Sea salt
- Freshly ground black pepper
- 2 tablespoons butter

Instructions

1. In a large skillet over medium-high heat, cook the bacon until crispy, about 5 minutes.
2. While the bacon is cooking, in a large bowl, mix together the squash, celeriac, Parmesan cheese, garlic, and thyme. Season the mixture generously with salt and pepper, and set aside.
3. Remove the cooked bacon with a sloted spoon to the rosti mixture and stir to incorporate.
4. Remove all but 2 tablespoons of bacon fat from the skillet and add the buter.
5. Reduce the heat to medium-low and transfer the rosti mixture to the skillet and spread it out evenly to form a large round paty about 1 inch thick.
6. Cook until the botom of the rosti is golden brown and crisp, about 5 minutes.
7. Flip the rosti over and cook until the other side is crispy and the middle is cooked through, about 5 minutes more.
8. Remove the skillet from the heat and cut the rosti into 8 pieces.

CREAMED SPINACH
Nutrition: Cal 195;Fat 20 g; Carb 3 g;Protein 3 g
Serving 4; Cook time 40 min

Ingredients

- 1 tablespoon butter
- ½ sweet onion, very thinly sliced
- 4 cups spinach, stemmed and thoroughly washed
- ¾ cup heavy (whipping) cream
- ¼ cup Chicken Stock
- Pinch sea salt
- Pinch freshly ground black pepper
- Pinch ground nutmeg

Instructions

1. In a large skillet over medium heat, add the buter.
2. Sauté the onion until it is lightly caramelized, about 5 minutes.
3. Stir in the spinach, heavy cream, chicken stock, salt, pepper, and nutmeg.
4. Sauté until the spinach is wilted, about 5 minutes.
5. Continue cooking the spinach until it is tender and the sauce is thickened, about 15 minutes.

CELERY SPINACH STEW
Nutrition: Cal 280;Fat 28 g; Carb 5 g;Protein 2.5 g
Serving 4; Cook time 25 min

Ingredients

- 2 cups fresh spinach, chopped
- 1 small onion, chopped
- 1 cup celery leaves, chopped
- 2 cups heavy cream
- 1 tbsp. fresh lemon juice
- 2 tbsps. butter
- 1 cup celery stalks, chopped
- 2 garlic cloves, minced
- 1/2 tsp. black pepper, ground
- 1 tbsp. fresh mint, torn
- 1 tsp. salt

Instructions

1. In a large colander, combine spinach and celery. Rinse well under running water and drain. Transfer to a cutting board cut into bite-sized pieces. Set aside.
2. Plug with your instant pot and press the "Sauté" button. Add butter and stir constantly until melts.
3. Add celery stalks, garlic, and onions. Cook for just two minutes and add celery leaves and spinach. Sprinkle with salt and pepper. Cook for 2 - 3 minutes and pour inside the heavy cream.
4. Securely lock the lid and press the "Manual" button. Adjust the steam release handle and hang up the timer for 5 minutes. Cook on high pressure.
5. When you hear the cooker's end signal, perform a quick release with the pressure and open the pot.
6. Stir within the mint and lemon juice. Let it chill for 5 minutes before serving.

SIMPLE BASIL PESTO ZUCCHINI
Nutrition: Cal 215;Fat 17 g; Carb 8 g;Protein 5 g
Serving 4; Cook time 15 min

Ingredients

- 1 cup mozzarella cheese
- 1 large red bell pepper, cut into strips
- 2 medium-sized zucchinis, thinly sliced
- 2 tbsps. organic olive oil
- 1 medium-sized eggplant, thinly sliced
- 1 tsp. Italian seasoning
- 1 cup vegetable stock

FOR THE BASIL PESTO:

- ½ tsp garlic powder
- 2 tsps. balsamic vinegar
- ½ tsp. black pepper, freshly ground
- 2 tbsps. fresh basil, finely chopped
- 2 tbsps. sour cream
- 3 tbsps. organic olive oil
- ¼ tsp. mustard seeds

Instructions

1. Combine sliced zucchinis, stripped red bell pepper, and sliced eggplant in a large bowl. Drizzle with olive oil and Italian seasoning. Optionally, add a pinch of salt and mix well using your hands. Set aside.
2. Combine all pesto
3. Ingredients in a blender and blend until smooth and creamy. Then schedule.

4. Plug inside the Instant Pot add vegetables within the stainless-steel insert. Pour within the vegetable stock and close the lid. Adjust the steam release handle and press the "Manual" button. Set the timer for 8 minutes and cook on high pressure.
5. When done; perform a quick pressure release by moving the valve on the "Venting" position.
6. Open the pot and transfer the vegetables to a serving plate. Top with basil pesto and serve immediately.
7. Optionally, garnish with some fresh basil leaves and get!

CHEESY MASHED CAULIFLOWER
Nutrition: Cal 183;Fat 15 g; Carb 6 g;Protein 8 g
Serving 4; Cook time 20 min

Ingredients
- 1 head cauliflower, chopped roughly
- ½ cup shredded Cheddar cheese
- ¼ cup heavy (whipping) cream
- 2 tablespoons butter, at room temperature
- Sea salt
- Freshly ground black pepper

Instructions
1. Place a large saucepan filled three-quarters full with water over high heat and bring to a boil.
2. Blanch the cauliflower until tender, about 5 minutes, and drain.
3. Transfer the cauliflower to a food processor and add the cheese, heavy cream, and butter. Purée until very creamy and whipped.
4. Season with salt and pepper.

VEGETABLES À LA GRECQUE
Nutrition: Cal 326;Fat 25 g; Carb 8 g;Protein 15 g
Serving 4; Cook time 15 min

Ingredients
- 2 tablespoons organic olive oil
- 2 garlic cloves, minced
- 1 red onion, chopped
- 0.6 pounds button mushrooms, thinly sliced
- 1 eggplant, sliced
- ½ teaspoon dried basil
- 1 teaspoon dried oregano
- 1 thyme sprig, leaves picked
- 2 rosemary sprigs, leaves picked
- ½ cup tomato sauce
- ¼ cup dry Greek wine
- ¼ cup water
- 0.5 pounds Halloumi cheese, cubed
- 4 tablespoons Kalamata olives, pitted and halved

Instructions
1. Press the "Sauté" button to heat your Instant Pot; now, heat the extra virgin olive oil. Cook the garlic and red onions for one to two minutes, stirring periodically.
2. Stir in the mushrooms and then sauté a different 2 to 3 minutes.
3. Add the eggplant, basil, oregano, thyme, rosemary, tomato sauce, Greek wine, and water.
4. Secure the lid. Choose "Manual" mode and low pressure; cook for 3 minutes. Once cooking is complete, use a quick pressure release; carefully remove the lid.
5. Top with cheese and olives.

SAUTÉED CRISPY ZUCCHINI
Nutrition: Cal 94;Fat 8 g; Carb 1 g;Protein 4 g
Serving 4; Cook time 25 min

Ingredients
- 2 tablespoons butter
- 4 zucchini, cut into
- ¼-inch-thick rounds

- ½ cup freshly grated Parmesan cheese
- Freshly ground black peppe

Instructions
1. Place a large skillet over medium-high heat and melt the buter.
2. Add the zucchini and sauté until tender and lightly browned, about 5 minutes.
3. Spread the zucchini evenly in the skillet and sprinkle the Parmesan cheese over the vegetables.
4. Cook without stirring until the Parmesan cheese is melted and crispy where it touches the skillet, about 5 minutes

MUSHROOMS WITH CAMEMBERT
Nutrition: Cal 161;Fat 13 g; Carb 4 g;Protein 9 g
Serving 4; Cook time 20 min

Ingredients
- 2 tablespoons butter
- 2 teaspoons minced garlic
- 1 pound button mushrooms, halved
- 4 ounces Camembert cheese, diced
- Freshly ground black pepper

Instructions
1. Place a large skillet over medium-high heat and melt the buter.
2. Sauté the garlic until translucent, about 3 minutes.
3. Sauté the mushrooms until tender, about 10 minutes.
4. Stir in the cheese and sauté until melted, about 2 minutes.
5. Season with pepper and serve

MEXICAN-STYLE ZUCCHINI AND POBLANOS
Nutrition: Cal 250;Fat 20 g; Carb 2 g;Protein 14 g
Serving 6; Cook time 15 min

Ingredients
- 1 tablespoon vegetable oil
- 2 poblano peppers, seeded and cut lengthwise into ½-inch strips
- 2 teaspoons unsalted butter
- ½ onion, thinly sliced
- 1 tablespoon minced garlic
- 1-pound ground pork
- 1 zucchini, cut into thick rounds
- 1 yellow crookneck squash, cut into thick rounds
- ½ cup chicken broth
- ½ teaspoon ground cumin
- 1 teaspoon salt
- 1 tablespoon Mexican crema or sour cream

Instructions
1. Select "Sauté" to preheat the Instant Pot and adapt to high heat. When the hot, add the oil and invite it to shimmer. Add the poblano strips in a single layer, working in batches if necessary, and char on each side, flipping only occasionally, for around 10 minutes.
2. Add the butter for the pot. Once melted, add the onion and garlic, and sauté until soft, 2 to 3 minutes.
3. Add the soil pork and break it into chunks, mixing it well using the vegetables. Cook before lumps are finished in the meat, and it's half-way cooked, about four or five minutes.
4. Add the zucchini, squash, broth, cumin, and salt on the pot.
5. Lock the lid. Select "Pressure Cook" or "Manual" as well as set pressure to low. Cook for two main minutes. When the cooking is complete, quick-release pressure. Unlock the lid.
6. Stir inside cream, therefore it fully incorporates in the sauce.

ASPARAGUS WITH COLBY CHEESE
Nutrition: Cal 170;Fat 12 g; Carb 8 g;Protein 8 g
Serving 4; Cook time 10 min

Ingredients
- 1 ½ pounds fresh asparagus
- 2 tablespoons organic olive oil
- 4 garlic cloves, minced

- sea salt, to taste
- ¼ teaspoon ground black pepper
- ½ cup Colby cheese, shredded

Instructions
1. Add 1 cup of water as well as a steamer basket in your Instant Pot.
2. Now, put the asparagus around the steamer basket; drizzle your asparagus with olive oil. Scatter garlic in the top in the asparagus. Season with salt and black pepper.
3. Secure the lid. Choose "Manual" mode and questionable; cook for 1 minute. Once cooking is complete, work with a quick pressure release; carefully eliminate the lid.
4. Transfer the prepared asparagus to some nice serving platter and scatter shredded cheese in the top.

VEGGIE SCRAMBLE
Nutrition: Cal 200;Fat 5 g; Carb 9 g;Protein 20 g
Serving 4; Cook time 30 min

Ingredients
- 4 egg whites
- 1 egg yolk
- 2 tbsps. almond milk
- 1 cup spinach
- 1 tomato, chopped
- ½ white onion, chopped
- 3 fresh basil leaves, chopped
- salt and pepper, to taste
- ghee

Instructions
1. In a bowl, whisk the egg yolk and whites while using milk. Stir well.
2. Heat the ghee in the pan over medium heat. Add the onions and sauté until fragrant.
3. Add inside tomato to the pan with all the spinach and cook prior to the spinach is almost wilted.
4. Pour the egg mixture within the spinach and cook until firm (or before the egg sets). Stir constantly. Season with salt and pepper.

PRESSURE COOKER QUINOA AND RICE
Nutrition: Cal 100;Fat 0,6 g; Carb 0,7 g;Protein 3 g
Serving 4; Cook time 15 min

Ingredients
- Rice (white, freckled or brow, 1 ¾ cups)
- Quinoa (5 tbsp)
- Water (3 cups)

Instructions
1. Add the rinsed rice and quinoa and water inside Pressure cooker; close the top's and set to "High pressure" for 3 minutes.
2. Once the timer signalizes, the cooking ends, release pressure to succeed naturally for 10 minutes.
3. Open the lid, stir the rice and quinoa somewhat bit and serve while it's hot.

CHICKPEA CURRY AND RICE
Nutrition: Cal 290;Fat 5,6 g; Carb 50 g;Protein 9 g
Serving 4; Cook time 20 min

Ingredients
- Chickpeas (1 cup, make sure these were soaked in water overnight)
- Oil (by choice, 1 tbsp)
- Water (1 cup)
- Tomatoes pure or sauce (about 2 cups)
- Onion (1, chopped)
- Spice mix Chana Masala (2 tbsp)
- Ginger (1 tbsp, chopped)
- Garlic (1 tbsp, chopped)
- Salt (1 teaspoon)

Instructions

1. Pour water and add the rice in a very pot that's heatproof and cover it which has a foil.
2. The pressure cooker should be pre-heated if you add inside oil and also the onion. Set it to "Sauté" and cook the onion till it glazes and softens up a bit bit.
3. Add the garlic, ginger and chana masala spice mix to pressure cooker and cook for half one minute.
4. Now add the chickpeas, water, and tomatoes and mix the ingredients.
5. Place the trivet inside pressure cooker (on the
6. ingredients) and on the top than it add the heatproof pot or container (make certain they can fit inside). Close and secure the coverage and hang to "High pressure" for twenty minutes.
7. Release pressure naturally for 10 mins once it's cooked; open the lid and serve the rice as well as the chickpeas in bowls.

VEGIES, LENTILS AND MILLET PRESSURE COOKER MIX
Nutrition: Cal 300;Fat 13 g; Carb 58 g;Protein 20 g
Serving 4; Cook time 30 min

Ingredients
- Leek (1 cup)
- Asparagus (1 cup)
- Sugar snap peas (1 cup)
- Bok Choy (half cup, chopped)
- Lentils (half cup)
- Mushrooms (any kind, half cup)
- Millet (1 cup)
- Garlic (2 cloves, chopped)
- Parsley, garlic chives and onion chives mix (1/4 cup)
- Lemon juice
- Salt

Instructions
1. Set the pressure cooker to "Sauté" and add inside the mushrooms and garlic and sauté to get a short while. Then add the lentils and millet and cook for one more minute. Then add the vegetable stock.
2. Close and secure the cover and hang it to "High pressure"; allow it to go cook for 10 mins and after that release pressure naturally.
3. Open the lid and add the peas, asparagus, and bok choy (you might be free to utilize some other vegetable by choice, obviously).
4. Close the superior again and allowed this to mix sit for a little bit.
5. The millet has to be well cooked (it ought to be yellow).
6. Stir, add the parsley and chives mix and serve in a very bowl. Squeeze some lemon juice and add salt by taste.

BAKED BEANS
Nutrition: Cal 230;Fat 6 g; Carb 40 g;Protein 2 g
Serving 8; Cook time 1 hour

Ingredients
- Beans (1 bag)
- Onion (half cup, chopped)
- Garlic (1 clove, chopped)
- Green bell pepper (half cup, chopped)
- Bacon (4 slices, cut in squares)
- Water (8 cups)
- Barbecue sauce (2 cups)
- Olive oil (1 tbsp)
- Mustard (optional, 2 tbsp)
- Salt and pepper to taste

Instructions
1. Pour water inside pressure cooker and adding the beans. Close and secure the lead, place it to "Manual" or "High Pressure" for 25 minutes.
2. Let the pressure out naturally.
3. Open the lid and strain the beans; wash it with cold water and hang up it aside in another pot or bowl.
4. Clean and dry pressure to succeed cooker then add the organic olive oil and the bacon. Add salt and pepper and sauté for 5 minutes (the bacon should be well fried.

5. Add the bell pepper and onion, stir and cook until the onion caramelizes.
6. Pour within the beans, mustard, garlic and barbecue sauce.
7. Close the cover and set to "High pressure" and cook for an additional fifteen minutes.
8. Release the pressure naturally. Open it, stir after which serve.

BLACK BEANS AND RICE
Nutrition: Cal 270;Fat 9 g; Carb 39 g;Protein 10 g
Serving 8; Cook time 70 min

Ingredients
- Black beans (1 along with a half cup)
- Rice (white or brown, 1 plus a half cup)
- Water (3 cups)
- Vegetable broth (3 cups)
- Onion (half, chopped)
- Garlic (4 cloves, chopped)
- Olive oil (2 teaspoons)
- Paprika (1 as well as a half teaspoons)
- Cumin (2 teaspoons)
- Oregano (1 as well as a half teaspoons)
- Chili powder (optional, 2 teaspoons)
- Lime juice
Instructions
1. Set pressure to succeed cooker to "Sauté"; add the essential olive oil and once it's hot enough add the onion and cook it till it's tender.
2. Add the paprika, cumin, garlic, oregano, salt, and chili powder and cook for half one minute, then shut off pressure cooker.
3. Pour inside water, vegetable broth, rice, and beans, stir and after that close and secure the cover, set to "High pressure" and cook for half an hour. Once you hear the timer, release pressure naturally for 10-fifteen minutes.
4. Open the lid, squeeze the juice of half lime, season with salt and pepper by taste, stir and serve. You will add avocado slices if you need, as well.

NO-COOK FALAFEL
Nutrition: Cal 106;Fat 9 g; Carb 2,5 g;Protein 5,5 g
Serving 10; Cook time 10 min

Ingredients
- ¾ cup (120g) hulled hemp seeds
- 1 tablespoon dried parsley leaves
- 1½ teaspoons ground cumin
- 1 teaspoon granulated onion
- ½ teaspoon granulated garlic
- ¼ teaspoon cracked black pepper
- Grated zest of 1 lemon
- ¼ cup (64g) tahini, room temperature
Instructions
1. Line a rimmed baking sheet with parchment paper.
2. Using a food processor or blender, grind the hemp seeds until a coarse meal forms.
3. Transfer the hemp meal to a medium-sized mixing bowl, then add the rest of ingredients except the tahini and whisk together until combined.
4. Stir in the tahini and continue to mix until the ingredients are well combined and a somewhat crumbly dough forms. It will have the texture of pie dough and should hold together when pinched.
5. Using your hands, roll the mixture into 10 balls, about 1 tablespoon each. Place the balls on the lined baking sheet.
6. Chill in the freezer for at least 30 minutes or in the refrigerator for 2 hours so the falafel balls hold together.

LUPINI HUMMUS
Nutrition: Cal 162;Fat 15 g; Carb 4 g;Protein 5 g
Serving 2; Cook time 5 min.

Ingredients

- 1½ cups (250g) jarred lupini beans (packed in brine), drained
- ½ cup (120 ml) extra-virgin olive oil
- ½ cup (120 ml) water
- ¼ cup (64g) tahini, room temperature
- Juice of 1 lemon
- 1 teaspoon crushed garlic
- 1 teaspoon ground cumin
- Paprika, for sprinkling
Instructions
1. Put the lupini beans, olive oil, water, tahini, lemon juice, garlic, and cumin in a food processor or high-powered blender and blend until smooth, 2 to 3 minutes. Transfer to a serving bowl and sprinkle with paprika.

CUCUMBER AVOCADO PINWHEELS
Nutrition: Cal 201;Fat 16 g; Carb 10 g;Protein 7 g
Serving 2; Cook time 10 min.

Ingredients
- 1 medium Hass avocado (7½ ounces/212g)
- 2 sheets sushi nori
- 2 tablespoons (20g) sesame seeds
- ½ cup (50g) thinly sliced cucumbers
- ½ cup (30g) broccoli sprouts
DIPPING SAUCE SUGGESTIONS:
- Low-sodium tamari or coconut aminos with sliced scallions (green parts only)
- Tangy Avocado Mayo (here) or vegan mayo of choice
Instructions
2. Cut the avocado in half and remove the pit. Scoop the flesh into a small dish and mash with a fork.
3. Lay each sheet of nori on a flat surface and spread half of the mashed avocado on each sheet, leaving 1 inch (2.5 cm) of space at the far end of each sheet.
4. Sprinkle a tablespoon of the sesame seeds over the avocado on each sheet.
5. Lay out half of the cucumber slices on each sheet and top each with half of the broccoli sprouts.
6. Wet the far edge of each nori sheet with a little water. Starting at the edge closest to you, roll up the sheet into a roll. Press gently along the seam to make sure the wet edge of nori is sealed up against the roll.
7. Slice each roll into 6 to 8 pieces (depending on your preference), running the knife under water before each cut.
8. Serve with the dipping sauce of your choice.

CURRY TOFU SALAD BITES
Nutrition: Cal 148;Fat 10 g; Carb 6.5 g;Protein 11 g
Serving 8; Cook time 10 min.

Ingredients
- 1 (14-ounce/397-g) package extra-firm tofu, drained
- ¼ cup (60 ml) Tangy Avocado Mayo (here) or vegan mayo of choice
- ¼ cup (25g) diced celery
- 2 teaspoons curry powder or chili powder
- ¼ teaspoon salt
- 32 thin slices cucumber (about 1 cup/100g)
- Cracked black pepper
- 2 scallions (green parts only), sliced
Instructions
1. In a large mixing bowl, mash together the tofu, mayo, celery, curry powder, and salt until uniformly mixed.
2. Scoop about 1 tablespoon of the tofu mixture on top of each cucumber slice.
3. Top with freshly ground pepper and sliced scallions and serve.

CARROT GINGER SOUP

Nutrition: Cal 234;Fat 20 g; Carb 7.7 g;Protein 20 g
Serving 4; Cook time 30 min.

Ingredients
- 2 tablespoons (30 ml) extra-virgin olive oil
- 1½ cups (190g) sliced carrots
- 1 tablespoon grated fresh ginger
- 1½ cups (360 ml) vegetable broth
- 1 (13.5-ounce/400-ml) can full-fat coconut milk
- Grated zest of 1 lemon
- ¼ teaspoon freshly ground black pepper

Instructions
1. Heat the oil in a large saucepan over medium heat. Add the carrots and ginger and cook for about 5 minutes, stirring occasionally, until the carrots begin to soften.
2. Add the broth and coconut milk to the pan and cover. Continue to cook for 20 minutes, until the carrots are tender and can easily be pierced with a knife.
3. Pour the soup into a blender and blend until smooth, about 2 minutes.
4. To serve, divide the soup among 4 bowls and top with the lemon zest and freshly ground black pepper

SPICY COCONUT SOUP

Nutrition: Cal 162;Fat 15 g; Carb 5 g;Protein 7 g
Serving 4; Cook time 30 min.

Ingredients
- 1 (14-ounce/397-g) block extra-firm tofu
- ½ cup (50g) sliced red bell peppers, plus extra for garnish
- ½ cup (30g) shredded red cabbage, plus extra for garnish

FOR GARNISH (OPTIONAL):
- Microgreens
- 1 stalk lemongrass, sliced
- Grated lime zest

Instructions
1. Heat the coconut milk, broth, tamari, chili paste, garlic, ginger, and lime juice in a large saucepan over medium heat, stirring just to mix the ingredients, about 5 minutes.
2. Drain, press, and cut the tofu into 1-inch (2.5-cm) cubes and add to the soup. Add the sliced peppers and shredded cabbage, cover, and continue to simmer for 15 minutes, until the peppers and cabbage are soft.
3. Remove from the heat and portion into bowls to serve. Garnish as desired.
4. To store: Refrigerate in a tightly sealed container for up to 4 days or freeze for up to a month.
5. To reheat: Warm in a covered saucepan over medium-low heat until the desired temperature is reached.

CREAMY CAULIFLOWER SOUP

Nutrition: Cal 289;Fat 20 g; Carb 10.5 g;Protein 16 g
Serving 4; Cook time 25 min.

Ingredients
- 2 tablespoons (30 ml) extra-virgin olive oil
- 4 cups (400g) cauliflower pieces
- 3 cups (720 ml) vegetable broth
- ¾ cup (120g) hulled hemp seeds
- ¼ cup (20g) nutritional yeast
- 1 tablespoon chopped fresh chives

TOPPING SUGGESTIONS:
- Additional chopped fresh chives or sliced scallions (green parts only)
- Sauerkraut
- Freshly ground black pepper

Instructions
1. Heat the oil in a large saucepan over medium heat. Add the cauliflower and cook for about 5 minutes, stirring occasionally, until the pieces begin to soften.
2. Add the broth and continue to cook until the cauliflower is tender and can easily be pierced with a knife.
3. Carefully pour the soup into a heat-safe high-powered blender and add the hemp seeds, nutritional yeast, and chives. Blend until smooth, 2 to 3 minutes.
4. To serve, divide the soup among serving bowls and top as desired.

DESSERTS

SAMOA BARS
Nutrition: Cal 216;Fat 20 g; Carb 7 g;Protein 3 g
Serving 16; Cook time 30 min.

Ingredients
Crust
- 1 1/4 cups almond flour (125 g)
- 1/4 cup Swerve Sweetener
- 1/4 tsp salt
- 1/4 cup butter, melted

Chocolate Filling and Drizzle
- 4 oz sugar-free dark chocolate, chopped
- 2 TBSP coconut oil or butter

Coconut Caramel Filling
- 1 1/2 cups shredded coconut
- 3 TBSP butter
- 1/4 cup Swerve Brown
- 1/4 cup Bocha Sweet or additional Swerve Brown
- 3/4 cup heavy whipping cream
- 1/2 tsp vanilla extract
- 1/4 tsp salt

Instructions
Crust

1. Preheat the oven to 325°F. In a medium bowl, whisk together the almond flour, sweetener, and salt. Stir in the melted butter until the mixture begins to come together.
2. Turn out the mixture into an 8x8 baking pan and press firmly into the bottom. Bake about 15 to 18 minutes, until just golden-brown. Remove and let cool while preparing the filling.

Chocolate Filling/Drizzle

3. In a small microwave-safe bowl, melt the chocolate and coconut oil in 30 second increments, stirring in between, until melted and smooth. Alternatively, you can melt it double boiler style over a pan of barely simmering water.
4. Spread about 2/3 of the chocolate mixture over the cooled crust.

Coconut Filling

5. In a medium skillet over medium heat, spread the coconut. Stirrin frequently, toast until light golden-brown. Set aside.
6. In a large saucepan over medium heat, combine the butter and sweeteners. Cook until melted and then bring to a boil. Boil 3 to 5 minutes, until golden.
7. Remove from heat and add the cream, vanilla, and salt. The mixture will bubble vigorously—this is normal. Stir in the toasted coconut. Spread the mixture over the chocolate-covered

crust. Let cool completely (about 1 hour), then cut into squares. Gently reheat remaining chocolate mixture and drizzle over the bars.

LEMON BARS
Nutrition: Cal 190;Fat 19 g; Carb 2 g;Protein 4 g
Serving 16; Cook time 20 min.

Ingredients
Crust
- 6 TBSP butter
- 2 cups superfine blanched almond flour
- 1/3 cup granulated sugar substitute (I used Swerve)
- 1 TBSP freshly-grated lemon zest

Filling
- 1/2 cup butter
- 1/2 cup granulated sugar substitute (I used Swerve)
- 1/2 cup fresh lemon juice
- 1/4 cup grated lemon zest
- 6 egg yolks
- 1/2 tsp xanthan gum
- 2 TBSP unflavored collagen powder (or 1 tsp unflavored gelatin)

Instructions
Crust

1. Preheat the oven to 350°F.
2. Melt the butter in the microwave or a small saucepan.
3. Add the almond flour, sweetener, and lemon zest, stirring until fullycombined.

4. Press the dough evenly along the bottom and 1/2 inch up the sides of an 8 x 8 inch square pan. For best results line the pan with parchment paper or foil first, then you can simply lift out the completed lemonbars.
5. Bake for 10 minutes.
6. Remove and cool while you make the filling.

Filling

7. Melt the butter in a small saucepan on low heat.
8. Remove from heat and whisk in sweetener, lemon juice, and lemonzest until dissolved.
9. Whisk in the egg yolks and return to the stove over low heat.
10. Whisk continually until the curd starts to thicken.
11. Remove from the heat and strain into a small bowl.
12. Whisk in the the xanthan gum and collagen (or gelatin) untildissolved and smooth.
13. Pour the filling over the pre-baked crust and spread out evenly to theedges of the pan.
14. Bake the bars at 350°F for 15 minutes.
15. Remove and cool.
16. Sprinkle with Powdered Swerve before serving, if desired.
17. Cut into sixteen 2 x 2 squares.

ALMOND PECAN SHORTBREAD COOKIES
Nutrition: Cal 190;Fat 19 g; Carb 2 g;Protein 3 g
Serving 20; Cook time 2 hours 20 min.

Ingredients
- 2 cups pecans
- 1 cup almonds
- 1 cup pastured butter, melted
- 3 TBSP Swerve
- 1 tsp vanilla extract

Instructions
Crust

1. Preheat oven to 350°F.
2. In a large food processor mix almond and pecans until they turn into a coarse flour.
3. Add butter and rest of ingredients to the food processor and blend until a dough is formed.
4. Now remove the dough from the food processor and with the aid of parchment paper shape it into a roll.
5. Put in the refrigerator for 2 hrs min, until dough hardens.
6. Now slice in to 1 inch-thick rounds.
7. Place on a cookie sheet on top of parchment paper.
8. Bake at 325°F for 10 minutes.
9. Be careful not to overbake or bottom will burn! Let cool before moving from the cookie sheet. If too crumbly, refrigerate before eating!

LEMON POPPYSEED COOKIES
Nutrition: Cal 190;Fat 15 g; Carb 8 g;Protein 5 g
Serving 8; Cook time 30 min.

Ingredients
Cookies
- 1 cup almond flour
- 1/4 cup coconut flour
- 3 TBSP poppyseeds
- 1 tsp baking powder
- 1/8 tsp salt
- 6 oz cream cheese, softened
- 1/2 cup Swerve Sweetener (granulated or confectioners)
- 1 large egg, room temperature
- Zest of one lemon
- 2 TBSP lemon juice
- 1/4 tsp liquid stevia extract

Glaze (optional)
- 1/4 cup confectioner's Swerve Sweetener
- 2 to 3 TBSP lemon juice

Instructions
Cookies

1. Preheat oven to 325°F and line a large baking sheet with parchment

paper.

2. In a medium bowl, whisk together the almond flour, coconut flour, poppy seeds, baking powder, and salt.

3. In a large bowl, beat cream cheese, sweetener, egg, lemon zest, lemon

4. juice, and stevia extract. Beat in almond flour mixture until well combined.

5. Form by hand 8 to 10 even balls. Flatten with the palm of your hand to about 1/2 inch-thick circles.

6. Bake about 20 minutes, until set and just barely brown around the edges. Remove and let cool on pan.

Glaze

7. In a small bowl, whisk together sweetener and enough lemon juice to make a thin glaze. Drizzle over cooled cookies.

THIN MINT MACAROON COOKIES
Nutrition: Cal 56;Fat 5 g; Carb 4 g;Protein 7 g
Serving 24; Cook time 20 min.

Ingredients
- 2 cups desiccated unsweetened coconut
- 1/2 cup unsweetened almond milk
- 1 1/2 tsp peppermint extract
- 1/2 cup granulated sweetener
- 3 egg whites
- 1/4 tsp xanthan gum
- 1 oz 90% or greater cacao dark chocolate

Instructions

1. Combine the coconut, almond milk, peppermint extract, and sweetener in a medium bowl and stir well.

2. In a separate large bowl whisk the egg whites and xanthan gum-together until soft peaks form.

3. Fold the egg mixture into the coconut mixture until fully combined.

4. Drop the dough mixture by scoop or tablespoon into 24 mounds onto a parchment-lined cookie sheet. Flatten into disks with your hand or aflat spatula.

5. Bake in a preheated 325°F oven for 16 minutes or until slightly firm.

6. Remove and cool.

7. Place the chocolate in a ziplock bag and melt in the microwave for 30seconds at a time until just liquid. Snip a tiny corner off of the bag and squeeze the chocolate out onto the cookies in a circular (or any) pattern. Cool and serve.

CHOCOLATE CHUNK COOKIES
Nutrition: Cal 140;Fat 12 g; Carb 6 g;Protein 4 g
Serving 18; Cook time 50 min.

Ingredients
- 2 cups / 6.3 oz / 190 g blanched almond flour/meal
- ¼ tsp fine grain sea salt
- ½ tsp baking soda
- ¼ cup / 2 oz / 55 g coconut oil, melted
- 2 TBSP honey (or maple syrup)
- 1 TBSP vanilla extract
- ¾ cup / 3.5 oz / 100 g coarsely chopped +70% dark chocolate

Instructions

1. Preheat oven at 350°F (175°C), place a rack in the middle. Line a baking sheet with parchment paper and set aside.

2. In the bowl of a food processor combine almond flour, salt, and baking soda. Pulse in coconut oil, honey (or maple syrup) and vanilla extract until dough forms.

3. Remove the blade from the food processor and stir in chocolate chunks by hand. The dough will be very moist and oily—don't worry, that's how it's supposed to be.

4. Let the dough rest in the refrigerator for 30 minutes. The resting time will make the dough easier to handle.

5. Take the dough out of the fridge and scoop one level tablespoon at a time onto the prepared baking sheet.

6. With your hands, press balls of dough down gently and give them a look-alike cookie shape.

7. Bake in the oven for about 7 minutes (8 minutes for darker cookies).

8. Let cookies cool on the baking sheet (without touching) for 15 minutes, then with the help of a spatula place cookies onto a rack and let cool completely.

ICED LEMON SUGAR COOKIES
Nutrition: Cal 96;Fat 8 g; Carb 4 g;Protein 7 g
Serving 40; Cook time 30 min.

Ingredients
Sanding "Sugar"
- 2 TBSP Swerve Sweetener or other granulated erythritol or xylitol
- 1 drop yellow gel food coloring

Dough
- 1 1/2 cups almond flour
- 1/4 cup coconut flour
- 1 tsp baking powder
- 1/2 tsp xanthan gum
- 1/4 tsp salt
- 6 TBSP butter, softened
- 1/2 cup Swerve Sweetener (or other erythritol sweetener)
- 1 large egg, room temperature
- 3 TBSP fresh lemon juice
- Zest of one lemon

Glaze
- 6 TBSP powdered Swerve sweetener (or other powdered erythritol)
- 3 TBSP fresh lemon juice

Instructions

1. For the sanding "sugar," combine granulated sweetener and gel food coloring in a small bowl. Use the back of a spoon to work food coloring into sweetener granules. Set aside.

2. For the dough, whisk together almond flour, coconut flour, baking powder, xanthan gum, and salt in a medium bowl.

3. In a large bowl, beat butter with sweetener until well combined. Beat in egg, lemon juice, and lemon zest.

4. Add almond flour mixture and beat until dough comes together. Turn out dough onto a large piece of parchment paper. Pat into a rough circle and then top with another piece of parchment. Roll out to about 1/4-inch thickness. Place on a cookie sheet and chill in refrigerator for 30 minutes.

5. Preheat oven to 325°F and line another baking sheet with parchment. Cut out cookies into desired shape and lift carefully with a small, offset spatula or knife. Place cookies at least 1/2 inch apart on prepared baking sheet. Reroll your dough and cut out more cookies (if your dough gets too soft to work with, you can put it in the freezer for a bit to harden up).

6. Bake 12 to 14 minutes, or until just golden-brown and firm to the touch.

7. Let cool on pan 10 minutes, then transfer to a wire rack to cool completely.

8. For the glaze, stir powdered sweetener and lemon juice in a small bowl until smooth.

9. Spread a thin layer of glaze over each cookie and sprinkle with sanding sugar.

RASBERRY ALMOND THUMBPRINT COOKIES
Nutrition: Cal 180;Fat 16 g; Carb 4 g;Protein 4 g
Serving 24; Cook time 35 min.

Ingredients
Cookies
- 1 3/4 cup almond flour
- 1 TBSP coconut flour
- 1/2 tsp baking powder
- 1/2 cup butter, softened
- 1/2 cup confectioner's Swerve Sweetener
- 1 egg yolk
- 1 tsp almond extract
- 1/4 cup Raspberry Chia Seed Jam

Glaze
- 3 TBSP confectioner's Swerve Sweetener
- 1/4 tsp almond extract

•1 to 2 TBSP water

Instructions

Cookies

1.Preheat oven to 325°F and line a baking sheet with parchment or a silicone liner.

2.In a medium bowl, whisk together almond flour, coconut flour, and baking powder.

3.In a large bowl, beat butter with sweetener until well combined and fluffy. Beat in egg yolk and almond extract. Beat in almond flour mixture until well incorporated.

4.Form dough into scant 1 inch balls and place two inches apart on prepared baking sheet. Press each ball down to about 1/2 inch high. Using your thumb, press an indentation into the center of each cookie.

5.Spoon about 1/2 teaspoon of jam into each and bake until just barely browning around the edges, 10 to 12 minutes. Cool on pan. The cookies will not seem set but will continue to firm up as they cool.

Glaze

6.In a small bowl, whisk together sweetener, almond extract, and water until a pourable consistency is achieved. Drizzle over cooled cookies.

GINGERBREAD COOKIES
Nutrition: Cal 130;Fat 11 g; Carb 4 g;Protein 3 g
Serving 20; Cook time 35 min.

Ingredients

•1/2 cup butter, softened
•2 eggs
•1 tsp vanilla extract
•1 tsp cinnamon liquid stevia
•1/4 cup heavy cream
•1 TBSP molasses
•2 cups sunflower seeds ground, or almond flour
•1/2 cup coconut flour
•1/4 cup Swerve or erythritol
•1 tsp baking powder
•1 tsp cinnamon
•1 tsp ground ginger
•1/4 tsp ground nutmeg
•1/4 tsp ground cloves
•1/4 tsp salt

Instructions

1.Preheat oven to 350°F.

2.Place the first 6 ingredients into a stand mixer and blend on high until incorporated.

3.Whisk the rest of the ingredients together in a bowl.

4.Slowly pour the dry ingredients into the wet in the stand mixer.

5.Blend until combined. It will be sticky so place dough in plastic wrap and refrigerate for at least one hour.

6.Flour surface of counter with gluten-free flour and your hands with flour then pat down dough or use a rolling pin until it's 1/2 inch in thickness.

7.Use cookie cutouts for gingerbread men and place on a silpat-lined baking sheet.

8.Add chocolate chip eyes and buttons, if desired.

9.Bake for 12 minutes.

10.Allow to cool for 10 minutes before removing gently from pan.

ALMOND BUTTER CHOCOLATE CHIP COOKIES
Nutrition: Cal 130;Fat 9 g; Carb 12 g;Protein 4 g
Serving 10; Cook time 35 min.

Ingredients

•1 large egg
•1 cup almond butter
•1/2 cup light brown sugar, lightly packed
•1 tsp baking soda
•1 cup dark chocolate chips

Instructions

1.Set oven to 350°F

2.Crack the egg into a medium bowl and beat it lightly. Add in the almond butter, baking soda, and sugar and mix everything together well.

3.Fold in the chocolate chips.

4.Scoop the dough onto a parchment or silpat-lined baking sheet. I use a (1 3/4 inch) scoop, but you can use a tablespoon. Space the cookies well apart, and flatten them slightly with the back of a spoon.

5.Bake for 8 to 10 minutes. Don't overbake these; the cookies will look underdone, but they will firm up as they cool.

6.Let them cool for a couple of minutes on the baking sheet, then transfer them carefully to a cooling rack.

ALMOND CRESCENT COOKIES
Nutrition: Cal 185;Fat 11 g; Carb 6 g;Protein 5 g
Serving 15; Cook time 35 min.

Ingredients

•1 stick salted butter, softened (1/2 cup)
•Pinch of kosher salt
•1/2 cup granulated erythritol sweetener
•1/2 tsp vanilla extract
•1 tsp almond extract
•2 cups superfine almond flour
•1/3 cup sliced almonds

Instructions

1.Beat the butter, salt, and sweetener until fluffy. Add the vanilla and almond extracts and blend well.

2.Add the almond flour and beat until just blended to a stiff dough.

3.Divide the dough into 12 balls.

4.Roll each ball into a 3 inch log.

5.Spread the sliced almonds onto a clean surface and crush slightly into smaller pieces with the heel of your hand.

6.Roll the logs in the almond pieces and then bend the two ends in and pinch slightly to create a crescent shape.

7.Place the almond crescents on a parchment-lined cookie sheet and bake in apreheated 350°F oven for 15 minutes. Remove and cool before serving.

MAPLE CREAM SANDWICH COOKIES
Nutrition: Cal 215;Fat 17 g; Carb 6 g;Protein 8 g
Serving 24; Cook time 40 min.

Ingredients

Cookies

•2 cups almond flour
•1/3 cup Swerve Sweetener
•1 tsp baking powder
•1/4 tsp salt
•1 large egg
•2 1/2 TBSP butter, melted
•1 tsp maple extract
•1/8 tsp stevia extract

Filling

•1/4 cup butter, softened
•1 cup powdered Swerve Sweetener
•2 TBSP cream, room temperature
•3/4 tsp maple extract

Instructions

Cookies

1.Preheat oven to 275°F and line two baking sheets with parchment paper.

2.Whisk almond flour, sweetener, baking powder, and salt together in a large bowl. Stir in egg, butter, maple extract, and stevia extract until dough comes together.

3.Turn dough out onto a large piece of parchment paper and pat into a rough rectangle. Top with another piece of parchment.

4.Roll dough out to about 1/8 inch thickness. Using a 2-inch maple leaf cookie cutter (or whatever shape you prefer) to cut out as many shapes as possible. Dough can be re-rolled multiple times to get more cookies.

5.Place half the cookies face up and half face down on the prepared baking sheet (if your cookie cutter is slightly irregular, this allows you to match them up properly after they are baked).

6.Bake about 20 minutes, until light golden-brown and firm to the touch. Watch them carefully, they can easily get too dark.

7.Remove from oven and let cool completely.

Filling

8.Beat butter and powdered sweetener together in a medium bowl until smooth. Beat in cream and maple extract to achieve a spreadable consistency.

9.To assemble, take one cookie and spread the backside with about a teaspoon of filling. Top with another cookie, backside towards the filling.

MATCHA FUDGE FAT BOMBS
Nutrition: Cal 194;Fat 19 g; Carb 1 g;Protein 1 g
Serving 20; Cook time 15 min.

Ingredients
- 3.5 oz cocoa butter
- 1/2 cup coconut butter
- 1/2 cup sugar-free maple syrup
- 1/3 cup heavy cream
- 3 TBSP coconut oil
- 2 scoops matcha mct powder
- 2 tsp vanilla essence

Instructions

1.Place all the ingredients in a small saucepan and place over low heat.

2.Heat until the cocoa butter has melted, stir to combine all ingredients.

3.Pour the mixture into an 8x8 inch square cake pan, lined with parchment paper.

4.Set in the fridge for 3 hours, or until firm.

5.Cut into 24 pieces and serve.

STRAWBERRY & CREAM FAT BOMBS
Nutrition: Cal 160;Fat 17 g; Carb 1 g;Protein 3 g
Serving 10; Cook time 15 min.

Ingredients
- 6 oz cream cheese, softened
- 5 fl.oz double cream
- 1 oz vanilla collagen protein powder
- 3 TBSP coconut oil, plus extra 2 tsp for rolling
- 1 tsp strawberry essence

Instructions

- Mix all ingredients with a hand mixer for 5 minutes, until well combined.
- Set the mixture in the fridge for 1 hour.
- When the mixture is set, rub your hands with a little coconut oil and shape the mix into 10 evenly-sized fat bombs. The coconut oil will stop the mix from sticking to your hands.
- Store the fat bombs in an airtight container in the fridge or freezer.

ZESTY LEMON FAT BOMBS
Nutrition: Cal 140;Fat 13 g; Carb 3 g;Protein 1 g
Serving 10; Cook time 15 min.

Ingredients
- 1 oz coconut butter
- 1 oz coconut oil
- 1 oz unsalted butter
- 1 TBSP sukrin melis
- 1 lemon zest & juice

Instructions

1.Place all the ingredients into a small saucepan over low heat. Heat until just melted, then remove from the heat.

2.Pour into silicone molds.

3.Place in the fridge and chill for 1 hour, until set.

VANILLA STRAWBERRY FUDGE FAT BOMBS
Nutrition: Cal 150;Fat 16 g; Carb 1 g;Protein 1 g
Serving 25; Cook time 15 min.

Ingredients
Vanilla Layer
- 8 oz cream cheese, softened
- 8 oz butter, softened
- 2 tsp vanilla extract
- 3 TBSP erythritol

Strawberry Layer
- 8 oz cream cheese, softened
- 8 oz butter, softened
- 1 oz strawberry protein powder (low or no carb)

Instructions
Vanilla Layer

1.Line a baking tray with parchment paper and set aside.

2.Place the softened cream cheese, softened butter, vanilla extract, and erythritol in a bowl and mix with a hand mixer on low speed, slowly building up to medium/high speed until all ingredients are really well combined.

3.Pour the vanilla layer into the lined tray and smooth out as evenly as possible, set in the fridge for at least 30 minutes.

Strawberry Layer

4.As you did with the vanilla layer, place the softened cream cheese, butter, and strawberry protein powder in a bowl. Mix on low speed with a hand mixer and slowly increase the speed to medium/high until all ingredients are really well combined.

5.Pour the strawberry layer on top of the vanilla layer, smooth it out and set in the fridge for 1 hour.

6.Cut your fudge into bite-sized pieces and keep it cool, as it will soften very quickly in warm temperatures.

CHOCOLATE CHEESECAKE KISSES FAT BOMBS
Nutrition: Cal 97;Fat 9 g; Carb 1 g;Protein 1 g
Serving 25; Cook time 25 min.

Ingredients
- 8 oz cream cheese, softened
- 2 oz natvia icing mix
- 1 tsp vanilla essence
- 7 oz heavy cream
- 5 oz sugar-free chocolate

Instructions

1.Add the chocolate to a small heatproof bowl and place over a small saucepan of simmering water, ensuring that the bowl doesn't touch the water.

2.Melt the chocolate completely and remove from the heat. Set aside.

3.Place the softened cream cheese in a bowl, using your hand mixer, mix on medium speed until smooth.

4.Add the Natvia Icing Mix and vanilla essence and mix on low speed until combined.

5.Add the heavy cream and mix on medium speed until smooth and beginning to thicken.

6.Pour in the melted chocolate and mix on medium speed, until all ingredients are completely combined and the mixture is firm enough to pipe.

7.Add the mixture into a piping bag with a star nozzle. Pipe evenly into mini cupcake papers. We filled 24 cupcake paper, depending on your piping skills, you may get more or less.

8.Cover the kisses and set in the fridge for at least 3 hours, or overnight for best results.

LEMON & POPPYSEED FAT BOMB
Nutrition: Cal 160;Fat 12 g; Carb 1 g;Protein 1 g
Serving 18; Cook time 25 min.

Ingredients
- 8 oz cream cheese, softened
- 3 TBSP erythritol

- 1 TBSP poppy seeds
- 1 lemon zest only
- 4 TBSP sour cream
- 2 TBSP lemon juice

Instructions
1. Place all ingredients in a bowl and using a hand mixer, mix on low speed; when ingredients are combined, mix on medium/high speed for 3 minutes.
2. Gently spoon mixture into mini cupcake cases or place into a piping bag and pipe into mini cupcakes cases. Refrigerate for at least 1 hour.
3. These cups will soften quickly in warm weather, we recommend to keep them refrigerated.

PINA COLADA FAT BOMBS
Nutrition: Cal 120;Fat 8 g; Carb 1 g;Protein 2 g
Serving 16; Cook time 25 min.

Ingredients
- 2 tsp pineapple essence
- 3 tsp erythritol
- 2 TBSP gelatin
- 1/2 cup boiling water
- 1/2 cup coconut cream
- 1 tsp rum extract
- 2 scoops MCT Powder (Optional)

Instructions
1. Dissolve the gelatin and erythritol in the boiling water in a heat-proof jug and add the pineapple essence.
2. Allow to cool for 5 minutes.
3. Add the coconut cream and rum extract and continue stirring for 2 minutes.
4. Pour into silicon molds and set for at least 1 hour, depending on the size of your mold.
5. Gently remove from the mold and enjoy. Store in the fridge.
6. Optional: If you want to get a real kick out of your fat bombs recipe try adding a scoop or two of MCT Powder, but be sure to mix it well in the hot water first (that may require a stick blender).

RED VELVET FAT BOMBS
Nutrition: Cal 160;Fat 8 g; Carb 1 g;Protein 2 g
Serving 24; Cook time 40 min.

Ingredients
- 100 g 90% dark chocolate
- 125 g cream cheese, softened
- 100 g butter, softened
- 3 TBSP natvia
- 1 tsp vanilla extract
- 4 drops red food coloring
- 1/3 cup heavy cream, whipped

Instructions
1. Melt the chocolate in a heat-proof bowl over a small pot of simmering water. Make sure that the bowl isn't touching the water, as this will cause the chocolate to burn.
2. While the chocolate is melting, mix together the remaining ingredients with a hand mixer on medium speed for 3 minutes. Ensure the mix is fully combined.
3. With the hand mixer on low speed, slowly add the chocolate mixture to the other ingredients. Mix on medium speed for 2 minutes.
4. Add the mixture to a piping bag and pipe the fat bomb mixture onto a lined tray. Set in the fridge for 40 minutes.
5. Add the heavy cream to whipping canister and apply whipped cream to the fat bombs.

RASPBERRY CREAM FAT BOMBS
Nutrition: Cal 160;Fat 8 g; Carb 1 g;Protein 2 g
Serving 24; Cook time 40 min.

Ingredients
- 1 (9 g packet) raspberry sugar-free jello
- 15 g gelatin powder
- 1/2 cup water, boiling
- 1/2 cup heavy cream

Instructions
1. Dissolve gelatin and jello in boiling water.
2. Add the cream slowly while stirring and continue to stir for 1 minute. If you add the cold cream in all at once and don't thoroughly mix, the jellies will split, creating a layered affect.
3. Pour the mixture into candy molds and set in the fridge for at least 30 minutes.

MAPLE PECAN FAT BOMBS
Nutrition: Cal 147;Fat 15 g; Carb 1 g;Protein 3 g
Serving 9; Cook time 25 min.

Ingredients
- 4 oz unsalted butter
- 2 oz pecan butter
- 1 scoop vanilla collagen powder
- 2 TBSP sugar-free maple syrup
- 9 pecan nuts

Instructions
1. Place all ingredients (except the pecans) into a small saucepan over low heat.
2. Whisk together until combined, then remove from heat. Allow to cool for 5 minutes.
3. Pour into a small heat-proof dish lined with parchment paper.
4. Sprinkle over the pecans then put in the fridge to chill.
5. Cool for 1-2 hours until set firm.
6. Cut into squares and enjoy.

CHOCOLATE ZUCCHINI BREAD
Nutrition: Cal 185;Fat 17 g; Carb 6 g;Protein 5 g
Serving 12; Cook time 50 min.

Ingredients
Dry Ingredients
- 1 1/2 cup almond flour (170 g)
- 1/4 cup unsweetened cocoa powder (25 g)
- 1 1/2 tsp baking soda
- 2 tsp ground cinnamon
- 1/4 tsp sea salt
- 1/2 cup sugar-free crystal sweetener (Monk fruit or erythritol) (100 g) or coconut sugar if refined sugar-free

Wet Ingredients
- 1 cup zucchini, finely grated measure packed, discard
- juice/liquid if there is some - about 2 small zucchini
- 1 large egg
- 1/4 cup + 2 TBSP canned coconut cream (100 ml)
- 1/4 cup extra virgin coconut oil, melted (60ml)
- 1 tsp vanilla extract
- 1 tsp apple cider vinegar

Filling (optional)
- 1/2 cup sugar-free chocolate chips
- 1/2 cup chopped walnuts (or nuts you like)

Instructions
1. Preheat oven to 180°C (375°F). Line a baking loaf pan (9 inches x 5 inches) with parchment paper. Set aside.
2. Remove both extremity of the zucchinis, keep skin on.
3. Finely grate the zucchini using a vegetable grater. Measure the amount needed in a measurement cup. Make sure you press/pack them firmly for a precise measure and to squeeze out any liquid from the grated zucchini, I usually don't have any! If you do, discard the liquid or keep for another recipe.
4. In a large mixing bowl, stir all the dry ingredients together: almond flour, unsweetened cocoa powder, sugar free crystal sweetener, cinnamon, sea salt, and baking soda. Set aside.

5. Add all the wet ingredients into the dry ingredients: grated zucchini, coconut oil, coconut cream, vanilla, egg, apple cider vinegar.
6. Stir to combine all the ingredients together.
7. Stir in the chopped nuts and sugar-free chocolate chips.
8. Transfer the chocolate bread batter into the prepared loaf pan.
9. Bake 50 - 55 minutes—you may want to cover the bread loaf with a piece of foil after 40 minutes to avoid the top to darken too much, up to you.
10. The bread will stay slightly moist in the middle and firm up after fully cooled down.
11. Transfer pan to a wire rack; let bread cool 15 minutes before removing from pan.

CINNAMON ALMOND FLOUR BREAD
Nutrition: Cal 221;Fat 15 g; Carb 10 g;Protein 9 g
Serving 8; Cook time 30 min.

Ingredients
- 2 cups fine blanched almond flour (I use Bob's Red Mill)
- 2 TBSP coconut flour
- 1/2 tsp sea salt
- 1 tsp baking soda
- 1/4 cup flaxseed meal or chia meal (ground chia or flaxseed, see notes for how to make your own)
- 5 eggs and 1 egg white whisked together
- tsp apple cider vinegar or lemon juice
- 2 TBSP maple syrup or honey
- 2–3 TBSP of clarified butter (melted) or coconut oil (divided). Vegan butter also works.
- 1 TBSP cinnamon, plus extra for topping
- Optional: Chia seeds to sprinkle on top before baking

Instructions
1. Preheat oven to 350°F. Line an 8×4 bread pan with parchment paper at the bottom and grease the sides.
2. In a large bowl, mix together your almond flour, coconut flour, salt, baking soda, flaxseed meal or chia meal, and 1/2 tablespoon of cinnamon.
3. In another small bowl, whisk together your eggs and egg white. Then add in your maple syrup (or honey), apple cider vinegar, and melted butter (1.5 to 2 tablespoons).
4. Mix wet ingredients into dry. Be sure to remove any clumps that might have occurred from the almond flour or coconut flour.
5. Pour batter into a your greased loaf pan.
6. Bake at 350°F for 30-35 minutes, until a toothpick inserted into center of loaf comes out clean. Mine came to around 35 minutes, but I am at altitude.
7. Remove from the oven.
8. Next, whisk together the other 1 to 2 tablespoons of melted butter (or oil) and mix it with 1/2 tablespoon of cinnamon. Brush this on top of your cinnamon almond flour bread.
9. Cool and serve, or store for later.
10. Transfer pan to a wire rack; let bread cool 15 minutes before removing from pan.

BLUEBERRY ENGLISH MUFFIN BREAD
Nutrition: Cal 156;Fat 13 g; Carb 4 g;Protein 5 g
Serving 12; Cook time 45 min.

Ingredients
- 1/2 cup almond butter, cashew, or peanut butter
- 1/4 cup butter ghee or coconut oil
- 1/2 cup almond flour
- 1/2 tsp salt
- 2 tsp baking powder
- 1/2 cup almond milk, unsweetened
- 5 eggs, beaten
- 1/2 cup blueberries

Instructions
1. Preheat oven to 350°F.

2. In a microwavable bowl melt nut butter and butter together for 30 seconds, stir until combined well.
3. In a large bowl, whisk almond flour, salt, and baking powder together. Pour the nut butter mixture into the large bowl and stir to combine.
4. Whisk the almond milk and eggs together then pour into the bowl and stir well.
5. Drop in fresh blueberries or break apart frozen blueberries and gently stir into the batter.
6. Line a loaf pan with parchment paper and lightly grease the parchment paper as well.
7. Pour the batter into the loaf pan and bake 45 minutes or until a toothpick in center comes out clean.
8. Cool for about 30 minutes then remove from pan.
9. Slice and toast each slice before serving.1/2 cup chopped walnuts (or nuts you like)

ZUCCHINI BREAD WITH WALNUTS
Nutrition: Cal 200;Fat 18 g; Carb 3 g;Protein 5 g
Serving 16; Cook time 60 min.

Ingredients
- 3 large eggs
- ½ cup olive oil
- 1 tsp vanilla extract
- 2 1/2 cups almond flour
- 1 1/2 cups erythritol
- ½ tsp salt
- 1 1/2 tsp baking powder
- ½ tsp nutmeg
- 1 tsp ground cinnamon
- ¼ tsp ground ginger
- 1 cup grated zucchini
- ½ cup chopped walnuts

Instructions
1. Preheat oven to 350°F. Whisk together the eggs, oil, and vanilla extract. Set to the side.
2. In another bowl, mix together the almond flour, erythritol, salt, baking powder, nutmeg, cinnamon, and ginger. Set to the side.
3. Using a cheesecloth or paper towel, take the zucchini and squeeze out the excess water.
4. Then, whisk the zucchini into the bowl with the eggs.
5. Slowly add the dry ingredients into the egg mixture using a hand mixer until fully blended.
6. Lightly spray a 9x5 loaf pan, and spoon in the zucchini bread mixture.
7. Then, spoon in the chopped walnuts on top of the zucchini bread. Press walnuts into the batter using a spatula.
8. Bake for 60-70 minutes at 350°F or until the walnuts on top look browned.

KETO BAGEL
Nutrition: Cal 168;Fat 17 g; Carb 8 g;Protein 5 g
Serving 4; Cook time 45 min.

Ingredients
- 1 cup (120 g) of almond flour
- 1/4 cup (28 g) of coconut flour
- 1 TBSP (7 g) of psyllium husk powder
- 1 tsp (2 g) of baking powder
- 1 tsp (3 g) of garlic powder
- Pinch of salt
- 2 medium eggs (88 g)
- 2 tsp (10 ml) of white wine vinegar
- 2 1/2 TBSP (38 ml) of ghee, melted
- 1 TBSP (15 ml) of olive oil
- 1 tsp (5 g) of sesame seeds

Instructions
1. Preheat the oven to 320°F (160°C).
2. Combine the almond flour, coconut flour, psyllium husk powder, baking powder, garlic powder, and salt in a bowl.

3. In a separate bowl, whisk the eggs and vinegar together. Slowly drizzle in the melted ghee (which should not be piping hot) and whisk in well.
4. Add the wet mixture to the dry mixture and use a wooden spoon to combine well. Leave to sit for 2-3 minutes.
5. Divide the mixture into 4 equal-sized portions. Using your hands, shape the mixture into a round shape and place onto a tray lined with parchment paper. Use a small spoon or apple corer to make the center hole.
6. Brush the tops with olive oil and scatter over the sesame seeds. Bake in the oven for 20-25 minutes until cooked through. Allow to cool slightly before enjoying!

CHOCOLATE COCONUT MOUNDS PIE
Nutrition: Cal 242;Fat 21 g; Carb 12 g;Protein 5 g
Serving 8; Cook time 60 min.

Ingredients
• 2 cups unsweetened coconut milk
• 4 eggs
• 1 tsp vanilla extract
• 1-1/2 tsp coconut stevia
• 2 cups unsweetened shredded coconut
• 1/2 cup unsweetened cocoa powder
• 1/4 cup coconut flour
• 1/2 tsp salt

Coconut Cream Topping
• 1 can (15 oz) coconut milk (opened, overnight in fridge)
• Optional: 2 ounces Lily's sugar-free coconut chocolate Bar

Instructions
1. In a stand mixer with a whisk attachment blend the first 4 ingredients together.
2. Change to the paddle attachment and add the rest of the ingredients on low speed.
3. Pour mixture into a pie plate and bake for 40 minutes.
4. Allow to cool before adding coconut cream topping.
5. Keep refrigerated.

BROWNIE TRUFFLE PIE
Nutrition: Cal 370;Fat 33 g; Carb 6 g;Protein 8 g
Serving 4; Cook time 60 min.

Ingredients
Crust
• 1 1/4 cup almond flour
• 3 TBSP coconut flour
• 1 TBSP granulated Swerve Sweetener
• 1/4 tsp salt
• 5 TBSP butter chilled and cut into small pieces
• 2-4 TBSP ice water

Filling
• 1/2 cup almond flour
• 6 TBSP cocoa powder
• 6 TBSP Swerve Sweetener
• 1 tsp baking powder
• 2 large eggs
• 5 TBSP water
• 1/4 cup melted butter
• 1 TBSP Sukrin Fiber Syrup (optional, but helps create a more gooey center)
• 1/2 tsp vanilla extract
• 3 TBSP sugar-free chocolate chips

Topping
• 1 cup whipping cream
• 2 TBSP confectioner's Swerve Sweetener
• 1/4 tsp vanilla extract
• 1/2 oz sugar-free dark chocolate

Instructions
Crust

1. Preheat oven to 325ºF and grease a glass or ceramic pie pan.
2. In a large bowl, combine almond flour, coconut flour, sweetener, and salt. Cut in butter using a pastry cutter or two sharp knives until mixture resembles coarse crumbs. Add two tablespoons water and mix until dough comes together. Add more water only if necessary to get dough to come together.
3. Press evenly into the bottom and up the sides of prepared pie pan, crimp edges, and prick bottom all over with a fork. Bake 12 minutes.

Filling
4. In a large bowl, whisk together the almond flour, cocoa powder, sweetener, and baking powder. Stir in eggs, water, melted butter, and vanilla extract until well combined. Stir in chocolate chips.
5. Pour batter into crust and bake 30 minutes, covering with foil about halfway through. Remove and let cool 10 minutes, then refrigerate half an hour until cool.

Topping
6. Combine cream, sweetener, and vanilla extract in a large bowl. Beat until cream holds stiff peaks. Spread over cooled filling. Shave dark chocolate over top. Chill another hour or two until completely set.

COCONUT KEY LIME PIE
Nutrition: Cal 460;Fat 42 g; Carb 6 g;Protein 11 g
Serving 9; Cook time 50 min.

Ingredients
Crust
• 2 cups raw hazelnuts
• 1 egg
• 4 TBSP chia seeds
• 4 TBSP organic butter, melted
• 1 TBSP coconut oil
• 1 TBSP Swerve

Filling
cup coconut cream
• 1.5 cup sour cream
• 3 large eggs
• 1 cup fresh key lime juice
• 3 TBSP Swerve
• 1 TBSP key lime zest
• ½ cup unsweetened coconut shavings

Instructions
1. Pre heat oven to 375ºF.
2. In a food processor grind the hazelnuts until they turn in to a flour, then add the chia seeds, Swerve, egg, and melted butter. Mix everything together until a dough is formed.
3. Now grease a 6 by 9 inch pyrex with coconut oil.
4. Press the crust flat into the pyrex.
5. Bake for 20 min at 375ºF.
6. In the meantime, prepare the filling.
7. In a large bowl mix all the filling ingredients and blend with an immersion blender until smooth and frothy.
8. Remove the crust from the oven once done.
9. Pour filling onto crust and put back in the oven at 350ºF.
10. Bake for 45 minutes.
11. Remove from the oven, and let cool, then sprinkle evenly with the coconut flakes. Then refrigerate overnight.

SWEET RICOTTA CHEESE PIE
Nutrition: Cal 270;Fat 12 g; Carb 4 g;Protein 14 g
Serving 8; Cook time 50 min.

Ingredients
• 1 1/2 cups almond flour, sifted
• 3 TBSP low carb sugar substitute (I used Swerve)
• 1/4 tsp salt
• 1/4 cup butter, melted
• 1 egg
• 1 tsp vanilla extract
• 4 eggs, beaten

- 1 tsp vanilla extract
- 15 oz ricotta cheese
- 1 TBSP coconut flour
- 3/4 cup Swerve (add more if desired; up to 1 cup)
- 2 TBSP low carb sugar substitute or 24 drops liquid stevia to help round out sweetness

Instructions
1. In deep dish pie plate, mix together almond flour, 3 tablespoons equivalent sugar substitute and 1/4 teaspoon salt.
2. Pour in butter, 1 egg and 1 teaspoon vanilla.
3. Mix until dough forms.
4. Press into pie plate. Bake at 350 degrees F for 10 minutes.
5. Set on rack to cool slightly.
6. In a large bowl mix 4 beaten eggs, 1 teaspoon vanilla, ricotta cheese, coconut flour, 1 cup equivalent sugar substitute and 2 tablespoons other sweetener.
7. Beat until smooth.
8. Pour into crust and bake at 350°F for 45 minutes or until lightly browned and firm.

CHAYOTE SQUASH MOCK APPLE PIE
Nutrition: Cal 190;Fat 16 g; Carb 6 g;Protein 2 g
Serving 16; Cook time 45 min.

Ingredients
Crust
- 1/2 cup butter, melted
- 1 1/2 cup almond flour
- 3/4 cup coconut flour
- 4 eggs
- 1 TBSP whole psyllium husks
- 1/2 tsp salt

Filling
- 5 medium chayote squash
- 3/4 cup low carb sugar substitute
- 1 1/2 tsp cinnamon
- 1/4 tsp ginger
- 1/8 tsp nutmeg
- 1 TBSP xanthan gum
- 1 TBSP lemon juice
- 2 tsp apple extract (optional)
- 1/3 cup butter cut in small pieces

Topping
- 1 egg
- Low carb sugar substitute

Instructions
Crust
1. Mix crust ingredients to form dough.
2. Separate into two dough balls.
3. Roll each crust ball out into pie crust.
4. Transfer one crust to 9 inch pie dish. Smooth out any cracks.
5. Reserve remaining crust for pie top.
6. **Filling**
7. Peel chayote and cut into slices.
8. Boil sliced chayote until fork tender. Drain. Return to pot.
9. Add sweetener, xanthan gum, lemon juice, and apple extract to cooked chayote squash.
10. Pour chayote mixture into prepared pie crust. Dot filling with butter.
Topping
11. Cover filling with reserved pie crust.
12. Flute edges of pie crust together and cut slits on pie top.
13. Brush egg on top crust and sprinkle with additional sweetener, if desired.
14. Bake at 375°F for 30-35 minutes (I took mine out after 30 minutes).

LEMON MERINGUE PIE
Nutrition: Cal 218;Fat 17 g; Carb 7 g;Protein 6 g
Serving 12; Cook time 60 min.

Ingredients

Pastry Crust
- 1 1/4 cup almond flour
- 2 TBSP coconut flour
- 2 TBSP arrowroot starch OR 2 TBSP oat fiber for THM
- 1 TBSP granulated Swerve Sweetener
- 1 tsp xanthan gum
- 1/4 tsp salt
- 5 TBSP butter, chilled and cut into small pieces
- 2-4 TBSP ice water

Filling
- 1 cup plus 2 TBSP water, divided
- 1 cup granulated Swerve Sweetener
- 2 tsp lemon zest
- 1/4 tsp salt
- 4 large egg yolks
- 1/3 cup lemon juice
- 3 TBSP butter
- 1/2 tsp xanthan gum
- 1 TBSP grassfed gelatin (can use 1 envelope Knox gelatin)

Meringue Topping
- 4 large egg whites at room temperature
- 1/4 tsp cream of tartar
- Pinch of salt
- 1/4 cup powdered Swerve Sweetener
- 1/4 cup granulated Swerve Sweetener
- 1/2 tsp vanilla extract

Instructions
Crust
1. Preheat oven to 325°F.
2. Combine almond flour, coconut flour, arrowroot starch, sweetener, xanthan gum, and salt in the bowl of a food processor. Pulse to combine.
3. Sprinkle surface with butter pieces and pulse until mixture resembles coarse crumbs.
4. With processor running on low, add ice water, one tablespoon at a time until dough begins to clump together.
5. Place a large piece of parchment on work surface and dust liberally with additional almond flour. Turn out dough and pat into a circle. Sprinkle with more almond flour and over with another large piece of parchment.
6. Roll out carefully into an 11-inch circle. Remove top layer of parchment. Place a 9-inch pie pan upside down on crust and then carefully flip both over so crust is lying in the pie pan. Remove parchment. (Alternatively, you can skip rolling out the pastry and simply press the crust into the bottom and up the sides of the pan.)
7. You may get some cracking and tears. Simply use small pieces of pastry from the overhang to patch them up. Crimp the edges of the crust and prick all over with a fork.
8. Bake crust 12 minutes, then remove and let cool.
Lemon Filling
9. In a medium saucepan over medium heat, combine 1 cup of the water, sweetener, lemon zest, and salt. Bring to just a boil, whisking frequently, until sweetener dissolves.
10. In a medium bowl, whisk egg yolks until smooth. Slowly add about 1/2 cup of the water to the egg yolks, whisking constantly. Then gradually whisk the egg yolks back into the pan and lower the heat to low. Cook for 1 minute more, stirring continuously.
11. Stir in lemon juice and butter and whisk until smooth. Sprinkle surface with xanthan gum and whisk vigorously to combine.
12. In a small bowl, stir together the remaining two tablespoons of water and the gelatin. Let sit 2 minutes until gelled, then stir into hot lemon mixture, whisking until well combined. Cover and set aside while making the meringue.
Meringue Topping
13. In a large bowl, beat egg whites with cream of tartar and salt until frothy. With beaters going, slowly add sweeteners and vanilla extract and continue to beat until stiff peaks form.
To Assemble
14. Preheat oven to 300°F.
15. Pour warm filling into crust. Dollop with meringue and spread right to the edges so that the meringue meets the crust. Swirl the top with the back of a spoon.

16. Bake 20 minutes or until meringue topping is golden andьjust barely firm to the touch. Remove and let pie cool 20 minutes, then refrigerate at least 3 hours to set

GRASSHOPPER MOUSSE PIE
Nutrition: Cal 261;Fat 26 g; Carb 5 g;Protein 3 g
Serving 12; Cook time 45 min.

Ingredients
No-bake Chocolate Pie Crust
- 3/4 cup unsweetened shredded coconut
- 1/4 cup unsweetened cocoa powder
- 1/2 cup sunflower seeds raw, unsalted
- 4 TBSP butter, softened
- 1/4 tsp salt
- 1/4 cup Swerve confectioners

Filling
- 1/2 cup water
- 1 tsp gelatin
- 5 oz avocado, mashed
- 8 oz cream cheese, softened
- 1 tsp peppermint extract
- 1 tsp peppermint liquid stevia
- Pinch of salt
- 1 cup heavy cream

Instructions
Crust
1. Combine all ingredients into a food processor and blend just enough to combine. Don't over blend or you will have the texture of peanut butter.
2. Taste crust to see if you need more salt or sweetness.
3. Using your fingers spread and mold crust onto bottom and sides of pie plate. Set aside.

Filling
1. Pour the water into a small saucepan and sprinkle the gelatin on top.
2. Turn on low heat, stirring constantly until gelatin is dissolved. Let cool.
3. Place the avocado, cream cheese, peppermint extract, stevia, and salt into a stand mixer and blend on high until smooth.
4. Taste and adjust sweetness if needed.
5. Pour in heavy cream in another bowl and use an electric mixer to blend on high until soft peaks form. Fold into the cream cheese mixture.
6. Gradually pour in the cooled gelatin and stir until combined.
7. Pour filling into pie crust.
8. Refrigerate at least 2 hours, loosely covered or up to 1 day.
9. When ready to serve add optional chocolate drizzle if desired.

COCONUT FLOUR CHOCOLATE CUPCAKES
Nutrition: Cal 270;Fat 22 g; Carb 6 g;Protein 6 g
Serving 12; Cook time 40 min.

Ingredients
Cupcakes
- 1/2 cup butter, melted
- 7 TBSP cocoa powder
- 1 tsp instant coffee granules (optional, enhances chocolate flavor)
- 7 eggs room temperature
- 1 tsp vanilla extract
- 2/3 cup coconut flour
- 2 tsp baking powder
- 2/3 cup Swerve Sweetener
- 1/2 tsp salt
- 1/2 cup unsweetened almond milk (more if your batter is too thick)

Espresso Butter cream
- 2 TBSP hot water
- 2 tsp instant espresso powder or instant coffee
- 1/2 cup whipping cream
- 6 TBSP butter, softened
- 4 oz cream cheese, softened
- 1/2 cup powdered Swerve Sweetener

Instructions
Cupcakes
1. Preheat oven to 350°F and line a muffin tin with parchment or silicone liners
2. In a large bowl, whisk together the melted butter, cocoa powder, and espresso powder.
3. Add the eggs and vanilla and beat until well combined. Then add the coconut flour, sweetener, baking powder and salt and beat until smooth.
4. Beat in the almond milk. If that batter is still very thick, beat in more almond milk 1 tablespoon at a time until it thins out a bit (batter will still be thick, but should be of scoopable consistency; it will not be pourable).
5. Divide batter among prepared muffin tins and bake in center of oven for 20 to 25 minutes. Cupcakes are done when the top is set and a tester inserted into the middle comes out clean. Cool in pan for 5-10 minutes and then transfer to a wire rack to cool completely.

Butter cream
1. In a small bowl, stir together hot water and espresso until coffee dissolves. Set aside.
2. With an electric mixer, whip cream until it forms stiff peaks. Set aside.
3. In a medium bowl, beat butter, cream cheese, and sweetener together until creamy. Add coffee mixture and beat until combined. With a rubber spatula, fold in whipped cream carefully until well combined.
4. Spread frosting on cooled cupcakes with a knife or offset spatula, or pipe on with a decorating bag.

PUMPKIN PIE CUPCAKES
Nutrition: Cal 170;Fat 12 g; Carb 5 g;Protein 3 g
Serving 6; Cook time 45 min.

Ingredients
- 3 TBSP coconut flour
- 1 tsp pumpkin pie spice
- 1/4 tsp baking powder
- 1/4 tsp baking soda
- Pinch of salt
- 3/4 cup pumpkin puree
- 1/3 cup Swerve Brown or Swerve Granular
- 1/4 cup heavy whipping cream
- 1 large egg
- 1/2 tsp vanilla

Instructions
1. Preheat oven to 350°F and line 6 muffin cups with silicone or parchment liners.
2. In a small bowl, whisk together the coconut flour, pumpkin pie spice, baking powder, baking soda, and salt.
3. In a large bowl, whisk pumpkin puree, sweetener, cream, egg, and vanilla until well combined. Whisk in dry ingredients. If your batter seems very thin, whisk in an additional tbsp of coconut flour.
4. Divide among prepared muffin cups and bake 25 to 30 minutes, until just puffed and barely set. Remove from oven and let cool in pan (they will sink...that's okay, all the better for plopping your whipped cream on top!).
5. Refrigerate for at least one hour before serving. Dollop whipped cream generously on top.

PEANUT BUTTER MOLTEN LAVA CAKES
Nutrition: Cal 270;Fat 22 g; Carb 6 g;Protein 10 g
Serving 4; Cook time 40 min.

Ingredients
- 1/4 cup butter
- 1/4 cup peanut butter
- 2 TBSP coconut oil
- 6 TBSP powdered Swerve Sweetener
- 2 large eggs2 large egg yolks
- 1/2 tsp vanilla extract

- 6 TBSP almond flour
- Low carb chocolate sauce

Instructions

1. Preheat oven to 350°F and grease 4 small (about 1/2 cup capacity each) ramekins very well. I used both butter and coconut oil spray.
2. In a medium-sized microwave safe bowl, combine butter, peanut butter, and coconut oil. Cook on high in 30 second increments until melted. Stir together until smooth.
3. Whisk in powdered sweetener until smooth. Whisk in eggs, egg yolks, and vanilla extract. Then whisk in almond flour until smooth.
4. Divide batter among prepared ramekins and bake 12 to 15 minutes, until sides are set but the center still jiggles a bit. Remove and let cool a few minutes.
5. Run a sharp knife around the inside of the ramekin to loosen the cakes. Cover each with an upside-down plate and flip over to turn the cake out onto the plate (you may need to give it one good shake, holding the plate and ramekin together tightly).
6. Drizzle with low carb chocolate sauce and serve immediately.

TEXAS SHEET CAKE
Nutrition: Cal 230;Fat 20 g; Carb 6 g;Protein 6 g
Serving 12; Cook time 40 min.

Ingredients
Cake
- 2 cups almond flour
- 3/4 cup Swerve Sweetener
- 1/3 cup coconut flour
- 1/3 cup unflavoured whey protein powder
- 1 TBSP baking powder
- 1/2 tsp salt
- 1/2 cup butter
- 1/2 cup water
- 1/4 cup cocoa powder
- 3 large eggs
- 1 tsp vanilla extract
- 1/4 cup heavy cream
- 1/4 cup water

Frosting
- 1/2 cup butter
- 1/4 cup cocoa powder
- 1/4 cup cream
- 1/4 cup water
- 1 tsp vanilla extract
- 1 1/2 cups powdered Swerve Sweetener
- 1/4 tsp xanthan gum
- 3/4 cup chopped pecans

Instructions

Cake

1. Preheat oven to 325°F and grease a 10x15 inch rimmed sheet pan very well.
2. In a large bowl, whisk together the almond flour, sweetener, coconut flour, protein powder, baking powder, and salt. Break up any clumps with the back of a fork.
3. In a medium saucepan over medium heat, combine the butter, water, and cocoa powder, stirring until melted. Bring to a boil and then remove from heat. Add to the bowl.
4. Add eggs, vanilla extract, cream and water and stir until well combined. Spread in prepared baking pan.
5. Bake 15 to 20 minutes, until cake is set and a tester inserted in the center comes out clean.

Frosting

6. In another medium saucepan, combine butter, cocoa powder, cream, and water. Bring to a simmer, stirring until smooth. Stir in vanilla extract. Add powdered sweetener 1/2 a cup at a time, whisking vigorously to dissolve any clumps. Whisk in xanthan gum.
7. Pour over warm cake and sprinkle with pecans. Let cool until frosting is set, about 1 hour.

GINGERBREAD CAKE ROLL
Nutrition: Cal 206;Fat 18 g; Carb 4 g;Protein 6 g
Serving 12; Cook time 40 min.

Ingredients
Cake
- 1 cup almond flour
- 1/4 cup powdered Swerve Sweetener
- 2 TBSP cocoa powder
- 1 TBSP grassfed gelatin
- 2 tsp ground ginger
- 1 tsp ground cinnamon
- 1/4 tsp ground cloves
- 4 large eggs room temperature, separated
- 1/4 cup granulated Swerve Sweetener, divided
- 1 tsp vanilla extract
- 1/4 tsp salt, divided
- 1/4 tsp cream of tartar

Vanilla Cream Filling
- 2 oz cream cheese, softened
- 1 1/2 cups whipping cream, divided
- 1/4 cup powdered Swerve Sweetener
- 1/2 tsp vanilla extract

Instructions

Cake

1. Preheat oven to 350°F and line an 11x17 inch rimmed baking sheet with parchment paper. Grease the parchment paper and pan sides very well.
2. In a medium bowl, whisk together the almond flour, powdered sweetener, cocoa powder, gelatin, ginger, cinnamon, and cloves.
3. In another medium bowl, beat the egg yolks with 2 tablespoons of the granulated sweetener until lighter yellow and thickened. Beat in the vanilla extract
4. Using clean beaters and a large clean bowl, beat the egg whites with the salt and cream of tartar until frothy. Beat in the remaining two tablespoons sweetener until stiff peaks form.
5. Gently fold the egg yolk mixture into the whites. Then gently fold in the almond flour mixture, taking care not to deflate them, until no streaks remain.
6. Spread the batter evenly into the prepared baking pan and bake 10 to 12 minutes, until the top springs back when touched.
7. Remove from the oven and let let cool a few minutes, then run a knife around the edges to loosen. Cover with another large piece of parchment paper and then a kitchen towel. Place another large baking sheet overtop and flip over.
8. Gently peel the parchment from what is now the top of the cake. While still warm, gently roll up inside the kitchen towel, starting from one of the shorter ends. Don't roll too tightly or it will crack. Let cool while preparing the filling.

Vanilla Cream Filling

9. In a small bowl, beat the cream cheese with 1/4 cup whipping cream until smooth.
10. In a large bowl, beat the remaining whipping cream with the sweetener and vanilla until it holds soft peaks. Then add the cream cheese mixture and continue to beat until stiff peaks form. Do not over-beat. Remove ½ cup and set aside for decorating.
11. Gently and carefully unroll the cake. Do not try to lay it completely flat, let it curl up on the ends. Spread with the remaining filling to within 1/2 inch of the edges. Gently roll back up without the kitchen towel. Place seam side down on a serving platter.
12. Sprinkle with some more powdered sweetener, if desired. Pipe remaining vanilla cream mixture in stars or other shapes down the center of the top of the cake.
13. Refrigerate 1 hour before slicing. Store in the refrigerator.

MINI CINNAMON ROLL CHEESECAKES

Nutrition: Cal 240;Fat 20 g; Carb 5 g;Protein 5 g
Serving 6; Cook time 40 min.

Ingredients
Crust
- 1/2 cup almond flour
- 2 TBSP Swerve Sweetener
- 1/2 tsp cinnamon
- 2 TBSP melted butter
- Cheesecake Filling
- 6 oz cream cheese, softened
- 5 TBSP Swerve Sweetener, divided
- 1/4 cup sour cream
- 1/2 tsp vanilla extract
- 1 large egg
- 2 tsp cinnamon

Frosting
- 1 TBSP butter, softened
- 3 TBSP confectioners Swerve Sweetener
- 1/4 tsp vanilla extract
- 2 tsp heavy cream

Instructions
Crust
1. Preheat the oven to 325°F and line a muffin pan with 6 parchment or silicone liners.
2. In a medium bowl, whisk together the almond flour, sweetener and cinnamon. Stir in the melted butter until the mixture begins to clump together.
3. Divide among the prepared muffin cups and press firmly into the bottom. Bake 7 minutes, then remove and let cool while preparing the filling.

Cheesecake Filling
4. Reduce oven temperature to 300°F. In a large bowl, beat the cream cheese and 3 tablespoons of the sweetener together until smooth. Beat in the sour cream, vanilla and egg until well combined.
5. In a small bowl, whisk together the remaining 2 tablespoons sweetener and the cinnamon.
6. Dollop about 3/4 tablespoon of the cream cheese mixture into each of the muffin cups and sprinkle with a little of the cinnamon mixture. Repeat 2 more times. If you have any leftover cinnamon "sugar," reserve to sprinkle on after the cheesecakes are baked.
7. Bake 15 to 17 minutes, until mostly set but centres jiggle slightly. Turn off the oven and let them remain inside for 5 more minutes, then remove and let cool 30 minutes. Refrigerate at least 2 hours until set.

Frosting
8. In a medium bowl, beat butter with powdered sweetener until well combined. Beat in vanilla extract and heavy cream.
9. Transfer to a small ziplock bag and snip the corner. Drizzle decoratively over the chilled cheesecakes.

CHOCOLATE PEANUT BUTTER LAVA CAKES

Nutrition: Cal 345;Fat 30 g; Carb 7 g;Protein 8 g
Serving 3; Cook time 35 min.

Ingredients
- 1/4 cup butter
- 1 oz unsweetened chocolate chopped
- 3 TBSP Swerve Sweetener
- 1 large egg
- 1 large egg yolk
- 3 TBSP almond flour
- 1/4 tsp vanilla extract
- Pinch of salt
- 2 TBSP peanut butter

Instructions
1. Preheat oven to 375°F and grease 3 small ramekins. Dust the ramekins with cocoa powder and shake out the excess.
2. In a microwave safe bowl, melt butter and chocolate together, whisking until smooth. Alternatively, you can melt it carefully over low heat.
3. Add the sweetener and whisk until combined. Then add the egg and egg yolk and whisk until smooth.
4. Whisk in the almond flour, vanilla extract, and salt until well combined.
5. Divide about 2/3 of the batter between the three ramekins, making sure to cover the bottom.
6. Divide peanut butter between the ramekins, placing in center of the batter. Cover with remaining batter. Bake 10 to 12 minutes, or until the edges of the cakes are set but the center still jiggles slightly.
7. Remove and let cool 5 to 10 minutes. Then run a sharp knife around the edges and flip out onto platesIn a medium-sized microwave safe bowl, combine butter, peanut butter, and coconut oil. Cook on high in 30 second increments until melted. Stir together until smooth.

PECAN PIE CHEESECAKE

Nutrition: Cal 340;Fat 30 g; Carb 5 g;Protein 6 g
Serving 10; Cook time 35 min.

Ingredients
Crust
- 3/4 cup almond flour
- 2 TBSP powdered Swerve Sweetener
- Pinch of salt
- 2 TBSP melted butter

Pecan Pie Filling
- 1/4 cup butter
- 1/3 cup powdered Swerve Sweetener
- 1 tsp Yacon syrup or molasses optional, for color and flavor
- 1 tsp caramel extract or vanilla extract
- 2 TBSP heavy whipping cream
- 1 large egg
- 1/4 tsp salt
- 1/2 cup chopped pecans

Cheesecake Filling
- 12 oz cream cheese, softened
- 5 TBSP powdered Swerve Sweetener
- 1 large egg
- 1/4 cup heavy whipping cream
- 1/2 tsp vanilla extract

Topping
- 2 TBSP butter
- 2 1/2 tbsp powdered Swerve Sweetener
- 1/2 tsp Yacon syrup or molasses
- 1/2 tsp caramel extract or vanilla extract
- 1 TBSP heavy whipping cream
- Whole toasted pecans for garnish

Instructions
Crust
1. In a medium bowl, whisk together the almond flour, sweetener, and salt. Stir in the melted butter until the mixture begins to clump together.
2. Press into the bottom and partway up the sides of a 7-inch springform pan. Place in the freezer while making the pecan pie filling.

Pecan Pie Filling
3. In a small saucepan over low heat, melt the butter. Add the sweetener and Yacon syrup and whisk until combined, then stir in the extract and heavy whipping cream.
4. Add the egg and continue to cook over low heat until the mixture thickens (this should only take a minute or so). Immediately remove from heat and stir in the pecans and salt.
5. Spread mixture over the bottom of the crust.

Cheesecake Filling
6. Beat the cream cheese until smooth, then beat in the sweetener. Beat in the egg, whipping cream, and vanilla a extract.
7. Pour this mixture over the pecan pie filling and spread to the edges.

To Bake

8. Wrap the bottom of the springform pan tightly in a large piece of foil. Place a piece of paper towel over the top of the springform pan (not touching the cheesecake) and then wrap foil around the top as well. Your whole pan should be mostly covered in foil to keep out excess moisture.
9. Place the rack that came with your Instant Pot or pressure cooker into the bottom. Pour a cup of water into the bottom.
10. Carefully lower the wrapped cheesecake pan onto the rack (there are ways to do this with a sling made out of tin foil but I didn't bother with that).
11. Close the lid and set the Instant Pot to manual mode for 30 minutes on high. Once the cooking time is complete, let the pressure to release naturally (do not vent it).
12. Lift out the cheesecake and let it cool to room temperature, and then refrigerate for 3 or 4 hours, or even overnight.

Topping

13. In a small saucepan over low heat, melt the butter. Add the sweetener and Yacon syrup and whisk until combined, then stir in the extract and heavy whipping cream. Drizzle over the chilled cheesecake and garnish with toasted pecans.

PEANUT BUTTER MUG CAKES
Nutrition: Cal 210;Fat 20 g; Carb 6 g;Protein 7 g
Serving 6; Cook time 10 min.

Ingredients
- 1/3 cup peanut butter
- 1/4 cup butter
- 2/3 cup almond flour
- 1/3 cup Swerve Sweetener
- 2 tsp baking powder
- 2 large eggs
- 1/2 tsp vanilla extract
- 1/4 cup water
- 3 TBSP sugar-free chocolate chips

Instructions
1. In a microwave-safe bowl, melt peanut butter and butter together until smooth.
2. In a medium bowl, whisk together the almond flour, sweetener, and baking powder. Stir in the eggs, vanilla extract, melted peanut butter mixture and water until well combined. Stir in chocolate chips.
3. Divide among 6 ramekins or mugs and microwave each for 1 minute, until puffed and set. Serve warm.

KENTUCKY BUTTER CAKE
Nutrition: Cal 310;Fat 27 g; Carb 6 g;Protein 7 g
Serving 16; Cook time 60 min.

Ingredients
Cake
- 2 1/2 cups almond flour
- 1/4 cup coconut flour
- 1/4 cup unflavored whey protein powder
- 1 TBSP baking powder
- 1/2 tsp salt
- 1 cup butter, softened
- 1 cup Swerve Granular
- 5 large eggs room temperature.
- 2 tsp vanilla extract
- 1/2 cup whipping cream
- 1/2 cup water

Butter Glaze
- 5 TBSP butter
- 1/3 cup Swerve Granular
- 2 TBSP water
- 1 tsp vanilla extract

Garnish
- 1 to 2 TBSP Confectioner's Swerve

Instructions

1. Preheat oven to 325°F. Grease a bundt cake pan VERY well and then dust with a few tbsp of almond flour.
2. In a medium bowl, whisk together the almond flour, coconut flour, whey protein, baking powder, and salt.
3. In a large bowl, beat the butter and the sweetener together until light and creamy. Beat in the eggs and vanilla extract.
4. Beat in the almond flour mixture and then beat in the whipping cream and water until well combined.
5. Transfer the batter to the prepared baking pan and smooth the top. Bake 50 to 60 minutes, until golden brown and the cake is firm to the touch. A tester inserted in the center should come out clean.
6. Butter Glaze:In a small saucepan over low heat, melt the butter and sweetener together. Whisk until well combined. Whisk in the water and vanilla extract.
7. While the cake is still warm and in the pan, poke holes all over with a skewer. Pour the glaze over and let cool completely in the pan.
8. Gently loosen the sides with a knife or thin rubber spatula, then flip out onto a serving platter. Dust with powdered sweetener.
9. Serve with lightly sweetened whipped cream and fresh berries.

CHOCOLATE WALNUT TORTE
Nutrition: Cal 343;Fat 31 g; Carb 9 g;Protein 9 g
Serving 1; Cook time 45 min.

Ingredients
Torte
- 1 1/2 cup walnuts
- 3/4 cup Swerve Sweetener
- 1/4 cup cocoa powder
- 1 tsp espresso powder (optional, enhances chocolate flavor)
- 1/2 tsp baking powder
- 1/4 tsp salt
- 1/2 cup butter
- 4 oz unsweetened chocolate
- 5 large eggs
- 1/2 tsp vanilla extract
- 1/2 cup almond milk

Glaze
- 1/2 cup whipping cream
- 2 1/2 oz sugar-free dark chocolate chopped
- 1/3 cup walnut pieces

Instructions
Torte
1. Preheat oven to 325°F and grease a 9-inch round baking pan. Line the bottom with parchment paper and grease the paper.
2. In a food processor, process walnuts until finely ground. Add sweetener, cocoa powder, espresso powder, baking powder, and salt and pulse a few times to combine.
3. In a large saucepan set over low heat, melt butter and chocolate together until smooth. Remove from heat and whisk in eggs and vanilla extract. Add almond milk and whisk until mixture smooths out. Stir in walnut mixture until well combined.
4. Spread batter in prepared baking pan and bake about 30 minutes, until edges are set but center still looks slightly wet. Let cool 15 minutes in pan, then invert onto a wire rack to cool completely. Remove parchment paper.

Glaze
5. In a small saucepan over medium heat, bring cream to just a simmer. Remove from heat and add chopped chocolate. Let sit to melt 5 minutes, then whisk until smooth.
6. Cool another 10 minutes, then pour the glaze over the cake, smoothing the sides. Sprinkle top with walnut pieces and chill until chocolate is firm, about 30 minutes.

CINNAMON ROLL COFFEE CAKE
Nutrition: Cal 222;Fat 20 g; Carb 5 g;Protein 7 g
Serving 8; Cook time 45 min.

Ingredients
- Cinnamon Filling
- 3 TBSP Swerve Sweetener

- 2 tsp ground cinnamon
- Cake
- 3 cups almond flour
- 3/4 cup Swerve Sweetener
- 1/4 cup unflavored whey protein powder
- 2 tsp baking powder
- 1/2 tsp salt
- 3 large eggs
- 1/2 cup butter, melted
- 1/2 tsp vanilla extract
- 1/2 cup almond milk
- 1 TBSP melted butter
- Cream Cheese Frosting
- 3 TBSP cream cheese, softened
- 2 TBSP powdered Swerve Sweetener
- 1 TBSP heavy whipping cream
- 1/2 tsp vanilla extract

Instructions

1. Preheat oven to 325°F and grease an 8x8 inch baking pan.
2. For the filling, combine the Swerve and cinnamon in a small bowl and mix well. Set aside.
3. For the cake, whisk together almond flour, sweetener, protein powder, baking powder, and salt in a medium bowl.
4. Stir in the eggs, melted butter and vanilla extract. Add the almond milk and continue to stir until well combined.
5. Spread half of the batter in the prepared pan, then sprinkle with about two thirds of the cinnamon filling mixture. Spread the remaining batter over top and smooth with a knife or an offset spatula.
6. Bake 35 minutes, or until top is golden brown and a tester inserted in the center comes out with a few crumbs attached.
7. Brush with melted butter and sprinkle with remaining cinnamon filling mixture. Let cool in pan.
8. For the frosting, beat cream cheese, powdered erythritol, cream and vanilla extract together in a small bowl until smooth. Pipe or drizzle over cooled cake.

BUTTER CAKE
Nutrition: Cal 269;Fat 24 g; Carb 5 g;Protein 6 g
Serving 15; Cook time 40 min

Ingredients
Cake
- 2 cups almond flour
- 1/2 cup Swerve Sweetener
- 2 TBSP unflavored whey protein powder
- 2 tsp baking powder
- 1/4 tsp salt
- 1/2 cup butter, melted
- 1 large egg
- 1/2 tsp vanilla extract

Filling
- 8 oz cream cheese, softened
- 1/2 cup butter, softened
- 3/4 cup powdered Swerve
- 2 large eggs
- 1/2 tsp vanilla extract
- Powdered Swerve for dusting

Instructions

1. Preheat the oven to 325°F and lightly grease a 9x13 baking pan.
2. In a large bowl, combine the almond flour, sweetener, protein powder, baking powder, and salt. Add the butter,egg, and vanilla extract and stir to combine well. Press intothe bottom and partway up the sides of the prepared baking pan.
3. In another large bowl, beat the cream cheese and butter together until smooth. Beat in the sweetener until well combined, then beat in the eggs and vanilla until smooth.
4. Pour the filling over the crust. Bake 35 to 45 minutes, until the filling is mostly set, but the center still jiggles, and the edges are just golden-brown.
5. Remove and let cool, then dust with powdered Swerve and cut into bars.

CLASSIC NEW YORK KETO CHEESECAKE
Nutrition: Cal 284;Fat 24 g; Carb 3 g;Protein 7 g
Serving 8; Cook time 1 hour 30 min.

Ingredients
- 24 oz cream cheese, softened
- 5 TBSP unsalted butter, softened
- 1 cup powdered Swerve Sweetener
- 3 large eggs, room temperature
- 3/4 cup sour cream, room temperature
- 2 tsp grated lemon zest
- 1 1/2 tsp vanilla extract

Instructions

1. Preheat the oven to 300°F and generously grease a 9-inch springform pan. Cut a circle of parchment to fit the bottom the pan and grease the paper. Wrap 2 pieces of aluminum foil around the outside of the pan to cover the bottom and most of the way up the sides.
2. In a large bowl, beat the cream cheese and butter until smooth, then beat in the sweetener until well combined. Add the eggs, once at a time, beating after each addition. Clean the beaters and scrape down the sides of the bowl as needed.
3. Add the sour cream, lemon zest, and vanilla extract and beat until the batter is smooth and well combined. Pour into the prepared springform pan and smooth the top.
4. Set the pan inside a roasting pan large enough to prevent the sides from touching. Place the roasting pan in the oven and carefully pour boiling water into the roasting pan until it reaches halfway up the sides of the springform pan.
5. Bake 70 to 90 minutes, until the cheesecake is mostly set but still jiggles just a little in the center when shaken. Remove the roasting pan from the one, then carefully remove the springform pan from the water bath. Let cool to room temperature.
6. Run a sharp knife around the edges of the cake to loosen, the release the sides of the pan. Refrigerate for at least 4 hours before serving.

ITALIAN CREAM CAKE
Nutrition: Cal 335;Fat 30 g; Carb 6 g;Protein 6 g
Serving 12; Cook time 45 min.

Ingredients
Cake
- 1/2 cup butter, softened
- 1 cup Swerve Sweetener
- 4 large eggs, room temperature, separated
- 1/2 cup heavy cream room temperature
- 1 tsp vanilla extract
- 1 1/2 cups almond flour
- 1/2 cup shredded coconut
- 1/2 cup chopped pecans
- 1/4 cup coconut flour
- 2 tsp baking powder
- 1/2 tsp salt
- 1/4 tsp cream of tartar

Frosting
- 8 oz cream cheese, softened
- 1/2 cup butter, softened
- 1 cup powdered Swerve Sweetener
- 1 tsp vanilla extract
- 1/2 cup heavy whipping cream, room temperature

Garnish
- 2 TBSP shredded coconut, lightly toasted
- 2 TBSP chopped pecans, lightly toasted

Instructions
Cake

1. Preheat the oven to 325°F and grease two 8 inch or 9 inch round cake pans very well (the 8 inch pans will take a little longer to cook but the layers will be higher and I think they will look better). Line the pans with parchment paper and grease the paper.
2. In a large bowl, beat the butter with the sweetener until well combined. Beat in the egg yolks one at a time, mixing well after each addition. Beat in the heavy cream and vanilla extract.

3. In another bowl, whisk together the almond flour, shredded coconut, chopped pecans, coconut flour, baking powder, and salt. Beat into the butter mixture until just combined.
4. In another large bowl, beat the egg whites with the cream of tartar until they hold stiff peaks. Gently fold into the cake batter.
5. Divide the batter evenly among the prepared pans and spread to the edges. Bake 35 to 45 minutes (or longer, depending on your pans), until the cakes are golden on the edges and firm to the touch in the middle.
6. Remove and let cool completely in the pans, then flip out onto a wire rack to cool completely. Remove the parchment from the layers if it comes out with them.

Frosting
7. In a large bowl, beat the cream cheese and butter together until smooth. Beat in the sweetener and vanilla extract until well combined.
8. Slowly add the heavy whipping cream until a spreadable consistency is achieved.

To Assemble
9. Place the bottom layer on a serving plate and cover the top with about 1/3 of the frosting. Add the next layer and frost the top and the sides.
10. Sprinkle the top with the toasted coconut and pecans. Refrigerate at least half an hour to let set.

COCONUT-ALMOND CAKE
Nutrition: Cal 231;Fat 19 g; Carb 12 g;Protein 3 g
Serving 8; Cook time 50 min.

Ingredients
- nonstick cooking spray
- 1 cup almond flour
- ½ cup unsweetened shredded coconut
- ⅓ cup Swerve
- 1 teaspoon apple pie spice
- 2 eggs, lightly whisked
- ¼ cup unsalted butter, melted
- ½ cup heavy (whipping) cream

Instructions
1. Grease a 6-inch round cake pan while using cooking spray.
2. In a medium bowl, mix together the almond flour, coconut, Swerve, and apple pie spice. Add the eggs, then the butter, and then your cream, mixing well after each addition.
3. Pour the batter in to the pan and cover with aluminum foil. Pour 2 glasses of water to the inner cooking pot, then place a trivet inside pot. Place the pan around the trivet.
4. Latch the lid. Select "Pressure Cook" or "Manual" and hang pressure to high and cook for 40 minutes. After enough time finishes, allow ten mins to naturally release pressure to succeed. For any remaining pressure, just quick-release it. Open the lid.
5. Carefully get the pan and allow it to cool for 15 to twenty minutes. Invert the dessert onto a plate. Sprinkle with shredded coconut, almond slices, or powdered sweetener, if desired, and serve.

DARK CHOCOLATE CAKE
Nutrition: Cal 225;Fat 20 g; Carb 4 g;Protein 5 g
Serving 6; Cook time 30 min.

Ingredients
- 1 cup almond flour
- ⅔ cup Swerve
- ¼ cup unsweetened powered cocoa
- ¼ cup chopped walnuts
- 1 teaspoon baking powder
- 3 eggs
- ⅓ cup heavy (whipping) cream
- ¼ cup coconut oil
- nonstick cooking spray

Instructions

1. Put the flour, Swerve, cocoa powder, walnuts, baking powder, eggs, cream, and coconut oil inside a large bowl. Using a hand mixer on very fast, combine the
2. Ingredients until the mix is well incorporated and appearance fluffy. This step will keep your cake from being too dense.
3. With the cooking spray, grease a heatproof pan, such like a 3-cup Bundt pan, that fits with your Instant Pot. Pour the dessert batter in the pan and cover with aluminum foil.
4. Pour 2 servings of water to the inner cooking pot, then place a trivet within the pot. Place the pan for the trivet.
5. Latch the lid. Select "Pressure Cook" or "Manual" and hang pressure to high and cook for 20 mins. After time finishes, allow 10 minutes to naturally release pressure to succeed. For any remaining pressure, just quick-release it. Carefully remove the pan and allow it to go cool for 15 to 20 mins. Invert the wedding cake onto a plate. It can be served hot or at room temperature. Serve having a dollop of whipped cream, if desired.

VANILLA CREAM WITH RASPBERRIES
Nutrition: Cal 302;Fat 30 g; Carb 4 g;Protein 4 g
Serving 4; Cook time 50 min.

Ingredients
- 1 ½ cup coconut milk, full-fat
- 1 tbsp. almond flour
- 2 tbsps. butter
- ¼ cup raspberries
- 3 egg yolks
- 3 tbsps. Swerve
- 1 tbsp. agar powder
- 1 vanilla bean
- 2 tsps. vanilla flavoring

Instructions
1. Using a sharp paring knife, slice the vanilla bean lengthwise and take away the seeds, schedule.
2. Plug inside instant pot and press the "Sauté" button.
3. Grease the inner pot with butter and add coconut milk. Warm up, stirring constantly, and adding egg yolks, swerve, and vanilla flavor.
4. Cook for 3 - 4 minutes, stirring constantly.
5. Finally, add agar powder, and vanilla seeds. Give it a good stir and then cook for an additional little bit, or until the mixture thickens.
6. Press the "Cancel" button and remove the cream in the pot. Divide between serving bowls and optionally top with a few whipped cream or fresh strawberries.
7. Plug inside instant pot and pour in the milk. Press the "Sauté" button and warm up. Add Swerve, cocoa powder, coconut cream, and vanilla extract.
8. Bring it to a boil, stirring constantly, and adding agar powder. Continue in order to smoke for 1 - 2 minutes.
9. Press the "Cancel" button and stir in finely chopped almonds.
10. Transfer the mix to a large mixing bowl and pour in the whipping cream. Beat well on high-speed for two main - 3 minutes.
11. Finally, divide the amalgamation between serving bowls and top each with raspberries. Serve cold.

KETO CHOCOLATE CAKE
Nutrition: Cal 300;Fat 12 g; Carb 7 g;Protein 8 g
Serving 6; Cook time 40 min.

Ingredients
- Almond flour (1 cup)
- Cocoa powder (unsweetened, ¼ cup)
- Coconut oil (1/4 cup)
- Eggs (3)
- Artificial sweetener by choice (2/3 cups)
- Walnuts (1/4 cups, chopped)
- Baking soda (1 teaspoon)

Instructions
1. All with the ingredients go in a very bowl and must be mixed which has a hand mixture (till everything gets to be a fluffy homogeny texture).

2. Pick a pan which will fit in the pressure cooker, grease it and pour the batter inside.
3. Pour water (2 cups) inside the pressure cooker, adding the steamer rack and ahead of it place the pot with the amalgamation.
4. Close and secure the lid, set to "High pressure" for 20 minutes; when cooking is completed, release the pressure naturally for 10 mins.
5. Cut it in pieces and serve.

PECAN PIE CHEESECAKE
Nutrition: Cal 340;Fat 31 g; Carb 5 g;Protein 6 g
Serving 10; Cook time 30 min.

Ingredients
FOR PECAN PIE FILLING
• Egg (1)
• Butter (1/4 cup)
• Artificial sweetener by choice (1/3 cup)
• Vanilla extract (1 teaspoon)
• Pecans (chopped)
• Heavy cream (2 tbsp)
• Salt (1/4 teaspoon)
• For cheesecake filling
• Cream cheese (12 oz.)
• Egg (1)
• Artificial sweetener by choice (5 tbsp)
• Heavy cream (1/4 cup)
• Vanilla extract (1/2 teaspoon)
FOR THE CRUST
• Almond flour (3/4 cups)
• Butter (2 tablespoons)
• Artificial sweetener by choice (2 tablespoons)
• Salt
Topping
• Toasted pecans
• Butter (2 tablespoons)
• Molasses (half tablespoon)
• Vanilla extract (half teaspoon)
• Heavy cream (1 tablespoon)
Instructions
Pecan pie filling
• Melt the butter and adding the artificial sweetener, stir and adding the heavy cream.
• Add the egg and cook on low heat (it should thicken). Remove it after a minute and atart exercising . the pecans and salt and stir.
• This mixture goes on the crust.
• Cheesecake filling
• Add the artificial sweetener to the cheese cream and beat well. Then add the egg, vanilla flavor and whipping cream and beat well.
• Add this mix within the pecan pie mix and spread well (over the crust).
For baking
• The entire pan (crust, pecan pie, and cheesecake spreading) must be covered with foil.
• Make sure the container will fit inside pressure to succeed cooker.
• Pour water in the cooker after which put the rack inside; place the pan on the top from the rack.
• Close the cover and hang the cooker to "Manual" for 30 minutes.
• Release pressure naturally.
• Take out the cheesecake, cool it to room temperature and after that input it in the fridge for 3-4 hours.
Topping:
• Melt the butter and add the artificial sweetener, you can add the Molasses; whisk well and after that pour inside heavy cream.
• Pour it over the cheesecake and top by incorporating more pecans (previously toasted). Serve and get!

CARROT CAKE
Nutrition: Cal 268;Fat 25 g; Carb 6 g;Protein 6 g
Serving 8; Cook time 60 min.

Ingredients
• Eggs (3)
• Carrots (1 cup, chopped)
• Artificial sweetener by choice (2/3 cups)
• Baking powder (1 teaspoon)
• Almond flour (1 cup)
• Coconut oil (1/4 cup)
• Cinnamon (1.5 teaspoons)
• Walnuts (half cup, chopped)
• Heavy cream (half cup)
Instructions
1. Use the coconut oil to grease a pan (be sure it's sufficient to suit within the pressure cooker).
2. Mix all of the Ingredients by using a hand mixer (the batter ought to be fluffy).
3. Pour the dough inside pan and place aluminum foil over it.
4. Pour two cups of water, add the steamer rack and put the pan while using batter into it.
5. Set pressure to succeed cooker to "Cake" and hang the timer for 40 minutes.
6. Release the stress naturally for ten minutes.
7. Let it cool well.
8. Serve with some extra heavy cream or any other toppings by choice.

CHOLATE MINT CAKE
Nutrition: Cal 214;Fat 19 g; Carb 8 g;Protein 6 g
Serving 8; Cook time 3 hours.

Ingredients
• Chocolate chips (make sure they may be reduced carbohydrate, 1/3 cup)
• Almond flour (1 cup)
• Almond milk (unsweetened, 2/3 cup)
• Artificial sweetener by choice (half cup)
• Cocoa powder (unsweetened, 1/3 cup)
• Butter (unsalted, 6 tablespoons)
• Eggs (3)
• Baking powder (1 ½ cup)
• Peppermint extract (half teaspoon)
• Salt (a pinch)
Instructions
1. Mix the powered cocoa, almond flour, artificial sweetener, salt, and baking powder.
2. Add the beaten eggs for this dry mix, almond milk, peppermint extract, chocolate chips, and melted butter.
3. The batter goes inside a previously greased pan or bowl that fits in the pressure cooker.
4. Set it to "Low" and let it bake for two-3 hours.
5. Let it cool for around 30 minutes (inside pressure cooker) and serve it while it's still warm.

MINI CHOCO CAKE
Nutrition: Cal 156;Fat 11 g; Carb 10 g;Protein 7 g
Serving 2; Cook time 15 min

Ingredients
• Eggs (2, beat them previously)
• Artificial sweetener by choice (2 tbsp)
• Baking cocoa (1/4 cup)
• Baking powder (half teaspoon)
• Vanilla extract (1 teaspoon)
• Heavy cream (2 tbsp)
Instructions
1. Mix the dry
2. Ingredients in the bowl and atart exercising . the wet
3. Ingredients and whisk well and soon you have a smooth batter.
4. Get bowls (ensure they can fit inside pressure cooker) and grease them.
5. Pour the dough inside the bowls (up on the half).

6. Add a cup full of water in the pressure cooker, put within the trivet and place the bowls inside.
7. Close and secure the lid; set to "High pressure" for 9 minutes.
8. Quick-release pressure to succeed then obtain the bowls out.
9. Serve with heavy cream.

COCONUT CUSTARD
Nutrition: Cal 174;Fat 14 g; Carb 6 g;Protein 6 g
Serving 4; Cook time 30 min.

Ingredients
- Eggs (3)
- Coconut milk (unsweetened, 1 cup)
- Vanilla extract (3 drops)
- Artificial sweetener by choice (1/3 cup)

Instructions
1. Mix well the milk, artificial sweetener, vanilla flavor, and eggs; work with a heatproof bowl and cover it with aluminum foil.
2. Put two cups inside the pressure cooker, put inside trivet and place the bowl over it.
3. Set to "High pressure" for 30 minutes once it's cooked release pressure naturally.
4. Cool the custard inside the fridge (until it's well set).
5. Serve in bowls and eat cooled.

AVOCADO PUDDING
Nutrition: Cal 251;Fat 21 g; Carb 3.7 g;Protein 6 g
Serving 2; Cook time 10 min.

Ingredients
- ½ ripe avocado, cut into cubes
- 1 tsp. agar powder
- 1 cup whole milk
- ¼ cup coconut cream
- 2 tsps. Stevia powder
- 1 tsp. vanilla extract

Instructions
1. Combine avocado and coconut cream in a food processor or a high-speed blender. Pulse until smooth and creamy. Then put aside.
2. In a large mixing bowl, combine milk, agar powder, Stevia, and vanilla flavor. Mix until well combined and then add avocado mixture. Stir all well and pour into an oven-safe bowl.
3. Pour 1 cup of water inside the metal insert of your Instant Pot. Set the trivet around the bottom make the bowl on the top.
4. Securely lock the lid as well as set the steam release handle by moving the valve on the "Sealing" position. Set the timer for 3 minutes for the "Manual" mode.
5. When you hear the cooker's end signal, perform a quick pressure release and open the pot.
6. Transfer the bowl to a wire rack and allow it to cool completely.
7. Refrigerate for 30 minutes before serving

SALTED CARAMEL PEANUT DELIGHT MILKSHAKE
Nutrition: Cal 220;Fat 16 g; Carb 3 g;Protein 6 g
Serving 1; Cook time 10 min.

Ingredients
- 1 cup Coconut Milk
- 7 Ice Cubes
- 2 tbsp. Peanut Butter
- 2 tbsp. SF Torani Salted Caramel
- 1 tbsp. MCT Oil
- 1/4 tsp. Xanthan Gum

Instructions
1. Add all ingredients to a blender.
2. Blend 1-2 minutes.

NUTTY COOKIE BUTTER
Nutrition: Cal 174;Fat 14 g; Carb 6 g;Protein 6 g
Serving 1; Cook time 20 min.

Ingredients
- 1 cup Raw Macadamias
- 3/4 cup Raw Cashews
- 1 tsp. Vanilla
- 1/4 tsp. Cinnamon
- 1/4 tsp. Ginger
- 1/8 tsp. Nutmeg
- 1/8 tsp. Cloves
- 2 tbsp. Butter
- 2 tbsp. Heavy Cream
- 2 tbsp. Swerve, powdered
- Pinch Salt

Instructions
1. In a food processor, blend together macadamia nuts and cashews until smooth.
2. In a saucepan, begin to brown butter along with the Swerve.
3. Once browned, mix in heavy cream.
4. Remove from heat.
5. To nut mixture, add vanilla and spices, cream and butter.
6. Process again, ensuring no lumps.
7. Add in caramel sauce and process until desired consistency is reached.

CHOCOLATE CHIA RASPBERRY PUDDING
Nutrition: Cal 246;Fat 12 g; Carb 7 g;Protein 23 g
Serving 1; Cook time 40 min.

Ingredients
- 3 tablespoons Chia Seeds
- 1 cup Unsweetened Almond Milk
- 1 scoop Chocolate Protein Powder
- 1/4 cup Raspberries fresh or frozen
- 1 teaspoon Optional : Honey

Instructions
1. Mix together almond milk and protein powder.
2. Mix in chia seeds.
3. Let rest 5 minutes before stirring.
4. Refrigerate 30 minutes.
5. Top with raspberries.

LEMON COCONUT VANILLA BEAN
Nutrition: Cal 246;Fat 16 g; Carb 7 g;Protein 20 g
Serving 1; Cook time 40 min.

Ingredients
- ½ cup extra virgin coconut oil, softened
- ½ cup coconut butter, softened
- zest and juice of one lemon
- seeds from ½ a vanilla bean

Instructions
1. Whisk ingredients in an easy to pour cup.
2. Pour into lined cupcake or loaf pan.
3. Refrigerate 30 minutes.
4. Top with lemon zest.

CARAMEL CHOCOLATE BROWNIES
Nutrition: Cal 320;Fat 7 g; Carb 12 g;Protein 10 g
Serving 8; Cook time 30 min.

Ingredients
- 2 cups Almond Flour
- 1/2 cup Unsweetened Cocoa Powder
- 1/3 cup Erythritol
- 1/4 cup Coconut Oil
- 1/4 cup Maple Syrup
- 2 large Eggs
- 1 tbsp. Psyllium Husk Powder
- 2 tbsp. Torani Salted Caramel
- 1 tsp. Baking Powder
- 1/2 tsp. Salt

Instructions
1. Preheat oven to 350 degrees.
2. In a bowl, beat together wet ingredients.
3. To the wet ingredients, slowly beat in dry ingredients.
4. Bake in an 11x7 well-greased brownie pan for 20 minutes.

WHITE CHOCOLATE SUMMER BERRY CHEESECAKE
Nutrition: Cal 280;Fat 14 g; Carb 6 g;Protein 14 g
Serving 2; Cook time 15 min.

Ingredients
- 8 oz. cream cheese, softened
- 2 oz. heavy cream
- 1 teaspoon Stevia Glycerite
- 1 teaspoon low sugar raspberry preserves
- 1 tablespoon Da Vinci Sugar Free Syrup, White Chocolate flavor

Instructions
1. Whip together ingredients to a pudding consistency.
2. Put in cups.
3. Refrigerate.

AUTUMN SPICE SCONE COOKIES
Nutrition: Cal 240;Fat 8 g; Carb 12 g;Protein 8 g
Serving 12; Cook time 60 min.

Ingredients
- 1 Sweet Lightning Winter Squash (or 1 1/4 cup Pumpkin Puree, strained)
- 2 tsp. Cinnamon
- 2 tsp. Garam Masala
- 1 tbsp. Coconut Oil Cooking Spray
- 2 large Eggs
- 1 tsp. Vanilla Extract
- 1 tsp. Baking Powder
- 1 cup Almond Flour
- 1/4 cup Butter
- 1/4 cup Pumpkin Pie Spice

Instructions
1. Preheat oven to 400 degrees.
2. Remove flesh from squash.
3. Slice squash.
4. Spray with coconut oil.
5. Place on parchment paper
6. Season with cinnamon and garam marsala.
7. Bake until tender 30-35 minutes.
8. Remove and place in food processor and process along with other ingredients.
9. Bake at 350 degrees.

DECADENT COCONUT MACAROONS
Nutrition: Cal 320;Fat 7 g; Carb 12 g;Protein 10 g
Serving 8; Cook time 30 min.

Ingredients
- 4 large egg whites
- 1 tsp. vanilla
- 1/4 tsp. cream of tartar
- 1/8 tsp. salt
- 1 cup erythritol
- 16 ounces finely shredded, unsweetened dried coconut
- 8 ounces cream cheese, softened
- 2 ounces heavy cream
- 2 ounces Da Vinci Sugar Free White Chocolate Syrup
- 2 ounces Enjoy Life Semi-Sweet Mini Chocolate Chips

Instructions
1. Preheat oven to 325 degrees.
2. Line 2 large baking sheets with parchment paper.
3. In a large mixing bowl, on low, beat together egg whites, vanilla, cream of tartar and salt until soft peaks form.
4. Add erythritol a tablespoon at a time.
5. Beat until stiff peaks form.
6. Fold in coconut.
7. Beat together cream cheese and cream until smooth.
8. Mix in syrup.
9. Add in coconut mixture, a little at a time.
10. Fold in chocolate chips.
11. Using a small ice cream scoop, place mixture on baking sheet.
12. Bake 20-25 minutes.
13. Turn off oven leaving cookies in for 30 minutes.
14. Move to wire rack.

RASPBERRY COCONUT PANCAKES
Nutrition: Cal 280;Fat 14 g; Carb 6 g;Protein 14 g
Serving 2; Cook time 15 min.

Ingredients
Pancakes:
- 2 large eggs
- 1 tbsp. fine coconut flour
- 2 tbsp. desiccated coconut (unsweetened)
- ¼ tsp. baking soda
- 3 tbsp. coconut milk
- ½ tsp. pure vanilla bean extract
- 1 tbsp. extra virgin coconut oil
- 3-6 drops liquid Stevia extract

Topping:
- ½ cup plain organic yogurt
- ½ tsp. pure vanilla bean extract
- ⅓ cup fresh raspberries
- 1 tsp. desiccated coconut (unsweetened)

Instructions
1. Beat eggs.
2. In a separate bowl, combine coconut flour, coconut, vanilla bean extract and baking soda.
3. Add to eggs.
4. Add coconut a little at a time.
5. Mix well.
6. Add sweetener.
7. In a separate bowl, mix the yogurt.
8. Grease a pan with coconut oil and turn heat to low.
9. Pour half a ladle of batter into the pan.
10. Flip when bubbles form.
11. Cook for 1 minute.
12. Top with coconut.

NO CRUST CHOCOLATE CHEESECAKE
Nutrition: Cal 310;Fat 18 g; Carb 3 g;Protein 14 g
Serving 2; Cook time 15 min.

Ingredients
- 8 oz. cream cheese, softened
- 2 oz. heavy cream
- 1 teaspoon Stevia Glycerite
- 1 teaspoon (packet) Splenda or other powdered or liquid low carb sweetener
- 1 ounce Enjoy Life Mini chocolate chips

Instructions
1. Whip together all ingredients except chocolate until a pudding consistency.
2. Fold in chocolate chips.
3. Refrigerate in serving cups.

PEANUTTY FROZEN DESSERT
Nutrition: Cal 340;Fat 22 g; Carb 7 g;Protein 20 g
Serving 1; Cook time 40 min.

Ingredients
- 1 Cup Cottage Cheese
- 1 Scoop Protein Powder
- 2 Tbsp. Peanut Butter
- 2 Tbsp. Heavy Cream
- 6 Drops Splenda
- 1 Hand blender or food processor

Instructions
1. In a food processor, blend together ingredients except protein powder.
2. When smooth mix in protein powder, blend to remove chunks.
3. Freeze for 40 minutes.

CHOCOLATE CARAMEL CHIP MUFFINS
Nutrition: Cal 250;Fat 7 g; Carb 12 g;Protein 8 g
Serving 1; Cook time 40 min.

Ingredients
- 2 cups Almond Flour
- 1/8 cup erythritol
- 1/2 tsp. baking soda
- 1/2 tsp. salt
- 1/2 tsp. xanthan gum
- 2 large eggs, lightly beaten
- 1 cup sour cream
- 2 T butter, melted, and slightly cooled
- 1 tsp. stevia glycerite
- ½ cup of Walden Farms SF Caramel Dip
- ¾ cup Enjoy Life Semi-Sweet Chocolate Chips

Instructions
1. Preheat oven to 350 degrees.
2. Using paper liners, line 45 muffin cups.
3. In a medium sized bowl, whisk almond flour, erythritol, baking soda, salt and xanthan gum.
4. In a separate bowl, lightly beat eggs.
5. Add sour cream, cooled butter and stevia
6. Stir liquid into flour and mix well.
7. Fill each muffin cup 3/4 full.
8. Bake 20-25 minutes until tops are light brown and springs to touch.

CREAM CHEESE FILLED CHOCOLATE ROLL CAKE
Nutrition: Cal 280;Fat 12 g; Carb 10 g;Protein 12 g
Serving 1; Cook time 40 min.

Ingredients
- 1 cup Almond Flour
- 4 tbsp. Butter, melted
- 3 large Eggs
- 1/4 cup Psyllium Husk Powder
- 1/4 cup Cocoa Powder
- 1/4 cup Coconut Milk
- 1/4 cup Sour Cream
- 1/4 cup Erythritol
- 1 tsp. Vanilla
- 1 tsp. Baking Powder
- Cream Cheese Filling:
- 8 oz. Cream Cheese
- 8 tbsp. Butter
- 1/4 cup Sour Cream
- 1/4 cup Erythritol
- 1/4 tsp. Stevia
- 1 tsp. Vanilla

Instructions
1. Preheat oven to 350 degrees.
2. Stir together dry ingredients.
3. Slowly mix in wet ingredients.
4. Spread dough on a baking sheet.
5. Bake 12-15 minutes.
6. Mix together cream cheese filling.
7. Spread cream cheese filling over cake.
8. Roll tightly.

CHOCOCHERRY NO BAKE CHEESECAKE
Nutrition: Cal 340;Fat 22 g; Carb 7 g;Protein 20 g
Serving 1; Cook time 40 min.

Ingredients
1. 8 oz. cream cheese, softened
2. 2 oz. heavy cream
3. 1 teaspoon Stevia Glycerite
4. 1 tablespoon Dutch process cocoa powder
5. 1 tablespoon Da Vinci Sugar Free Syrup, Cherry flavor
6. 3-5 drops EZSweet liquid Splenda

Instructions
7. Whip together all ingredients except Ezsweet until a pudding consistency.
8. Sweeten to taste with Ezsweet.
9. Refrigerate in small cups.

BROWN BUTTER BLACKBERRY CAKE
Nutrition: Cal 240;Fat 16 g; Carb 7 g;Protein 20 g
Serving 1; Cook time 40 min.

The Cake
- 1 1/2 cups Almond Flour
- 1/4 cup Erythritol, powdered
- 2 tbsp. Psyllium Husk Powder
- 1/2 cup Sour Cream
- 1/3 cup Salted Butter
- 2 large Eggs
- 1 1/2 tsp. Baking Powder
- 2 tbsp. Poppy Seeds
- Zest of 1 Lemon
- 1 tsp. Vanilla Extract
- 1/4 tsp. Liquid Stevia

The Icing
- 2 tbsp. Lemon Juice
- 1/2 cup Erythritol, powdered
- 1/2 cup Blackberries, strained
- 1/4 cup Heavy Cream
- 6 tbsp. Butter

Instructions
1. Preheat oven to 350 degrees.
2. Over medium low heat, brown butter.
3. Mix together all dry ingredients.
4. In separate bowl, mix together all wet ingredients.

5. Add brown butter to wet ingredients.
6. Slowly mix in dry ingredients to wet ingredients
7. Mix until dough forms.
8. Put dough into greased round cake pan.
9. Bake 20-25 minutes.
10. Let cool on cooling rack.
11. In a food processor, purée blackberries.
12. Mix with lemon and erythritol.
13. Cream together, butter and heavy cream.
14. Mix into blackberry purée.
15. Ice the cake and refrigerate 20-30 minutes.

DARK CHOCOLATE PEPPERMINT FROZEN CREAM
Nutrition: Cal 290;Fat 16 g; Carb 3 g;Protein 20 g
Serving 2; Cook time 30 min.

Ingredients
- 1 Cup Heavy Cream
- ½ Cup Light Cream
- ½ tsp. Liquid Stevia Extract
- ½ tsp. Vanilla (Optional)
- Several Drops Peppermint Extract (Optional)
- 1 Square Dark Chocolate (Optional)
- Several Drops Green food coloring (Optional)

Instructions
1. Whisk together all ingredients except chocolate.
2. Freeze for 5 minutes.
3. Add to ice-cream maker.
4. Add shavings before ice cream has set.

KETO CHOCOLATE CHUNK AVOCADO ICE CREAM
Nutrition: Cal 310;Fat 18 g; Carb 3 g;Protein 20 g
Serving 2; Cook time 30 min.

Ingredients
- 2 ripe Hass Avocados
- 1 cup Coconut Milk (from carton)
- 1/2 cup Heavy Cream
- 1/2 cup Cocoa Powder
- 2 tsp. Vanilla Extract
- 1/2 cup Erythritol, Powdered
- 25 drops Liquid Stevia
- 6 squares Unsweetened Baker's Chocolate

Instructions
1. Scoop avocado into a bowl.
2. Add coconut milk, cream, and vanilla extract.
3. With an immersion blender, proceed to cream together.
4. Add Erythritol, stevia, and cocoa powder to the avocado mixture and mix well.
5. Add chop bakers chocolate.
6. Chill 6-12 hours, then about 20 minutes before you're ready to serve, add mixture to ice cream machine as per manufacturer's instructions.

KETO BLACKBERRY PUDDING DELIGHT
Nutrition: Cal 310;Fat 18 g; Carb 3 g;Protein 20 g
Serving 2; Cook time 40 min.

Ingredients
- 1/4 cup Coconut Flour
- 1/4 tsp. Baking Powder
- 5 large Egg Yolks
- 2 tbsp. Coconut Oil
- 2 tbsp. Butter
- 2 tbsp. Heavy Cream
- 2 tsp. Lemon Juice
- Zest 1 Lemon
- 1/4 cup Blackberries
- 2 tbsp. Erythritol
- 10 drops Liquid Stevia

Instructions
1. Preheat oven to 350 degrees.
2. Mix together dry ingredients.
3. Add butter and coconut oil to a bowl
4. Beat egg yolks until pale and add erythritol and Stevia.
5. Beat until well mixed.
6. Add heavy cream, lemon juice, lemon zest, coconut oil and butter and beat until fully mixed.
7. Sift dry ingredients into wet and mix well.
8. Put batter into two ramekins.
9. Push in 2 tbsp. blackberries.
10. Bake for 20-25 minutes.

COCONUT MACAROONS BITES
Nutrition: Cal 240;Fat 3 g; Carb 6 g;Protein 15 g
Serving 2; Cook time 25 min.

Ingredients
- 4 Egg Whites (1/2 Cup)
- 1 tsp. Vanilla
- ½ tsp. EZ-Sweet (Or equivalent of 1 cup artificial sweetener)
- 4½ tsp. Water
- 2 Cups Unsweetened Coconut

Instructions
Pre-heat to 375 degrees.
Mix together egg whites and liquids
Mix in coconut.
Put into whoopee pie pan.
Put in oven and reduce to 325 degrees.
Bake 14 minutes.

BAKED KETO STRAWBERRY CHEESECAKE
Nutrition: Cal 280;Fat 18 g; Carb 6 g;Protein 15 g
Serving 2; Cook time 120 min.

Ingredients
Crust:
- ¾ Cup Pecans (84g)
- ¾ Cup Almond Flour
- 4 Tbsp. Butter
- 2 Tbsp. Splenda
Filling:
- 1½ lbs. Cream Cheese
- 4 Eggs
- ½ Tbsp. Liquid Vanilla
- ½ Tbsp. Lemon Juice
- ½ tsp. EZ-Sweetz (Equivalent to 1 cup sugar, if Splenda, use 1 cup)
- ¼ Cup Sour Cream
- 9 Strawberries

Instructions
1. Preheat to oven to 400 degrees.
2. Crush the pecans.
3. In a saucepan, melt butter and add pecans, Splenda and flour.
4. Mix for several minutes.
5. Grease a 9" spring form pan and add the dough.
6. Cook for 7 minutes until it starts to brown.
7. Combine all ingredients at room temperature
8. Mix well.
9. Slice and Place strawberries along the sides of the crust and fill with filling.
10. Place in oven and lower heat to 250 degrees.
11. Bake 60-90 minutes.

CREAMY CHOCOBERRY FUDGE SAUCE
Nutrition: Cal 320;Fat 20 g; Carb 3 g;Protein 17 g

Serving 2; Cook time 15 min

Ingredients
- 4 ounces cream cheese, softened
- 1-3.5 ounce bar Lindt 90% chocolate, chopped
- 1/4 cup powdered erythritol
- 1/4 cup of heavy cream
- 2 tbsp. Monin sugar free Raspberry Syrup

Instructions
1. Melt together cream cheese and chocolate.
2. Once melted, stir in sweetener.
3. Remove from heat and let cool.
4. Once cool, mix in cream and syrup.
5. Mix well.

EASY CHOCO-COCONUT PUDDING
Nutrition: Cal 246;Fat 16 g; Carb 7 g;Protein 15 g
Serving 1; Cook time 50 min.

Ingredients
- 1 cup coconut milk (full fat, canned)
- 2 tbsp. cacao powder or organic cocoa
- 1/2 tsp. stevia powder extract
- Or 2 Tbsp. honey or maple syrup
- 1 Tbsp. quality gelatin
- 2 Tbsp. water

Instructions
1. Over medium heat whisk together coconut milk, cocoa, and sweetener.
2. In a separate bowl, mix the gelatin and water.
3. Add to pan and stir until fully dissolved.
4. Pour into small dishes and refrigerate 30-45 minutes.

MICROWAVE TIRAMISU
Nutrition: Cal 270;Fat 16 g; Carb 9 g;Protein 17 g
Serving 1; Cook time 15 min.

Ingredients
- 1 tbsp. eryrithol or any sweetener of choice
- 1/2 tsp. of LC sweet brown sugar without the carbs, you can omit this if you want
- 1 tbsp. of unsalted soften butter
- 3 tbsp. of almond flour (honeyville brand)
- 2 tbsp. of vanilla whey protein powder
- 1/4 tsp. of baking powder
- 1 tbsp. of almond milk
- 2 tbsp. of beaten egg or egg whites

Coffee Mixture:
- 1 tbsp. of instant coffee
- 2 tbsp. of water

Filling:
- 2 oz. cream cheese or if you have mascarpone cheese use it
- 2 tbsp. whipped cream or heavy cream
- 1 tsp. of eyrithol

Garnish:
- 1 tsp. unsweetened cocoa powder
- 1 tsp. of unsweetened grated chocolate

Instructions
1. First, mix together the sweetener and the softened butter.
2. Next, mix in the rest of the ingredients.
3. Divide into 2 ramekins.
4. Wait 1 minute for baking powder to activate.
5. Microwave for 1 minute.
6. Melt cream cheese in microwave for 30 seconds and mix in cream and sweetener.
7. Cut cake in half.
8. Dip 2 pieces of cake into coffee.
9. Layer the cake with the filling and sprinkle with cocoa and grated chocolate.

HAZELNUT CHEESECAKE BALLS
Nutrition: Cal 315;Fat 20 g; Carb 4 g;Protein 20 g
Serving 4; Cook time 30 min.

Ingredients
- 8 oz. package cream cheese
- 1/4 cup cocoa powder
- Stevia to taste
- 1 or 2 tbsp. Sugar Free Hazelnut syrup
- 1/4 cup ground hazelnuts

Instructions
1. Mix together all ingredients at room temperature except for the hazelnuts.
2. Roll into 16 balls.
3. Cover in hazelnuts.

BERRY LAYER CAKE
Nutrition: Cal 246;Fat 16 g; Carb 7 g;Protein 15 g
Serving 1; Cook time 15 min.

Ingredients15
- 1/4 of the lemon pound cake
- 1/4 cup of whipping cream
- 1/2t Truvia
- 1/8t orange flavor
- Mixed berries

Instructions
1. Cut lemon cake into small cubes.
2. Cut strawberries into small pieces.
3. Whip together whipping cream, Truvia, and orange flavor.
4. Layer fruit, cake and cream in a clear cup.

COCONUT CREAM MACAROONS
Nutrition: Cal 246;Fat 12 g; Carb 5 g;Protein 17 g
Serving 2; Cook time 35 min.

Ingredients
- 1 teaspoon vanilla
- 4 or 5 egg whites
- 1/4 teaspoon cream of tartar
- 9 ounces cream cheese
- 1 cup erythritol
- 3 ounces heavy cream
- 1/8 teaspoon salt
- 18 ounces dried coconut

Instructions
1. Preheat oven to 325 degrees.
2. Whisk together egg whites, cream of tartar, vanilla and salt.
3. Occasionally add erythritol.
4. Add coconut.
5. Whisk together cream cheese, heavy cream and chocolate syrup.
6. Mix in egg mixture.
7. Mix in chocolate.
8. Scoop into baking sheet.
9. Bake 25 minutes.

RICH BROWNIE CHEESECAKE
Nutrition: Cal 320;Fat 18 g; Carb 12 g;Protein 15 g
Serving 2; Cook time 35 min.

Ingredients
Brownie:
- ½ cup Kerry Gold Butter
- 2 oz. chopped unsweetened chocolate
- ½ cup almond flour
- 1/4 cup cocoa powder
- ⅛ tsp. salt
- 2 eggs

- ¾ cup sweetner equivalent to sugar (we used liquid Splenda)
- ¼ tsp. vanilla
- ¼ cup chopped Pecans

Cheesecake:
- 1 lb. softened Cream Cheese
- 2 large Eggs
- ½ cup sweetener equivalent to sugar (again we used liquid Splenda)
- ¼ cup Organic Heavy Cream
- ½ tsp. Organic Vanilla Extract

Instructions
1. Preheat oven to 325 degrees.
2. Butter a pie pan.
3. Melt butter and chocolate together in the microwave.
4. In a bowl, mix almond flour, cocoa powder and salt.
5. In separate bowl, mix eggs, sweetener and organic vanilla extract.
6. Add in almond flour mix.
7. Mix in melted butter and chocolate and pecans.
8. Pour into pie pan.
9. Spread out evenly.
10. Bake 15 minutes.
11. Cool 15 minutes.
12. Reduce heat to 300.
13. Beat softened cream cheese
14. Add eggs, sweetener, cream, and vanilla extract.
15. Mix well.
16. Pour over brownie crust.
17. Bake around 40 minutes until center hardly jiggles.
18. Drizzle chocolate sauce on top.

CREAMY BANANA FAT BOMBS
Nutrition: Cal 134;Fat 12 g; Carb 1 g;Protein 3 g
Serving 12; Cook time 70 min.

Ingredients
- 1&¼ cups cream cheese, at room temperature
- ¾ cup heavy (whipping) cream
- 1 tablespoon pure banana extract
- 6 drops liquid stevia

Instructions
1. Line a baking sheet with parchment paper and set aside.
2. In a medium bowl, beat together the cream cheese, heavy cream, banana extract, and stevia until smooth and very thick, about 5 minutes.
3. Gently spoon the mixture onto the baking sheet in mounds, leaving some space between each mound, and place the baking sheet in the refrigerator until firm, about 1 hour.
4. Store the fat bombs in an airtight container in the refrigerator for up to 1 week.

BLUEBERRY FAT BOMBS
Nutrition: Cal 115;Fat 12 g; Carb 1 g;Protein 1 g
Serving 12; Cook time 3 hours 10 min.

Ingredients
- ½ cup coconut oil, at room temperature
- ½ cup cream cheese, at room temperature
- ½ cup blueberries, mashed with a fork
- 6 drops liquid stevia
- Pinch ground nutmeg

Instructions
1. Line a mini mufn tin with paper liners and set aside.
2. In a medium bowl, stir together the coconut oil and cream cheese until well blended.
3. Stir in the blueberries, stevia, and nutmeg until combined.
4. Divide the blueberry mixture into the mufn cups and place the tray in the freezer until set, about 3 hours.
5. Place the fat bombs in an airtight container and store in the freezer until you wish to eat them

SPICED-CHOCOLATE FAT BOMBS
Nutrition: Cal 117;Fat 12 g; Carb 2 g;Protein 2 g
Serving 12; Cook time 15 min.

Ingredients
- ¾ cup coconut oil
- ¼ cup cocoa powder
- ¼ cup almond butter
- ⅛ teaspoon chili powder
- 3 drops liquid stevia

Instructions
1. Line a mini mufn tin with paper liners and set aside.
2. Put a small saucepan over low heat and add the coconut oil, cocoa powder, almond buter, chili powder, and stevia.
3. Heat until the coconut oil is melted, then whisk to blend.
4. Spoon the mixture into the mufn cups and place the tin in the refrigerator until the bombs are firm, about 15 minutes.
5. Transfer the cups to an airtight container and store the fat bombs in the freezer until you want to serve them

CHOCOLATE-COCONUT TREATS
Nutrition: Cal 43;Fat 5 g; Carb 1 g;Protein 1 g
Serving 16; Cook time 35 min.

Ingredients
- ⅓ cup coconut oil
- ¼ cup unsweetened cocoa powder
- 4 drops liquid stevia
- Pinch sea salt
- ¼ cup shredded unsweetened Coconut

Instructions
1. Line a 6-by-6-inch baking dish with parchment paper and set aside.
2. In a small saucepan over low heat, stir together the coconut oil, cocoa, stevia, and salt for about 3 minutes.
3. Stir in the coconut and press the mixture into the baking dish.
4. Place the baking dish in the refrigerator until the mixture is hard, about 30 minutes.
5. Cut into 16 pieces and store the treats in an airtight container in a cool place.

ALMOND BUTTER FUDGE
Nutrition: Cal 204;Fat 22 g; Carb 3 g;Protein 3 g
Serving 36; Cook time 2 hours 10 min.

Ingredients
- 1 cup coconut oil, at room temperature
- 1 cup almond butter
- ¼ cup heavy (whipping) cream
- 10 drops liquid stevia
- Pinch sea salt

Instructions
1. Line a 6-by-6-inch baking dish with parchment paper and set aside.
2. In a medium bowl, whisk together the coconut oil, almond butter, heavy cream, stevia, and salt until very smooth.
3. Spoon the mixture into the baking dish and smooth the top with a spatula.
4. Place the dish in the refrigerator until the fudge is firm, about 2 hours.
5. Cut into 36 pieces and store the fudge in an airtight container in the freezer for up to 2 weeks

NUTTY SHORTBREAD COOKIES
Nutrition: Cal 105;Fat 10 g; Carb 2 g;Protein 3 g
Serving 18; Cook time 50 min.

Ingredients
- ½ cup butter, at room temperature, plus additional for greasing the baking sheet
- ½ cup granulated sweetener

- 1 teaspoon alcohol-free pure
- vanilla extract
- 1&½ cups almond flour
- ½ cup ground hazelnuts
- Pinch sea salt

Instructions

1. In a medium bowl, cream together the buter, sweetener, and vanilla until well blended.
2. Stir in the almond four, ground hazelnuts, and salt until a firm dough is formed.
3. Roll the dough into a 2-inch cylinder and wrap it in plastic wrap. Place the dough in the refrigerator for at least 30 minutes until firm.
4. Preheat the oven to 350°F. Line a baking sheet with parchment paper and lightly grease the paper with buter; set aside.
5. Unwrap the chilled cylinder, slice the dough into 18 cookies, and place the cookies on the baking sheet.
6. Bake the cookies until firm and lightly browned, about 10 minutes.
7. Allow the cookies to cool on the baking sheet for 5 minutes and then transfer them to a wire rack to cool completely.

VANILLA-ALMOND ICE POPS
Nutrition: Cal 166;Fat 15 g; Carb 4 g;Protein 3 g
Serving 8; Cook time 4 hours 10 min.

Ingredients

- 2 cups almond milk
- 1 cup heavy (whipping) cream
- 1 vanilla bean, halved lengthwise
- 1 cup shredded unsweetened Coconut

Instructions

1. Place a medium saucepan over medium heat and add the almond milk, heavy cream, and vanilla bean.
2. Bring the liquid to a simmer and reduce the heat to low. Continue to simmer for 5 minutes.
3. Remove the saucepan from the heat and let the liquid cool.
4. Take the vanilla bean out of the liquid and use a knife to scrape the seeds out of the bean into the liquid.
5. Stir in the coconut and divide the liquid between the ice pop molds.
6. Freeze until solid, about 4 hours, and enjoy.

RASPBERRY CHEESECAKE
Nutrition: Cal 176;Fat 18 g; Carb 3 g;Protein 6 g
Serving 12; Cook time 1 hours 10 min.

Ingredients

- ⅔ cup coconut oil, melted
- ½ cup cream cheese, at room temperature
- 6 eggs
- 3 tablespoons granulated sweetener
- 1 teaspoon alcohol-free pure vanilla extract
- ½ teaspoon baking powder
- ¾ cup raspberries

Instructions

1. Preheat the oven to 350°F. Line an 8-by-8-inch baking dish with parchment paper and set aside.
2. In a large bowl, beat together the coconut oil and cream cheese until smooth.
3. Beat in the eggs, scraping down the sides of the bowl at least once.
4. Beat in the sweetener, vanilla, and baking powder until smooth.
5. Spoon the bater into the baking dish and use a spatula to smooth out the top. Scater the raspberries on top.
6. Bake until the center is firm, about 25 to 30 minutes.
7. Allow the cheesecake to cool completely before cuting into 12 squares.

PEANUT BUTTER MOUSSE
Nutrition: Cal 280;Fat 28 g; Carb 4 g;Protein 6 g
Serving 4; Cook time 40 min.

Ingredients

- 1 cup heavy (whipping) cream
- ¼ cup natural peanut butter
- 1 teaspoon alcohol-free pure
- vanilla extract
- 4 drops liquid stevia

Instructions

1. In a medium bowl, beat together the heavy cream, peanut butter, vanilla, and stevia until firm peaks form, about 5 minutes.
2. Spoon the mousse into 4 bowls and place in the refrigerator to chill for 30 minutes.

CAULIFLOWER CHAFFLE
Nutrition: Cal 246;Fat 16 g; Carb 7 g;Protein 20 g
Serving 2; Cook time 30 min.

Ingredients

- 2 cups cauliflower florets, grated
- ½ teaspoon garlic powder
- ½ teaspoon salt
- ½ teaspoon ground black pepper
- 1 teaspoon Italian seasoning
- 2 eggs, pasteurized, at room temperature
- 1 cup mozzarella cheese, full-fat, shredded
- 1 cup parmesan cheese, full-fat, shredded

Instructions

5. Switch on the waffle maker and set it to preheat according to the manufacturer's instructions.
6. Meanwhile, prepare the batter and for this, take a medium-sized bowl, add all the ingredients to it, and whisk well by using an electric mixer at medium speed until incorporated and smooth batter comes together.
7. Grease the waffle maker with avocado oil spray, sprinkle 2 tablespoons of parmesan cheese on waffle trays until covered, and ladle the prepared batter on top.
8. Shut the waffle maker with its lid and let cook for 5–8 minutes until waffle turns firm and golden-brown.
9. When done, remove waffles by using a tong or a fork and repeat with the remaining batter.
10. Let waffles cool slightly and serve.

PARMESAN AND GARLIC CHAFFLES
Nutrition: Cal 352;Fat 24 g; Carb 2 g;Protein 18 g
Serving 4; Cook time 30 min.

Ingredients

- 1 teaspoon garlic powder
- 2 cups mozzarella cheese, full-fat, shredded
- 4 teaspoons Italian seasoning
- 4 eggs, pasteurized, at room temperature
- 1 cup parmesan cheese, full-fat, grated

Instructions

1. Switch on the waffle maker and set it to preheat according to the manufacturer's instructions.
2. Meanwhile, prepare the batter and for this, take a medium-sized bowl, add all the ingredients (except for cheese), whisk until incorporated, and fold in cheese until mixed.
3. Grease the waffle maker with avocado oil spray and ladle the prepared batter on waffle trays.
4. Shut the waffle maker with its lid and let cook for 5–8 minutes until waffle turns firm and golden-brown.
5. When done, remove waffles by using a tong or a fork and repeat with the remaining batter.
6. Let waffles cool slightly and serve.

PIZZA CHAFFLE
Nutrition: Cal 337;Fat 24 g; Carb 7 g;Protein 25 g
Serving 4; Cook time 30 min.

Ingredients

- 4 eggs, pasteurized, at room temperature
- 2 cups mozzarella cheese, full-fat, shredded
- ¼ teaspoon Italian seasoning
- 4 tablespoons pizza sauce, sugar-free
- ½ cup parmesan cheese, grated
- Pepperoni slices, as needed for topping

Instructions

1. Switch on the waffle maker and set it to preheat according to the manufacturer's instructions.
2. Meanwhile, prepare the batter and for this, take a medium-sized bowl, crack eggs in it, add Italian seasoning and mozzarella cheese, and whisk well by using an electric mixer at medium speed until incorporated and smooth batter comes together.
3. Grease the waffle maker with avocado oil spray, sprinkle 1 tablespoon of parmesan cheese on waffle trays until covered, and ladle the prepared batter on top.
4. Shut the waffle maker with its lid and let cook for 5–8 minutes until waffle turns firm and golden-brown.
5. When done, remove waffles by using a tong or a fork and repeat with the remaining batter.
6. Let waffles cool slightly, spread pizza sauce over each waffle, and top with pepperoni and some more mozzarella cheese.
7. Microwave each waffle for 20 seconds at a high heat setting and then serve.

BUFFALO CHICKEN CHAFFLE

Nutrition: Cal 465;Fat 24 g; Carb 8 g;Protein 35 g
Serving 4; Cook time 30 min.

Ingredients

- ½ cup celery, diced
- ½ cup almond flour
- 1 cup chicken, pasteurized, shredded
- 2 teaspoons baking powder
- ½ cup Frank red hot sauce and more for topping
- 4 eggs, pasteurized, at room temperature
- ½ cup mozzarella cheese, full-fat, shredded
- ½ cup feta cheese, full-fat, crumbled
- 1 ½ cup cheddar cheese, full-fat, shredded

Instructions

1. Take a small bowl, place flour in it, and stir in the baking powder until mixed, set aside until required.
2. Switch on the waffle maker and set it to preheat according to the manufacturer's instructions.
3. Meanwhile, prepare the batter and for this, take a medium-sized bowl, crack eggs in it, and whisk until blended.
4. Beat in red hot sauce, beat in flour mixture until incorporated, beat in all the cheeses until well combined, and then fold in chicken.
5. Grease the waffle maker with avocado oil spray and ladle the prepared batter on waffle trays.
6. Shut the waffle maker with its lid and let cook for 5–8 minutes until waffle turns firm and golden-brown.
7. When done, remove waffles by using a tong or a fork and repeat with the remaining batter.
8. Let waffles cool slightly, top with some more hot sauce and feta cheese, and serve.

CHEDDAR CHAFFLES

Nutrition: Cal 240 Fat 14 g; Carb 4 g;Protein 14 g
Serving 4; Cook time 30 min.

Ingredients

- 4 tablespoons almond flour
- 2 cups cheddar cheese, full-fat, shredded
- 4 eggs, pasteurized, at room temperature

Instructions

1. Switch on the waffle maker and set it to preheat according to the manufacturer's instructions.

2. Meanwhile, prepare the batter and for this, take a medium-sized bowl, add all the ingredients, and whisk well by using an electric mixer at medium speed until incorporated and smooth batter comes together.
3. Grease the waffle maker with avocado oil spray and ladle the prepared batter on waffle trays.
4. Shut the waffle maker with its lid and let cook for 5–8 minutes until waffle turns firm and golden-brown.
5. When done, remove waffles by using a tong or a fork and repeat with the remaining batter.
6. Let waffles cool slightly and serve.

EGG AND MOZZARELLA CHAFFLE

Nutrition: Cal 258 Fat 19 g; Carb 2 g;Protein 20 g
Serving 4; Cook time 30 min.

Ingredients

- 4 eggs, pasteurized, at room temperature
- 2 cups mozzarella cheese, full-fat, shredded

Instructions

1. Switch on the waffle maker and set it to preheat according to the manufacturer's instructions.
2. Meanwhile, prepare the batter and for this, take a medium-sized bowl, crack eggs in it, add cheese, and whisk well until incorporated and smooth batter comes together.
3. Grease the waffle maker with avocado oil spray and ladle the prepared batter on waffle trays.
4. Shut the waffle maker with its lid and let cook for 5–8 minutes until waffle turns firm and golden-brown.
5. When done, remove waffles by using a tong or a fork and repeat with the remaining batter.
6. Let waffles cool slightly and serve.

JALAPENO AND CHEDDAR CHAFFLE

Nutrition: Cal 258 Fat 19 g; Carb 2 g;Protein 20 g
Serving 4; Cook time 30 min.

Ingredients

- 4 tablespoons jalapenos, chopped
- 4 tablespoons almond flour
- 4 eggs, pasteurized, at room temperature
- 2 cups cheddar cheese, full-fat, shredded

Instructions

1. Switch on the waffle maker and set it to preheat according to the manufacturer's instructions.
2. Meanwhile, prepare the batter and for this, take a medium-sized bowl, crack eggs in it, add remaining ingredients, and whisk well by using an electric mixer at medium speed until incorporated and smooth batter comes together.
3. Grease the waffle maker with avocado oil spray and ladle the prepared batter on waffle trays.
4. Shut the waffle maker with its lid and let cook for 5–8 minutes until waffle turns firm and golden-brown.
5. When done, remove waffles by using a tong or a fork and repeat with the remaining batter.
6. Let waffles cool slightly and serve.

BEEF AND ONION BUN CHAFFLE

Nutrition: Cal 593 Fat 40 g; Carb 2 g;Protein 55 g
Serving 4; Cook time 30 min.

Ingredients

Sauce

- 8 tablespoons horseradish
- 8 teaspoons erythritol sweetener
- 1 teaspoon salt
- 2 cups mayonnaise, full-fat

Chaffle

- 4 tablespoons white onion, minced

- ½ teaspoon salt
- 2 cups mozzarella cheese, full-fat, grated
- 4 eggs, pasteurized, at room temperature
- 16 ounces deli roast beef

Instructions

1. Prepare the sauce and for this, take a medium-sized bowl, place all of its ingredients in it, and whisk until combined. Set aside until needed.
2. Switch on the waffle maker and set it to preheat according to the manufacturer's instructions.
3. Meanwhile, prepare the batter and for this, take a medium-sized bowl, crack eggs in it, add onion, salt, and cheese, and whisk well by using an electric mixer at medium speed until incorporated and smooth batter comes together.
4. Grease the waffle maker with avocado oil spray and ladle the prepared batter on waffle trays.
5. Shut the waffle maker with its lid and let cook for 5–8 minutes until waffle turns firm and golden-brown.
6. When done, remove waffles by using a tong or a fork and repeat with the remaining batter.
7. Let waffles cool slightly, drizzle 2 tablespoons of the horseradish sauce over two waffles, top with beef, and cover the other waffles.
8. Serve chaffle buns with the remaining horseradish sauce and then serve.

BELGIAN CHAFFLES
Nutrition: Cal 400 Fat 28.5 g; Carb 3 g; Protein 28 g
Serving 4; Cook time 30 min.

Ingredients

- 3 cups cheddar and jack cheese blend, full-fat, shredded
- 4 eggs, pasteurized, at room temperature

Instructions

1. Switch on the waffle maker and set it to preheat according to the manufacturer's instructions.
2. Meanwhile, prepare the batter and for this, take a medium-sized bowl, crack eggs in it, and whisk until blended.
3. Add cheese blend into the eggs and stir until combined.
4. Grease the waffle maker with avocado oil spray and ladle the prepared batter on waffle trays.
5. Shut the waffle maker with its lid and let cook for 5–8 minutes until waffle turns firm and golden-brown.
6. When done, remove waffles by using a tong or a fork and repeat with the remaining batter.
7. Let waffles cool slightly and serve.

BROCCOLI AND CHEESE CHAFFLE
Nutrition: Cal 340 Fat 26 g; Carb 4 g; Protein 24 g
Serving 4; Cook time 30 min.

Ingredients

- 4 tablespoons almond flour
- 1 cup broccoli florets, chopped
- 1 teaspoon garlic powder
- 4 eggs, pasteurized, at room temperature
- 2 cups cheddar cheese, full-fat, shredded

Instructions

1. Switch on the waffle maker and set it to preheat according to the manufacturer's instructions.
2. Meanwhile, prepare the batter and for this, take a medium-sized bowl, crack eggs in it, add flour, cheese, and garlic powder, and then whisk well by using an electric mixer at medium speed until incorporated and smooth batter comes together.
3. Grease the waffle maker with avocado oil spray, spread half the broccoli into the waffle tray, and ladle the prepared batter on top.
4. Shut the waffle maker with its lid and let cook for 5–8 minutes until waffle turns firm and golden-brown.
5. When done, remove waffles by using a tong or a fork and repeat with the remaining batter and broccoli.
6. Let waffles cool slightly and serve.

BACON CHAFFLES
Nutrition: Cal 380 Fat 29 g; Carb 4 g; Protein 24 g
Serving 4; Cook time 30 min.

Ingredients

- 4 tablespoons green onion, chopped
- 1 tablespoon almond flour
- ½ cup bacon, pasteurized, chopped
- ½ teaspoon baking powder
- 4 eggs, pasteurized, at room temperature
- 1 cup cheddar cheese, full-fat, shredded
- 1 cup mozzarella cheese, full-fat

Instructions

1. Switch on the waffle maker and set it to preheat according to the manufacturer's instructions.
2. Meanwhile, prepare the batter and for this, take a medium-sized bowl, crack eggs in it, add flour, baking powder, and both kinds of cheese, and whisk well until incorporated.
3. Add bacon and onion, and stir until mixed and smooth batter comes together.
4. Grease the waffle maker with avocado oil spray and ladle the prepared batter on waffle trays.
5. Shut the waffle maker with its lid and let cook for 5–8 minutes until waffle turns firm and golden-brown.
6. When done, remove waffles by using a tong or a fork and repeat with the remaining batter.
7. Let waffles cool slightly and serve.

CANNABIS CHAFFLES
Nutrition: Cal 422 Fat 37 g; Carb 4 g; Protein 17 g
Serving 4; Cook time 30 min.

Ingredients

- 2 tablespoons melted cannabutter
- 1 cup mozzarella cheese, full-fat, shredded
- 1 cup cream cheese, full-fat, softened
- 4 eggs, pasteurized, at room temperature

Instructions

- Switch on the waffle maker and set it to preheat according to the manufacturer's instructions.
- Meanwhile, prepare the batter and for this, take a medium-sized bowl, crack eggs in it, add remaining ingredients, and whisk well by using an electric mixer at medium speed until incorporated and smooth batter comes together.
- Grease the waffle maker with avocado oil spray and ladle the prepared batter on waffle trays.
- Shut the waffle maker with its lid and let cook for 5–8 minutes until waffle turns firm and golden-brown.
- When done, remove waffles by using a tong or a fork and repeat with the remaining batter.
- Let waffles cool slightly and serve.

Conclusion

I hope you liked my cookbook.

Ketogenic diet utilizes this process as a quick and healthy way to lose weight. By greatly reducing your sugar and carbohydrate intake which, instead of using the recently consumed sugars and carbs as energy, forces your body to burn it's previously stored fat to use as energy throughout the day.

At last, I want to wish you a very happy keto journey ahead. I hope you will achieve all your weight loss goals and overcome your health issues as well.

1. **So here are some final tips:**

2. **Minimize Your Carb Consumption**

3. **Include Coconut Oil in Your Diet**

4. **Ramp up Your Physical Activity**

5. **Increase Your Healthy Fat Intake**

6. **Try a Short Fast or a Fat Fast**

7. **Maintain Adequate Protein Intake**

8. **Test Ketone Levels and Adjust Your Diet as Needed**

Thanks again for purhasing this book, I hope you enjoyed it!

Sandra Grant
2022

Printed in Great Britain
by Amazon

86165369R00081